OXFORD STUDIES IN EUROPEAN LAW

Constitutional Pluralism in the EU

OXFORD STUDIES IN EUROPEAN LAW

Series Editors: Paul Craig, Professor of English Law at St John's College, Oxford and Gráinne de Búrca, Professor of Law at New York University School of Law

The aim of this series is to publish important and original research on EU law. The focus is on scholarly monographs, with a particular emphasis on those which are interdisciplinary in nature. Edited collections of essays will also be included where they are appropriate. The series is wide in scope and aims to cover studies of particular areas of substantive and of institutional law, historical works, theoretical studies, and analyses of current debates, as well as questions of perennial interest such as the relationship between national and EU law and the novel forms of governance emerging in and beyond Europe. The fact that many of the works are interdisciplinary will make the series of interest to all those concerned with the governance and operation of the EU.

OTHER TITLES IN THIS SERIES

European Law and New Health Technologies
Edited by Mark L Flear, Anne-Maree Farrell, Tamara K Hervey, and Thérèse Murphy

The Legal Effect of EU Agreements
Mario Mendez

The Enforcement of EU Law
The Role of the European Commission
Stine Andersen

European Agencies
Law and Practices of Accountability
Madalina Busuioc

The Foundations of European Union Competition Law
The Objective and Principles of Article 102
Renato Nazzini

The Emergence of EU Contract Law
Exploring Europeanization
Lucinda Miller

Participation in EU Rule-making
A Rights-Based Approach
Joana Mendes

Regulating Cartels in Europe
Second Edition
Christopher Harding, Julian Joshua

Religion and the Public Order of the European Union
Ronan McCrea

Governing Social Inclusion
Europeanization through Policy Coordination
Kenneth A Armstrong

Judicial Control in the European Union
Reforming Jurisdiction in the Intergovernmental Pillars
Alicia Hinarejos

EU Counter-Terrorist Policies and Fundamental Rights
The Case of Individual Sanctions
Christina Eckes

From Dual to Cooperative Federalism
The Changing Structure of European Law
Robert Schütze

Conflicts of Rights in the European Union
A Theory of Supranational Adjudication
Aida Torres Pérez

Judicial Deliberations
A Comparative Analysis of Transparency and Legitimacy
Mitchel de S-O-l'E Lasser

Racism and Equality in the European Union
Mark Bell

Constitutional Principles of EU External Relations
Geert De Baere

Civil Procedure and EU Law
A Policy Area Uncovered
Eva Storskrubb

Constitutional Pluralism in the EU

KLEMEN JAKLIC

OXFORD
UNIVERSITY PRESS

OXFORD
UNIVERSITY PRESS

Great Clarendon Street, Oxford, OX2 6DP,
United Kingdom

Oxford University Press is a department of the University of Oxford.
It furthers the University's objective of excellence in research, scholarship,
and education by publishing worldwide. Oxford is a registered trade mark of
Oxford University Press in the UK and in certain other countries

First Edition published in 2014

Published in the United States of America by Oxford University Press
198 Madison Avenue, New York, NY 10016, United States of America

British Library Cataloguing in Publication Data
Data available

Library of Congress Control Number: 2013952041

ISBN 978–0–19–870322–8

For Blanka, Neža Ana, and Sara Kate

Acknowledgments

My first and warmest thanks go to my wife Blanka. Without her patience and support this book would not only not have been written, but, even if written, would not mean to me what it now does. Exact same thanks go to our daughters Neža Ana and Sara Kate. Life has been a blessing since you've been here. Because of the work on this book I may have often been much-too-absent, and absent-minded, husband and dad, but I am also both immensely joyful and grateful that I can now dedicate it to all three of you.

My biggest thanks are owed to Professor Paul Craig. Without him this book would not have begun. Without his sharp judgment and insight, scholarly guidance and advice, his genuine kindness, patience, understanding, his compelling criticism and just as sincere encouragement, the book would never have been written. For all that I've learned from him, on so many levels, there are no adequate words of acknowledgment. Let me just say that lucky are they whose paths cross with his own, and that I am forever grateful that I, too, can be among those indebted to him.

The first of this book's three main parts is the mapping analysis of the leading authors on constitutional pluralism and their different strands of thought. The idea of this part has been to provide the first comprehensive analysis of the terrain as a precondition to both further scholarship on the topic as well as my own two additional objectives within this book. When finished, each of the draft mapping chapters has been discussed with the respective author of each analyzed strand. I am thus very grateful to Profs Neil MacCormick, Joseph Weiler, Neil Walker, and Miguel Maduro for having read the respective chapters and for their priceless discussions with me over 2006, and on other occasions. The same thanks go to Prof Mattias Kumm for our email exchange that has helped me with his strand. Those discussions helped take my readings of their theories further than it would have otherwise been possible. Several of these exchanges have gone beyond the mapping analysis and have had an impact also on the shaping of some key parts of the book's main argument, as acknowledged in the text.

Help from the European pluralists has been crucial to this book. But the role of my American mentors has been indispensable to it in even more fundamental ways. Prof Frank Michelman was the one who opened my doors to the academic world back in 1999. There is no way to repay my debt for all his attentive help, guidance, understanding, and support over all this time ever since. Without any of those this book would never have seen the light of day. Moreover, most of the contents in Chapters 9 and 10 were written under his mentorship, after my return from Oxford in the period between 2008–2011. Those were added to the book's current form in the process of substantially reworking my older Oxford D.Phil. dissertation (from 2007) into the monograph. Among my warmest thanks are also those to Prof Larry Tribe who acted as my field supervisor in the earlier years.

Without the enormous privilege of learning from him in many different ways, and without his precious capacity to enlighten and refine you, while at the same time understanding and supporting you, my research at Harvard would also not have been the same, nor would I have had the opportunity to see Oxford other than as a tourist. Without him too, you would not be reading this book today.

Many have helped through offering teaching opportunities, some of which contributed decisively to my further improvement of this book. Huge thanks for this and other reasons are due to Profs Glyn Morgan, Michael Sandel, Mathias Risse, Chris Robichaud, and various departments across Harvard University. I am especially grateful to the faculty of Harvard Law, in particular again to Prof Frank Michelman, Vice Deans Prof Bill Alford and Prof Andrew Kaufman, as well as Prof Martha Minow, the Dean, for the opportunity to teach as Lecturer on Law (spring 2012) the subject of my choice: Europe and the Future of Democracy. This teaching directly on constitutional pluralism has infused me with enormous energies at the right time and proven invaluable to the progress on the book. It has been during this period and appointment that I have been able to complete the major part of my refining work, wrap it all up, and now submit. The most valuable aspect of teaching has however been the truly remarkable hundreds of bright student minds who in their own special ways together taught me more about my own topic than I ever could have taught any of them about theirs. Space does not permit me to thank all of them in person, but I do want to single out those whose feedback, challenges, and criticisms most directly improved some of my arguments in the book: Liz Freedman, Tarek Austin, Patrick Withers, Patrick Johnson, Luke Raffin, Jamie Walsh, Oliver Schoppe, Guillermo Gapel, Danielle Singleton, Severin Randall, Livio Valenti, Haitham Al-Salama, Jirka Jelinek, Jann Spiess and Duval Guimaraes—thanks a million!

Neither this book, nor anything at all, would however have been possible for me without the following individuals who helped when it mattered most: Prof Dr Marjetka Uršič Vrščaj, Prof Dr Russell Nauta, Dr David Odell, Dr James Ku, Prof Dr Matthew Kulke, Prof Dr Branko Zakotnik, Dr Roger Lange and Dr Laima Zarins. Prof Inka Stritar, Dr Vladislav Bevc, and Profs Dr Lovro Šturm, Dr Miro Cerar, and Dr Peter Jambrek have all helped in their own different ways as well, as have many personal colleagues, friends, and family members (listed in no particular order): Max Fontes, Michele Gigli, Manuel d'Empaire, Prof Dr Kerem Cem Sanli, Prof Dr Cengiz Sisman, Dr Octavio Sanchez, Prof Dr Vlad Perju, Assistant Dean Jeanne Tai, Walter Popper and Fleet Hill, Klemen Babnik, Niko Šutić, Aleš Malerič, Gorazd Čibej, Andrej Grum, Andrej Crček, Jure Vanič, Matej and Anja Pristavec, Igor Salmič, Florjan Frčej, Tomaž Vernik, Jana Bambič, Lucija Repanšek, Dr David Movrin, Suresh Gurdev, Dejan Steinbuch, Dr Simon Dobnik, Marko and Tina Babnik, Brina Babnik, Darko, Irena, Jernej and Lovro Iskra, Arif Sulejmanović, Tomaž and Manja Jaklitsch, Monika and Marko Zupanc, Mojca and Matej Godnič, Tone and Nataša Corel, Katja Corel and Mario Frančešević, Jurij and Emina Jaklič, Nada and Štefan Simončič, Angelca Klanšek, Tone and Marica Klanšek, Ernest and Rezka Jaklitsch, and many others.

Many thanks also to the anonymous reviewers, and to all at OUP (Natasha Flemming, Clare Kennedy, Catherine Cragg, Katherine Marshall, and many others) who have helped with the editing, page proofing, and other aspects of the production process that has been carried out so professionally. A big thanks also goes to Alan McConnell Duff, Mikael Strugar, Ajda Pirš, and especially Cherry Mosteshar and her team from The Oxford Editors, for their prior precious help on the same front and for all their patience with me. I am also very grateful to Prof Stephen Weatherill and, again, the late Prof Neil MacCormick, who both examined a whole earlier version of this text—my D.Phil. dissertation—and offered exceptionally useful feedback. Same thanks go to the editor of this series, Prof Gráinne de Búrca who co-examined my Harvard S.J.D. dissertation: her feedback there further improved both chapters that were later added to this book. Finally, thank you to the late Prof Peter Birks, head of Oxford Law postgraduate department. Besides few others it was him who, in a letter compiled in the last days before his passing, stood up for the plan of this concurrent research strategy that has been the key. One result of that "last will", and trust, of his is this book.

The plan and detailed chapter-by-chapter descriptions of this project were completed in 2003, my first year at Oxford. According to the program, all that was then assessed and confirmed at an examination by two Faculty members in 2004. The plan of the project and chapter descriptions explained in some detail the idea of the comprehensive mapping of the pluralist branch, its analysis and assessment. They also identified the different pluralist strands and clarified the main differences between them and their distinct orientations. The first draft mapping analysis was completed by late 2004 and early 2005, and it was the whole of 2006 that I then spent discussing the chapters with the examined pluralists. The very idea of mapping and analyzing the terrain of constitutional pluralism as presented in those materials, as well as selected individual chapter drafts, were shared with them in 2005–2006, and with a younger colleague at his request in late 2004. Moreover, I appreciate the interest of Profs John Erik Fossum and Augustin Menéndez with whom I shared the first completed manuscript in the summer of 2007. Section 1 of Chapter 9 is composed of parts of my article on "Liberal Legitimacy and the Question of Respect" that appears in Ratio Juris (accepted in 2012, published September 2014) as the original publication. Thanks to John Wiley & Sons Ltd (Blackwell Publishing) for the permission to reproduce them here.

In the end thoughts lead back home once more. Now to my mother and father, brother and sister. They are the only ones who have followed and shared the entirety of the good and less good times of my journey into constitutional pluralism. They alone know what it took as they too have given *their* all into it. So thank you mom Marijana and dad Tine, I hope you'll enjoy reading your work. Same deepest thanks go to dear brother Mark, whose care for me and my girls has been endless and, above all, to my sister Tina who has taught us all how to never give up.

Klemen Jaklic

Cambridge, MA, spring 2012

Series Editors' Preface

The literature on constitutional pluralism has grown very considerably over the last two decades. The publication within this series of a monograph that seeks to take stock of the existing scholarship, assess it and then propose a particular conception of constitutional pluralism that the author regards as preferable is therefore to be welcomed. This is, in broad terms, the agenda of Klemen Jaklic's book.

In the first part of the work he carefully analyses the meaning of constitutional pluralism used by leading authors in this field, including Neil MacCormick, Neil Walker, Joseph Weiler, Miguel Poaires Maduro, and Mattias Kumm. The objective is to provide a map of the overall intellectual terrain in a way that has not been done hitherto. This careful exercise reveals, moreover, the different strands of thought that exist within the frame of constitutional pluralism. The author shows that while each of the principal contributions can justly be regarded as a theory about constitutional pluralism, they are nonetheless very different, often focusing on different questions, with the consequence that the respective contributions do not sit easily with each other.

Jaklic does not shy away from the difficulty posed by the very heterogeneity of thought within constitutional pluralism. He acknowledges the critique that there may be no common core to this branch of thought and responds by positing what he believes is the central core of constitutional pluralist thought, and revealing how existing theories fit into this new picture. He acknowledges also the critique from those who subscribe to monist interpretations of the constitutional order, and provides a detailed response to such arguments. In the final part of the book Jaklic makes the case for what he conceives to be the superior theory of constitutional pluralism and the ground on which it can be claimed to be a new branch of constitutional thought.

This work will be of interest to all those who are concerned with EU law and the relationship between its legal orders.

Paul Craig and Gráinne de Búrca

Contents

Introduction

Over the last couple of decades a substantial body of literature dealing with the subject of the European Union's constitutionalism has emerged. One way of making analytical sense of this rising new scholarship is to observe and categorize the main distinct branches within it. One such categorization is introduced in what follows, and serves to illustrate the place and general meaning of constitutional pluralism within the body of this scholarship. The categorization sees three main branches among the existing theories. These are classified according to the criterion of how they associate the concept of constitutionalism with the development at the European level, and of how a possible constitutionalism at that level would properly relate to the nation-state constitutionalism.

The constitutional discussion in Europe has started to thrive; especially after the advancement of the so-called transformation thesis in the early 1990s.[1] The claim of the thesis was that the EU had already gone through the transformation from an international legal order to a constitutional one. The claim has been supported mainly by the European Court of Justice's (ECJ) elaboration of the doctrines of direct effect, supremacy, pre-emption, and implied powers, by its protection of fundamental rights and principles of good administration, as well as by the existing system of judicial review. In addition to that, the story of the EU's constitutionalization has been backed by certain typical constitutional features provided for by the Treaties themselves, and by a subtle transformation of the language the Court has used throughout the years.[2]

I

Some have reacted quite sceptically to the transformation idea and have claimed that Europe cannot be understood as having a constitution in the real sense of this

[1] The classic account is, for example, J. Weiler, "The Transformation of Europe" (1991) 100 Yale LJ 2403. The path-breaking early account is E. Stein, "Lawyers, Judges and the Making of a Transnational Constitution" (1981) 75 American Journal of American Law 1; also F. Mancini, "The Making of a Constitution for Europe" (1989) 26 CML Rev 595. For a succinct account of the transformation thesis, the counter-argument, as well as a response to the counter-argument, see P. Craig, "Constitutions, Constitutionalism, and the European Union" (2001) 7 ELJ 125.

[2] Craig (n 1) at 128–30.

word.[3] These sceptical reactions have gradually evolved into what is the first branch in our categorization. It comprises positions that insist that constitutionalism either has not, cannot, or should not yet, spread beyond the confines of a state, be that a nation or pluri-nation-state.[4] This is the common core of this branch, but its individual strands, as well as variants within the strands, have their own particular emphases within this common core.

One strand of the scepticism has thus been based on the view that the state can be the only possible, or major, source of constitutional authority as a consequence of its exclusive capacity to form and nourish a sufficiently homogeneous sovereign *demos* that would be capable of forming a democratic will. A radical variant of this argument comes close to suggesting that only a more ethno-centric *demos* could warrant the existence of a sufficiently democratic constitution. Since such homogeneity is not the case at the Union level, any attempt to form constitutionalism at that level must fail.[5] A milder variant, however, distances itself from such a potentially ethno-centric claim, although it continues to maintain vigorously that because of certain structural preconditions of democracy which can only be met in a state, the concept of a constitution is still inextricably bound up with the idea of the state.[6] Since the EU does not yet meet—as it is not a state—those structural preconditions of democracy, such as the Europeanized party system, European media, European civil society, etc, it also cannot yet claim constitutionalism in the real sense of this word. The argument concludes that at the moment when the EU would meet the preconditions, it could indeed have a constitution too, but would at the very same moment automatically become a state.

Another strand within the same branch of scepticism shares the main concerns raised earlier about the lack of legitimation through a popular constituent power. Its rejection of the transformation thesis is, however, primarily focused on the claim that international law remains the only appropriate legal register within which we can conceive of European integration.[7] The insistence of the second strand on explaining all the transformations of the EU exclusively within the

[3] See, for example, D. Grimm, "Does Europe Need a Constitution?" (1995) 1 ELJ 282; J. Isensee, "Staat und Verfassung" in J. Isensee and P. Kirchof (eds), *Handbuch des Staatsrecthts* (Heidelberg: Müller 1987); P. Kirchof, "Der deutsche Staat im Prozes der europäischen Integration" in J. Isensee and P. Kirchof (eds), *Handbuch des Staatsrechts*, Vol VII (1992); A. Pellet, "Les Fondements Juridiques Internationaux du Droit Communautaire" in Academy of European Law (ed.), *Collected Courses of the Academy of European Law*, Vol V (1994), Book 2; T. Schilling, "The Autonomy of the Community Legal Order: An Analysis of Possible Foundations" (1996) 17 Harv Int LJ 389; T. Hartley, *Constitutional Problems of the European Union* (Oxford: Hart Publishing, 1999).

[4] Cf Craig, who uses the term "constitutional Euro-scepticism" to describe the variety of these sceptical positions ((n 1) at 163).

[5] European constitutional scholarship associates a certain degree of this radical, and much criticized ethno-centric conception of a *demos*, with the decision of the German Federal Constitutional Court in *Brunner v The European Treaty* [1994] 1 CMLR 57. For criticism of the allegedly "Carl-Schmittian" rationale behind the decision see J. Weiler, "The State 'Über Alles': Demos, Telos and the German Maastricht Decision" in O. Due et al. (eds), *Festschrift für Ulrich Everling* (Baden-Baden: Nomos Verlag) at 651.

[6] Grimm (n 3).

[7] Pellet (n 3); Schilling (n 3); Hartley (n 3).

traditional paradigm of international, and not constitutional, law denies the claim of a self-standing and constitutional EU legal system. Consequently, it limits constitutionalism to the internal domain of a state, just as is also the case under the first strand.

The common feature of the two sceptical strands is the proposition that the ultimate authority over the state's territory does and should remain with the member states and their constitutions. The member states are hierarchically superior to the non-constitutional legal order of the Union, and the member states thus also remain "masters" of such an order. In the ultimate sense it is and should be for them to determine its course, validity, and content. From the perspective of constitutionalism this view can, therefore, be characterized as "nation-state constitutional monism."[8]

II

There have been numerous responses to the preceding reasoning. Advocates of a rival school of thought share the idea that Europe has been transformed into a hierarchical constitutional legal order. They explain that the foundation of Europe's constitutional authority is now fully independent of, and not derived from, the constitutional authority of the nation-states, which it hierarchically overrides or, at any rate, ought to override. The jurisprudence of the ECJ has provided the modern foundation for this school of thought. In the founding decision of the Court in *Van Gend en Loos*[9] the Treaty is, for instance, presented as much more than an agreement between states or an agreement between the Union and states. It is an agreement between the peoples of Europe that establishes a direct relationship between EU law and those peoples. That source of direct legitimacy authorizes the claim of independent normative authority, both political and legal, which means that the EU is, in the words of the Court, endowed with sovereign rights. This, combined with other aspects of the Court's jurisprudence,[10] has provided the impetus for the view of some that we are witnessing the forging of

[8] For similar characterizations of these approaches see, for example, N. Walker, "The Idea of Constitutional Pluralism" (2002) 65 ML Rev 337; N. MacCormick, "Beyond the Sovereign State" (1993) 56 ML Rev 1, 8; "Risking Constitutional Collision in Europe" (1998) 18 OJLS 517, 527. M. La Torre, "Legal Pluralism as Evolutionary Achievement of Community Law" (1999) 12 Ratio Juris 182, 192–3.

[9] Case 26-62 NV *Algemeine Transport-en Expeditie Onderneiming van Gend & Loos v Netherlands Inland Revenue Administration* [1963] ECR 3.

[10] Case 11/70 *Internationale Handelsgesellschaft mbH v Einfuhr-und Vorratsstelle für Getreide und Futtermittel* [1970] ECR 1125: "The law stemming from the Treaty, an independent source of law, cannot because of its very nature be overridden by rules of national law, however framed, without being deprived of its character at Community Law and without the legal basis of the Community itself being called into question. Therefore the validity of a Community measure or its effect within a Member State cannot be affected by allegations that it runs counter to either fundamental rights as formulated by the Constitution of that state or the principles of a national constitutional structure." See also, Case 6/64 *Flamino Costa v ENEL* [1964] ECR 585; Case 106/77 *Amministrazione delle Finanze dello Stato v Simmenthal SpA* [1978] ECR 629.

some deep European constitutional authority that is, by its very nature, the ultimate constitutional foundation on the territory of Europe. It is thus also hierarchically superior to the constitutional authorities of the nation-states. Whether or not such an authority might already exist, proponents of such a view agree that this state of affairs should at least be the desired result of the *finalité* of European integration. Like the proponents of the first branch, they too are thus preoccupied with finding, or establishing, the *one* ultimate constitutional foundation over a given territory. It is in this sense that the second branch can also be characterized as a version of monism—as "European constitutional monism."

There are clearly also variants within the branch of European constitutional monism. Those belonging to a stronger strand argue for a continuing and intensified constitutionalization of the EU to a degree that it would eventually represent a full-blown European state.[11] For proponents of the second branch it is not, however, necessary to argue for a European state. Based on the declared independent nature of the EU legal order, a milder strand might thus at least implicitly assume that, while not being a type of state constitutionalism, EU constitutionalism would still need to be the one with the foundational ultimate authority on the territory of Europe. It would thus also be for this legal order to decide with final authority about, for example, the content and validity of its laws as the supreme laws of the land, its relation to other legal orders, as well as its future development as such.

III

Neil MacCormick, in a short article in 1993,[12] was the first to express reservations about both of the monist visions. He explained how monist accounts actually assume that ultimately all law of a given territory emanates from a single source of authority. Thus, on a territory governed by a particular constitutional authority, only *it* has the authority to regulate the conduct of citizens, except insofar as it has delegated part of its authority over a defined subject matter to some other entity. International law, canon law, church law, the law of universities, firms, families, and the law of other social institutions, have all traditionally been seen as falling within that delegated sphere of law. Thus, in this way all these areas of law are seen as deriving in some ultimate sense from that single source of constitutional authority. MacCormick explained that this idea of one ultimate source of legal/political authority, that is this deepest assumption of monism, has completely

[11] The idea is an old one, and continues to attract notable contemporary proponents. Examples include F. Mancini, "Europe: The Case for Statehood" (1998) 4 Eur LJ 29; J. Fishcher, "From Confederation to Federation: Thoughts on the Finality of European Integration," (2000) Federal Trust European Essay No 8; G. Morgan, *The Idea of a European Superstate* (Princeton, NJ: Princeton University Press, 2005); G. Verhofstadt, *De Verenigde Staten van Europa* ("The United States of Europe") (Antwerp: Houtekiet, 2005); see also his, "Forging 'United States of Europe' is Key to the Future," Statement (November 2005). See also Chapter 9, n 64, this book.

[12] MacCormick (n 8).

dominated our legal/political tradition and thought. He reminded us how it is already apparent in the work of Bodin and Hobbes and then "runs through many successor variations, whether it is Rousseau locating it in the general will," or indeed "Kant in the constitutional but absolute and irresistible state . . . , Bentham and Austin with their sovereign *legibus solutus*, or Dicey and the constitutional tradition of the sovereignty of Parliament."[13] One of the idea's most elaborate affirmations is indeed to be found also in Kelsen, whose work has provided the groundwork of continental legal thought.

In that 1993 article, and other contributions that followed, MacCormick then set out to argue that the developments of the new Europe represent a fundamental challenge to the concept of monism. He maintained that in these circumstances we should no longer understand that there is one ultimate source of constitutional authority on each state territory; namely, those states' individual constitutions, from which all legal and political authority of that territory should be seen as ultimately emanating. Nor should we understand, MacCormick contended, that the latter have been, or should be, replaced by the European constitution as the ultimate single source of constitutional authority over the territory of Europe. His conviction was that both of these monist views must be wrong, and that they ought to give way to a third, pluralist vision. According to this, the European constitution is not ultimately derived from, and so hierarchically inferior to, national constitutional authority. Nor are the national constitutions ultimately grounded in, and thus hierarchically subordinated to, the European constitutional authority. Instead, both of these are and should be self-standing, and thus coequal, sources of constitutional authority that overlap *heterarchically* over a shared piece of territory so that neither of them is really the ultimate authority. This plurality is understood as avoiding the one-sided domination characteristic of the hierarchical strategies of either of the monisms described above.

But such an idea of heterarchy as opposed to hierarchy of sources of constitutional authority is a highly abstract construct. Standing alone it appears almost mysterious, begging questions as to the more concrete meaning of such pluralism (heterarchy) as distinct from monism (hierarchy). That is probably why it actually figures only as the abstract principled ground, the deepest pluralist basis in MacCormick's theory, from which he developed his more tangible conception and meaning of constitutional pluralism.

MacCormick's was not the only contribution to the topic. Soon after his 1993 article, additional proposals started to emerge that also claimed to be pluralist as opposed to monist. Gradually, several contributions appeared under the common label of "constitutional pluralism." The authors often cited one another and gave the impression that their proposals were similar to, and corroborative of, each other. A common view started to prevail among them and many non-participant observers, namely, that all these contributions initiated and belonged to a new common branch within constitutional thought. The branch of constitutional pluralism was

[13] MacCormick (n 8) at 15.

born; one that claims to bring a novel and normatively superior understanding of the concept of constitutionalism to Europe, and to constitutional thought in general.

At the heart of the alleged new branch is the insistence that we need to change our whole assumed basic framework of constitutional discourse. In a sense the new pluralist context in Europe that can no longer be explained in monist terms simply serves the pluralists' argument that the old monistic approach to constitutional discourse neither can, nor should, reign any longer. It should be replaced with the pluralist framework as a whole new setting in which to place and engage in constitutional discourse. The immediate focus of constitutional pluralists is thus on explaining constitutional authority in a new and superior manner, which would offer that whole new foundational framework to constitutional discourse. It is not, however, that pluralists are interested in the issue of authority alone. The new pluralist approach would not necessarily change the topics of the traditional constitutional discourse, though it would clearly also add several new ones. The idea is rather that it would profoundly restructure the way in which we should approach those topics in our alleged new pluralist age. Over the years the pluralist claims have gained immense popularity among European scholars, so much so that in Europe constitutional pluralism has now become the dominant branch of constitutional thought.

The claims of constitutional pluralism are important and far-reaching. Yet the discourse that has so far evolved consists mainly of numerous individual parts of contributions by each of the pluralist authors that are still rather dispersed throughout the literature. There has been practically no attempt thus far to construct a more integrated picture of each version of the theory. Nor has anyone yet conducted an overarching inter-theoretical analysis and assessment of the theories. The current trend of making and collecting partial individual contributions, without at the same time meticulously clarifying the whole, continues. This tendency only adds to the puzzles and doubts that have begun to surround the idea of constitutional pluralism. An in-depth overarching examination of the branch of constitutional pluralism indeed does not exist, nor has it been attempted to date. Yet, as this book shows, it is only through such an overarching analytical approach that the most fundamental and pressing questions about constitutional pluralism can be successfully addressed and answered. To provide such an overarching examination of the branch is the idea of this work. That being so, the work consists of three main aims or themes.

The *first main aim* concerns the mapping analysis. The idea is to map out comprehensively all the leading contributions in the field, and to do so in a particular way that will also help unravel the formidable labyrinth they currently form. This goes beyond mere restatements of the proposals.

Firstly, the various different individual contributions by a given leading pluralist author, which are currently still quite dispersed through the literature, are pulled together into a coherent whole to construct a more complete picture (and my own reading) of the given author's pluralist theory. Such a constructivist collation aims at closing gaps and resolving inconsistencies between the different pieces by the individual author. This proceeds by further pursuing the internal logic of the theory's central axioms as stated by its respective author, as well as by drawing on several interviews with the pluralist authors under scrutiny that were conducted for this specific purpose. The result is a careful construction of a more complete picture of each different version of constitutional pluralism; a construction that goes beyond the current literature, but is at the same time inevitably predetermined by the theory's own internal logic. In all cases the theories are thus upgraded and further clarified, while in some the material is pulled together into a concrete conception of pluralism for the first time. This shows why exactly the given author, who might or might not assign himself to the branch, should nonetheless be regarded as one of the leading pluralists.

Secondly, by introducing a unique decoding device elaborated for this specific purpose, "Ariadne's Thread," it is possible to conduct the mapping analysis in a manner that shows that the various contributions hiding under the umbrella of "constitutional pluralism" are strikingly different projects, much more so than has been commonly assumed and represented. In important respects they actually appear within wholly different discourses and deal with different sets of questions. When they are making contributions within the same topic, their positions often contradict one another, so much so that each author would clearly consider the other proposals as monist when judged by his own standards. The particular mapping analysis does not just starkly reveal these different uses of the same term; doing so in a unique and new way that later enables us to unravel the maze. It also actively develops the different discourses that these distinct uses of the term "constitutional pluralism" constitute. This, at the same time, poses an immediate and pressing further question that is part of the second aim of this work.

The *second main aim* of the work is a comprehensive assessment of the pluralist theories thus elaborated and separated. This aim also consists of several sub-parts.

Firstly, there is the puzzle concerning the existence versus the non-existence of the common branch. If the theories are actually so significantly different as the mapping suggests, then to what, if anything at all, does the branch really amount? Can we really speak of a novel common branch of constitutional pluralism? Or is the latter, as one recent critique has now also explicitly suggested, only empty rhetoric masking a group of different proposals with no common core that could bring that claimed uniqueness and superiority? It is argued that if these different proposals are indeed to be seen as currently belonging to the same branch, the latter needs to be understood in a particular way; quite differently from what has been assumed by any of the current proposals. This will clarify for the first time what truly constitutes the common core or trunk of the pluralist branch, while showing how all of these very different conceptions of pluralism actually fit into this new picture. Relying on the unique Ariadne's Thread mapping analysis, this part of the assessment thus decodes the pluralist branch and unravels the labyrinth.

Secondly, the assessment turns to the several lines of the recent fundamental critique of the very idea of pluralism: the position purporting to disprove its distinctiveness from monism. It is argued, however, that after the common branch is decoded and all its ramifications are mapped, those important lines of the critique appear in a wholly new light and must be rejected. The sound core of constitutional pluralism does carry an idea that is a true novelty within constitutional thought, and cannot be dismissed by any of those current criticisms. Some slightly different critical concerns that are not quite yet elaborated by these current lines of criticism might nonetheless be able to harm some of the less sound parts of the existing branch. This nevertheless leaves its core, and a fully sound, superior conception that can potentially still flow from it, intact.

Thirdly, the assessment does not focus only on the branch as such, but also on each of the theories. This runs through the mapping analysis, where each individual theory is first appraised internally at the end of its own chapter. Such an intra-theoretical assessment examines coherence and such other internal aspects of each individual theory that do not yet include comparisons with the rest of the pluralist theories. Its part is also the elaboration of the exact variant of ultimate values underlying each different version of the theory. This is later followed by a confrontation and assessment of the theories *inter se*. This is conducted through separate chapters designated specifically to this key comprehensive *inter*-theoretical assessment. The latter, an element that has been profoundly missing from current discourse, is crucial since it reveals several serious weaknesses in the existing versions of pluralism, in some more than others, that have not been identified thus far. The detailed examination of these weaknesses serves at the same time as a springboard from which to determine whether or not a potential sound path for pluralism still exists and, if it does, in what direction the current discourse thus should be reoriented.

This leads to the *third and final main aim* of the work. The preceding inter-theoretical assessment identifies the "bare" sub-branches of pluralism. They are those through which the distinctive pluralist idea cannot succeed to a satisfying extent. This at the same time also carves out the one and indeed the only fully sound general direction that still remains open to pluralism, while avoiding the identified difficulties. Two of the current sub-branches are more compatible with this orientation than others. Neither of them, however, yet makes use of its full potential so that constitutional pluralism could truly work for the benefit of all humanity, not just the Europeans alone. The possibility of this more universalist path, based on a truly genuine equality, is then further explored. The study that results involves an elaboration of a unique and sound conception of constitutional pluralism within this approach. It is argued that that is the superior among the conceptions of the new branch. This is not solely because it is the only one sufficiently distinct from monism. Nor is it "merely" because through such a more universalist approach alone is it possible to avoid all those various other decisive problems besetting the rest of the conceptions. Rather, its superiority lies also in its capacity to unleash a unique new democratic potential implicit in Europe's new post-sovereign context. Through this sound conception of constitutional pluralism, the post-sovereign Europe can be seen as the seed of a new historic advancement of democracy for the Europeans and non-Europeans alike that has been unavailable thus far throughout our monist age; and in part because of monism. This opportunity would likewise be lost were we to adopt one of the "bare" sub-branches of pluralism. The work concludes by showing how the sound pluralist model of democracy would gradually, but inevitably, arise out of the particular sound foundation of constitutional pluralism. The branch of constitutional pluralism, thus reoriented and refined, has the potential rightfully to be considered the superior new approach within constitutional thought.

PART I

MAPPING ANALYSIS

Ariadne's Thread

When Theseus, an Athenian, sailed to Crete and entered the labyrinth, the Cretan king Minos' daughter, Ariadne, gave him a ball of thread that served as a navigation tool and led the Athenian through the labyrinth. There he managed to defeat the Minotaur, who had feasted on human flesh for years, and then found a way out of the labyrinth by following the path of the thread.[1]

The branch of thought known as constitutional pluralism is itself a labyrinth. Its intricate passageways and dead alleys, reflected in the heavily intertwined yet distinct, separate versions of the theory, seem a perfect setting for getting lost. Once inside these theoretical constructs, without some metaphorical ball of thread in hand you may believe you are heading towards decoding the labyrinth, but are in fact being led astray. You find two versions and their individual features in a particular relationship, and they appear to have particular meanings. But appearances are deceptive. The true picture would have revealed itself in a different light were you to analyse the versions with the right decoding tool designed to constantly read into your picture the parameters ordinary observation leaves out.

The decoding tool I have developed for the case of constitutional pluralism will help us navigate through the maze. It is not possible to clarify the pluralist branch without the use of such a tool. This is because, as we will see, the pluralists engage in different types of discourses while using a similar-sounding rhetoric, which often gives the false impression that they are working on the same thing within the same sector of the labyrinth.

The decoding tool posits four different discourses (sectors of the labyrinth). The first is about the proper *subject* of decision-making authority. It deals with the institutional question of "*who*"—the nation-state or European institutions—should have the (final) authority to decide in a disputed case. The question of "who decides who decides," is thus constitutive of the first discourse as defined by the decoding tool. I will also refer to it as the discourse of the *who*.

[1] Cretan king Minos, the son of Zeus and Europa, had a famed Greek craftsman, Daedalus, build the labyrinth. Ovid writes that Daedalus confused the usual passages and deceived the eye with a conflicting maze of various wandering paths ("*in errorem variarum ambage viarum*"), and that the famous craftsman himself was barely able to return to the entrance, so deceptive was the place ("*tanta est fallacia tecti*") (Ovid, *Metamorphoses*, Book 8, lines 160–67).

The second discourse centers on a substantially distinct question. It is not primarily engaged with the question of determining the right institutional *who* of decisions, but rather the question of *how* any institutional *who*—be that a nation-state or a European constitutional actor—should or should not go about determining its decisions. The "*how*" here refers to the right manner, or method, through which the constitutional discourse should take place, and so the second discourse is about the quest for the right *form* of constitutional discourse in Europe. In this light, it also deliberately avoids the more direct question over the right content (the "*what*") of constitutional discourse. Its whole point is that direct discussions and decisions on such issues are to be left to the existing constitutional identity holders themselves, so as to avoid imposing on them any particular content from such further substantive discourse.

The third discourse is directly concerned with ascertaining the right *content* of constitutional discourse. To a substantial degree it is about determining the right substantive *what* of the existing constitutional identities in Europe. While the second discourse deliberately avoids the substantive question of constitutional discourse in Europe, this third discourse intentionally focuses on that very question and attempts to make a pluralist proposal within that sphere. I will refer to it as the discourse of the *what*.

There is also a fourth discourse defined by the tool. While this cannot be equated with any of the first three, it is the most abstract of the discourses and can accommodate the others. It deals with the question concerning the relationship between different constitutional orders at the most abstract foundational level that does not yet by itself reach the more specific questions of the *who*, *how*, and *what*. It must be emphasized though that the "foundational discourse" I have in mind here is specifically defined. It does not embrace just any contribution to foundational constitutional theory, or to foundational constitutional questions as such, that is more foundational than the rest of a pluralist theory of some author in question. Rather, the term "foundational discourse" denotes the fact that someone has elaborated a distinctive pluralist conception—actually explained the notion of *heterarchy*—at the deepest systemic level. Such a conception also needs to be a unique and sufficiently elaborated proposal as to the specific pluralist relationship between both constitutional orders within that clearly distinct type of discourse that cannot be equated with the discourses of the *who*, the *what*, and the *how*. Only some pluralists will have such conceptions sufficiently elaborated and defined at such a foundational level. MacCormick's abstract account of constitutional heterarchy, as distinct from hierarchy, is an example of a germ of his own foundational conception that we will be able to explicate more fully within this last type of discourse.

The four discourses are interrelated, but at the same time distinct. Different pluralists work within different discourses, and their proposals are normally not limited to a single one. The decoding tool should thus enable us to separate the various contributions and to conduct meaningful comparisons. We should thus be able to avoid being swallowed up by the labyrinth, and eventually be able to map and decode the whole branch.

1

MacCormick and the Idea of Pluralism

1. Preliminary Clarifications

It was Neil MacCormick who, in a short article published in 1993, first suggested that the development of the new Europe might harbor the potential for pluralist novelty transcending the traditional monist understandings of constitutional power and authority. Only a brief abstract account of his pluralist alternative has been provided thus far,[2] but as has been hinted, MacCormick expanded on that abstraction to develop his more tangible conception of constitutional pluralism. Before beginning the exploration of his fuller conception, some preliminary clarifications would be useful.

MacCormick's conception is about dispersal of authority over a given territory so that there is no longer one single and final authority from which all law of that territory would ultimately originate. The authority is understood in both the political sense, as de facto obedience to a single power source, and in the legal sense, as some normative ground, as opposed to the mere fact of obedience, which confers near absolute legislative power on a single source. In MacCormick's work this notion of ultimate authority appears under the name of sovereignty, and he mainly operates using this term. The central target of his critique is thus best described as the idea that in some ultimate sense, all law always originates (sovereignty in the political sense) or should originate (sovereignty in the legal sense) "in a single power source, like a sovereign."[3] His argument for the dispersal of authority so that no one can any longer claim the ultimate authority, or sovereignty, leads to his desired condition described as "beyond sovereignty."

Relying on Austin, MacCormick explains that a sovereign in the predominantly political sense exists, "where somebody has the power to issue commands but is not subject to a power of commanding by other people," and whereby "the power of commanding rests simply on the habits of a population, not upon any kind of legal or normative grant of authority to command."[4] Thus, "for Austin, the idea of sovereignty is a matter of fact, a matter of politics."[5] By contrast, sovereign in the predominantly legal sense exists where somebody has near-absolute legislative power conferred by normative terms. Here, an underlying normative legal theory

[2] Introduction, pp. 4–5.

[3] N. MacCormick, "Beyond the Sovereign State" (1993) 56 ML Rev 1, 8.

[4] MacCormick (n 3) 12.

[5] MacCormick (n 3) 12.

is required "that explains what it is for there to be a position of normative power defined by some highest-order legal rules or norms that put, or sometimes put," that single somebody in the defined position of sovereignty.[6]

MacCormick's immediate focus is on the concept of a sovereign state, which could be seen as such an ultimate single authority—the sovereign—in its political and legal sense.[7] The sovereign state, MacCormick explains, is "a territorial political order coupled with a legally defined position of near-absolute legislative power."[8] There are two aspects to the concept. Firstly, a state is sovereign in the external sense if the exercise of power on its territory is not subject to some external superior power or legal constraints.[9] Secondly, we can speak of a sovereign state in the internal sense when a particular agency within a state has such a position of near-absolute legislative power.[10]

Moreover, sovereign states have "monopoly of normative power, in the sense that only they have legal authority to regulate the conduct of citizens, except in so far as they have explicitly delegated some power of the regulation over some defined subject-matter."[11] In areas of delegation we have, for instance, international law; primitive law; canon law; and church law; and the law of social institutions like universities, firms, and families.[12] Note, however, that by being *delegated* by the will of the sovereign state, all these areas of law, too, are seen as ultimately residing in the sovereign state. MacCormick reminds us here of the old idea that "[c]ivil society is impossible unless you construct an order in which power is vested absolutely in a sovereign or in the state," and explains how this thought "runs through many successor variations, whether it is Rousseau locating all in the general will, or Kant in the constitutional but absolute and irresistible state," or indeed authors like "Bentham and Austin with their sovereign *legibus solutus*, or Dicey and the constitutional tradition of the sovereignty of Parliament."[13]

2. The New Europe as a Challenge to Sovereignty

MacCormick observes how—even if recent jurisprudence seems to have downplayed the idea of sovereignty as foundational for law—the press, politicians, and popular opinion have not followed this path. There is still widespread belief

[6] MacCormick (n 3) 12.

[7] While the sovereign state could be seen as the starting point of his preoccupation with pluralism, we will see throughout this book that MacCormick's project is about sovereignty as such. I thus understand that he includes under the concept of the sovereign all of the following: a particular institution of ultimate power and authority within a state (eg UK Parliament), or the state itself (the sovereign state), or, indeed crucially, some underlying body in which the state or institutional sovereignty ultimately resides, like the people of the state, or the Austinian aggregate of the UK electorate, plus monarch, plus lords, to which MacCormick refers (MacCormick (n 3) at fn 6). It will be argued what else must fall under his concept of the sovereign and sovereignty that needs to be dispersed. See pp. 28–9.

[8] MacCormick (n 3) at 14.

[9] MacCormick (n 3) at 14.

[10] MacCormick (n 3) at 14.

[11] MacCormick (n 3) at 14.

[12] MacCormick (n 3) at 14.

[13] MacCormick (n 3) at 15.

that "there are a lot of sovereign states in the world, that this is a good thing, that the United Kingdom is one, and that it will be a bad thing if the UK ceases to be so."[14] MacCormick reminds us, for instance, how the British Prime Minister "assured the House of Commons that the 'Sovereignty of this House' is in no way infringed by the Maastricht Treaty," or how the Danish electorate voted down the Maastricht Referendum due to, as was said, "concern about national sovereignty."[15] In light of this background MacCormick sets out to revisit the issue in the specific context of the new Europe, which, according to him, poses the fiercest challenge to the idea of sovereignty and its assumed foundational link with law and politics. The question is thus whether the new Europe "finally torpedoes" the idea that political and legal systems "comprise all and only the rules that emanate from sovereign commands," and with this torpedoes the existence of sovereign states in Europe themselves.[16]

Developments after the Second World War have, indeed, dramatically changed the legal and political landscape in Europe. Legal regimes have evolved—that of the EU and Council of Europe—which seem to have supremacy over domestic law, even if only within the limited range of defined subjects. In the view of the European Court of Justice (ECJ), the law stemming from the EU Treaties thus "cannot because of its very nature be overridden by rules of national law, however framed, without being deprived of its character as Community Law and without the legal basis of the Community itself being called into question."[17] The principles of the supremacy of EU law and its direct applicability have been accepted by national institutions and are now regarded as part of the normal state of affairs. Similarly, the European Convention on Human Rights, as interpreted by the Strasbourg Court, also seems to have, at least de facto, the status of binding higher law in Europe. In practice, its decisions tend to be followed by member states of the Council of Europe even when they contradict domestic law.[18] Indeed, it is because of such developments that the Strasbourg Court has declared the European Convention on Human Rights "the constitutional instrument of European public order" in the field of human rights.[19]

It is clearly in the light of these new circumstances that MacCormick asks whether it is not that "the realities of our modern Europe" challenge the continuing existence of sovereign states in Europe, and the idea of sovereignty as the ultimate source of law in general.[20] His inquiry starts by addressing the question from the perspective of sovereignty understood in the political sense. At first glance, he speculates, it perhaps seems possible to put away the challenge through this

[14] MacCormick (n 3) at 1. [15] MacCormick (n 3) at 2. [16] MacCormick (n 3) at 2–3.

[17] Case 11/70 *Internationale Handelsgesellschaft mbH v Einfuhr- und Vorratsstelle für Getreide und Futtermittel* [1970] ECR 1125, para 3.

[18] See, eg P. Leuprecht, "The Execution of Judgments and Decisions" and G. Ress, "The Effects of Judgments and Decisions in Domestic Law," both in R. Macdonald et al (eds), *The European System for the Protection of Human Rights* (Dordrecht: Kluwer Academic Publishers, 1993).

[19] *Loizidou v Turkey* (App no 15318/89) (1995) Series A no 310, paras 27, 31.

[20] MacCormick (n 3) at 4.

Austinian understanding of sovereignty. One might reason that the "Parliament has delegated power to the Community's law-making organs, hence the commands they issue are binding on UK citizens in virtue of their pre-adoption by the sovereign body."[21] "It might be possible," MacCormick writes, "to be satisfied with this, so to say, monocular, view."[22] On this reading, "the European Community is sufficiently accounted for on the thesis that somebody here once said, 'let these Community organs be obeyed as to those matters *quoad* the United Kingdom', and now all these organs are being obeyed as a matter, ultimately, of obedience to our own native sovereign."[23] So, the sovereign is still ultimately in charge; the ultimate authority is still in its hands, one might think.

At the same time, however, McCormick urges that we be reminded of the contrary reasoning coming from the side of the European organs. They insist on the view that the EU is already a "new" and "independent legal order."[24] In light of these contrary views, "the ultimate test"[25] that could really determine sovereignty in the political sense would be something like the following: "whether Parliament could if it chose unilaterally enact legislation directly revoking British membership of the European Community and have it generally obeyed in the UK."[26] But if this is the ultimate test then one needs to take into account the fact that even proponents of national sovereignty reasoning concede that such direct revocation of membership "is not at all likely to happen, because of the huge economic damage the UK would suffer in circumstances of such a (purported) unilateral revocation."[27] So what then, MacCormick asks, is the answer to the question of the Austinian political sovereignty?[28] His answer is that "in these murky and conjectural waters" one probably needs to "concede that it is an open question either way whether Parliament and those who respond to Parliament's enactments have or have not a practice of habitual obedience to Community legislation."[29] There is after all "a certain consciousness of sanctions that would be incurred in the event of unilateral rather than amicably negotiated renunciation."[30]

So, our immediate response to the challenge of the new Europe—one that endeavored to explain obedience of Union organs still wholly through the sovereign member state—was too narrow a view.[31] It implicitly took for granted that under the "ultimate test" the habitual obedience would automatically go its way. After MacCormick's analysis, however, one sees that under the ultimate test and the circumstances of economic sanction the habitual obedience could well also be understood as going the other way. In such a case, the Austinian theory would work the other way around: "[i]nstead of... the bureaucrats of Brussels... being delegates of the UK sovereign, the UK authorities are mere delegates of the

[21] MacCormick (n 3) at 3. [22] MacCormick (n 3) at 4. [23] MacCormick (n 3) at 4.

[24] MacCormick (n 3) at 4. The two cited phrases are from Case 11/64 *Costa v ENEL* [1964] ECR 585, 593, 602–3.

[25] MacCormick (n 3) at 3. [26] MacCormick (n 3) at 3. [27] MacCormick (n 3) at 3.

[28] MacCormick (n 3) at 3. [29] MacCormick (n 3) at 3–4.

[30] MacCormick (n 3) at 3–4.

[31] "Yet is this account a very convincing one? Or does it not proceed with too narrow a perspective?" (MacCormick (n 3) at 4).

Euro-sovereign."[32] But while there may be Union officials and others who would find this idea of EU sovereignty "not unattractive," MacCormick reminds us that "that just shifts us from one monocular view to another."[33] From the perspective of the member states such a position would be "as unacceptable and implausible a solution as single-state sovereignty is from the Community viewpoint."[34]

So, in the end, neither of these "monocular"[35] accounts is very convincing for MacCormick. Both imply "too narrow a perspective."[36] The situation in the new Europe thus seems "too complex to be satisfactorily solved either way in terms of habit-of-obedience [ie political understanding of] sovereignty."[37] The conclusion seems to be that in these circumstances it is meaningless to speak of whether the habit-of-obedience rests with one side or the other, because at best it would be speculation—and does not the very act of speculation cut against the idea of political sovereignty as a *fact* of power, as actual obedience? The old Austinian approach to the analysis of the new circumstances along the lines of political sovereignty must be abandoned.

3. The Alternative Approach Leading to Pluralism

These findings lead MacCormick to focus on "other models which may enable us to account for legal complexity in a different way."[38] He points to an alternative avenue for analysing the new Europe and addressing the challenge it poses to the idea of sovereignty and sovereign states. This avenue, according to MacCormick, stresses more the legal understanding of sovereignty and "the kind of normative system law is," as opposed to merely some "set of power relations."[39] The focus now is not so much on the criterion of *actual obedience* in some ultimate-test situations, but more on the *normative* question. Should the national and European institutions, the described developments notwithstanding, still be understood as being grounded in one ultimate source of normative authority of a given territory (the situation of sovereignty); or would it be more appropriate in these circumstances to see them as deriving their authority from different "ultimate" sources of normative authority over the same territory (beyond sovereignty)?[40] This

[32] MacCormick (n 3) at 4 (footnote omitted). [33] MacCormick (n 3) at 5.

[34] MacCormick (n 3) at 5. MacCormick explains that the same story can also be told with respect to the European Convention on Human Rights (MacCormick (n 3) at 4).

[35] MacCormick (n 3) at 5. [36] MacCormick (n 3) at 4. [37] MacCormick (n 3) at 5.

[38] MacCormick (n 3) at 5. [39] MacCormick (n 3) at 8.

[40] Although the legal approach to sovereignty differs from the political one, a degree of effectiveness of a normative order (of observance of the purportedly authoritative ordinances) as a criterion for its existence must still be present in this approach. This is crucial for MacCormick's understanding of law and goes hand in hand with his understanding that the concept of sovereignty is both a political and legal concept ("Janus faced," as he writes), and that it is only a matter of which of the two components is stressed more. Hence, he actually describes this distinction as one between a "predominantly legal" and "predominantly political" understanding of sovereignty and normative order.

predominantly legal approach allows for the possibility that different constitutional orders, distinguished by their different respective sources of normative validity, coexist on a given territory: that they "overlap and interact, without necessarily requiring that one be subordinate or hierarchically inferior to the other" or to some third, similar order.[41]

So is there in Europe, and in each of the member states' territories, now only one ultimate source of normative authority in this predominantly legal sense; only one constitutional order? Or does each of the territories already include different and coexisting sources of such authority and thus also different constitutional orders? If the former is the case, the challenge to monism by the new Europe is rebutted and we still have sovereignty and sovereign states in Europe in some predominantly legal sense. But if the latter case holds, we have gone beyond sovereignty into circumstances in which there are now different, independent, but overlapping constitutional orders (and their normative validity sources) within each member state and the EU.

MacCormick's answer within this legal avenue of approaching the question is linked to his understanding of law as an institutional normative system. It is hence closely dependent on his institutional theory of law,[42] which, decisively for this case, insists "on a degree of sociological realism."[43] He thus seems to rely on the following two factors as determinative of the existence/non-existence of an independent constitutional order.

Firstly, existence of a developed constitutional order in part inescapably depends on self-referential attributes:

> [O]n the one hand, the existence of institutions with powers of law-making or adjudication or law-enforcement depends on norms of competence which are themselves to be regarded as elements of the system; on the other hand, the function of those very institutions is to legislatively determine, or to adjudicate upon and interpret, or to uphold, the very norms that constitute the system. In a sense, the laws make the institutions, and yet at the same time the institutions make the laws. Legal systems in their modern, developed form, exhibit the apparently paradoxical character of being self-referential ... The self-referential, or partially self-referential, character of a legal system has been associated in recent work by Luhmann, Teubner, and others of their school with the idea of *"autopoiesis"*, the idea of the system as self-generating and regenerating, transforming information received into the system's own terms before absorbing it. This seems somewhat exaggerated, though the idea is suggestive.[44]

Indeed, for MacCormick's purposes the idea of self-referentiality is suggestive to the extent that, under such an understanding, it becomes possible to see how constitutional orders might coexist without one necessarily being the ultimate source of

[41] MacCormick (n 3) at 8.

[42] N. MacCormick and O. Weinberger, *An Institutional Theory of Law* (Dordrecht: D. Reidel Publishing, 1986).

[43] N. MacCormick, "The Maastricht-Urteil: Sovereignty Now" (1995) 1 ELJ 259, 264.

[44] MacCormick (n 43) at 261–2 (footnote omitted).

the other.[45] The EU clearly possesses this first characteristic; notoriously, its institutions have been endorsing the understanding that their authority is ultimately grounded not in the nation-state constitutions but in the Treaties—that is, in the Union's constitution itself.[46]

But according to the institutional theory of law, a mere self-referential attribute is not enough for an alleged system to qualify as a self-standing constitutional order. MacCormick does not agree with exaggerations of the paradox of the self-referential quality of legal systems as some authors, in his view, have unduly advocated. For in reality the situation is, as his institutional theory teaches, "not too paradoxical," since the systems' "institutional existence is only 'in part' dependent on their own norms; it is also dependent upon at least some measure of efficacy."[47] The latter is thus the second necessary attribute institutional theory expects to be met by a would-be system for it to reasonably qualify as a self-standing constitutional order. Such efficacy requires, MacCormick explains, "some amalgam of the following two things: legitimacy in the eyes of those whom the putative norms of the order regulate; and power or influence over the conduct of the human beings to whom the norms are addressed."[48] For MacCormick, a plausible claim to the existence of a normative order and its self-standing source of normative authority is thus not merely equal to "a claim about some abstract normative claim of right" by an order, but "also requires a high degree of observance of the purportedly authoritative ordinances," which includes "the sense of right and wrong" of those over whom the institutional power is being exercised.[49]

This is why, in MacCormick's view, the national institutions' insistence on rejecting the European institutions' claims that they are already grounded in their own existing constitutional order and its authority, is unwarranted. The institutional efficacy of the self-referential EU institutions is not undermined when the reality is that their ordinances are implemented in the European and national everyday practice. At a minimum, in such circumstances, that efficacy is not undermined to any greater degree than is the efficacy of the member state institutional orders. For MacCormick, this suggests the conclusion that, as an external fact of social reality, there already exist two self-standing constitutional orders. A mere contrary *will* of the national institutions could not undermine that. Nor would, of course, a will of the European institutions suffice, if they claimed that their order had ultimate authority over the national orders and, so willed, depriving the latter of their self-standing character and subordinating them to mere *sub*-units of their own order. The point about the existence or non-existence of a normative order is not in what is willed but in whether the two attributes described by the institutional theory exist. Or in MacCormick's words, "[m]any norms do arise from acts of will performed in or through institutions of one kind and another. But they are

[45] MacCormick (n 43) at 262.

[46] N. MacCormick, *Questioning Sovereignty: Law, State and Nation in the European Commonwealth* (Oxford: Oxford University Press, 1999) 114.

[47] MacCormick (n 43) at 261–2.

[48] MacCormick (n 43) at 262.

[49] N. MacCormick, "Questioning Post-sovereignty" (2004) 29 EL Rev 852, 861.

normative, not because willed, but because expressive of an authority whose final sources are non-voluntaristic in character."[50] In this non-monocular view, the fact that there are different ultimate rationales underlying both orders' decisions that are actually being implemented does not undermine the independent existence of either of the two orders, and especially not the existence of only one of them. On the contrary, it tends to confirm the coexistence of both.

If this is so, MaCormick argues, then the challenge to our traditional monist understanding of constitutional power and authority (ie to legal sovereignty) by the development of the new Europe indeed has bite. He consolidates it by a further observation, namely, that these are not simply different orders but ones that also interact in a particular way. This interaction is not of the ordinary type, such as operates between monistic states, that is compatible with legal sovereignty and is exhibited by international private law. In the latter case, MacCormick explains, "foreign law" is treated as a matter of "fact" and must be appropriately proved in the domestic legal system in which it is to be applied.[51] "English law as understood and applied by a Swedish or German court," he argues, "may differ from 'the same' English law as understood and applied by an English court; and an English court may come to a holding about German law different from that to which a German court would have come."[52] MacCormick maintains this interaction is different to the relationship that exists between the EU and member states. It represents the type of interaction in which "one legal system, when it applies norms from another system, treats them not as simple matters of 'fact', but rather as norms of *law* valid within the system."[53] "The accession of a state to the Community," thus, "entails its recognition of EC law as constituting valid law in the state, and its recognition that relevant future decisions by the competent Community organs will constitute law binding within the state."[54]

Moreover, the overlap between both orders is *constitutional* in nature. The EU order claims to enjoy a direct link with the European people(s) themselves and its constitution is thus the direct representation of that source of authority. At the same time, the member state orders also claim a direct legitimation link for themselves and their constitutions, except that they do so in relation to their own respective *demoi*. Thus, even though MacCormick often uses the rhetoric of confrontation between self-standing legal systems, what he actually means by that is the confrontation between constitutional orders. His pluralism is, in other words, not a mere pluralism of legal systems, or legal pluralism: it is constitutional pluralism.

All that has been said thus far contributes towards MacCormick's conclusion that the new Europe has come to a condition in which it can no longer be understood in traditional, monistic constitutional terms, but is only explicable in some novel, pluralist sense. The most abstract presentation of his pluralist alternative would amount to the following. We should no longer understand

[50] MacCormick (n 49) at 861.
[51] MacCormick (n 43) at 262.
[52] MacCormick (n 43) at 262.
[53] MacCormick (n 43) at 262.
[54] MacCormick (n 43) at 262.

there to be but one ultimate source of constitutional authority in each state territory—namely, those states' individual constitutions—from which all law and political power of that territory ultimately emanates. This position could be termed nation-state constitutional monism. Nor should we understand that the latter has been replaced by the European constitution as a single ultimate source of constitutional authority in the territory of Europe. This position could be termed European constitutional monism. Neither of these monocular monist accounts recognizes the central finding of MacCormick's legal approach to analysing sovereignty: the externally valid fact of social reality. This reveals that, alongside the existing self-standing nation-state constitutional orders, we also have a self-standing European constitutional order. Both of the unrealistic monist accounts should therefore give way to a third, pluralist understanding. Accordingly, the European constitution does not derive from, nor is hierarchically inferior to, the national constitutions, which are themselves not grounded in, nor hierarchically subordinate to, some ultimate all-European source of authority. Instead, and as a matter of external social fact, a nation-state and the EU both have autonomously rooted sources of constitutional authority that simultaneously coexist and overlap in a given shared territory. They are thus heterarchically rather than hierarchically related. The crucial consequence of such a pluralist alternative is that both types of orders should now make appropriate changes to their old explanatory monistic accounts, which they are no longer free to follow without qualification. There is, in other words, a need for some kind of *concessions* in this respect by the orders and their constitutional authorities.

Before explaining the kinds of concessions MacCormick had in mind, I shall pause briefly to recall that this abstract notion of pluralism is precisely the one referred to in my introduction when outlining the general placement of MacCormick's pluralist alternative to both monisms. That account sounded, I wrote, almost mysterious in its high abstraction. As such it is not yet exactly the same thing as MacCormick's version of pluralism, that is, not the same as his fuller understanding of constitutional heterarchy. It is rather a higher abstraction that we can extract from the notion of pluralism (heterarchy) as he defines it. Yet it is critical for our purposes of decoding the branch in Chapter 6 to distinguish and explain precisely this minimal abstracted part from MacCormick's concept of pluralist heterarchy, although neither MacCormick nor any other pluralist attempts to define this element. Henceforth, I shall be referring to it as the minimized understanding of heterarchy, or, "heterarchy minimized."

In order to distinguish the notion of the minimized understanding of constitutional heterarchy from further, more elaborated meanings of heterarchy, it should be stressed that it points only in the *general* sense to the need for concessions by the coexisting and overlapping constitutional orders. It implies that the orders need to recognize that they coexist with one another and, accordingly, now need to adopt *some* concessions that would reflect this. The point is, while the minimized understanding of heterarchy requires such concessions, it remains silent about the more precise meaning, type, and strength of the concessions. Those could either be merely procedural, or substantive, or both. In addition, they could be extremely thin, or relatively thick, made only with respect to one particular level of constitutional discourse, or to some, or all levels.[55] There just needs to be some concessions *as such.*

As we will see in this book, none of the pluralists has a conception of pluralism that is constituted by the mere minimal understanding of heterarchy. They all imply either this or that type of more specific concessions, and see *those* as being constitutive of pluralism. We will see in Chapter 2, for instance, how Neil Walker's epistemic pluralism requires concessions that are strictly procedural in nature, implying that these constitute pluralism. According to his view, the coexisting and territorially overlapping systems thus have to recognize that it could not be *externally* correct, and thus not *inter*-systemically valid, to claim that either one or the other has the ultimate constitutional authority in relation to which the authority of the other is only derivative. They both need to concede that all such claims now have to be understood as valid only in the *internal* sense; that is, from the point of view of each of these systems' own and peculiar *episteme*. These concessions are procedural because they only require the adjustment in the alleged nature of the claims. They assert the *internal* instead of *external* validity of sovereignty claims. Thus, they do not demand any substantive division of authority between the coequal constitutional systems.[56]

But with MacCormick, things are different in this respect. His pluralism requires substantive concessions; that is, it does not require some mere procedural concessions that dictate adjustment in the alleged nature of the constitutional systems' sovereignty claims while leaving the choice for possible substantive concessions and adjustments of such claims to the systems themselves. Rather, it assumes concessions that demand that each of the self-standing constitutional systems limits the scope of its claim to ultimate authority to a particular substantively confined sphere within a given shared territory. On the one hand, it should thus be conceded that the old absolute ultimate authority (sovereignty) of the nation-states that extended over the entire sphere within the nation-state territory has now become a limited (no longer the ultimate) authority over the given territory. It is now confined exclusively to the *non*-EU sphere within that territory. "The point is," MacCormick writes, that the nation-states now "have a new sovereignty that is old sovereignty restricted as to the topics of its possible or permissible exercise."[57] On the other hand, the European federal ambition of some all-European constitutional authority evolving into the ultimate authority over the whole territory of Europe is also tamed, and its scope confined to the EU substantive sphere within each nation-state territory. For just as

[55] We will see in the following chapters that different pluralists imply very different types of concessions.

[56] See Chapter 2, pp. 33–40, especially 36 and 39–40.

[57] N. MacCormick (n 49) at 863. In this light, MacCormick also criticizes one but not the other possible rationale behind the German Federal Constitutional Court's decision in *Brunner*: "So far as the Constitutional Court was denying that sovereignty has passed to organs of the European Community or Union, we may agree with it on the grounds here argued. But so far as it asserted a resultant continuing sovereignty of a German people, we may doubt it... [We have] to deny that it [ie sovereignty] is a continuing property of any Member State" (MacCormick (n 43) at 265).

the nation-state had to make substantive concessions, so too such substantive concessions are needed by the European side. "If [the pluralist] view is well founded," MacCormick writes, then "it suggests that the doctrine of supremacy of Community law is not to be confused with any kind of all-purpose subordination of Member State law to Community law."[58] "Rather, the case is that [the EU] constitutes in its own context and over the relevant range of topics a source of valid law superior to other sources recognised in each of the Member States."[59] The EU must recognize this. While the territorial overlap (heterarchy) defined only procedurally will be enough for Walker's epistemic pluralism (anything more he would consider as a monist move),[60] MacCormick sees territorial overlap (heterarchy) in the substantive sense as the constitutive feature of pluralism. This is then his fuller understanding of heterarchy which, as stated above, goes further than the minimized understanding of the concept (the heterarchy minimized).

It is precisely his understanding of pluralism (heterarchy) in the sense of such *substantive* concessions, and that alone, that enables MacCormick to conclude that Europe is already in the condition of "beyond sovereignty,"[61] or "post-sovereignty."[62] Only within this kind of understanding does it seem "*obvious*" to claim, as MacCormick does, "that no state in Western Europe any longer is a sovereign state,"[63] and possible to justify it in the following way:

> None [of the Member States] is in a position such that all the power exercised internally in it, whether politically or legally, derives from purely internal sources. Equally, of course, it is not true that all the power which is exercised either politically or normatively is exercised by, or through, or on the grant of, one or more organs of the European Community. Nor has the Community as such the plenitude of power politically or normatively that could permit it remotely to resemble in itself a sovereign state or sovereign federation of states. The observation that there are no remaining sovereign states in the Community does not in any way entail the proposition that therefore there must instead be a sovereign Community ["a sovereign super-state," as MacCormick also names it] . . . Where at some time past there were, or may have been, sovereign states, there has now been a pooling or a fusion within the communitarian normative order of some of the states' powers of legislation, adjudication and implementation of law in relation to a wide but restricted range of subjects. Some matters fall to be handled within one normative system or normative order, while other parts remain rooted or based in other normative systems or normative orders, with arrangements designed (so far, rather successfully) to prevent incompatibility in areas of overlap.[64]

Indeed, it seems that sovereignty can no longer be understood as representing a vital concept only when it is limited in some rather stronger sense, like the one implied in MacCormick's *substantive* concessions. What clearly eliminates the territorial

[58] MacCormick (n 43) at 264. [59] MacCormick (n 43) at 264.

[60] P. 22. See more in Chapter 2, pp. 34–40 and 50–1. [61] See, eg MacCormick (n 49) at 854.

[62] MacCormick (n 49) at 853; also MacCormick (n 46) at 123. MacCormick uses both expressions as synonyms.

[63] MacCormick (n 3) at 6 (emphasis added).

[64] MacCormick (n 3) at 6. The term "overlap" that MacCormick used in the last sentence is the type of overlap I later characterize as "judicial overlap." I do so in order to distinguish it from the other type of overlap that his conception also implies, namely, substantive territorial overlap. See Chapter 7, pp. 195–7.

all-purpose subordination is the division of the territory's substantive spheres between the distinct authority sources. By contrast, the mere procedural concessions of epistemic pluralism seem insufficient for downgrading sovereignty so much as to say that the concept has wholly lost its utility in the circumstances of the new Europe. After all, in the case of the procedural concessions the nation-states can continue claiming all-purpose foundational sovereignty, extending it over all their old substantive spheres or even expanding those further, as long as they formally concede that such a sovereignty is now justified only from the internal *episteme*.[65] This explains why sovereignty is still a very relevant concept for Walker. It also explains that the condition of "late sovereignty" (the term used by Walker to describe the new situation under his epistemic pluralism) is not yet quite the same as that of "beyond sovereignty" (MacCormick's account of the conditions under his version of pluralism).[66] The distinction between the two authors' foundational understandings of pluralism, as have just been described, in terms of procedurally versus substantively defined heterarchy and territorial overlap, indeed explains their disagreement about whether the death of sovereignty has been much exaggerated and its continued vitality unduly dispelled, as suggested by Walker, or whether these *are* the circumstances in which the concept has lost its utility for politics and public law, as MacCormick believes.[67]

I shall end my explication of this point by clarifying that MacCormick's pluralism and his condition of "beyond sovereignty" do not mean that every attribute of sovereignty has been removed in the Europe of post-sovereign states. "The Member States," MacCormick writes, "no doubt enjoy a kind of residual sovereignty in the sense of an ability to renounce membership of the Union and return to their former independence, though," as he also adds, "it is doubtful if any could effectively do this politically in present circumstances."[68] In mentioning that residual "last-resort power"[69] of the member states "over their own constitutions"[70] MacCormick goes even further to characterize it as "desirable that this be so."[71] He argues that it is so despite the fact that his conception of pluralism, which he considers the correct explanatory account of the current situation in Europe, teaches that there is no ultimate sovereignty in the Europe of post-sovereign states. But how could that possibly be, one might ask? That is, does not the very position of pluralism and the superiority implied in the view that we should read the new Europe as eliminating the ultimate authority, necessarily exclude the possibility that it be *desirable* that there still is, after all, some residual ultimate authority? Does that

[65] Under procedural concessions a system needs only admit the internal nature of its claims but can fully retain, or even enhance the substantive domain that it claims for itself. See pp. 39–40.

[66] N. Walker, "Late Sovereignty in the European Union" in N. Walker (ed.), *Sovereignty in Transition* (Oxford: Hart Publishing, 2003) 2; MacCormick (n 49) at 853.

[67] MacCormick (n 49); Walker (n 66). I am indebted to both Neil MacCormick and Neil Walker for their generous discussions on this point that helped me elaborate this distinction in their views and the underlying reason for it.

[68] MacCormick (n 43) at 265; cf MacCormick (n 49) at 863.

[69] MacCormick (n 49) at 863.

[70] MacCormick (n 49) at 863.

[71] MacCormick (n 49) at 863.

not, in the end, undermine the pluralist conception and, with it, the essence of MacCormick's project?[72]

On the contrary, I think that it is the last and critical step by which MacCormick attempts to secure the true pluralist nature of his conception of pluralism. What we seem to have here is a similar strategy as will be later observed also in Weiler's pluralism; that is, retaining the non-exercised residual sovereignty in the background means precisely that MacCormick's pluralism—as in any true pluralism—can only be *proposed*. Although it claims to be the correct explanation for the current situation in Europe and, as we shall also see, the normatively desired state of affairs for the future, his pluralism does not impose itself. The choice about whether or not to observe the claimed superiority of the pluralist conception, as MacCormick understands it, is left with the actors themselves. What rests with MacCormick's theory of pluralism is the notion that if the actors chose to exercise their residual sovereignty this would, provided they were successful, at the same time immediately terminate the conditions of pluralism. The existence of a free choice for inferior monism or superior pluralism that lies in the background of the pluralist concept is, thus, not in conflict with the teachings of the conception but the very confirmation of its pluralist spirit.

Yet if the nation-states, along with Europe, do not adopt the conception of pluralism as MacCormick understands it and take the position of substantive concessions, they have not established pluralism, but remain within monism. This is thus exactly the opposite of Walker's understanding: that constitutional pluralism is already established, and only has been so, by binding the actors with no more than his procedural concessions. To require from them the thicker substantive concessions as the very precondition of pluralism would, in his view, actually move such a conception to monism.

4. Towards Normative Pluralism

This account of MacCormick's pluralism is an explanatory one. It explains how the situation in the new Europe is best understood as a matter of existing social reality (explanatory pluralism). While it clearly involves some normative considerations, it does not yet focus fully on the normative question. The explanatory account does not yet say much about whether this new situation in Europe is a good thing (that would be normative pluralism), or whether we should return to the previous state of affairs, or perhaps move forward to some new one.

After proposing his explanatory pluralism, MacCormick also makes the further step into normative pluralism. He acknowledges that we could either go forward, stay, or return:

[72] Some who contributed their essays to Walker's edited book *Sovereignty in Transition* (n 66) seem to assume so; cf MacCormick (n 49) at 863.

> Either we are fated to go forward to a situation in which there is a massively centralised European Community which takes over the dominant place in legal imagination. . . . The other way would be the way back. No doubt many are tempted by it. Their siren voices urge us to go back to the good old world in which we did not face the loss of sovereignty through its being granted somewhere else. The quest is to go back to a European order of fully sovereign states, with no links stronger than those of treaties that bind only *rebus sic stantibus*.[73]

MacCormick is not keen on either of these two monist options. He prefers his pluralist "sideways move."[74] This is the current arrangement, in which we have diffused centers of power and authority understood as grounded in different and self-standing sources, of which none is any longer the *ultimate* source of authority to the other. If, in order to qualify as a normative pluralist, one would need to consider this pluralist understanding and its claimed actual realization in contemporary Europe as being more valuable than either of the two monistic alternatives, then MacCormick is clearly in this camp. This is already evident in his groundbreaking article from 1993, where he writes of pluralism that "[i]n a whole variety of ways, to do as you would expect of someone with my personal political stance or attitude,[75] this seems to me to be a good thing and a great historic opportunity for many things which I personally would regard as good."[76] But in that early contribution, MacCormick does not further explain the crucial "variety of ways" he believes the pluralist understanding to be normatively superior to either of the monist opposites. Instead, he briefly and very generally remarks that he is opposed to the "return to the old polycentric sovereignties of Europe" as well as to the potential move towards "a European mega-sovereignty,"[77] due to the greater risk such monist understandings could pose to peace. Thus, he is "unwaveringly opposed to the road back" because "[o]ne of the main upshots of the universal sovereign statehood was two disasters—world wars, one of which dominates my own earlier memories, the other of which scarred the lives of my parents' generation, only for the medicine to be repeated, yet worse, twenty-one years later."[78] But as the term "variety of ways" signalled, there was actually more to it than just this abstract reference to the value of peace. Analysis of some of MacCormick's other contributions reveals the more elaborate meaning and justification for his normative pluralism.

This will be examined in Chapter 6,[79] along with what more precisely was meant by the "variety of ways" in which MacCormick's pluralism claims normative superiority to the monist alternatives. We will also explore how exactly it is

[73] MacCormick (n 3) at 17. [74] MacCormick (n 3) at 17.

[75] MacCormick explicitly refers here to his 1990 article, "Can Nationalism be Philosophically Credible?" in W. Twinning (ed.) *Issues of Self-Determination* (Aberdeen: Aberdeen University Press, 1991).

[76] MacCormick (n 3) at 17. [77] MacCormick (n 3) at 18.

[78] MacCormick (n 3) at 17.

[79] See also Chapter 8, pp. 254–6. As for democracy, which was also one of the fields for which MacCormick sensed that it could offer one of the strongest justifications for his pluralism, see MacCormick (n 46) at 145–55. See also Chapter 8, pp. 259–60 and Chapter 10.

understood to secure peace more effectively than the monist options.[80] In this chapter, however, let us first make use of the fact that MacCormick claims to be a normative pluralist in order to explicate more fully his basic concept of pluralism as such. For if his described pluralist conception is to be understood in normative terms, regardless of what exactly those normative grounds are, this seems to require an important further development in the meaning of MacCormick's basic conception of pluralism and its notion of heterarchy.

As MacCormick acknowledges, the theory of sovereignty—of a sovereign state or sovereign institution within the state—can, and normally does, rest on some normative ground offering some valuable underpinning that justifies the position of sovereignty. There are many theoretical candidates, but in a modern democratic European state, it normally means that the state is sovereign because, and only because, it derives its authority from the self-determined and self-governing people of that state. The same is understood to be true regarding the sovereignty of some nation-state institutions, such as a parliament. This is considered sovereign only because, and in as much as, it is the representative of the self-determined people of that state. The self-determination and self-government (sovereignty) of the nation-state *demos* is, then, normally considered the ultimate valuable underpinning of the sovereignty of that state and its institutions. That, after all, is the whole point in (self) representations of these states as *democratic* states, and of their constitutions as *democratic* constitutions.

However, if something like this normatively underlies the monist idea of sovereignty of the European nation-states and sovereignty of some of their institutions, then a proponent of pluralism, claiming to have found the more valuable *normative* alternative to such sovereignty, needs to engage with the suggested valuable normative grounds that are said to constitute sovereignty. An alternative normative ground needs to be proposed, and it must be demonstrated why that would make a more valuable alternative to the one said to constitute the statal and institutional sovereignty.

This realization is important for our attempt to unfold more fully MacCormick's abstract pluralist conception. It suggests that this could not be read as merely posing a challenge to the sovereign states and their sovereign institutions. Because MacCormick's pluralism is characterized as normative, it seems that one has to understand it to mean that the new conception also puts the particular sovereigns *themselves* under siege. This must be so to the degree to which the meaning of their sovereignty is associated with the notion of their ultimate authority on the territory of their respective nation-states. For it seems that under the pluralist reading, a particular state *demos* would need to cease to be the ultimate authority unto itself; that is, the omnipotent sovereign within the particular territory of its nation-state. Instead, there would need to be another equally relevant source of self-standing authority that would, independently of that particular state *demos*, now exercise its share of authority within that very same territory. Neither of the sources

[80] See Chapter 6, p. 186.

of authority would under this view remain the ultimate source of authority over the other.

So, despite the fact that MacCormick speaks mainly of sovereignty of states and institutions,[81] this extended reading of his pluralist conception seems to hold. This is not just because otherwise he could not hope to propose a *normative* alternative to the old monist accounts, but also because one can, indeed, also find traces of this fuller understanding of pluralism in MacCormick's own text. For instance, when describing the post-revolutionary world of modernity as the world of sovereign states that now need to be decoupled from sovereignty, he explains that these "were nation states asserting the inalienable sovereignty of a sovereign nation or people."[82] Furthermore, when discussing the idea of sovereignty in general, in the work of Bodin and Hobbes and their attempts to ground "political certainties in the unquestionable word of the sovereign," he also refers to Rousseau and his identification of this sovereign in the nation or people as a whole, that is, in their "general will."[83] Finally, by stating that "[t]he principle of national self-determination becomes morally and practically problematic because (or when) it is coupled to the concept or doctrine of the absolutely sovereign state,"[84] he announces his later detailed revision of the traditional ("sovereign-tist") understanding of a nation or people as characteristic of a sovereign state.

Therefore, when speaking of his dispersal of authority, of abolishing sovereignty, MacCormick must not only have in mind sovereign states and sovereign institutions of the states. He must inevitably address also the deeper origins of that sovereignty, indeed, the ultimate sovereigns *themselves*, with a *demos* being just the most common modern example. When more fully explicated, the particular extended meaning of MacCormick's pluralism thus comes down to something like this: a particular state *demos*, such as the Germans, or British, or French, on its "own" state territory, can no longer be considered sovereign. Such a *demos* no longer has the ultimate authority on that state territory. Now other sources exercise their self-standing and coordinate authority in that territory as well, and what was previously the substantive sphere under one ultimate source of authority is now dispersed in some balanced way to at least two substantive spheres. These are governed by different, self-standing sources of authority that coexist over a shared territory and are represented by the distinct but overlapping constitutional orders.

So what could these two distinct sources be? Firstly, it is important to clarify that MacCormick does not imply a renunciation of self-determination of a *demos* as such. On the contrary, while requiring abolition of its traditional form (the

[81] Although, on the other hand, he often uses "sovereignty" and "the sovereign" in their abstract sense.

[82] N. MacCormick, "Liberalism, Nationalism, and the Post-sovereign State" (1996) XLIV Political Studies 553, 553.

[83] MacCormick (n 3) at 15.

[84] N. MacCormick, "What Place for Nationalism in the Modern World" (1994) 2 Hume Papers on Public Policy 79, 93. Again, for the revision of the idea of a sovereign nation-state *demos* and the corresponding detailed explication of the normative dimension of MacCormick's pluralism, see Chapter 6, pp. 177–87.

sovereign statal *demos*) that is bound up with the idea of statal and institutional sovereignty, he also requires that it be retained in a new, reinterpreted understanding and form. In other words, a self-determined *demos* as one of the sources of authority now stands in a revised and adjusted (specifically limited) form that is compatible with another equally important and self-standing—all European—source of authority. It now shares, or indeed divides, authority on that same territory with this other source. Secondly, what more precisely the second source amounts to in MacCormick's conception seems more intriguing. It is, no doubt, a democratic source, so some kind of a people, a *demos*, is implied. But what exact kind of a *demos* is it? On my reading MacCormick leaves the question subtly open. As we will see, he is very elaborate as to the content and nature of the mandatory principles that this source generates.[85] However, the exact identification of the source itself, such as in the case of the precisely defined state *demos* on the nation-state side, seems to persistently evade the reader's grasp.[86] Whoever and whatever that is, it is inherently bound up with some kind of a "new European identity." This is a notion that the very idea of a self-standing European constitutional order, in MacCormick's words, "presuppose[s] or require[s]."[87] In other words, regardless of how the subject of that source is defined, MacCormick understands that it produces certain particular principles, and these he does identify and define.[88] These are understood as representing this independent self-standing second source and do not owe their validity to the first coordinate source.

Be that as it may, for a sound conception of pluralism developed later in this work, the question will be clarified in due course. What is more relevant here is to realize that we now have the whole of MacCormick's basic conception of pluralism. It is his fuller, substantive understanding of constitutional heterarchy, whereby the old sovereignty (monism), which must now be dispersed between two substantive spheres and their different actors (pluralism), is to be understood in the sense of state sovereignty and institutional sovereignty, as well as in the sense of the sovereignty of the sovereigns themselves. It is a conception of heterarchy that, somewhere deep down, also includes one part that was called heterarchy minimized: a minimal understanding of the concept of constitutional heterarchy. We get this by

[85] Chapter 6, pp. 179–85.

[86] MacCormick comes closest to identifying the source bound up with this new identity when agreeing that it could "even" be "a European Demos" in its specific form (ie that of European *demoi*) as some authors have proposed. Here he has in mind Weiler and his idea of the multiple *demoi*: "the claim . . . [of] self-standing legal order can be held to presuppose or to require the constructing of a new European identity, or even, as Joseph Weiler puts it in this volume, the actualization of a European Demos. Such an identity, such a Demos would play somehow the same role that national identity, or the identity of the people as a self-aware Demos, plays in the legitimation of the institutions of a state" (MacCormick (n 82) at 553). That "even" suggests to me that while allowing the identification of some sort of European *demos* as the second source, MacCormick also remains open to possible other identifications of this second democratic source itself, and so leaves space for those who would imagine something else than the specifically European *demos*. On the reading that I will endorse in Chapters 9 and 10, this other *demos* could, in order for pluralism to succeed, only be conceived as fully open-ended and universal, which means that it will go beyond the mere *European demos*.

[87] MacCormick (n 82) at 553.

[88] Chapter 6, pp. 179–85.

abstracting MacCormick's fuller understanding of heterarchy to the degree that the latter actually loses some of its key constitutive elements, like the substantive, as distinct from the merely procedural, concessions. While MacCormick himself did not single out and elaborate this particular minimal concept of heterarchy, we needed to. The reasons for this will become apparent in Chapter 6, where we will try to solve the riddle of the pluralist labyrinth.

The first step towards that end is, however, already completed. Our decoding tool—the Ariadne's Thread—has already been helpful in mapping MacCormick's understanding of pluralism. We can see that the meaning of his "constitutional pluralism," as explained here, appears fully within the fourth sector of the labyrinth—what the Ariadne's Thread defined as the "foundational discourse."[89] It is an analysis of a heterarchical relationship between constitutional orders, both as legal and political orders, at their deepest theoretical level. That is, the level of their coexisting sources at which those sources and their respective constitutional formations are divided through a unique pluralist solution—MacCormick's specific version of foundational heterarchy. This foundational discourse is not yet the same as the discourse on the institutional question of *who* (some nation-state institution, a European one, or some third kind instead) should ideally have the final say in deciding constitutional cases in Europe. It is also different from the question of *how* exactly, in order to get things right, to engage in constitutional interpretation in Europe. And it is likewise different from the discourse over *what* exactly should be the content of the substantive identities that Europe (the Europeans) and its nation-states (the national citizens) ought to adopt at their respective constitutional sites.

Having completed the construction of the essence of his understanding of pluralism, let us now leave MacCormick for a while and turn to Neil Walker to try to decipher in greater detail what exactly *he* has in mind when he utters the phrase "constitutional pluralism." By attempting to pull together various elements of Walker's scholarship into a coherent whole, the following chapter aims at unfolding a fuller picture of his pluralism that flows from the theory's own internal logic.[90] This also enables the assessment of the individual theory.

[89] See p. 12.

[90] I am indebted to Neil Walker for his willingness to engage with me in several discussions over earlier drafts of the following chapter. The insights gained in this way have been invaluable for my construing attempts in what follows. Any errors, however, are my own.

2

Epistemic Pluralism

1. Explaining the Theory

1.1 The basic idea

Constitutional discourse has perhaps never been under greater challenge than it is today, notes Neil Walker.[1] There are several strands of attack. One is the criticism that, in its traditional understanding, constitutional discourse has been too state-centered.[2] Another is that it has amounted to unwarranted constitutional fetishism, which "frustrates, obstructs or at least diverts attention from other mechanisms through which power and influence are effectively wielded and political community is formed."[3] There is also the related but more general criticism of constitutionalism's supposedly inherent normative bias; that is, its "tendency to favour certain interests and values over others and its failure to provide a level playing field within which all relevant interests and values may be authentically and fairly engaged."[4] And there is the objection of the widespread ideological exploitation of the ideas of constitutionality and constitutionalism: "the propensity of many to clothe their interests, ideas or aspirations in constitutional garb, not because of the commitment to certain normative standards which may be represented or suggested by constitutionalism but because of the symbolic authority which they hope to draw upon by so doing."[5]

The combination of these individual critiques, coupled with various responses to them, lead to a comprehensive challenge that eventually threatens to undermine the ideas of constitutionality and constitutionalism. The formidable challenge is that, within our age, these ideas have become wholly imbued by deep, radical disagreement. Constitutionalism has become a "highly protean notion,"[6] "an increasingly polymorphic idea,"[7] and "its field of possible signification increasingly wide and diverse."[8] It seems to represent a wholly "debased conceptual currency."[9] Walker fears that as a result of radical disagreement, constitutionalism has become "too indeterminate a discourse to be of any compelling or even persuasive normative

[1] N. Walker, "The Idea of Constitutional Pluralism" (2002) 65 ML Rev 317, 317.
[2] Walker (n 1) at 319, 320–4.
[3] Walker (n 1) at 319, 324–7.
[4] Walker (n 1) at 319, 328–31.
[5] Walker (n 1) at 319, 331–3.
[6] Walker (n 1) at 319.
[7] Walker (n 1) at 333.
[8] Walker (n 1) at 319.
[9] Walker (n 1) at 333.

value in principle" or even "to provide a viable point of reference for the mobilisation of a broad consensus of public and political opinion in practice."[10]

He devotes attention to, and discusses, each of the individual critiques and their collective force.[11] One of the best contexts in which to observe the thoroughness and intensity of their challenge is probably indeed the new Europe; the primary locus of Walker's attention. Here the traditional meaning of the concept of constitutionalism has recently been tested the most. Claims to a constitutional status are even made by non-state entities, and by interests that escape even the most axiomatic confines of traditional constitutionalism (such as that of "we the people") previously taken for granted. Of course, the traditionalists resist what they conceive as unwarranted corruptions of their cherished concept. Thus, there is in Europe deep disagreement over the right meaning of the concept of constitutionalism, which has materialized in the threat of actual conflicts between the highest tribunals of the member states and that of the EU. Indeed, the disagreement that threatens to make ideas of constitutionalism and constitutionality a "debased conceptual currency" is most manifest precisely in our post-Westphalian context of the new Europe.[12]

Walker's goal is to find a way out of these problems. At the core of his project is the ambition of redeeming the ideas of constitutionalism and constitutionality from the formidable challenge of disagreement. Walker argues that this can best be accomplished through a version of constitutional pluralism that he develops and describes as epistemic constitutional pluralism.[13]

The basic idea is to instil an axiom of epistemic incommensurability into the highly disputed discourse about constitutionalism and constitutionality. While operationalization and the force of the application of the axiom vary, depending on the particular level of the discourse into which it is instilled, epistemic pluralism starts as a second-order thesis. That is, it is concerned with the question of how to develop and secure the most legitimate conception of the idea of constitutionalism, in the face of the deep disagreement about this issue. The goal is thus to find a conception that would avoid privileging in advance some of the views of the concept at the expense of other, "demeaned" images or visions. In other words, the second-order question to which epistemic pluralism first and foremost applies is the issue of what can legitimately be seen as constituting the concept of constitutionalism. This involves consideration as to what should be best thought as falling within legitimate outer boundaries of constitutional discourse, and what should those boundaries be.[14]

10 Walker (n 1) at 319.

11 Walker (n 1) at 319.

12 Walker (n 1) at 320, fn 13.

13 Walker (n 1) at 339.

14 These second-order questions concerning a legitimate common conception of constitutionalism are always inseparably related to further substantive questions of constitutionality (as is the question of what is the proper content of prescriptive constitutional norms or their best interpretation in a particular community), and to structural constitutional rules (questions over the best institutional architecture within a particular constitution). Epistemic pluralism thus inevitably applies to these first-order constitutional discourses as well. We will observe that later in some detail (subsection 1.5).

Each legal system that claims to be a constitutional system asserts its own ultimate authority in determining its foundational recognition rules: the rules of recognition, change, and adjudication. In Europe, these rules that define constitutional systems embody very different and highly conflicting underlying visions of what constitutes, or should properly constitute, the concept of constitutionalism. The nation-states have their own understandings, the EU has its own vision, and there are also other non-state entities with their own claims. It is these different and conflicting underlying understandings of the concept of constitutionalism that are responsible for the European systems' *conflicting* authority claims concerning who ultimately controls whose foundational recognition rules. Thus, for instance, one view holds that the EU, since it is not a state, cannot have a constitutional status because only a state can nourish a sufficiently homogenous *demos*, which this view understands as a precondition to constitutionalism. On this understanding the authority to determine foundational recognition rules of the EU legal system lies within the nation-states that ground those ultimate recognition rules in their constitutions. The opposite view holds that because the EU has established a direct link with the *demoi* of Europe it has also developed into a constitutional system. This is clearly possible, some proponents of this view maintain, even in the absence of a common European *demos*. Others go further and explain that such a constitutional system possesses the ultimate authority to determine its own rules of recognition, change, and adjudication. Some of those argue that those rules are ultimately superior because they give expression to a more inclusive all-European source of constitutional authority, and that this is the reason why they should control whatever lower-rank foundational rules the nation-states may choose and determine for themselves. And there are other lines of reasoning and claims aplenty. So which of the conflicting authoritative assertions should then prevail as defending the more correct underlying understanding of the concept of constitutionalism?

At the core of the epistemic pluralist position is the endorsement of the axiom that the different constitutional authority and knowledge claims of the different sites claiming constitutional status in Europe should be seen as epistemically incommensurable. In particular, this should hold true with respect to the sites' assertions of their own constitutional rules of recognition, change, and adjudication.[15] So when the European nation-states, for example, assert their own ultimate constitutional authority (sovereignty), declare their rules of recognition and change as the overriding ones, and assert their courts' power to adjudicate with final authority, these claims are to be treated as epistemically no more or less correct than the opposite claims of the same type as asserted by the EU and its institutions. Together with the constitutionalism-defining views that they embody and defend,

[15] "Certainly, if we think of the different norm types within constitutional orders in terms of polity identifying rules (rules of recognition, change and adjudication); substantive rules (content of prescriptive norms); and structural rules (institutional architecture), then the key fault-line between different sites—the single cell in the matrix of possible relations between orders where their different points of departure are incommensurable and where conflict in principle most intractable, is where the polity identifying rules are at stake on either side" (N. Walker, "Late Sovereignty in the European Union" in N. Walker (ed.), *Sovereignty in Transition* (Oxford: Hart Publishing 2003) at 28).

these authoritative claims should all be seen as system self-referential, as plausible only from their system's own internal *episteme*.[16] As such, neither of the two internal conflicting epistemic justifications is to be accepted as being more correct from the point of view of some *external*, common *episteme*. The same must hold for any other proposal for epistemic reconciliation on these issues, even if it claimed to be externally correct. Such a proposal would produce no more than another equally incommensurable internal view. For, as epistemic pluralism further explains, there is no common epistemic scale on which the plausibility of these conflicting claims from different constitutional sites could be measured, assessed, and reconciled.[17] The endorsement of the axiom about the lack of any firm external epistemic ground and so of possible epistemic reconciliation on these issues—that is, inter-systemic epistemic scepticism—is thus central to the concept of epistemic pluralism. This is the reason for the theory's conclusion about the equal but internal epistemic plausibility of such claims.

1.2 Two ways in which the axiom avoids external arbitration

Given the central goal of Walker's project of redeeming constitutionalism from the challenges, the key point must be that this kind of strategy evades external arbitration in favor of some of the constitutionalism-constitutive claims and against other such claims, views, and aspirations. Epistemic pluralism is said to avoid either privileging or demeaning conservative claims about constitutionalism, made by those defending the traditional view and assumptions of constitutionalism. In the same way, as the argument goes, it also treats the more progressive and transformative claims made by those expanding constitutionalism far beyond the nation-state confines, or indeed any other claims reasonably aspiring constitutional status. This alleged greater neutrality of epistemic pluralism is implied in two important senses.

First, it is meant in the sense that under the axiom of epistemic incommensurability a wide spectrum of the differing and conflicting second-order constitutional claims now comes to the table of constitutionalism. That is, they all count as views of the concept of *constitutionalism* and they are all recognized as part of the *common constitutional* discourse. However, this is so provided that they first meet a set of thin minimal standards defined by epistemic pluralism, with an additional requirement that will be considered. This set of seven "minimal standards" draws the outer boundary of the concept of constitutionalism. For it is not the case that just anything, even under epistemic pluralism, can legitimately be presented as a particular vision of constitutionalism. However, these outer inter-systemic standards are in fact thinly defined. As a result, a truly wide scope of claims can now

[16] "*Episteme*": a given historical condition that both enables and shapes the perception of knowledge and deliberation within a particular historical place and time. M. Foucault was the first to use this term in the described meaning in his, *The Order of Things* (M. Foucault, *The Order of Things: An Archaeology of the Human Sciences*, tr. A. Sheridan (New York, NY: Pantheon, 1970).

[17] Walker (n 1) at 338; N. Walker, "Sovereignty and Differentiated Integration in the European Union" (1998) 4 ELJ 355, 361–2; N. Walker, "All Dressed Up?" (2001) 21 OJLS 563, 569.

qualify. All the relevant conflicting claims in Europe meet the standards without difficulty, as the latter "stretch" the idea of constitutional discourse "in a manner... which is relevant to state polity, post-state and even post-polity or non-polity settings."[18]

The first of the minimal standards requires that a particular claim be associated with a polity or political process that has developed an explicit constitutional discourse—"the emergence of a constitutional self-consciousness on the part of those associated with the polity or political process with respect to that polity or political process."[19] The second standard is that in that polity or political process there is also "the claim to foundational legal authority, or sovereignty."[20] This claim is not to be understood in the traditional (Westphalian) sense of sovereignty or foundational legal authority, which associates these notions with territorial exclusivity. Rather, it is about sovereignty and ultimate authority understood in the qualified, pluralist sense, as will be explained.[21] The third is a developed "jurisdictional scope—the delineation of a sphere of competence." The fourth is the existence of "the claim to interpretive autonomy—to the entitlement of an organ internal to the polity or political process to construe the meaning and extent of these competences." The fifth requires that "there is the constitution and regulation of an institutional structure to govern the polity."[22] The sixth insists that there is "the specification of the status, conditions and incidents of membership of or association with the polity—the criteria and rights and obligations of 'citizenship'—broadly defined."[23] Finally, the seventh requires that "there is the manner in which and procedures by which the voice of the membership registers—the mechanisms, democratic or otherwise, by which their interests and aspirations are articulated and taken into account."[24]

Secondly, and as mentioned, the competing claims must meet a further inter-systemic requirement. External epistemic incommensurability not only widens the scope of potentially legitimate claims so that it minimizes the outer standards for constitutional claims, but also itself becomes one of the standards the claims need to respect. This not only assures that a wide scope of claims can reach the table of legitimate conceptions of constitutionalism. It means in addition that they cannot attain that status unless they also understand each other as all *equally* legitimate second-order visions of the concept. In other words, all of the claims on the table have to accept, as a further precondition for access to the table, that in the *external* sense they would all understand and treat each other's weights as epistemically incommensurable: they are thus all equal in this further particular sense. This is the essential feature of epistemic pluralism and needs further clarification.

The axiom of epistemic incommensurability implies that beyond meeting the minimal standards, any potential second-order constitutional claim must also, in

[18] Walker (n 1) at 342. [19] Walker (n 1) at 342. [20] Walker (n 1) at 342.
[21] Pp. 36–7. [22] Walker (n 1) at 342.
[23] Walker (n 1) at 343. [24] Walker (n 1) at 343.

order to be really recognized as falling within legitimate constitutional discourse, not "close off or demean" the alternative, often conflicting, constitutionalism-constitutive claims. "Close off or demean" here does not mean that a particular site's constitutionalism-constitutive claims cannot maintain from its internal perspective to be the correct and so more acceptable view of the concept of constitutionalism. Rather, it means that such superiority cannot be asserted from some inter-systemic (external) perspective. None of the claims can be understood as the best from some common historical or other kind of *external episteme* supposedly underlying all constitutional sites and their different perspectives.[25] They have to *mutually concede* that the question of inter-systemic superiority to which they all strive should be *left open and undecided.* Or so the axiom dictates.

There does not, however, need to be any further mutual deference in the normative sense on the constitutional sites' second-order level. This is the level where the sites define their own respective rules of recognition, change, and adjudication in a way that embodies and defends a particular vision of constitutionalism. Therefore, these different constitutionalism-defining claims may continue to disagree and contradict, according to Walker's version of constitutional pluralism.

This degree of mutual deference at the second-order level is what links epistemic pluralism to the agonistic approach to solving the puzzle of deep disagreement in constitutional politics:[26] the minimal mutual concession is precisely about keeping a supposedly important part of the debate in controversy. By choosing not to claim external epistemic superiority about the nature of its own assertion, each site chooses to leave this part of disagreement open, subject to the ongoing future joint consideration.[27] In a supposedly important way this is understood to be less aggressive and more conciliatory than would be an assertion, against other claims, of external epistemic superiority by this or that individual conflicting claim. And it is exactly in this sense in which epistemic pluralism seems to understand that

[25] Walker describes the theory's requirement of "inclusive normative coherence" as providing that "constitutionalism should be defined in a sufficiently inclusive and open-ended way as not to militate in favour of some and against other constitutional aspirations or claims, provided that these aspirations or claims meet certain minimal standards." He further explains that the "inclusive normative coherence should exclude or challenge those positions which themselves do not comply with the standard of inclusive normative coherence—which seek, whether within a transformative discourse or within a particular existing constitutional framework, to close off or demean alternative constitutional aspirations (which themselves should meet the standards of inclusive normative coherence) and which do not permit interested parties 'to enter into processes of contestation and negotiation of the rules of recognition'" (Walker (n 1) at 335–6).

[26] Cf J. Tully, *Constitutionalism in an Age of Diversity* (Cambridge: Cambridge University Press, 1995); J. Tully, "The Agonic Freedom of Citizens" (1999) 28 Economy and Society 161; J. Tully, "The Unfreedom of the Moderns in Comparison to their Ideals of Constitutional Democracy" (2002) 65 ML Rev 204; J. Tully, "Struggles over Recognition and Distribution" (2002) 7 Constellations 469.

[27] Such a future joint consideration would need to be considered as a counterfactual ideal. That is, an epistemic pluralist would need to understand that the sites and their claims will never actually get to a solution of the controversy in such a future joint consideration, while they would, nevertheless, always need to strive after such a solution. The fact that there will be no resolution does not mean that the counterfactual ideal has no point. On the contrary, it obviously helps to shape the sites' own reasoning and conclusions.

privileging one second-order conception of constitutionalism as externally superior would be to "demean" or "close off" unduly the alternative conceptions and claims.

One of the main points of epistemic pluralism thus seems to become that, due to its axiom, the whole discourse can turn into a more fluid, plastic, and open-ended agonistic process. This can be the case primarily in the second-order constitutional discourse but consequently also the first, as we shall see.[28] This way, it is believed, those who hold a view will feel more prone and amenable to ongoing, open-ended negotiation that also includes negotiation about what part of the previously foreclosed, internal, non-negotiable core should nevertheless be negotiated.

In explicating this strategy I am not judging to what extent, if at all, it makes the discourse more plastic and fluid than do alternative strategies—those that require a more substantive elaboration of views on the external level. I am merely showing that the distinction in the degree of fluidity between this strategy and opposing ones has been implicitly posited.[29]

1.3 The case of Europe

We shall now move to observing the operation of epistemic pluralism within the new Europe. The traditional statist, as well as the transformative EU, vision of constitutionalism clearly both meet the seven minimal standards. They could thus both potentially qualify as legitimate conceptions of constitutionalism. However, they could only do so if they ceased to be demeaning to each other and to other potential claims and aspirations. Both sites would need to recognize that neither the nation-states' nor the EU's monist claim to ultimate authority of their foundational recognition rules is better or worse in the sense of some common, objectively valid (ie external) *episteme*. Thus, neither the intergovernmental-delegation idea, which elevates the nation-state monist view of constitutionalism over the alternatives, nor some vision of the all-European constitutional monism, which does the same with the European vision of constitutionalism, can win the external battle. Only if the visions ceased to be so demeaning could they be accepted as belonging

[28] Subsection 1.5, pp. 43–50.

[29] Or, as Frank Michelman has already observed in a related context: "We may have some sense that ostensibly procedural propositions, taken as a class, are in some important way less aggressive, more conciliatory, than are propositions of substantive policy or value. A reason for that may be that any proposition identifiable as procedural has to be one that leaves open for future joint consideration at least some part of what the parties are felt to be in disagreement about. Just because that is so, someone who pushes a procedural proposition, even one over which there is some level of disagreement, may stand a better chance of being seen to act within the bounds of a decent respect for the differing views of others than does someone who pushes a normative proposition of substance, even one over which there is no higher level of disagreement . . . This provides me with a possible answer to the question about what a deeply proceduralistic, liberal theory of legitimacy might look like. It would be a theory that starts out from a commitment to reciprocity among notionally free and equal persons rather than from a commitment to liberty. (I'm not saying such theories can succeed, I'm only saying that's what they are like)" (F. Michelman, "Proceduralism in Liberal Constitutional Theory: A Fragment," Annual Distinguished Lecture, Boston University School of Law, 14 April 2005, unpublished manuscript, 20). Cf the distinction between procedural versus substantive conceptions of democracy and constitutionalism, A. Teršek, *Ustavna Demokracija in Vladavina Prava* (Ljubljana: Famnit, 2002).

to a common, redeemed conception of constitutionalism wide enough potentially to encompass some tamed versions of both visions, as well as other possible views and aspirations.

Between the old externally understood monist extremes of intergovernmental delegation and federal European super-constitutionalism the space thereby opens for an array of legitimate visions of constitutionalism, previously excluded by the two extreme positions. This is hoped to have important consequences for the discourse. Walker admits that under his terms the future debate on the principle on which the EU is or should be founded may well remain fierce.[30] He reminds, however, that observance of the epistemic pluralist axiom would "provide a framework within which it [ie the debate] can at least be recognised *as* a common debate with manageable boundaries and with polar options excluded."[31] It would also crucially invigorate that debate. By the necessary and supposedly minimal exclusions of those who externally exclude, the theory of epistemic pluralism refuses to leave in place "a deep fault-line which undermines the very ground on which debate might take place."[32] It thus provides "a safety net encouraging the participation of those who might otherwise refuse engagement so as to avoid recognising and dignifying positions in polar opposition to their own."[33]

Epistemic pluralism thus rejects both of the monisms. Rejection of the intergovernmental-delegation idea means that the theory excludes the *external inter-systemic* vision of a European constitution as eventually grounded in the ultimate authority of the member states and their monist constitutions (states as the "Masters of the Treaties"). Similarly, rejection of the federal European constitutional vision corresponds to excluding the opposite *external inter-systemic* view—that the constitutions of the member states should in some ultimate sense derive their authority from the hierarchically superior, ultimate source of all-European constitutional authority. Instead of legitimizing either of these two options, epistemic pluralism posits that neither is correct. Instead, they must now both recognize two things. Firstly, the constitutional nature of their claims: that they are both legitimate claims about constitutionalism. Secondly, that neither of them can be understood as *externally* superior to the other.

When I say that the sites (systems) must recognize one another and accept these described concessions, I mean that the theory of epistemic pluralism would otherwise characterize them as being mistaken. At the same time, the theory allows for the practical possibility of some system not adopting these procedural concessions.[34] This

[30] N. Walker, "Europe's Constitutional Momentum and the Search for Polity Legitimacy" in J. Weiler and C. Eisgruber (eds), *Altneuland: The EU Constitution in a Contextual Perspective* (2004) Jean Monnet Working Paper No 5/04, 43.With its wide, common conception of constitutionalism, and within its alleged widely inclusive confines, epistemic pluralism reopens parts of previously closed areas of possible competing visions. The debate thus, arguably, becomes even more diverse.

[31] Walker (n 30) at 43. [32] Walker (n 30) at 43.

[33] Walker (n 30) at 43–4.

[34] One can characterize them as procedural concessions because they do not require any adjustment in substantive portions of the conflicting claims, but "only" both adjustments in the understanding of the nature of those claims. That is, the claims need to cease to regard themselves as superior in the

would not jeopardize the existence of the new pluralist configuration in its own terms: the situation would be regarded as one of "objective," but not yet "inter-subjective" pluralism. Epistemic pluralism can therefore live with a "system in denial" that would fail to accept the external incommensurability of its own sovereignty claims. But the epistemic pluralist would treat such monist views as mistaken: (a) as "based upon misreading or myopic reading" of the current situation in Europe, (b) as normatively "undesirable", and as being (c) "(hopefully) increasingly unlikely."[35]

It is by these mutual concessions that the epistemic pluralist stance can be distinguished from the position of monism.[36] The pluralist stance introduces a unique notion of *territorial overlap*: coexistence, over the same territory, of autonomous constitutional authorities and their respective self-standing sources, or, in Walker's words, "constitutional autonomy without territorial exclusivity."[37] Thus, we now have two different types of autonomously rooted and so heterarchically related constitutional authorities, which are coexistent within some shared territorial space and are self-defining. Though their self-definitions may conflict, none of the underlying authorities is exclusive. The concessions, such as those set out above, assure such mutual heterarchical presence. At the same time, these concessions are minimal under epistemic pluralism, as they only require the adjustment in the *nature* as opposed to *substance* of the site's claims.[38] The theory does not require, as a precondition to characterizing a configuration as pluralist, that the conflicting claims of foundational constitutional authority also acknowledge substantive mutual limitations. So, if the EU confines the claim to its foundational constitutional authority to the sphere within its functionally limited jurisdiction, this is not the normative requirement and constitutive feature of constitutional pluralism, as understood by epistemic pluralism. Similarly, it is not required by epistemic pluralism that the member state acknowledges any substantive limit to *its* foundational constitutional authority: for example as being confined to the sphere outside of the EU substantive sphere of constitutional authority. As long as the respective sites recognize that their foundational claims and aspirations are no longer meant to be understood in the sense of external epistemic validity, and so meet the concession about *external* epistemic incommensurability between such claims, they are free to define and assert their claims however they wish. They can even stick to their old monist claims and monopolizations of substantive spheres while merely conceding that these now have internal epistemic quality.[39] Beyond its loose, seven threshold criteria and the axiom of incommensurability at the external level, the

objectively valid *external* sense and can, even if substantively unchanged, continue to be asserted as long as they acknowledge that such views are now grounded only in their own *internal epistemes*.

[35] I am indebted to Prof Walker for a discussion on this point that has led to my understanding of the theory's aspect as described (EUI Florence, January 2006, and email correspondence, March 2006).

[36] For more on this key distinction, see Chapter 6, pp. 169–71 and Chapter 7, pp. 191–6.

[37] Walker (n 15) at 23; Walker (n 1) at 349.

[38] See pp. 35–7, and n 34.

[39] A discussion with Neil Walker on this point led to my understanding/elaboration of this aspect of his theory (see n 35). I am indebted to him.

theory of epistemic pluralism offers no further reconciliation at the foundational level between such internally valid claims or aspirations, and those may well continue to contradict radically. According to epistemic pluralism, the territorial overlap (the heterarchical relation between constitutional authorities over the same territory) is thus "merely" a procedurally as opposed to a substantively determined notion.[40]

But while substantive territorial overlap (heterarchy understood in the substantive sense) is not a constitutive element of pluralism under epistemic pluralism, it is one of several further options under this theory.[41] Because its thin understanding of constitutional pluralism leaves the choice for such further (substantive) reconciliation at the foundational level to the constitutional sites themselves, epistemic pluralism can at least explain and accommodate this phenomenon, if it perhaps occurs, while monism cannot. No matter how strong the factual reality, the monist readings would, by definition, continue to require the sites to claim the all-encompassing nature of their authorities. Those readings are unable to accommodate and explain the possible phenomenon of the EU as an autonomously rooted while functionally limited constitutional polity.

1.4 Explanatory and normative pluralism

Thus far I have only considered epistemic pluralism as the pluralist dimension of Walker's theory. While this dimension stands at the core of, and wholly imbues, Walker's version of constitutional pluralism, there are also two other pluralist aspects that are evident in his work and go hand in hand with the epistemic pluralist position. They are "explanatory" and "normative" pluralism.[42] The three pluralist dimensions are meant to apply to constitutionalism in general,[43] although Walker explicates them in the specific case of the EU, which in his view poses the most pressing challenge to constitutional monism.

While the particular epistemic pluralist dimension does not automatically flow from either the explanatory or normative pluralism, the converse does follow. Explanatory and normative pluralism both necessarily flow from epistemic pluralism. They also acquire specific content and meaning based on the fact that they are underpinned by the specific, *epistemic* pluralist view.[44]

The idea of epistemic incommensurability of knowledge and authority claims as emanating from the different constitutional sites in Europe thus means, for the

[40] Recall the analysis from Chapter 1, pp. 22–4 that showed how MacCormick, by contrast, assumed the substantive notion of constitutional heterarchy and its substantive idea of a territorial overlap. It will be observed later (pp. 91–2 and 166–7) how some other versions of pluralism also seem to require the stronger, substantive territorial overlap and concessions. This distinction will, however, not prevent us from discerning a common denominator to all the pluralist proposals, which will be discussed in Chapter 6, pp. 165–73.

[41] Discussion with Neil Walker (n 39).

[42] Walker (n 1) at 338–9; Walker (n 15) at 4; Walker (n 17) at 569–70.

[43] Walker (n 15) at 38–9.

[44] Walker (n 1) at 338.

explanatory dimension of pluralism, that as a matter of social reality there is no sure common basis of historical knowledge from which we can evaluate the force of conflicting authority claims expressed by the different constitutional sites.[45] Hence, we must "simply accept that the claims are each plausibly sustained and incommensurable and the strong version of explanatory pluralism that flows from that."[46] Explanatory pluralism thus holds that we can only explain adequately "what is going on within the new European constitutional configuration if we posit a framework which identifies multiple levels of constitutional discourse and authority."[47] The alternative would be to describe the reality in monistic terms: that "one claim continues to prevail over and subsume the other, in which case," as Walker reminds, we could not "meaningfully talk of a plurality of unit(ies) at all, but merely of the resilience or reassertion of an old (state-based) or emergence of a new (EU based) monistic unity."[48] Walker thus opts for the explanatory pluralism on the grounds that it is the more realistic reading of the current situation in Europe, congruent with his epistemic pluralist axiom that the claims of these sites are externally incommensurable. He makes it clear that "to try to explain the new emerging post-Westphalian order in one-dimensional terms, by reference to national delegation, inter-governmentalism, and the traditional law of international organisations," would be "to try to force square pegs into round holes, and to understate the extent and distort the character of the transformation which is underway."[49] On this reading, then, Walker is an explanatory pluralist while authors like Schilling[50] or Hartley[51] would be better described as explanatory monists.[52]

45 Walker (n 1) at 338; cf Walker (n 15) at 4. 46 Walker (n 1) at 338.

47 Walker (n 1) at 338. 48 Walker (n 1) at 338. 49 Walker (n 1) at 337.

50 T. Schilling, "The Autonomy of the Community Legal Order: An Analysis of Possible Foundations" (1996) 17 Harv Int LJ 389; T. Schilling, "Rejoinder: The Autonomy of the Community Legal Order" (1996) Harvard Jean Monnet Working Paper Series No 96/10; A. Pellet, "Les Fondements Juridiques Internationaux du Droit Communautaire" in Academy of European Law (ed.), *Collected Courses of the Academy of European Law*, Vol V (1994), Book 2. These positions defend the view that—as a matter of social reality—the EU can still be best described as an entity of international law. On this reading the states are still the "masters of the treaties." Walker himself mentions and cites Schilling as well as Pellet when distinguishing their explanatory monisms from his position of explanatory pluralism (see Walker (n 1) at 322, fn 19).

51 T. Hartley, "The Constitutional Foundations of the European Union" (2001) 117 LQR 225; T. Hartley, *Constitutional Problems of the European Union* (Oxford: Hart Publishing, 1999) ch 7. For a rebuttal of this position, see P. Craig, "Constitutions, Constitutionalism, and the European Union" (2001) 7 ELJ 125, 130–4.

52 And so would be also those authors who, even if implicitly, already presuppose some all-European single source of ultimate constitutional authority (sovereignty). Among this group of European monists Walker even sees authors such as Ingolf Pernice. Although the latter sets out to reconcile the idea of a poly-centered structure of political authority with the idea of an encompassing EU-wide unity, Walker explains that his "legal unity appears to presuppose a single source of sovereign authority," and that, hence, "it is difficult to see how the idea of a genuinely poly-centred structure may be sustained, since the multiple centres must, in the name of that unity, be reducible *in the final analysis* to one master principle of generative norm." Walker further describes Pernice's position as providing that, since the citizens of Europe taken as a whole are now Masters of the Treaties, no member state, regardless of its own self-understanding, any longer has the right of unilateral withdrawal from the EU. Walker concludes from this that authority within a multi-level system (such as the one proposed by Pernice) "would seem to inevitably gravitate towards the

While opting for explanatory pluralism entails some normative dimension, I follow Walker in nonetheless characterizing this pluralist dimension as "explanatory pluralism." This distinguishes it from an even stronger normative dimension which is termed "normative pluralism."

The normative dimension of pluralism is that "the only viable and the only acceptable ethic of political responsibility for the new configuration is one which is premised upon mutual recognition and interpenetration of constitutional sites located at different levels."[53] As a matter of the desired future development in Europe, this normative pluralism should lead "neither to a new unity or fixed hierarchy of constitutional authority nor, at the other extreme, to a fragmentation of authority."[54] Not everyone who is an explanatory pluralist is necessarily also a pluralist in normative terms. One might accept that, as a matter of social reality, there are multiple sites of heterarchical constitutional authority in the new Europe, but still advocate for monism as the better alternative—that we either "'rewind' to the earlier Westphalian order of fully sovereign states, or else 'fast-forward' to a full-blown European state which absorbs and replaces the existing member states."[55] Thus, for instance, Mancini's "Europe: The Case for Statehood" accepts explanatory pluralism, but argues for a monist solution in normative terms as regards further development of the new European constitutionalism.[56]

1.5 From second-order level to the first

It was noted at the inception of this chapter that epistemic pluralism is primarily a second-order thesis. It is also a thesis that primarily draws from, and deals with, the new constitutional situation in Europe, which is said to pose the most pressing challenge to constitutional monism, and to have provoked the emergence of the pluralist theory. Despite this, epistemic constitutional pluralism is a broader project, meant to apply beyond this primary focus. The theory is said to be applicable more broadly in two respects.

Firstly, it ranges beyond the particular focus of the EU. The elaboration of the "minimal standards" and the requirement of leaving the second-order constitutional debate open in the externally epistemic sense (the criteria of legitimate

federal level, even if, as with Pernice, it is the citizenry rather than the institutions which are the fount of authority and the custodians of sovereignty" (Walker (n 15) at 13–14, fn 31). There are other similar approaches to constitutionalism in Europe that, according to Walker, count as European monism. He explicitly refers to Armin Von Bogdandy, Deirdre Curtin, and Igge Dekker (Walker (n 15) at fn 30).

[53] Walker (n 15) at 4. [54] Walker (n 15) at 4; cf Walker (n 1) at 337–8.

[55] Walker (n 1) at 337–8.

[56] F. Mancini, "Europe: The Case for Statehood" (1998) 4 ELJ 29. Walker sees Mancini as an example of an explicit normative monist ("full federal statehood for the EU"). And he also detects the strand of more implicit normative monists, but still *monists* because their proposals presuppose a single source of sovereign authority. See Walker (n 15) at fnn 30 and 31.

constitutionalism as defined by epistemic pluralism) are meant as a general theory. Walker discusses not only the EU, but often also the WTO and even NAFTA as good candidates for, if not already good examples of, constitutionalism under his theory.[57] Indeed, despite some formidable potential difficulties with *directly* applying the idea of constitutional pluralism beyond the European context,[58] Walker has never abandoned his ambition of presenting the theory in general terms so as to make it equally relevant for the global context—although there its details would surely need to appear in some still further-adjusted form that he has not yet developed as of this point.[59]

The second respect in which epistemic pluralism is broadened is from a second-order to a first-order constitutional discourse. That is, it spills over also to first-order constitutional disagreement about the content and interpretation of this or that prescriptive constitutional rule (like freedom of expression, equal protection, right to privacy, and other constitutional norms) in everyday constitutional cases. And when it comes to such first-order constitutional disagreement, it applies to both first-order constitutional disagreement *between* the systems, as well as to *fully internal* contexts when a first-order constitutional resolution in a concrete case does not impinge upon another constitutional system's asserted constitutional domain.[60] The theory therefore comprehensively permeates constitutional discourse, and in doing so penetrates into each of the constitutional systems—that of the EU, those of the European nation-states, as well as any other individual constitutional system recognized as such by the second-order part of its thesis.

The application of the theory to the level of first-order constitutional knowledge claims indeed seems to be unavoidable for at least two reasons. Firstly, the levels are necessarily interconnected: second-order authority and knowledge claims control first-order constitutional knowledge claims within a constitutional system. To understand that second-order claims are system self-referential—that is, epistemically incommensurable—is not neutral to first-order constitutional knowledge claims and their respective resolutions of concrete constitutional cases. The question becomes rather: what exactly does that understanding do to the first-order

[57] Walker (n 1) at 339, 345, 347–8, 350, 355.

[58] See Chapter 9, pp. 220–5, 285–94, and 317–19; cf G. de Búrca and J. Weiler (eds), *The Worlds of European Constitutionalism* (Cambridge: Cambridge University Press, 2012), especially the Prologue and Dialogic Epilogue.

[59] Walker (n 1) at 339, 345, 347–8, 350, 355; see also his recent "Constitutionalism and Pluralism in Global Context," NYU Colloquium on Global and Comparative Public Law, December 2011, available at <http://www.reconproject.eu/main.php/RECON_wp_1003.pdf?fileitem=5455875>; and his, "The Place of European Law" in de Búrca and Weiler (n 58).

[60] Walker's articles are less explicit about widening the breadth of epistemic pluralism along this second axis. At several points in his literature one can nonetheless find indications that this must be the case; see, eg Walker (n 1) at 343, 351–2; also Walker (n 15) at 28. I am indebted to Neil Walker for discussions on this point that clarified my understanding (EUI, Florence, June 2003, July 2003, and January 2006).

constitutional disagreement and the actual decisions that have to be made in concrete cases notwithstanding the fact of that disagreement.[61]

Secondly, constitutional disagreement is above all a practical problem about making actual but disputed decisions concerning our and other people's lives. Where it becomes most decisive is exactly at the level of everyday, actual disputes with governmental authorities about whether something is or is not congruent with some provision of a constitution as the highest legal authority of that legal system. Here the problems of deep postmodern disagreement about the "right meaning" of this or that constitutional clause become most evident and pressing. Here they are materialized. So if the proponent of epistemic pluralism really wishes to engage seriously with the idea of redeeming constitutional discourse from the difficulties posed by disagreement, he must do something about this level of disagreement as well. The theory cannot just remain at the level of the more abstract second-order question of what range of claims legitimately get to the table as reckonable constitutional arguments: the question of what claims qualify as *constitutional* discourse. Redeeming constitutional discourse from the challenge of disagreement must be meant in the more comprehensive sense, or it fails at the outset.

If Walker's project thus cannot be read as being confined to the second-order constitutional discourse, this then raises the question of the exact way in which the incommensurability axiom applies to the domain of first-order constitutional discourse. Up until now, Walker has not yet elaborated on this point, although he agrees there must be such an elaboration, since this is necessary for the concrete level of everyday first-order constitutional disagreement. What follows is therefore my attempt to unfold this part of the theory as it flows from my understanding of both the theory's axioms and Walker's further explanations in our discussion on this point.

The key issue is whether epistemic pluralism simply copies its operationalization of the axiom of epistemic incommensurability from the second-order constitutional disagreement onto this level of first-order constitutional disputes, and so treats all claims within the latter discourse as equally incommensurable? This position would seem to bring it close to the camp of radical agonistic democrats, with writers like Chantal Mouffe or Ernesto Laclau,[62] or perhaps some from the CLS camp,[63] all of whom seem to assume that there is never any ethically valuable legacy for deciding questions of political morality. Or does epistemic pluralism distance itself from

[61] I am grateful to Neil Walker for a discussion on this particular aspect, which enabled me to elaborate the point and develop the application of the theory to the first-order level of constitutional discourse that follows (EUI, Florence, January 2006).

[62] E. Laclau and C. Mouffe, *Hegemony and Socialist Strategy: Towards a Radical Democratic Politics* (2nd edn, New York, NY: Verso, 2001); see also Mouffe's "Preface: Democratic Politics Today" in C. Mouffe (ed.), *Dimensions of Radical Democracy: Pluralism, Citizenship, Community* (New York, NY: Verso, 1992), and other contributions to that book.

[63] At least some of the authors from this branch endorse(d) a radical version of the indeterminacy thesis and its related scepticism about the possibility of a communicative public rationality, such as the one reflected in the concept of constitutional rights.

these camps by assuming that we nevertheless could and should do something more in normative terms once on the level of conflicting first-order constitutional claims?

It might be possible to argue in theory that an exact transposition of the foundational premise of epistemic pluralism from the second-order level to the first-order level is the only logically consistent position for an epistemic pluralist to take. After all, first-order claims are inherently interconnected with the second-order ones. So, if one posits that the second-order level is permeated with incommensurability, there might thereby inescapably be such same incommensurability also at the first-order level. Be that as it may, Walker would nonetheless not want that to be his position.[64] He assumes that, with respect to first-order constitutional questions, epistemic pluralism *should* be allowed to discriminate in some way between the reckonable constitutional arguments (the reckonable first-order constitutional arguments are those that originate only from the *legitimate* second-order conceptions). The particular meaning of incommensurability should thus not simply be copied from the second-order level to the first. Rather it should be operationalized in a particular way when applied to the first-order constitutional disagreement.

This distinction is due to the different circumstances at the two levels. There can be fierce conflict on the level of foundational constitutional rules while not at the same time endangering the viability of epistemic pluralism. This can be so provided that the actual outcomes of concrete decisions on the first-order constitutional level, while having different principled second-order rationales, are in congruence. It is therefore for an advocate of epistemic pluralism to insist that assertions of foundational recognition rules can, normatively speaking, continue to conflict. However, when it comes to dealing with conflict in concrete cases at the first-order level, the need for actual congruence becomes pressing. Otherwise the instances of constitutional collision would render the epistemic pluralist theory unviable. This seems to be one of the main reasons why the axiom of epistemic incommensurability is treated differently when it comes to the first-order constitutional disagreement, where any resolution of cases has to take into account that pressing need for congruence at this very concrete level.

Therefore, while epistemic incommensurability requires at the second-order level the adoption of certain procedural concessions,[65] the same axiom requires further mutual *substantive* concessions at the first-order level.

The fact that foundational recognition rules need to be understood as externally epistemically incommensurable, and that each constitutional system should recognize such self-referentiality by adopting procedural concessions, has a deeply destabilizing effect on constitutional knowledge. This destabilization "from

[64] Interview (n 61). My understanding is that Walker would tend to characterize his general approach as being more like that of J. Tully, who is a more moderate representative of the agonistic project and who would also want to distance himself from the more radical agonistic alternatives mentioned.

[65] Recall that under these procedural concessions the proponents of rival claims to sovereignty can no longer maintain that their claims are grounded in some objectively valid, external *episteme*, but must instead merely recognize that they are contingent in the internal epistemic sense.

below" does also have an impact on the level of first-order knowledge claims, both within and between systems. Some first-order solutions that were previously perhaps taken for granted, as they rested on the assumed external epistemic superiority of their underlying foundations, must now be reassessed. Their assumed superiority can no longer be seen as so strongly anchored. Their proponents must recognize that the world has changed in the new Europe, and that some of their most fundamental underlying assumptions have become epistemically contingent. Therefore, to continue to treat alternative first-order views as if nothing has changed would be to unduly demean the latter.

The realization of the self-referentiality and contingency of the second-order claims, coupled with the need for sufficient congruence at the first-order level, thus puts pressure on the conflicting first-order claims. This is the catalyst for a greater degree of substantive mutual concessions, whatever those happen to be. Parties to first-order constitutional disagreement realize that they must reopen negotiation on the substantive dimensions of their claims. Epistemic pluralism therefore generates a mutually reflexive constitutional discourse at the first-order constitutional level, a discourse that is exceptionally fluid and open-ended.[66] It is indeed in this way that advocates of epistemic pluralism hope to redeem constitutionalism from disagreement at the first-order level.

There is a particular internal relationship between the two ways in which the incommensurability axiom is operationalized at the two levels. This applies to procedural concessions at the second-order level, but procedural *and* substantive ones at the first-order level. Neither can exist without the other. The necessary corollary to retaining mere procedural concessions at the second-order level is to generate the need for substantive concessions at the first-order level. This enables sufficient congruence at the first-order level to be achieved, thereby allowing the second-order foundational rationales to continue to overlap and conflict without the need for substantive reconciliation. In analogous fashion the necessary corollary to retaining the intensely reflexive and fluid substantive discourse envisioned at the first-order level, is to hold on to the mere procedural concessions at the second-order level that come to spread epistemic destabilization all the way up to the first-order level.

While requiring substantive concessions *as such* at the first-order level, Walker does not, however, delve into this substantive discourse itself. This is in part because the very destabilization posited by the theory means that we cannot know what the substantive result would be. It is for the parties who are themselves engaged in the substantive discourse to determine their own chosen conclusion.[67] The theory simply highlights the process by which, that is *how*, the substantive

[66] N. Walker, "Constitutionalism and New Governance in the European Union: Rethinking the Boundaries" (2005) EUI Working Papers LAW No 2005/15, 15–16.

[67] Indeed, part of Walker's answer as to what epistemic pluralism amounts to in substantive terms would be that he does not know—ie epistemic pluralism should not externally impose—that result. I am indebted to him for a discussion that contributed to my understanding on this point (see n 61).

discourse takes place.[68] It is a process of mutual reflexivity, of reciprocal adjustments among equals, that implies some thin form of communicative rationality. That is, some variant of the notion of public reason, or *quasi*-public reason.[69]

This moves epistemic pluralism slightly away from the more radical strand mentioned earlier,[70] and brings it at least a little closer to a well-known group within the mainstream of liberal constitutional thought. Theories that assume communicative public rationality are normally rationalizations of what one would do under the best circumstances, and there are different understandings of what this entails. These usually amount to the replacing of what are felt to be inappropriate interpretive questions with new ones. As such, these modified interpretive questions represent thresholds for determining in the midst of disagreement those publicly legitimate arguments and resolutions that all would have reason to endorse. For example, in Rawls the old question concerning the best epistemic or metaphysical conception of the good is replaced by a counterfactual question. The question is, "which arguments and resolutions every party to a disagreement may be reasonably expected to endorse as being most conducive to the full development and exercise by every person of the two moral powers of the reasonable and rational?"[71] According to Rawls's version of communicative rationality, only sincere answers to the latter interpretive question can count as good public reasons. That very specification of the right interpretive question is his answer to the *how* of legitimate resolutions within the discourse. As another example, one may take Habermas's theory of communicative rationality, which offers a similar type of answer to the question of *how*. His specific version of the right interpretive question adopts a distinctly *intersubjectivist* reciprocal articulation. An argument or resolution counts as legitimate, as a good public reason, only if "it could be accepted by everybody from the perspective of each individual"; and this also needs to be judged in the counterfactual sense of the reasonable person.[72] However loose a constraint we may presume is imposed by these abstract *how* thresholds (ie public reason's right questions) on public decision-making under each version of the theory of communicative rationality, we must nevertheless presume that they exert some constraint.[73]

While epistemic pluralism follows this general path of public communicative rationality, and can thus be seen as belonging to this group of theories, it also occupies a significantly distinctive place within the group. Like the thresholds

[68] Walker agrees that, unlike with the mentioned substantive question of the *what* of the first-order constitutional discourse, epistemic pluralism cannot avoid answering the question of the *how* of that discourse (interview (n 61)).

[69] Interview (n 61). [70] See n 62.

[71] J. Rawls, *Political Liberalism* (New York, NY: Columbia University Press, 1993) ch 6. Cf F. Michelman, "Rawls on Constitutionalism and Constitutional Law" in S. Freeman (ed.), *The Cambridge Companion to John Rawls* (Cambridge: Cambridge University Press, 2002) 399–400.

[72] J. Habermas, *The Inclusion of the Other: Studies in Political Theory* (3rd edn, Cambridge, MA: The MIT Press, 2001) 31.

[73] F. Michelman, "The Problem of Constitutional Interpretive Disagreement: Can 'Discourses of Application' Help?" in M. Aboulafia et al (eds), *Habermas and Pragmatism* (London: Routledge, 2002) subsection C.

described above, epistemic pluralism also steers and regulates the way in which substantive concessions are to be made, and entails a mutually reflexive discourse, in which procedural as well as substantive concessions will be made. However, unlike the other theories in the group, epistemic pluralism does not impose a sacrosanct form of the *how*, that is, a specifically defined right question that would be the single correct approach for identifying legitimate arguments in all contexts. This is because epistemic pluralism, as a highly agonistic project, rejects the idea that there can be such sacrosanct approaches to the exercise of communicative rationality. For the epistemic pluralist the conditions for discourse and disagreement must be more fluid, and this extends even to the posited conditions, which ought to be open to constant renegotiation.[74] The epistemic pluralist does not assume a specific pre-given position of best circumstances before engaging in communicative ethics. By way of contrast, the epistemic pluralist maintains that we should use existing conditions as a forerunner for attempts to change the constitution, the institutional structure, and the like. This more agonistic approach to communicative rationality thus arguably leaves the legitimate constitutional discourse more open and fluid than do other proposals within the branch of communicative rationality. The more agonistic strategy of epistemic pluralism seems necessary, since only if it assumes some greater degree of incommensurability than the conventional theories, can it really hope to better redeem constitutionalism from disagreement at this first level.

Epistemic pluralism's constraint concerning public reason cannot therefore be specifically defined, but must remain as a mere abstract and flexible exhortation to highly reflexive negotiation. In this way the discourse can be kept as plastic (unfixed) as possible in circumstances where we have fundamental disagreement. But what, then, does this in practice mean for constitutional disagreement between systems as well as for fully intra-systemic contexts, that is, the interpersonal constitutional disagreement limited only to parties within a system?

In the case of *inter-systemic* disagreement, such as between the EU and member states, the abstract constraint, which requires high mutual reflexivity in the procedural and the substantive sense, generates a new spirit within the process of decision-making in circumstances of disagreement. This leads, it is implied, to a transformation of the terms of exchange, which becomes more dialogic. Walker points to developments in the relations between the EU and member states that represent the institutional germ of this more radical transformation and also

[74] Hence Walker's endorsement of the criticism of Rawls's theory as being still insufficiently inclusive of legitimate disagreement: "The fundamental weakness of Rawls's position, as Waldron brings out well, is not so much the lack of plausibility in his argument that it is possible to conceive of a 'free-standing' theory of justice (although that remains a standing objection, and part of the explanatory context for the subsequent pragmatic objection) within a hypothetical 'well-ordered society,' but that, more pragmatically, in 'the real world' no such agreement on the content of such a 'free-standing' theory exists and that instead our politics are, *inter alia*, 'dedicated quite explicitly to grappling with fundamental *dis*agreement about justice'" (Walker (n 1) at 335) (Walker's citations in this paragraph are from J. Waldron's *Law and Disagreement* (Oxford: Oxford University Press, 1999)). Cf Walker (n 30) at 6–7.

accelerate the substantive aspect of the transformation.[75] Among these institutional developments is the preliminary reference procedure of Article 267 TFEU;[76] development of cross-system mechanisms of exchange between representative, executive, monetary, and other institutions of the different systems;[77] the Comitology committee structure;[78] and the recent development of the Open Method of Coordination,[79] as well as other similar mechanisms for mutual inter-systemic learning and accommodation. These mechanisms helped produce a set of inter-ethical practices, which grew up into a highly mutually reflexive approach to inter-systemic disagreement. As envisioned by the theory, substantive mutual adjustments seem to have become the practice in everyday European reality at the first-order constitutional level, while at the level of second-order claims the respective sites continue to assert their sovereignty in conflicting ways. Because of the abstract constraint of a high degree of mutual reflexivity, and the development of the institutional mechanisms adumbrated earlier, epistemic pluralism can, it is claimed, deal with the inter-systemic first-order constitutional disagreement in a dialogic way. It thereby prevents such disagreement from undermining the viability of heterarchically coexisting authorities set as such at the foundational level. It is for these reasons that epistemic pluralism does not need to propose a particular answer to the question of "who decides who decides" in the case of first-order disagreement between the systems. That determination can and should, it is believed, remain for each individual system itself.

In the context of fully *intra-systemic* disagreement, that is, interpersonal and inter-institutional constitutional disagreement within a system, the theory's distinctively abstract and flexible public reason applies as well. Here too it functions as the criterion of the correct manner in which to engage in constitutional interpretation: the manner that would be consistent with epistemic pluralism as opposed to monism. Yet within the intra-systemic sphere this nonetheless still leaves us with a relatively wide sphere of disagreement. It might be unrealistic to assume that in this particular context the interpersonal disagreement between the actors, here meaning all the citizens and institutions subject to a given state's constitutional jurisdiction, could be reflexively fully tamed. Therefore, the interpretive criterion itself might not be enough in all cases to avoid the threshold question of who is to make the ruling in such circumstances of remaining intra-systemic disagreement. Yet even then epistemic pluralism does not pick its favorite institution—for example, the courts, majority rule, or some other kind of *who* threshold—that would in some

[75] Walker (n 15) at 29–30.
[76] Walker (n 15) at 29.
[77] Walker (n 15) at 29.
[78] "[T]he Comitology system creates inclusive decision-making contexts which allow for mutual accommodation and mutual learning between different types of national, supranational and non-aligned actors" (Walker (n 15) at 30).
[79] Similarly to the comitology committee structure, "the recent development of the Open Method of Co-ordination is in some measure at least in response to the indeterminacy and contestation of jurisdictional boundaries between state and EU in matters as diverse as employment policy and asylum policy. The OMC responds by side-stepping the hard questions of competence and substituting for compartmentalised decision-making hierarchy an inclusive policy cycle which lacks any authoritative end-point" (Walker (n 15) at 30).

normative sense be a priori best suited for the job. Instead, it leaves this issue open, and treats it as contingent upon the context of an individual community, while taking only an *indirect* normative stance on the issue. It requires that in cases of fundamental disagreements between people and institutions about a piece of legislation or a constitutional amendment, there should be low thresholds for reconsideration of such matters, through, for example, negotiation leading to the possibility of non-constitutional mechanisms of amendment. Nonetheless, this does not fundamentally alter the fact that, for the epistemic pluralist, the issue of who should decide fundamental disagreements should remain as contingent as possible and dependent on context. There should thus also not be any a priori preference for either majoritarianism or judicial review.

2. Situating the Theory

It might be helpful to conclude the exploration of Walker's theory by making further use of the decoding tool—our Ariadne's Thread—to see where exactly epistemic pluralism falls on the map of pluralism's labyrinth. We can observe at the outset that epistemic pluralism dealt in one part with what the tool tells us is the most abstract theoretical discourse on pluralism:[80] where Walker's theory engaged with the "second-order" level of discourse that included foundational rules of recognition. Like MacCormick's vision analysed in Chapter 1, it engaged in the theoretical discourse about the deepest foundations of the heterarchically as opposed to hierarchically related constitutional authorities and their sources. As observed, epistemic pluralism did imply a theoretical premise according to which the EU and member states' constitutional systems were autonomously rooted and coexistent over some shared territorial space. True, we saw that the meaning of this heterarchical coexistence at the foundational level differed in epistemic pluralism, from that in MacCormick's conception.[81] However, this does not by itself change the fact that this part of Walker's theory clearly also belongs to the foundational discourse; to the same sector of the labyrinth.

Yet it is already at this foundational level that one can notice in Walker a central further theme and meaning of pluralism. Above all, epistemic pluralism is preoccupied with what, using Ariadne's Thread, we described was the theme of the *how*. That is, by elaborating its own variant of a pluralist conception epistemic pluralism implies the meaning of constitutional heterarchy in which the principal preoccupation is to determine the proper *form* as opposed to *content* of constitutional discourse. It has already been observed that at the level of Walker's foundational discourse, his theory aims at avoiding external imposition of any particular constitutional content. The choices about the content itself were left entirely to the

[80] See p. 12.

[81] As does the specific central idea of the epistemic pluralist project, which is designed to redeem the ideas of constitutionalism and constitutionality from the challenge of deep and intractable postmodern disagreement in politics.

relevant constitutional sites themselves. Thus, epistemic constitutional pluralism is not concerned with the question of the *what*, and emphatically does not aim at engaging in discourse concerning that theme. Indeed, to engage in that theme and thereby externally arbitrate between different foundational claims would be seen, according to epistemic pluralism, as a paradigmatic example of the monist undertaking.

That epistemic pluralism is a theory primarily working within the *how* sector of constitutional discourse becomes even more obvious after recalling its explication as to the first-order level of discourse and that part of disagreement. There we saw that, by elaborating its own thinnest version of public rationality (even avoiding elaboration of a particular sacrosanct formula), epistemic pluralism attempts in some radical sense to avoid external imposition of the correct constitutional content and instead tries to be neutral as to the latter.[82] This was so with respect to both the inter-systemic and intra-systemic part of the constitutional discourse. Indeed, this is a paradigmatic example of a theory engaging with the question of the right interpretive method (the theme of the *how*) as opposed to the right substantive content (the theme of the *what*) of constitutional discourse. All this is perfectly congruent with the specific central aim of epistemic pluralism—to redeem the ideas of constitutionalism and constitutionality from deep and radical postmodern disagreement. As a result of this specific orientation and theme within which it works, epistemic pluralism then also implies a specific meaning of constitutional heterarchy, of constitutional pluralism, that is inseparably bound up with this particular theme. This is also why it follows that any other proposal that contradicts the new thin *form* of constitutional discourse at both its levels is quickly dismissed as a non-pluralist—that is, a monist—move.

While the discussion thus far reveals that Walker's project of constitutional pluralism is primarily about the second discourse from our Ariadne's Thread (the *how*, rather than the *what*), how about the theme of the *who*? Walker's theory is also not primarily addressed to the question of final interpretive authority ("who decides who decides?") and its discourse of the *who*. It is apparent from the preceding explications that the theory, however, is not silent on that theme either, and actually has profound implications for the dilemma of "who decides who decides." It is central to the epistemic pluralist view concerning the question of *foundational authority* that the different claims of the member states and the EU in their final *decision-making* (interpretive) authority are incommensurable. Walker believes that this dilemma cannot be resolved externally; he assumes there is no common, external epistemic scale on which the plausibility of these conflicting claims could possibly be measured and assessed. It is for this reason that he proposes the adoption of the epistemically pluralist stance towards the validity of both claims, that is, to recognize the absolute validity of both as measured from their internal perspectives, rather than try to reconcile one with another through some external balancing. Any such external balancing would necessarily always impose reasons

[82] Or, more accurately, this is the theory's attempt. Whether it can succeed in it or not, is another issue. See pp. 60–8 and Chapter 8, pp. 235–8, 239–50.

with which neither could agree, because there are no objective (inter-systemic, external), but only subjective (intra-systemic, internal), epistemic criteria for assessing the validity of both decision-making authority claims. For the epistemic pluralist, such an imposition would only provide a third, equally internal and incommensurable view.[83]

The consequence is that under epistemic pluralism the "who decides who decides" dilemma remains externally unresolved, and so is the very confirmation of the autonomies of the respective constitutional orders. Or, as Walker himself puts it:

> If ultimate authority in the post-Westphalian order is consistent with autonomy rather than exclusivity, so too the power of ultimate arbitration and interpretation in domains of overlapping jurisdiction need not be exclusive. Interpretive autonomy means precisely that. It does not necessarily mean that from an external point of view "only the institutions of that particular order are competent to interpret the constitutional and legal rules of that order" [citing Schilling, "The Autonomy of the Community Legal Order" (n 49)], but merely that this can be plausibly asserted from an *internal* point of view. In a configuration of overlapping and rival polities—in a landscape of contested boundaries—the supreme judicial authorities of these rival orders will each claim the right to police these contested boundaries in terms of the normative pedigree of their own order and by reference to the rules of adjudication associated with that normative pedigree. In other words, on a pluralist reading the assertion of rival plausible claims to have the last judicial word on an overlapping or disputed question of competence, provided these claims are also reasonably institutionally effective on their own terms, confirms rather than denies the interpretive autonomy of each of the polities or putative polities in question.[84]

There is an obviously pressing question here. Namely, how could such an arrangement possibly deal with the threat of an unbearable degree of collision that could result?[85] Part of Walker's answer has already been touched on.[86] There it was explained that the institutional germ of first-order conflict prevention is already present to a degree. To that one can add some doctrinal devices—like "the doctrine of pre-emption, or the technique of minimal harmonisation, or, more tentatively, the developing jurisprudence of procedural harmonisation in the area of domestic court enforcement of Community rules."[87] These doctrinal and institutional devices represent the so-called "bridging mechanisms"[88] that "seek to ensure that

[83] See, eg Walker's criticism of Weiler's proposal for a Constitutional Council of the Union, which would act as a "meta-forum" for resolving the competing jurisdictional claims of the ECJ and the highest national courts (Walker (n 17) at 387).

[84] Walker (n 1) at 349.

[85] The threat definitely seemed unbearable to Kelsen, who on this type of occasion simply played his trump card of "no one can serve two masters."

[86] Pp. 48–50. [87] Walker (n 17) at 376 (citations omitted).

[88] Walker (n 17) at 375–7; N. Walker, "Legal Theory and the European Union: A 25th Anniversary Essay" (2005) OJLS 581, 592; N. Walker, "The Migration of Constitutional Ideas and the Migration of the Constitutional Idea: The Case of the EU" (2005) EUI Working Paper LAW No 2005/04, 3.

the terms of mutual accommodation between the two levels of legal order prevent the outbreak of argument in the border regions *in the first place*."[89] Moreover, even the failure of the preventive bridging mechanisms is not thought to be fatal to epistemic pluralism. Drawing on Weiler's scholarship,[90] Walker highlights the fact that one should not underestimate the particular context in which actual collisions, if they arise, are situated within the new Europe. In this view, the stakes are high, and the kind of Cold War logic of "mutually assured destruction" makes it realistic that "neither side is likely to go further than merely threatening the use of its judicial 'nuclear weapon' to strike down a properly constituted rule of the other side."[91] The "fear of reprisal and the extremely hazardous consequences for all which would flow from this chain of activity" are said to explain why this is "in fact . . . how the principals have behaved in EU-state boundary disputes to date, the belligerent rhetoric masking a willingness to compromise in the final instance."[92]

Notwithstanding this position, Walker seems to acknowledge that even some almost perfect body of bridging mechanisms, coupled with a truly serious disincentive for mutual destruction, might not themselves suffice to leave the dilemma of "who decides who decides" unresolved. What is ultimately decisive is the high degree of "intense reflexivity"[93] that epistemic pluralism requires. The proposal would be viable only if the respective interpretive authorities embrace the strategy, making use of the relevant bridging mechanisms—especially where there is actual collision between the highest authorities. Only then would leaving open the question of "who decides who decides" really succeed. It is in this light that Walker writes that "interpretive autonomy remains a powerful index of constitutional maturity."[94] And this is also why he emphasizes that constitutional autonomy under pluralism is about *both* "making that claim to autonomy" as well as "accepting full responsibility . . . before both internal and external audiences."[95]

Whether one believes in the practical viability of such a proposal or not, one cannot but note here a third variation in Walker's meaning of pluralism. Within this theme of the *who*, for him pluralism is the situation in which neither some institution of the nation-state constitutional order, nor that of the EU, has the final say in deciding constitutional disputes between those orders. Any other solution, whereby such final decision-making authority would be exercised by one of these institutions, some common institution, some instance of another legal order like an institution of international law, or some explicit distribution of final decision-making authority between such institutions, Walker does not consider as pluralism, but monism. This is therefore quite a specific meaning of pluralism within this distinct and narrower theme of the *who*. Despite their obvious internal

89 Walker (n 17) at 376 (emphasis added).

90 J. Weiler, "The Reformation of European Constitutionalism" (1997) 35 Journal of Common Market Studies 97, 125–8.

91 Walker (n 17) at 377.

92 Walker (n 17) at 377.

93 Walker (n 66) at 15.

94 Walker (n 1) at 350.

95 Walker (n 66) at 15.

connections, it should nonetheless be distinguished from Walker's other two meanings of pluralism—the one within the foundational discourse and the one within the theme of the *how*. In the current literature the distinctions between these different meanings are almost always conflated. It is usually not clear to which of these meanings a commentator, or a pluralist author himself, is referring when making an observation or criticism. This contributes to a significant degree of confusion currently accompanying pluralist scholarship. Numerous observations and criticisms in the current literature that might perhaps be valid with respect to one of these meanings often do not hold for the other two. Judging a whole proposal as "not being pluralist" on the basis of a mere discussion within the theme of the *who* is, for instance, a classic mistake of that nature, often committed by critics and pluralists alike. We will observe this closely later in this work. It is thus critical to draw the distinctions discovered by using Ariadne's Thread and to keep using the tool for the rest of our analysis. This should enable us later to decode and make sense of the whole branch behind the new literature, provided of course such a branch exists in the first place.

3. Assessing the Theory

3.1 In search of the rationale

The core of the theory posits that foundational recognition claims and their underlying rationales are externally incommensurable: that they lack any common inter-systemic *episteme* by which they could be measured and assessed.

But why exactly this is or should be the case is not explicitly argued. The axiom is rather flatly stated by the theory as one aspect of the "elementary circumstances of constitutional politics," for which "it is axiomatic that [they be] acknowledged and respected."[96] This is so even though it seems that there could be several different understandings of the rationale behind (ie meanings of) the stated position of external epistemic incommensurability. So we have a situation in which the theory assumes its own superiority—that it is non-imposing, or less imposing than other proposals—because it imbues constitutional discourse with this particular axiom, while it does not at the same time engage in argumentation as to why exactly this axiom should be understood as such a superior choice. Rather, the axiom's superiority seems to be assumed *by default*. That is to say, while we have seen the operationalized implications of adopting the axiom for the second and first-order constitutional discourse, the question remains why exactly is the positing of the

[96] Walker (n 1) at 335. Cf also Walker (n 15) at 28: "A sovereign order must assume its own continuing or self-amending sovereignty within its sphere of authority (rules of recognition and change) and must retain interpretive autonomy (rules of adjudication), deciding the boundaries of that sphere of authority. This is the irreducible core, the non-negotiable given of any sovereign order— . . . the 'vanishing point' of perspective from which its 'sovereign' vision of the world is constructed or assumed but which itself cannot be seen and cannot be questioned in the construction of that vision" (footnote omitted).

underlying axiom, and not perhaps some other, similar or distinct version of it, warranted in the first place, so that the default superiority of epistemic constitutional pluralism is justifiably assumed together with its presented implications?

In the inter-theoretical assessment of the pluralist theories (see Chapter 8) we will see that all the theories assume different degrees of external commensurability. It is therefore the case that this key question could only be successfully addressed if possible rationales underlying the axiom of incommensurability are identified and explained prior to engaging in that kind of assessment. If there are different rationales and meanings behind the axiom of incommensurability, they could well lead to different final conclusions within such inter-theoretical assessment. The following *intra*-theoretical analysis will therefore prepare epistemic pluralism for the final, *inter*-theoretical evaluation of the different versions of constitutional pluralism that we will conduct in Chapter 8.

So why exactly does Walker think we should understand that the claims are epistemically incommensurable and ought to be treated as such? Why is he an epistemic sceptic, when numerous other authors—despite acknowledging the fact of disagreement—often conclude that there are sufficient reasons for striking a particular balance between some of the conflicting foundational constitutional claims, and so reconcile them epistemically?[97] There could be different possible rationales behind (meanings of) the axiom of external epistemic incommensurability.

The first candidate rationale, under which the assumption of default superiority of the axiom could be warranted, is the notion of uncertainty. One could reason along the following lines: certain arguments make sense to me when I look at the issue from one perspective; but the opposing arguments make sense when I look at the issue from another perspective. My further attempts to try to reconcile or balance the existing arguments, so that some third solution appears as externally preferable, do not provide any such superior argumentation. I am bewildered by the inability of any of these conceptions to demonstrate external superiority over the rest, and so declare that I am uncertain about what could be the right or best external epistemic choice.[98] I conclude that the issue is incommensurable: that there is no right external answer to it.

This kind of reasoning assumes that the conclusion of external epistemic incommensurability requires something less than any of the positive positions that compete with it. It assumes that incommensurability of conflicting foundational recognition claims, for example those of the EU and member states, is a "*theoretically less ambitious claim*" than any of the following three: that the EU should have ultimate hierarchical priority over national levels, that national levels should be seen as having that priority, or that any other substantive balancing or reconciling solution would be best. While something more must be known and explained about each of these three positive positions, no such further knowledge or

[97] This is, for instance, the case with those pluralists who belong to the camp that I characterize as "substantive pluralism." See pp. 74–89 (Weiler), pp. 177–87 (MacCormick), and pp. 251–6.

[98] R. Dworkin, "Objectivity and Truth: You'd Better Believe It" (1996) 25 Philosophy and Public Affairs 87, 131.

explanation is needed from the incommensurability strand. If so, then the failure of the substantive positive positions to supply that further knowledge is enough to establish the claim of incommensurability (the no-right-answer claim), which is thus true *by default*.[99]

Now, it is certainly possible that claims that we are—or should be—uncertain about some issue are "theoretically less ambitious" than claims of a stronger positive nature: these uncertainty positions "do hold by default" along the presented line of reasoning. If one analyses arguments on all sides of a given issue, and at the end just does not know what to think about them in the sense of external superiority, then one is perhaps entitled without further deliberation to declare that one is uncertain in that sense and has no view on the issue. In that case one neither needs to, nor can, provide further external reasons for claiming uncertainty, beyond one's report of failure to see the best external answer.[100]

However, the leap from declaring that, externally speaking, one has no view on the issue (conclusion of uncertainty) to the further claim that things should therefore be considered externally incommensurable (no-right-answer conclusion) cannot be assumed. Incommensurability, as a conclusion about no right or best external answer, is wholly different from the uncertainty position. In contrast to the agnostic stance of the uncertainty claim, the further incommensurability (no-right-answer) conclusion needs a positive substantive rationale in support.[101] It is itself a positive claim.[102] In addition to the positions from the EU and national levels, there are also numerous other positive positions that strike a substantive balance between both ends of the scale. However, one is just as much in need of an argument for the additional view—that none of these balances can be best because the issue is inter-systemically incommensurable—as one is for each of the above positive positions. In other words, with the exception of the uncertainty position, which is a positive claim to a lesser degree, the rest of the positions are all such claims to the same degree.

The tempting confusion of not distinguishing between the principle of uncertainty and incommensurability as the no-right-answer claim might perhaps explain the implicit tendency within epistemic pluralism to assume the axiom's default superiority.[103] At the same time, this clarifies that such a tendency and assumption cannot be warranted. The superiority of its axiom, and so of the theory itself, must

[99] Dworkin (n 98) at 131. [100] Dworkin (n 98) at 131–2.

[101] Dworkin (n 98) at 132.

[102] Were the axiom of epistemic incommensurability understood as no more than the principle of uncertainty, then epistemic pluralism as a theory would, in my view, face insurmountable difficulties. The less ambitious claim of uncertainty means that one has no view on the issue and is just not able to argue further for this or that solution of one's "theory" in the way that, for instance, epistemic pluralism currently does. In such circumstances no theory can be proposed at all. Under this scenario epistemic pluralism would thus amount to no more than a self-sufficient contemplative exercise without offering any proposal in the collective normative sense, and certainly not to something that claims to redeem ideas of constitutionalism and constitutionalism from disagreement *in some best way for all*, as it now declares.

[103] On the other hand, Walker's theory, which is to be understood as part of the trajectory of his work rather than the final proposal, might have intended to argue for the superiority of the axiom at some later stage. But see Chapter 8, section 2.2, especially pp. 240–5, and section 2.3. of that chapter.

instead be argued for and defended by a positive rationale underlying the axiom. This element is now missing from the theory. The uncertainty type of rationale behind the default superiority of the axiom would thus indeed leave the theory undefended at its very core. What is more, it would make it logically untenable.

If the external epistemic incommensurability thus cannot but be a positive claim, what positive rationale does actually lie behind this kind of axiom? Could it perhaps be the claim of "direct epistemic incommensurability"? According to this first positive candidate-rationale someone might think from the start, even prior to taking into account the factor of the need for comity towards others who disagree, that these are types of questions to which there simply are no right answers. That is, we would have an openly positive epistemic judgment claiming that the right external epistemic answer to these questions is that there is no right answer. Such a particular positive epistemic judgment, however, assumes its own external epistemic superiority in relation to all other positive accounts. In this light the incommensurability claim of epistemic pluralism would need to be fully explained and epistemically defended against the plethora of other openly epistemic proposals. These do claim greater commensurability and do propose substantive reasons underpinning their positions. Under this reading of the axiom, Walker's theory would thus need to address all of those proposals and explain why they are not capable of measuring the conflicting claims and why those substantive considerations must give way to its own positive account.

Under this understanding of the axiom, the problem for epistemic pluralism would not only be that it currently leaves out the necessary defense of epistemic justification. It would also be that any such direct epistemic defense would automatically seem to undercut its central claim that this is a theory that does not privilege any epistemic position as being externally best against its other epistemic competitors.[104]

If this first positive rationale does not prove to be the right candidate, could there be something more sophisticated behind the axiom of external epistemic incommensurability? Some slightly different rationale behind its positive no-right-answer conclusion, other than "direct epistemic incommensurability" discussed earlier? Could such a further option provide the missing reasons that could eventually explain in what sense epistemic constitutional pluralism can perhaps rightfully assume the default superiority among the various positive claims?

3.2 The theory's Eigenvalue

Could it be that the axiom requires suspension of our epistemic judgment due to reasons of civility or comity, that is, some kind of special respect towards others? Under this second, positive variant of the no-right-answer rationale you do have a

[104] My understanding from our exchanges is that, in part due to these difficulties, Walker would try to avoid the "direct epistemic incommensurability" as the rationale underlying the theory's axiom (interview, see n 61).

view about which answers are externally right, correct, better, and which are wrong, worse, etc. However, since you find that others disagree deeply about the issue, as well as perhaps with your epistemic method, you assume that a judgment of epistemic incommensurability, the inter-systemic no-right-answer conclusion, is the right one to adopt when those who disagree are affected by your decision. So you do think that there are epistemically right or better answers in the sense of some external, common *episteme*. You also think you have one in the case at hand, but in one form or another you nonetheless *suspend* your personal judgment because of existing disagreement between yourself and others, who you know are also knowledgeable and rational.[105] This is about the "unwillingness on [your] part to impose [your] own conviction about the merits upon others who disagree, and who disagree in ways that [you] cannot help respecting, and with whom [you] are desirous of maintaining—or perhaps feel obligated to maintain—mutually respectful and regardful relations."[106] So, while under the first rationale the no-right-answer conclusion is concerned only with your direct perception of epistemic obscurity regarding the issues in question, under the second rationale it is dictated by reasons of civility or comity towards others who disagree.[107]

A particular variant of such a "suspending of judgment" rationale indeed seems to be the best candidate for Walker's endorsement as the underlying ethical or moral source and so the meaning of his axiom of epistemic incommensurability.[108] On this reading, there is the deep moral or ethical Eigenvalue of reciprocal civility—reciprocal equal respect understood in a particular way—that inherently underpins the axiom and so the theory itself.[109] It is this value that dictates the whole external minimal arrangement (operationalization) as proposed by epistemic pluralism. At the same time, this means that such an external arrangement can also point to the precise variation of the value. So, for instance, it is this one and the same Eigenvalue that determines both the different types of particular concessions—that is, those that are merely procedural at the second-order level,

[105] Just like the first no-right-answer claim ("direct epistemic incommensurability"), so this type of no-right-answer conclusion (resting on the idea of suspending one's epistemic judgment) is also a positive claim. The term "suspending of judgment" is thus not to be understood as an escape from judgment; it is unlike the uncertainty position. For in deferring, in one form or another, to a judgment of others is, of course, still to act on one's own judgment. In other words, "[i]n answering the question of the proper reaction to disagreements, we are, inescapably providing an answer from the perspective of one point of view, one which we hold because we believe it to represent things as they are" (J. Raz, "Disagreement in Politics" (1998) 43 The American Journal of Jurisprudence 25, 27).

[106] Michelman (n 29) at 4. Cf Rawls on the "duty of civility" in Rawls (n 71) at 217–18, 242.

[107] Cf Michelman (n 29) at 3–4, where Michelman draws the distinction between the two possible general rationales behind propositions of incommensurability.

[108] I am indebted to Neil Walker for a reconfirming exchange on this point (n 61).

[109] "Eigenvalue": the deepest and often implicit value inherent at the very roots of a theory, one that wholly imbues it and makes it self-legitimating. Walker already used the term briefly in a related context in his, "From *Großraum* to Condominium: A Comment" in C. Joerges and N. Ghaleigh (eds), *Darker Legacies of Law in Europe: The Shadow of National Socialism and Fascism over Europe and Its Legal Traditions* (Oxford: Hart Publishing, 2003) 200. The term as defined here surely differs somewhat from its conventional meaning in mathematics (eg "a latent root of the characteristic equation of a matrix"), although the analogy seems instructive.

and those that are procedural plus openly substantive at the first-order level.[110] The concessions meanwhile, being exactly the particular ways in which the suspension of judgments operates in this theory, also clearly point back to the precise scope and strength of the particular Eigenvalue inherent in epistemic pluralism. The same is true with the described particular operationalizations of the theory as to fully internal (inter-personal) and cross-systemic (inter-systemic) contexts of constitutional disagreement.[111] These operationalizations are just different articulations of the same Eigenvalue, which at the same time indicate its exact particular variation as endorsed by the theory.[112] What we can also know from the theory about its variant of the Eigenvalue of reciprocal equal respect is that, beyond these supposedly minimal external arrangements proposed, the substance of the theory's equal respect is deliberately not defined objectively and so independently of whatever ongoing deliberation there is about that equal respect. Within this sphere of the *what*, the theory attempts to keep the substance of its equal respect fluid and unfixed, precisely for reasons of equal respect. It therefore endorses a variant of equal respect that does not pretend that we will ever finally agree on what the substance of that equal respect is and so, instead, attempts to preserve the highest degree of autonomy in this matter for the actors involved.[113]

This Eigenvalue is thus the value that lies at the deepest roots of the constitutional theory of epistemic pluralism. It is the only value entrenched at the externally valid meta-constitutional level. The theory thus makes it the single externally valid priority among all the constitutionally relevant values of the ethical universe. The priority is meant in the sense that compliance with the demands of this meta-constitutional Eigenvalue is understood as the precondition to anyone's pursuit of other constitutional values. You first need to satisfy all the needs of the Eigenvalue (ie its operationalized requirements) before you may move on to satisfy the needs of any other value. Such prioritization of this one value flows from Walker's understanding of the proper meaning and purpose of constitutionalism—that is, his understanding of the *why* we (should) get into (constitutional) politics in the first place. That, according to him, is about resolving our differences without unduly privileging one or more subjects of the disagreement over others,[114] and that goal is assured by instilling that particular understanding of fundamental reciprocal equal respect and therefore the highest corresponding autonomy of the subjects.

[110] Walker believes that the ethical impulse behind both different types of concessions is actually one and the same, and is the Eigenvalue of reciprocal equal respect (interview, see n 61).

[111] Pp. 48–50.

[112] In our exchanges Walker repeatedly, and correctly I think, made the point that civility between persons and civility between systems are in some last analysis not such radically different things, and so what we have here is again the same Eigenvalue with slightly different articulations (operationalizations) in these two respective contexts (interview, see n 61).

[113] I am grateful to Neil Walker for his exchange of thoughts and feedback on this issue (interview, see n 61). Cf pp. 47–50 and 51–3.

[114] Again, I am indebted to Neil Walker for his exchange and insight on this point (interview, see n 61).

Here we shall emphasize even further that it is a particular *kind* of the Eigenvalue of equal respect that Walker has in mind under the term "reciprocal equal respect." I will sometimes refer to it as the "ascetic version of mere reciprocity." This is meant to express two related characteristics. Firstly, the fact already discussed that reciprocity is the only externally valid value (ie the Eigenvalue) recognized as such by this theory. Thus, it is the only value entrenched at the externally valid meta-constitutional level. Secondly, that it is the particularly thin version of mere reciprocity that epistemic pluralism has in mind. Recall that it is the version of mere reciprocity that attempts to abstain in some radical way from making external arbitration into the substantive domain of the *what* itself. Those controversial determinations of substance, we saw, are to be left to the subjects themselves. So, the theory does not understand the single externally valid value of reciprocity in some thick sense, which would define its meaning in connection to various other substances and their values. Rather it takes a thin version of the abstract requirement of reciprocity that is independent of the element of potential truth involved in those other values. It is, indeed, an exceptionally ascetic version of mere reciprocity.[115] Only by distinguishing this particular sense behind the too general label of "reciprocal equal respect" can we capture accurately the meaning of the theory and its value underpinning. It is only on the basis of this specific ascetic version of mere reciprocity, respect for the other's views regardless of the potential element of truth involved in those views,[116] that we have those minimal procedural concessions on the second-order level, and the mere abstract and open-ended exhortation to further reciprocal substantive concessions at the first-order level of constitutional discourse. Likewise, it is "only" this specific sense of equal respect that the parties to disagreement must satisfy prior to moving on to argue for their own internally valid values and solutions.

3.3 Undercut and reoriented

The salient issue is therefore whether this further option could perhaps provide the missing reasons that could explain why epistemic constitutional pluralism can assume the default superiority among the various positive proposals, as it does at the moment.[117] I mean superiority in the sense of clearly being the least intrusive theory of constitutionalism that can redeem constitutional discourse from the challenges of disagreement, or at least redeem it to some greater degree than its competing proposals.[118] This is precisely because of its clearly less demeaning, or

[115] The term "mere reciprocity" was used before. See, eg F. Michelman, "Modus Vivendi Postmodernus? On *Just Interpretations* and the Thinning of Justice" (2000) 21 Cardozo Law Review 1954, 1966, where Michelman discusses Rosenfeld's argument against "a conception of justice as 'mere' reciprocity," such as that of John Rawls. Rosenfeld's meaning of the term is, however, slightly different from the one I am ascribing it here, and so an equation of the "ascetic mere reciprocity" with Rosenfeld's "mere reciprocity" should be avoided.

[116] That is, regardless of whether *I think* some controversial accompanying substantive values as true, and regardless of how deeply convinced *I am* that they are true.

[117] P. 54. [118] Pp. 31–2.

non-demeaning, treatment of the competing second and first-order constitutional claims, visions, and aspirations. In this concluding section of this chapter, I attempt to explain why I think that the third candidate rationale cannot justify the theory's assumption of such a default superiority either. The latter, I will maintain, is logically untenable even with such a foundation to the axiom.

We saw how the rationale of uncertainty was unable for its own reasons to sustain the theory's position of default superiority. But it seems that the default superiority could still be justified if it was beyond logical or ethical controversy that under this kind of a foundation the theory is either (1) externally non-imposing, or (2) in some way at least clearly less imposing than are other competing theories. Indeed, via either of these two routes, if they really worked, the theory's alleged redeeming, or highest degree of redeeming, of constitutionalism from disagreement would still be possible.

So is it the case, firstly, that epistemic pluralism is externally non-imposing? It was explained above that the theory's supposedly minimal arrangement at the second and first-order level was to be understood as the externally valid dimension of the theory in addition to its uncontroversial minimal standards. Indeed, it was clarified how those claims and visions that contradict the arrangement are considered objectively mistaken by the theory. We can recall Walker's example of the "system in denial," for instance. They are taken as either misreading the external reality of explanatory pluralism or mistakenly disregarding the external normative superiority of normative pluralism, or both.[119] So, let us leave no doubt: in its incommensurability axiom, that is the theory's operationalized arrangements at both levels of the discourse, the theory is itself understood as being externally valid. Further determination of the axiom through prioritization of the particular Eigenvalue, to which it actually amounts, only reaffirms the theory's claim to objective normative superiority. This also clarifies that epistemic pluralism's alleged minimal arrangement at both levels, and the Eigenvalue behind it, are not to be understood as externally fluid. This minimum of the theory is kept externally fixed.[120]

If this is so, then there is only one way to keep epistemic pluralism from being externally *non*-imposing, which is what would justify its default superiority and redeem constitutionalism from disagreement. Namely, the theory's external imposition (ie its Eigenvalue) needs to be somehow above the fray. It must lie beyond serious controversy as the obvious response to the problem of constitutional disagreement and the question of the best external constitutional conception. This is, however, clearly not the case. There is, of course, a whole plethora of not unreasonable competing proposals and visions; a tremendous fundamental disagreement about this issue. The external propositions of epistemic pluralism fall into this ring of full-blown rivalry at both levels of the discourse, as another highly contentious proposal among many. The competing theories disagree with the

[119] Pp. 38–9.

[120] Indeed, Walker at some point himself speaks of "the irreducible core," "the non-negotiable given" of any sovereign constitutional order (see n 96).

epistemic pluralist solution and its Eigenvalue.[121] So even though it is itself controversial, and in spite of its own ambition of not privileging and imposing one controversial view among many within the deep postmodern disagreement, epistemic pluralism in the last instance actually does the latter. It privileges and imposes its own controversial external arrangement, and the Eigenvalue behind it, with which the competing and not unreasonable theories, and their own underlying values, continue to disagree fiercely. Epistemic pluralism thus necessarily undercuts the possible claim to being a *non*-imposing theory that in some comprehensive way redeems the ideas of constitutionalism and constitutionality from their challenges.

Secondly, this explanation should not mean, of course, that the theory could not perhaps be understood as externally clearly *less* imposing than its competing alternatives. Its default superiority would be justified even if this route were the only one to work out. In this way, epistemic pluralism could still redeem constitutionalism to a higher degree than any other competing theory or vision of constitutionalism. So, indeed, a defendant of epistemic pluralism could try to say the following: "surely the theory privileges itself by default, and surely it is externally imposing as just described, I recognize that." But the defender might then try to go on to explain that this imposition is exactly what we should want from the theory. For, as the argument would go, this is a special, different kind of external imposition. It is obviously the *most minimal* external imposition, and so clearly the least privileging one in the sense that it shows greater respect, by being more fluid and less demeaning, towards all the conceptions than the latter show among themselves and to it. In other words, the theory's imposition of its external arrangement is made only on the level of the minimal thin framework (within the sphere of *how*) of constitutional discourse, and so leaves vast space *within* this framework (the sphere of *what*) externally non-arbitrated and fluid, in the hands of the ongoing discourse between all these different and not externally exclusive competing conceptions themselves. With this, the defender could conclude, the theory clearly institutes a greater degree of external non-imposition and fluidity, and so a higher degree of decent respect for the differing views of all than do the competing and thicker external impositions, some of which go as far as to engage in privileging within the sphere of the *what*.

The key to this kind of understanding is the assumption that the ascetic mere reciprocity (the thin *how*-type of framework arrangement that flows from it at both levels of discourse) is *clearly*, as a matter of logic or at least not seriously dubitable ethical proposition, the highest degree of reciprocal equal respect. Because this is clearly the least demeaning collective arrangement in relation to all the disagreeing but legitimate conceptions, claims, and aspirations, their holders all have better

[121] Not only authors like moral realists, Dworkinians, Razians, all the radical relativists, and others, but even the great majority of those from within Walker's own broader "family" of political or otherwise allegedly non-epistemic communicative rationality, like Rawls and Habermas, would disagree with the particular Eigenvalue as the proper response to disagreement. In the name of their own deep underlying values they would all prefer their own respective arrangements as the allegedly better answers to the same problem. As would those whose first-order claims and aspirations endorse, either consciously or unconsciously, those kinds of second-order understandings.

reason to adopt *it* as opposed to some other, more externally imposing common alternative. This is then the still workable minimum that stands the best chance of winning our collective agreement, while at least partly redeeming the ideas of constitutionalism and constitutionality from the challenges of disagreement. It seems, thus, that the default superiority succeeds.

Yet this attempt would also be logically untenable. At first glance it might indeed appear that epistemic pluralism's proposal for the Eigenvalue of mere reciprocity *self-evidently* institutes an externally less-imposing arrangement than do the other competing alternatives dealing with the same question over the best conception of constitutionalism, or constitutional pluralism. However, the appearance is deceptive. This is so simply because that assumption of the specific ascetic mere reciprocity *as the highest degree of reciprocal equal respect* is one of the very points fundamentally in controversy *as well*. For example, a great number of not unreasonable competing conceptions either explicitly argue or at least imply within their basic premises that only through some greater degree of external epistemic declaration of one's own identity can one start building a true, non-hypocritical reciprocal respect toward others who disagree. They understand that only by taking this route and claiming one's own external identity to a greater degree as required by some particular contexts, does one realize that one *is* and that the "other" is *different*. That is, that the "*I*" and "*the other*" really exist, and exist as autonomous entities. Only through this relatively "thicker" approach, they say, is it really possible to generate the authentic acceptance of the "other", and hence the only true and highest attainable reciprocal respect and autonomy for the "other" and myself.

This points to an understanding of the concept of reciprocal equal respect and its corollary of autonomy that are more substantively determined than in ascetic mere reciprocity. The latter, as we saw, deliberately attempts to stay away from any substantive garb from within the sphere of the *what*. These opposing understandings, by contrast, seem to require taking at least slightly more into account in their conceiving of the concept of reciprocal equal respect. They take more seriously into consideration the factor of truth or weight of the values involved in some specific context in which the questions of true and highest reciprocal respect and autonomy are being posed. In this view, the proper understanding and meaning of reciprocal equal respect cannot be formed in isolation and without some contribution from some of those more concrete and externally valid substantive values from within the sphere of the *what*.

We will see how Joseph Weiler, for example, understands his principle of constitutional tolerance[122] as embodying a much thicker substantive understanding of what counts as the only true and highest reciprocal equal respect. His theory declares as externally valid its own particular reconciliation of some substantive values in the rationales behind foundational recognition rules of the member states and Europe respectively. It rejects others, however, many of which Walker's thin conception would clearly not exclude, as unacceptable. Thus, for instance,

[122] Which can be seen as his own Eigenvalue, although one which is quite different from the one found in epistemic pluralism (see pp. 74–89).

nationhood understood solely in terms of the values of existential shield and originality can be part of the legitimate meta-blocks of the pluralist constitutionalism in Europe. Or, essential humanity understood in the very particular sense of human humility can also qualify as such. Other understandings of nationhood or essential humanity, which are abundant, are understood as unsound dimensions or blocks that should not co-constitute the new Europe's concept of constitutionalism. So the actors should not be free to self-define their respective constitutional identities around them.[123] It is crucial that such a reconciliation is not to be seen merely as an external choice for some but not other substantive ends from the sphere of *what.* While being the necessary substantive co-determinant, it is at the same time also understood as *the product* of the only right strategy for dealing with the "other," that of the highest possible degree of equal respect and autonomy.[124] This is because, for Weiler, this conception of highest reciprocal equality and its related true autonomy should not be understood as defined without external recognition of those relatively thick substantive ends that his theory proposes in its own external reconciliation. The opposite approach, leading to understanding equal respect only in terms of mere reciprocity, would seem in his view to unduly favor one identity over another, and hence precisely to hinder the true and highest mutual equal respect.[125]

All other pluralist proposals analysed in subsequent chapters will implicitly assume more substantive understandings of reciprocal equal respect, to varying degrees, than found in epistemic pluralism and its ascetic mere reciprocity. Moreover, there are also numerous authors from the general field of legal theory who explicitly reject such a thin mere reciprocity to be the highest realization of equal respect and autonomy.

Some variant of more substantive understanding of reciprocity is clearly behind Raz's complaint about how those who reply to the question of significance of disagreement with the suspending of judgment thesis (ie this or that version of mere reciprocity), give greater weight to the views of others than they give to their own. Raz writes:

If your reply to the question of the significance of disagreement is that we should refrain from this action or that because it is controversial, i.e. because others believe it to be wrong, or unfair, or unwise, then we refrain from that action not because the views of those others

[123] Pp. 74–7.

[124] The right strategy of dealing with the alien, Weiler writes, "is to acknowledge the validity [in the external sense, as his conception makes very clear] of certain forms of non-ethic bounded identity but simultaneously to reach across boundaries. [This way] the identity of the alien, as such, is maintained [i.e. externally recognized]. One is not invited to go out and, say, 'save him' by inviting him to be one of us . . . On the other hand, despite the boundaries which are maintained [i.e. recognized as such externally, valid for both of us], and constitute the I and the Alien, one is commanded to reach over the boundary and accept him, in his alienship, as oneself. The alien is accorded human dignity. The soul of the I is tended to not by eliminating the temptation to oppress but by learning humility and overcoming it." J. Weiler, "In Defence of the Status Quo: Europe's *Sonderweg*" in J. Weiler and M. Wind (eds), *European Constitutionalism Beyond the State* (Cambridge: Cambridge University Press, 2003) 19. For further explication, see pp. 96–101 in connection with pp. 78–89.

[125] For more on this, see pp. 96–101, and pp. 74–89.

are true, but simply because they are held by them, because they are their views, be they true or false. To the extent that that is our answer we give other people's views a weight which we do not give to our own . . . There is an asymmetry here between the role that my beliefs and those of others play in my reasoning. Giving weight to the views of others is not treating them the same way I treat myself. It is giving them, i.e. their views, greater weight than the weight I give myself. That is why deferring to others is not the obvious thing to do . . . True, in deferring to others I am also implying that others should defer to me. If I think that I should refrain from acting on my views simply because others disagree, I am committed to thinking that others should refrain from following the truth simply because I, among others, disagree. In this respect, I am not favoring others over myself. But that does not make deferring . . . any more plausible. It merely suggests a new way of stating the difficulty: If I do not think that the fact that I hold a view is a reason for me to follow it, why should I think that it is a reason for others? The answer to the question of the right response to the existence of widespread disagreement over principles is far from obvious.[126]

The element causing the "asymmetry" of which Raz speaks is the fact that such mere reciprocity, which he criticizes as not the highest equal respect by default, refuses to take into account any factor of relative truth of the views (weights of the values) involved. It a priori refuses to understand itself as a more substantivized, and arguably more meaningful, true reciprocity that should be defined in part also by building into itself—to some degree and in some way[127]—the relative weights of those factors. What seems to be behind Raz's reasoning is a different understanding of the highest reciprocal equal respect than the one we find assumed in epistemic pluralism's mere reciprocity.[128]

To give another example, John Finnis's claim that our practical reasoning is able to grasp certain human goods as the intelligible aspects of integral human flourishing for all, in its own way rejects justice as mere reciprocity. For him, true equal respect and autonomy are only conceivable by not leaving out of their meaning those intelligible basic goods themselves. Rejecting the view that this would mean "submit[ting] oneself to heteronomy (i.e. extrinsic constraints on one's autonomy,

[126] Raz (n 105) at 28–9. Even if what Raz might have in mind here is a Waldron-type of suspending thesis (deferring only to majority's view), the same applies also to Walker's variation of the thesis. The potential differences do not make Raz's analysis inapplicable also in Walker's case.

[127] That is something Raz does not go further to elaborate at that same point, but something that can, of course, be traced from other parts of his more openly substantive external theory of justice than is that of epistemic pluralism. See, eg his, *The Morality of Freedom* (Oxford: Clarendon Press, 1986).

[128] That Raz has in mind a more substantive understanding of reciprocal equal respect than just mere reciprocity can, I think, also be observed from his further response to Waldron's variant of the suspending thesis. As other variants of this thesis, the latter argues that—since we are not in possession of any uncontroversial moral epistemology—we should always suspend our judgment (in Waldron's case the suspension is in relation to the majority's view): "The . . . claim is true, but irrelevant. That sound moral epistemology is controversial does not mean that we cannot know what it requires. From the fact, if it is one, that its central precepts are controversial, it only follows that avoiding controversy is not a goal to be pursued. At least that follows unless there is an alternative and at least sufficiently attractive goal which is not subject to the same problem. Waldron's right of participation is not such an alternative. It is equally controversial. Having declared that right instrumentalism does not take seriously the problem of disagreement, Waldron seems oblivious to the fact that if valid the same charge can be levelled against his solution, as (quite likely) against all others" (Raz (n 105) at 47).

one's self-determination)," he argues that the intelligible external truth (value) of these substances makes them precisely the very "intrinsic point of one's autonomy." It is obvious that such a view must reject, as Finnis does explicitly, any understanding of equal respect and autonomy that conceives of these notions "only 'thinly' and with unjustified restrictions of content and scope."[129]

Thus, it cannot be simply assumed *by default* that the radically abstaining strategy of epistemic pluralism establishes the highest degree of reciprocal equal respect and non-imposition. There is deep fundamental disagreement among the reasonable about whether this or some other approach would actually be less imposing. Moreover, there is no a priori guarantee that the theory's axiom of privileging *by default* its own required abstention from external arbitration into the sphere of the *what* constitutes a lesser imposition than those more substantive external proposals, if they are privileged. While the minimum *how* strategy is indeed a different imposition into the domain of the *what*, one that requires the omission-like type of imposition within that sphere, the *different* imposition does not necessarily imply *lesser* imposition. In principle, an omission can be just as imposing as a commission and, depending on circumstances, even more so. The default superiority stance of epistemic pluralism equates these different notions (different versus lesser imposition) too quickly.[130]

The difficulty is reinforced when considered in the light of the very goal of epistemic pluralism—that of alleviating imposition and privileging from the domains of deep postmodern disagreement. When it actually cannot be shown by default why epistemic pluralism is less imposing and demeaning than its alternatives, but it nonetheless inevitably imposes its own particular value and effects into the sphere of the *what*, the theory undercuts itself. For, it is the very point of its own axiom that requires suspending of such an external privileging within the domain of the *what* in circumstances of widespread fundamental disagreement. Problems are exacerbated when one realizes that the thinner, that is, the more "minimal," such a theory aspires to be, the more controversial, and so the more imposing, it actually becomes, as judged by its own standards. From this view, epistemic pluralism threatens to eat itself, as it were, and cannot succeed in its aim of proposing a conception of constitutionalism that would be less imposing than other competing visions and proposals. The superiority of the strategy of building a minimum *how*-type of framework in order to accommodate as much disagreement as possible,[131] cannot be defended *by default*. Hence, by this

[129] J. Finnis, *The Fundamentals of Ethics* (Oxford: Clarendon Press, 1983) 124.

[130] This is why epistemic pluralism cannot succeed, in my view, in its attempt to build a minimal framework theory that would in some distinctively greater degree than other theories avoid external arbitration between a vast range of different proposals and aspiration in the field of second and first-order constitutional content. This is what I mean above (n 82) when I say that it is an attempt (not already an accomplished goal) of epistemic pluralism to build a minimal framework theory that would in some radical sense avoid external arbitration between a vast range of different proposals.

[131] Recall Walker's criticism of Rawls's framework as still not being encompassing enough (ie not sufficiently "minimal") to accommodate widespread disagreement by attracting collective agreement only about some less bold a minimum, which we need in order to redeem constitutionalism as a collective venture (see n 74).

conception, constitutionalism also cannot be redeemed from disagreement to some a priori greater degree than by some other more substantive conception.

Moreover, even if epistemic pluralism really were the conception prescribing the highest degree of respect and of fluidity between the existing second and first-order claims and proposals, this would not necessarily constitute the best pluralist approach. The question is why would such a highest fluidity—and not perhaps some other variant of it that would allow for accommodation of also some other values potentially relevant to pluralism—be the best pluralist approach?[132]

Epistemic constitutional pluralism cannot axiomatically posit that it is the least imposing or demeaning of the proposals, and that, hence, it is the best pluralist conception. Indeed, the theory's current proposal on these two points is equally controversial as are those implicit in other conceptions. This would normally not be a problem, but it is in the case of epistemic pluralism. By picking itself and merely axiomatically pointing to the particular and no less-contested value behind its own axiom, epistemic pluralism thereby contradicts itself. From among issues or theories that are equally controversial within the bounds of some not a priori unreasonable disagreement, one cannot choose one which is less imposing by default.

The project cannot be to try and establish default superiority of epistemic pluralism by positing this kind of axiom, either under its uncertainty, direct epistemic incommensurability, or Eigenvalue rationale, and to build upwards only from that unquestioned baseline some supposedly least or even non-imposing an arrangement for constitutional discourse. From its inception, such a project implants the seeds of its own destruction, so that in the final analysis it then always necessarily undercuts itself. In order to save itself as a coherent theory, epistemic pluralism would need to be reoriented from the project that seeks the *least imposing* arrangement whose superiority holds by default, to a project about the most *justifiably imposing* arrangement. Yet the latter has a different orientation. Having no real ambition to redeem constitutionalism from external disagreement, a project it treats as an impossible goal, it is rather primarily focused on a deeper exploration of the wider competing ethical and moral views on the very issue that divides. It thereby primarily and openly engages itself in an open inter-theoretical exchange with such alternative ethical and moral positions. This is the process that then also further shapes one's own conclusions as well as the minds of all who are involved in such a deeper and more inclusive exploration.

If so reoriented, however, it becomes clear that the theory of epistemic pluralism, as it currently stands, is not such a project. Seen from that perspective it is undefended. Relying on its default strategy (the supposedly uncontroversial assumption of being less controversial), the theory closes itself and is currently in fact oriented in the opposite direction. It does not engage in the inter-theoretical discourse over why exactly *it* might be superior despite the existence of all those different views on the key dividing issue.[133] In order to undertake the needed

132 See the inter-theoretical assessment in Chapter 8, pp. 235–60 and Chapter 9, sections 1 and 2.

133 Every pluralist author analysed in this work has a vision different from epistemic pluralism, and they are all—thought to varying respective degrees—substantively thicker conceptions.

reorientation of the project, epistemic pluralism must first make a step backwards, and get rid of the chains of its default assumption. Only that way would it be able to confront the opposing underlying values of the competing pluralist proposals freely and on openly ethical and moral grounds. This is, as we will see, needed for making any further progress on the topic. Such an inter-theoretical assessment will be explored in Chapter 8.

3

Substantive Pluralism

1. Explaining the Theory

1.1 The basics

Like MacCormick and Walker, Joseph Weiler is searching for the best conception of constitutionalism for Europe. Analysis will show that it is possible to discern from his writings that he, too, inevitably embraces some abstract idea of heterarchy as opposed to a hierarchy of constitutional sources at the foundational level. Whether he wants this or not, he in practice also therefore argues for a kind of constitutional pluralism to be the right answer to his quest. While Weiler may share with MacCormick and Walker some common notion of heterarchy at the foundational level, he certainly does not spend time directly explaining what precise features his own variant of heterarchy assumes at that deepest level of the discourse. That remains obscure at first, although it can be later at least partially discerned by inferring back from his more elaborate understanding of heterarchy: one that appears at other levels of the pluralist discourse, where Weiler makes his principal contribution.

Like Walker's, Weiler's contribution thus engages with those other discourses and has an emphatic focus on one of them. However, the following examination will show how Weiler's concrete understanding of heterarchy (constitutional pluralism) differs starkly from what was Walker's assumed understanding of this notion according to his epistemic pluralism. We will see that Weiler's focus, unlike Walker's, is not concentrated on the attempt to build a procedural framework that would, in the fullest way possible, avoid external arbitration between a myriad of candidates for a substantive constitutional identity in Europe in order that such a determination be wholly left to the constitutional actors themselves. By way of contrast, to a significant degree Weiler's further understanding of heterarchy, of pluralism, *itself* directly enters the discussion concerning the best substantive constitutional identity. It argues for its own external proposal within that discourse. Within the scheme of the mapping analysis, this is accorded the label of "substantive constitutional pluralism." The latter also claims to be a novel and unique approach to understanding the concept of constitutionalism.

It can be discerned from Weiler's scholarship how, from one angle, he sees the old Europe as providing an environment for building and intensifying deep identity boundaries within the Old Continent—national, ethnic, religious, and ideological.

Its history up until the end of the Second World War, as well as the first decades of European integration, was one in which strong sovereign states prevailed in Europe. Through their constitutions these states defended their "full sovereignty, autonomy, independence."[1] They adopted the logic of "relentless defense and maximization" of their own interest as understood through the lens of each particular sovereign and its idiosyncrasies.[2] Whatever occurred at the transnational level was at best understood in terms of classical international, not constitutional, law. This fully recognized the sovereignty and autonomy of the sovereign states and their constitutions, and provided a "neutral arena" for these independent constitutional actors to "prosecute their own . . . goals premised on power and self-interest."[3] This strategy pursued and intensified boundaries as they were seen from monocular perspectives of the idiosyncratic interests of the sovereign actors involved, that is, the states that were each, depending on the period, a personification of either their own national *demos* or a sovereign of another kind. At least in the case of the modern nation-state this seemed legitimate and proper, given the deeper and underlying noble idea, that of the ultimate sovereignty of the will of each *demos* as a full political unity with corresponding exclusive and ultimate authority to govern by and for itself. This monistic behavior thus rested, in normative terms, on the underlying monistic ground that assumed one single ultimate source of constitutional authority within a given sovereign-state territory. And, as Weiler implies, it was this statal constitutional monism that helped provide the favorable environment for fostering the high boundaries within the old Europe.[4]

From another angle, Weiler also observes an idea opposed to the nation-state constitutional monism, one that started to emerge after the Second World War with the rise of the new Europe and its integration. The choice for the European Community, he writes, not only had economic purposes, but also rested on a deeper, nobler goal. After witnessing one of the most horrific boundary abuses by the old Europe that manifested in the Second World War, founders of the Community saw the latter as "an antidote to the negative features" of this type of monistic "statal intercourse."[5] They understood it as the beginning of a process that would secure peace through integration.[6] A more straightforward version of the vision was to move gradually from the economic integration to an eventual "full political union."[7] This, then, would be a version of a "federal United States of

[1] J. Weiler, *The Constitution of Europe: "Do the New Clothes Have an Emperor?" and Other Essays on European Integration* (Cambridge: Cambridge University Press, 1999) 91 (quotation marks omitted).

[2] Weiler (n 1) at 91.

[3] Weiler (n 1) at 92.

[4] Weiler (n 1) at 92, in connection with J. Weiler, "In Defence of the Status Quo: Europe's Constitutional *Sonderweg*" in J. Weiler and M. Wind (eds), *European Constitutionalism beyond the State* (Cambridge: Cambridge University Press, 2003) 20.

[5] Weiler (n 1) at 91. For a more detailed account of this point, see, eg J. Weiler, *Christian Europe*, 89–93. All citations from this work are from the Slovenian version of the book, J. Weiler, *Krščanska Evropa: Raziskovalna Razprava*, tr. M. Požbolt (Claritas: Ljubljana 2005), henceforth *Christian Europe*.

[6] Weiler (n 1) at 91; Weiler (n 5) at 89–93.

[7] Weiler (n 1) at 91.

Europe," which would in the name of some *essential humanity*—the idea of a *transnational human* intercourse on a *European* scale—lead to the "final demise" of the sovereign states' relentless maintenance of identity boundaries.[8] The opposing strategy to sovereign-state monistic behavior is elimination of the relevance of idiosyncrasies, of replacing them with the idea of essential humanity cleansed of the identity boundaries that separate us and make us strangers. It is the strategy of Europeans becoming a political unity under the common superstate of Europe; something like the project of a liberal "neutral" state of the US.[9] Translated into constitutional terms, this means that the sovereign-state constitutional monism is replaced by a version of a European constitutional monism. A given state's sovereign, as the single and ultimate source of constitutional authority within the sovereign-state territory (eg each nation-state's *demos*), gives way to the all-European source (eg European *demos*) that now becomes the ultimate single source of constitutional authority across the territory of Europe. It is this monist normative ground that deep down underlies the newly envisioned constitutional monist behavior and intercourse, which is now the *all-European* monist behavior and intercourse. In it the identity boundaries tend to lose their previous relevance and the states' constitutions of now-federal units are subordinated to the superior European constitution of the sovereign union.[10]

Weiler is not happy with either of the monist alternatives. At the same time, however, he believes there are noble dimensions in both of them. For instance, the maintaining of certain identity boundaries by statal monism does not seem wholly mistaken to Weiler, as we shall see. Nevertheless, he shares with proponents of the European monist thought the horror of the particular way in which the strategy of statal constitutional monism erected and pursued certain boundaries throughout Europe's infamous past.[11] Furthermore, he does not see the strategy of the European monist project as being wholly mistaken. The general idea of removing the boundaries in the spirit of "come, be one of us" in the name of some essential humanity, "is noble," Weiler writes, "since it involves . . . elimination of prejudice, of the notion that there are boundaries between humans that cannot be eradicated."[12] But despite its good intentions, he crucially cautions, the "be one of us" strategy "is often an invitation to the alien to be one of us, by being one of us."[13]

[8] Weiler (n 1) at 91. See also J Weiler, "Does Europe Need a Constitution? Demos, Telos and the German Maastricht Decision" (1995) 1 ELJ 219, 248.

[9] Weiler (n 1) at 339, 341.

[10] Weiler is careful to note that this vision—by proposing "a federal structure of sorts"—still assumes a degree of internal pluralism "in which local interests and diversity would be maintained." "Thus, although Delors speaks in his October 17, 1990, speech of Europe as a federation, he is—in good faith—always careful to maintain respect for 'pluralism'" (see Weiler (n 1) at 92, fn 207). Weiler is referring here to "Jacques Delors at the College of Europe in Bruges," reprinted in *Europe*, Doc No 1,576 (21 October 1989) 1, 5.

[11] J. Weiler, "Europe: The Case against the Case of Statehood" (1998) 4 ELJ 43, 60; Weiler (n 4) at 18–19.

[12] Weiler (n 11) at 61; Weiler (n 4) at 19.

[13] Weiler (n 11) at 61; Weiler (n 4) at 19.

Weiler thus believes that the specific European monist strategy risks robbing the existing "other" of his identity.[14] It still manifests, he explains, arrogance of the "I" and belief in his superiority, hence, intolerance: "If I cannot tolerate the alien, one way of resolving the dilemma is to make him like me, no longer an alien."[15] While this surely is incomparably better than exclusion and repression, which represented the worst instances of boundary abuses within the old nation-state monist Europe, it is still a form of dangerous intolerance, Weiler maintains.[16] His fear is indeed that European constitutional monism would lead to a kind of common European "melting pot" of the US style. This would sweep away even some of the most valuable boundaries, such as those particular elements from the strategy of statal monism that he regards as noble and believes would need to be retained in some refined form.[17] For Weiler, it is thus not only the sovereign state and its powerful monist constitutionalism that, if not tamed, poses the threat of boundary abuse. For him, this potential is equally dangerous under the even more powerful monist constitutionalism of a European superstate.[18]

It is in reaction to these shortcomings of the rival monist narratives that Weiler can be viewed as developing his distinctive version of constitutional pluralism. In order to avoid the deficiencies of constitutional monism presented above, he goes back to redefine the monist foundations and strategies that spring from them. His pluralist alternative implies that neither of the two different kinds of ultimate sources of constitutional authority should prevail and ultimately subsume the other, so as to become the dominant force, generating either the first or the second monistic strategy. Instead, they need to be understood as coequal and mutually taming sources of constitutional authority that are capable of guarding against either of the two monist types of boundary abuse. Weiler speaks of the "principle of constitutional tolerance" as his pluralist alternative to both of the monist strategies. Therefore, national identity boundaries must be retained but redefined in a particular way so as to retain their sound dimensions while rejecting unsound ones. Equally, the notion of essential humanity must be retained as a goal, but it too must be refined so as to embody the right understanding of essential humanity.

Or, according to Weiler's own abstract description of the principle:

> The alternative strategy is to acknowledge the validity of certain forms of bounded identity but simultaneously to reach across boundaries. We acknowledge and respect difference (and what is special and unique about ourselves as individuals and groups) and yet we reach across differences in recognition of our essential humanity of being all born in the image of God.

[14] Weiler (n 11) at 61; Weiler (n 4) at 19.

[15] Weiler (n 11) at 61; Weiler (n 4) at 19.

[16] Weiler (n 11) at 61; Weiler (n 4) at 19; cf also Weiler (n 1) at 341.

[17] See his, *The Constitution of Europe* (n 1) at 339 (with respect to the boundary of nationality) and, *Christian Europe* (n 5) at 50, 104–11 (with respect to the boundary of religion).

[18] Weiler (n 1) at 341, 250, 269; Weiler (n 8) at 248; Weiler (n 11) at 62.

> This, I think, is the essence of Mosaic law on this issue [which provides that] *the stranger that dwelleth with you shall be unto you as one born among you, and thou shalt love him as thyself; for ye were strangers in the land of Egypt. I am the Lord your God [that is, God of both of you].* Herman Cohen (1842–1918), the great neo-Kantian philosopher of religion, in an exquisite modern interpretation of the Mosaic law on this subject captures its deep meaning in a way which retains its vitality even in today's Ever Closer Union . . .: "[T]his law of shielding the alien from all wrong is of vital significance . . . The alien was to be protected, not because he was a member of one's family, clan, religious community or people; but because he was a human being. In the alien, therefore, man discovered the idea of humanity." What is significant in this are the two elements I have mentioned: on the one hand, the identity of the alien, as such, is maintained. One is not invited to go out and, say, "save him" by inviting him to be one of you. One is not invited to recast the boundary. On the other hand, despite the boundaries which are maintained, and constitute the I and the Alien, one is commanded to reach over the boundary and love him, in his alienship, as oneself. The alien is accorded human dignity. The soul of the I is tended to not by eliminating the temptation to oppress but by maintaining it and overcoming it.[19]

Through the principle of constitutional tolerance, which Weiler sees as "the most fundamental or foundational principle of the Union,"[20] the new Europe thus

> seeks to dictate a different type of intercourse among the actors belonging to it, a type of self-limitation in their self-perception, a redefined self-interest, and hence, redefined policy goals. To the interest of the state must be added the interest of the community. But crucially, it does not extinguish the separate actors who are fated to live in an uneasy tension with two competing senses of the polity's self, the autonomous self and the self as part of a larger community, and committed to an elusive search for an optimal balance of goals and behaviour between the community and its actors.[21]

While it brings them all closer in an "ever-closer union" it also maintains and in a particular way refines their boundaries so that the union is *always* to remain one among distinct actors: "among distinct peoples, distinct political identities, distinct political communities."[22]

One can observe the level of generality in Weiler's descriptions of his pluralist alternative, of his notion of constitutional tolerance. This is a view "from a distance," as it were—a picture of the basics of Weiler's pluralist theory that I wanted to convey in this first section. Before further explicating the more concrete meaning of the notion in the next section, we should note here how constitutional tolerance does inherently imply that there are two equally important types of source of constitutional authority in Europe. Neither of these is more fundamental,

[19] Weiler (n 11) at 61–2; cf Weiler (n 4) at 104–11 and 117–22; J. Weiler, "Federalism without Constitutionalism: Europe's *Sonderweg*" in K. Nicolaïdis and R. Howse (eds), *The Federal Vision: Legitimacy and Levels of Governance in the US and EU* (Oxford: Oxford University Press, 2002) at 65–70; J. Weiler, "Why Should Europe Be a Democracy: The Corruption of Political Culture and the Principle of Constitutional Tolerance" in F. Snyder (ed.), *The Europeanisation of Law: The Legal Effects of European Integration* (Oxford: Hart Publishing, 2000) at 217–18; Weiler (n 1) at 337–43.

[20] Weiler, "Why Should Europe Be a Democracy" (n 19) at 217; Weiler (n 4) at 18.

[21] Weiler (n 1) at 93.

[22] Weiler (n 4) at 20; see also Weiler (n 1) at 93, fn 212; Weiler, "Why Should Europe Be a Democracy" (n 19) at 217.

nor is one of them hierarchically superior and the other subordinate. Neither must dominate the other. This means that they must instead be somewhat heterarchically related.[23] This is important to note, since it is this most abstract idea that Weiler's notion of constitutional tolerance inescapably implicitly shares with MacCormick's and Walker's constitutional pluralism. This is the idea that goes back to the abstract sense of pluralism characterized in the Introduction.[24] This confirms Weiler's membership within the pluralist family. Yet the exact features of his heterarchy at this foundational level are not yet clear; it is not yet for instance directly explained whether the tolerance (the distinction of pluralism versus monism) here requires only procedural, or perhaps already some substantive, concessions at this foundational level. Nor is it clear from this most abstract account whether Weiler's notion of heterarchy could be further understood in some more concrete terms like those from, say, one of the more specific discourses on pluralism that we know from our Ariadne's Thread. In fact, many often explain that Weiler's "Constitutional Tolerance" is an abstract concept alone and that Weiler "does not elaborate [further] on the ideal."[25] I believe this is mistaken. A closer and more integrated reading of his various contributions clearly discerns the rich, concrete picture of this central concept. Let us then take that closer look and attempt to construct a more specific meaning of Weiler's *heterachy* as is implied in his principle of constitutional tolerance.

1.2 Explicating Weiler's heterarchy

Chapter 2 explored how Walker's epistemic pluralism applied to both contexts, the inter-systemic (between EU and member states, and between member states

[23] When discussing both of the monistic strands and their modern proponents (monistic European federalists on the one hand and those who continue to defend the ultimate sovereignty of the member states), Weiler criticizes them as "unitarian" and "monolithic" in that they attempt to find one overall framework or source that "would encompass and explain the entire phenomenon." It is a discourse, he writes, "which reflects the Schmittian idea that it is exercise of power in the exceptional case which is politically defining" (footnote omitted). At the same time Weiler also reveals his endorsement of the alternative, ie of the pluralist foundations and its notion of heterarchy as opposed to hierarchy of ultimate authority (sovereignty): "I do not wish to belittle these [monistic] preoccupations. I find, however, MacCormick's trilogy on sovereignty—exploring its fragmented, divided and difficult fit to the modern state—far more compelling as a framework for understanding the Union" (footnote omitted; but what he cites are three of MacCormick's articles that brought the notion of pluralism and its abstract foundations) (Weiler (n 1) at 271). See his explicit endorsement of this pluralist foundations also at Weiler (n 1) at 233–4 and 328. Cf the section titled "Neither Kelsen nor Schmitt: the principle of European constitutional tolerance—concept and praxis" in Weiler (n 4) at 15.

[24] See p. 5. Note that, at this high level of abstraction of heterarchy, it is not yet important whether the European source of authority, as the counter-source to the national *demos*, is represented by the one European *demos* or by the multiple *demoi* together constituting that source. Both of these forms, and many more, are compatible with the most abstract idea of heterarchy as distinct from hierarchy. In both of these forms the EU enjoys the direct legitimation link with its own ultimate source that is not one and the same with the ultimate source of the nation-state. Cf MacCormick (see Chapter 1, n 86, this book); but see J. Weiler "Prologue: Global and Plural Constitutionalism—Some Doubts" in G. de Búrca and J. Weiler (eds), *The Worlds of European Constitutionalism* (Cambridge: Cambridge University Press, 2012) 13–14.

[25] See, eg P. Eleftheriadis, "The Idea of a European Constitution" (2007) 27 Oxford Journal of Legal Studies 1, 18.

themselves) as well as the fully intra-systemic one (interpersonal constitutional disagreement within a system). Similarly, Weiler's principle of constitutional tolerance is meant to apply to the relationship between the states, between the states and the Union, as well as spilling over to the peoples themselves and influencing relations among individuals.[26]

We also saw that the abstract notion of pluralist heterarchy in Walker's epistemic pluralism actually meant two minimal procedural rules, when observed from a closer perspective. With respect to the second-order level of discourse, the actors merely needed to adopt the axiom that none of their conflicting claims could be understood as being right in the objective, inter-systemic (external) sense. At the first-order level this rule was combined with a rather open exhortation to negotiation and reciprocal (reflexive) adjustment of substantive solutions between the actors. The two minimal rules were the only objective—inter-systemically or externally valid—meta-constitutional content under epistemic pluralism. To impose anything more in the external sense was understood as contrary to pluralism and its notion of constitutional heterarchy. In those two minimal procedural rules, indeed, lies the specified meaning of epistemic pluralism's heterarchy that, according to Walker, represents the normatively superior version of constitutionalism for Europe.

When Weiler's heterarchy, as implied within his pluralism and its constitutional tolerance, is observed from a closer perspective, it reveals a significantly different meaning and orientation. Even though both of the notions of heterarchy may have common features at some most abstract level, it will be explained how Weiler's pluralism through its constitutional tolerance actually requires adoption, at the objective, inter-systemic level, of some meta-constitutional content which is decisively thicker than are the mere minimal procedural rules of epistemic pluralism. It is possible to pull together various strands of Weiler's scholarship and to discern from that this more substantive pluralist strategy. It is the strategy of retaining certain boundaries from the old monistic pole, while redefining them in a particular way so as to make them congruent with the opposite pole of essential humanity that must also be refined and adjusted. If I am right then Weiler's general description of his constitutional tolerance actually implies a much more concrete substantive meaning of pluralism than either of the two theories (MacCormick's and Walker's) examined thus far. It consists of what I will characterize as various substantive "building blocks" inherent in his vision of the superior version of constitutionalism for Europe.

Closer scrutiny of Weiler's scholarship reveals which identity boundaries are to be maintained and which can be discarded, which of their dimensions need to be refined and which do not, as well as showing how should those that need refinement be refined. He considers the cluster of dimensions thus selected as the meta-constitutional essence of a European constitution, as its substantive transcendental core. It is the core that is understood to be valid externally and to bind

[26] Weiler (n 1) at 93.

normatively not only constitutional interpreters but even the constitution-makers themselves.[27] It is also not open to amendment, if Europe is to have the best possible plural constitution in the normative sense.[28] What is more, these ethical values represent the meaning of his constitutional tolerance, since it is the underlying heterarchy of equally important sources which serves to "mutually tame," "refine," and thus produce these substances. The ethical values do not simply represent one out of many possible and equally legitimate interpretations of the tolerance principle that lies at the center of the constitutional essence, but they *are* this meta-essence (the principle of tolerance) itself. These are the "building blocks" I shall be talking about, and they at the same time reveal the more precise meaning of Weiler's heterarchy, his constitutional pluralism. Such an external, but balanced, reconciliation (mutual refinement) of the substantive ethical blocks from opposing sources, instead of a monist pursuit of some substantive vision determined solely by a single and ultimate source of constitutional authority, is what I will characterize as "substantive pluralism."

Weiler, unlike Walker, clearly does engage in this type of discourse, and openly announces that the goal of his discussion of these substantive blocks is to ground his proposal in ethics: it is about "a refusal on my [ie Weiler's] part" to discuss these issues in other terms, "even if I am mindful of the fashionability of moral relativism, and the manipulability of ethics."[29] And it is a particular type of ethics, too, that he has in mind, namely, most of these substantive building blocks representing his constitutional tolerance ought to be seen as ethical ends in themselves, not merely as means: for Weiler, European constitutionalism should above all be about these ends, instead of just means, as some believe.[30] When discussing this *telos*, the ultimate ethical and meta-constitutional purpose of the European Union as he sees it, Weiler thus explains:

> For many... democracy is the objective, the end, of the European construct. This is fallacious. Democracy is not the end. Democracy, too, is a means, even if an indispensable means. The end is to try, and try again, to live a life of decency, to honour our creation in the image of God, or the secular equivalent. A democracy, when all is said and done, is as good or bad as people who belong to it. A democracy of vile persons will be vile... In the realm of the social... the relationship to the alien is at the core of such decency. It is difficult to imagine something normatively more important to the human condition.[31]

[27] Weiler (n 5) at 36.

[28] Cf Menéndez's similar reading of Weiler on this point: "It is important to notice that Weiler considers that *such a core* is not open to be amended, *not even in the process of writing a European constitution*" (A. Menéndez, "A Pious Europe? Why Europe Should Not Define Itself as Christian" (2004) Arena Working Paper No 10/04, 7).

[29] Weiler (n 1) at 243.

[30] See, eg Weiler's critical remarks on Mancini's understanding of democracy as the ultimate goal of the Europe project in Weiler (n 11) at 60. See also Weiler (n 1) at ch 7, explicitly at 262 and Weiler (n 5) at 116. Cf in this respect also Miguel Maduro's version of constitutional pluralism, which is precisely about enhancing democracy and so different from Weiler's in this very assumption (see Chapter 4, pp. 108–9 and 112–4).

[31] Weiler (n 11) at 60. Cf Weiler (n 5) at 116–17.

We can now turn in more detail to the building blocks of this pluralist tolerance, of these balanced and mutually refined ethical ends that will reveal what that "life of decency" is that a European constitution should foster, according to Weiler. This will enable us to clarify the more precise meaning of his pluralist heterarchy.

1.3 The building blocks

1.3.1 From the boundary of nationhood and essential humanity

Nationality and ethnicity are among the identity boundaries most deeply intensified within Europe's monist past, and Weiler focuses principally on them. He notes how the intensity of the monist strategy resulted in horrific abuses, and argues that the old monist regime of fully sovereign nation-states in Europe generated *a high potential* for such abuse. Weiler explains how this occurs at three levels.[32] The first is the level of the abuse against another state and its nation, whereby physical or any other kind of aggression is but the most violent form of this kind of abuse.[33] The second is the abuse of the state against its nation; its most egregious form occurs when the state ceases to be instrumental in relation to individuals and society, but instead becomes an end in itself.[34] The third is the most internal context of the abuse. This occurs when a sense of collective identity within a given state, which by definition implies "an other" within that same state, induces a sense of self-superiority against "the other."[35] The manifestations of all these types of abuse within a monist regime, Weiler writes, "are a living part of the history of the European nation-state" and are "so well known as to obviate discussion."[36]

History was so much about the abuse of nationality and ethnicity that it goes without saying why Weiler welcomes emphatically the "central plank"[37] of the new European project. It implies the ambition to control the excesses of the nation-state constitutional monism when it comes to the particular boundary of nationhood and ethnicity. Even the strategy of the new European monism, which knows no boundaries of this kind but puts in their place the notion of essential humanity regardless of our distinct nationalities, thus appears noble to Weiler. It puts pressure on and eliminates the full sovereignty of the nation-states—that is, the nation-state monism—that contributed towards the setting of such deep national and ethnic boundaries, which actually lead to their abuse. The right constitution for the new Europe, he explains, should indeed prevent rather than foster such grave national and ethnic excesses. It should, moreover, also go further and not simply prevent such carnage—that is "the easy part," as Weiler writes—but deal at a deeper level with the source of these attitudes, so as to prevent also the less egregious, but still deeply wrongful treatment of "the other" and disable the source of the monist abuse itself.

32 Weiler (n 1) at 340.
33 Weiler (n 1) at 340.
34 Weiler (n 1) at 340.
35 Weiler (n 1) at 340.
36 Weiler (n 1) at 341.
37 Weiler (n 1) at 341.

Yet, the type of "taming" that comes from this new European monist source, while being welcome and necessary, still does not appear entirely appropriate to Weiler. For he believes that not all dimensions inherent in the boundaries of nationhood should be constitutionally foregone by this particular understanding of boundless essential humanity. On the contrary, just as Weiler emphatically welcomes the new Europe's goal of exterminating the abuses of national boundaries, so he also no less vigorously defends certain sound dimensions of nationhood even in their statal form. He argues that there are two important human values in nationhood, which the new Europe and its monist source should be careful not to sweep away together with the unsound dimensions in nationhood. They are belongingness and originality.

"Belongingness," Weiler writes, "is inherent in nationhood; nationhood is a form of belonging. Nationhood is not an instrument to obtain belongingness, it *is* it."[38] And it means above all "a place, a social home," he explains.[39] In this sense "[i]t is like the 'bonds of blood' in family and tribe in that those who are of the nation have their place, are accepted, belong, independently of their achievements—by just being."[40] Herein, he argues, lies the "powerful appeal [of national belongingness]—it is a shield against existential aloneness. The power of this belongingness may be understood by the drama and awesomeness of its opposites: isolation, seclusion, excommunication."[41] Its value becomes even more obvious and critical when "nationhood offers a place to the familyless, to the tribeless."[42]

In addition to the virtue of existential shield, loyalty and autochthony could also, if not stretched too far, be seen, according to Weiler, as justifying belongingness as the sound value in nationhood. "But nationhood," he writes, also "transcends the family and tribe."[43] It

> not only offers a place to the familyless, to the tribeless, but . . . calls for loyalty . . . towards others which go beyond the immediate "natural" (blood) or self-interested social unit. And, indeed, belongingness of this type is a two-way street. It is not only a passive value: to be accepted. It is also active: to accept. Loyalty is one of those virtues which, if not abused, benefits those on both the giving and receiving ends.[44]

Such loyalty is not abused and can justify belongingness only if it is understood as being shed of its abusive "ethnic and culturally repressive baggage."[45] "Ironically . . . its artificiality gives it its bridging potential."[46]

Similarly, the virtue of autochthony can only have a justificatory role if it is understood in its non-abusive sense. "[T]he nexus to place and land," Weiler writes, has of course "horrific associations which need no exploring here."[47] But if we could separate the abusive hold that it has on perception and sensibility, and take instead just those dimensions in autochthony that are "an antidote to the

[38] Weiler (n 1) at 338.
[39] Weiler (n 1) at 338.
[40] Weiler (n 1) at 338.
[41] Weiler (n 1) at 338.
[42] Weiler (n 1) at 338.
[43] Weiler (n 1) at 338.
[44] Weiler (n 1) at 338–9.
[45] Weiler (n 1) at 339.
[46] Weiler (n 1) at 339.
[47] Weiler (n 1) at 339.

fragmentation of the post-modern condition," then, Weiler believes, this would be a further justificatory virtue to support the value of national belongingness.[48]

The other core element, which embodies a sound value that Weiler sees in nationhood alongside belongingness is, as noted, the claim about originality. This means that human potentialities should be realized in their "authentic," "original ways," "ways which humanity as a whole would be the poorer for not cultivating."[49] And in Weiler's view it is precisely the nation, "with its endlessly rich specificities, co-existing alongside other nations," that is the indispensable vehicle for realizing that important virtue.[50] On this reading, "the tower of Babel was not a sin against God but a sin against human potentiality; and the dispersal that came in its aftermath, not punishment, but divine blessing."[51]

Weiler believes that nation-state monism that linked nationhood with state into a fully sovereign nation-state, which then naturally fostered its own sovereign values, was not wrong in principle in advancing the ideas of belongingness and originality. It was wrong to the extent that its idea of sovereignty of the nation-state and its national *demos* inevitably led to fostering also the unsound dimensions of nationhood. This is why he concludes that the new Europe's monism, aimed against excesses of nation-state monism, should "not eliminate the national state," but rather "tame the national interest" in a particular way so as to keep the "pure and uncorrupted"[52] boundaries of nationhood while eliminating only the unsound ones. What we get out of this process of taming are two uncorrupted boundaries of nationhood—belongingness and originality—that ought to be preserved, according to Weiler, and in the favorable environment of a nation-state, albeit a tamed one, where the nation could most fully realize its sound potential.[53] At the same time, what we exclude as unsound are all other boundaries that nationality may assume. They are the "codified expressions"[54] in nationality, introduced by help from the formal monist logic within a nation-state and its consequently untamed nationalist reflexes.[55] These "artificial boundaries"[56] are things that go beyond the value of originality, and do not actually allow the "cultural differences to express themselves in their authentic, spontaneous form."[57] They also constitute an equally unsound "false consciousness which nationalism may create instead of belongingness."[58]

[48] Weiler (n 1) at 339. [49] Weiler (n 1) at 339.
[50] Weiler (n 1) at 339. [51] Weiler (n 1) at 339. [52] Weiler (n 1) at 341.
[53] Weiler (n 1) at 339: "[T]he state is to be seen principally as an instrument, the organizational framework within which the nation is to realize its potentialities . . . The well being and integrity of the state must, thus, be secured so that these functions may be attained. That is not a meagre value in itself. But to the extent that the state may claim, say, a loyalty which is more than pragmatic, it is because it is at the service of the nation with its values of belongingness and originality. (This conceptualization underscores, perhaps exaggerates, the difference with the American truly radical alternative liberal project of the non-ethno-national polity . . .)".
[54] Weiler (n 1) at 342.
[55] Such development seems to flow naturally, given monism's absence of the perception of an equally strong opposing source of constitutional authority that could tame the nation-state and its understanding of the nation as the single ultimate source of authority on a given state territory.
[56] Weiler (n 1) at 342. [57] Weiler (n 1) at 343. [58] Weiler (n 1) at 343.

It is important to note further that these two boundaries from nationhood are actually complementary to another value. Just as the "essential humanity" from the new European monism tames the "nationality" from the nation-state monism, thereby producing the sound value of refined nationhood, so the process also works in the opposite way. What was the ultimate source of constitutional authority within the nation-state also tames the opposing European monism. It thus produces a refined understanding of essential humanity that is no longer the "essential humanity" cleansed of national boundaries—that is, *boundless* essential humanity—but one that is congruent with those sound values in nationhood. For Weiler, the right understanding of essential humanity cannot be had without the latter reflecting precisely those two essentially human values from nationhood. Dimensions from essential humanity that dictate a nationality-blind understanding of this notion are thus excluded as corrupted and are replaced by a particular value of humility as one of its sound values stemming from the tamed European source of constitutional authority. The implication for Weiler is that it is this humility, which differs from the still-arrogant strategy of "melting" the boundaries, that requires our national difference to remain and be recognized as indispensable, while also demanding that I adopt humbleness and reach across difference in accepting the still different "other" as accepting myself.

For Weiler's pluralism, it is crucial that the process works both ways, since otherwise it is easy to see, as he explains, how the nation-state monism and its potential for boundary abuse could be replaced by a European monism and its no less-dangerous potential for the abuse: "It would be more than ironic," he states, "if a polity set up as a means to counter the excesses of [monistic] statism ended up coming round full circle and transforming itself into a [no less monistic] (super) state."[59] That is, "[i]t would be equally ironic if the ethos which rejected the boundary abuse of the nation-state gave birth to a polity with the same potential for abuse."[60] "The problem with this unity vision [ie European melting-pot monism] is that its very realization entails its negation."[61]

In contrast to either of the monistic visions, Weiler's pluralism requires that both of the monist sources mutually tame one another so as to arrive at a balanced reconciliation of substantive ethical blocks that flow from them respectively and join in the refined pluralist whole. Analysis so far suggests that we can already speak of three such refined building blocks of his pluralist, and allegedly normatively superior, meta-constitution of Europe. The first and second originate from the nation-state monistic source of constitutional authority. They are nationhood as belongingness (in its virtues of existential shield, loyalty, and autochthony, properly understood) and nationhood as originality. The third comes from the opposing, European monist source of constitutional authority and is a particular nationality-associated humility as the sound expression of essential humanity instantiated for the field of national boundaries.

[59] Weiler (n 1) at 341. [60] Weiler (n 1) at 341. [61] Weiler (n 1) at 341.

These externally balanced ethical blocks are actually principles that clearly point in specific substantive directions while excluding others. In this sense they truly are the "building blocks" of a European constitution since, on the one hand, they already determine the substantive dimension of that constitution and, on the other, their further balanced reconciliation is undertaken through the process of constitutional application by judges and other interpreters of a European constitution. Such substantive reconciliation is the reason why we have characterized Weiler's understanding of heterarchy as substantive constitutional pluralism. A monist pursuit of some substantive value that is determined solely by a single and ultimate source of constitutional authority is no longer possible. For in the new Europe's pluralist meta-constitution there is and should be, according to Weiler, this novel unique pluralist perception of two equally strong opposing sources of constitutional authority. This means that neither is hierarchically superior to the other and that, consequently, each has to tolerate and adjust to the other's values as described. We can see through this process the unfolding of Weiler's relatively thicker, substantive meaning of constitutional tolerance.

Moreover, there is a further feature that reinforces the pluralist character of Weiler's thesis. Namely, this pluralist substantive balance, while not concealing its claim to normative superiority as the best meta-constitution for Europe, is something that is nonetheless not imposed on any of the actors. As any true pluralism, this conception is merely being proposed.[62] In this sense Weiler explains that while in the still monist Canada, for instance, "[t]he Quebecois are told: in the name of the people of Canada, you are obliged to obey," in the new pluralist Europe "the French or the Italians or the Germans are told: in the name of the peoples of Europe, you are invited to obey."[63] That is, "[i]n both, constitutional obedience is [normatively] demanded."[64] But the key difference is that in Europe, "acceptance and subordination are voluntary," and so "they constitute an act of true liberty and emancipation [ie true pluralism] from collective self-arrogance and constitutional fetishism: a high expression of Constitutional Tolerance."[65]

1.3.2 From religious boundary and essential humanity

The monism of old Europe has also manifested itself in the intensity of religious boundaries. Though Weiler does not discuss this explicitly, it is clearly the monistic logic of fusion between sovereign political power and religion that played its own part in the history of abuse of religious boundaries in Europe. This history is notorious for its religious wars, imperialism under the cover of faith, oppressions of the "internal other," and all sorts of other instances of boundary abuse in this particular field. The most horrific abuses occurred in times when sovereignty did not yet rest with the nation-state *demos*, but with sovereigns of other kinds—monarchs, kings, feudal lords, privileged classes of citizenry, and the like. Traditional substantive principles from those times—as the "*une foi, un loi, un roi*," or

[62] Cf MacCormick, Chapter 1, this book, pp. 24–5.
[63] Weiler (n 4) at 21. [64] Weiler (n 4) at 21. [65] Weiler (n 4) at 21.

"*cuius regio eius religio*"—remind of how closely a particular pursuit of religious vision was tied up with the political rule of each sovereign in Europe's past. Indeed, it was that kind of intense monist logic of the era—the sovereign's will as the ultimate source of authority also as regards the choice for full-blown endorsement of this or that religious vision by the state or other political entity under his rule—that helped foster the high potential for abuse at all those three levels, which, as explained earlier, Weiler distinguishes while speaking of monism's impact on boundary abuse.[66]

Thus, Europe's history is full of instances of states and their sovereigns rising against other sovereign states in defending a particular "correct" religious vision. Examples range from princes and kings raising their armies against other sovereigns from different factions of the same creed, such as the wars between Catholic and Protestant states of the sixteenth and first half of the seventeenth century, to aggression against other religious identities demonstrated in the struggle between the Holy Roman Empire and the Turks, the *Reconquista* of the Christians versus Muslims on the territory of modern-day Spain and Portugal, and the like. This corresponds with the first of Weiler's levels at which the abuse of some identity boundary is against another sovereign political entity and its people, and where physical or any other kind of aggression is the most egregious form of this kind of abuse.[67]

But Europe's past is also replete with examples of states and their sovereigns abusing religious boundaries in relation to their people. When, under the regime of *cuius regio eius religio*, for instance, a new sovereign ruler of a different denomination took over, large groups had to convert and actually found this to be more realistic than facing repression by the sovereign state. Similarly, across the German states the real victims of the 30-year religious wars are often said to have been poor peasants who lost their crops, farms, and lives through starvation and slaughter as their local sovereign princes fought against each other as well as Spanish, French, Polish, Danish, and Swedish kings. The population of that German-speaking territory fell from 21 million people to 13 million during those 30 years. Indeed, examples such as these correspond fully with Weiler's second level at which the boundary abuse is that of the sovereign state against its people: when the sovereignty of the state ceases to be instrumental in relation to individuals and society, but instead becomes an end in itself.[68]

Weiler's third level at which boundary abuse is intensified under monism is fully internal and occurs, we observed, when a sense of collective identity within a given sovereign state "induces a sense of superiority and a concomitant sense of condescension or contempt for the other," that is, when it makes him "an inferior other."[69] Examples from European history of religious boundaries' abuse at this particular level are notorious as well, and range from all kinds of suppressions to expelling (or worse) of adherents of other religions and factions in a given sovereign state. Moreover, the particular imposing character of the common

[66] See p. 77. [67] See p. 77. [68] See p. 77. [69] Weiler (n 1) at 340.

Christendom that Europe surely maintained during that period—one with a too-excluding stance towards "the other" within itself—was itself an improper treatment of religious boundaries: a strategy of abuse against those who would not fall within its collective self.

We see that the monist boundary abuse in this field, and its intensity in the particular historic era, was not much less violent than in the case of nationality abuse. Although Weiler does not discuss this explicitly with respect to religion, I will expound his pluralist alternative as inevitably securing prevention from monism-associated abuse in this field as well. Yet, just as in the case of nationality, so here, too, we should not think just about how to prevent the carnage. "That's the easy part," Weiler wrote with regard to abuse of national boundaries, and it should clearly hold for religious ones as well.[70] An even more thorough and proper response is that we should, he believes, go further in the religious field, just as was the case in the national, and deal "at a deeper level with the source of these attitudes."[71] Only by instilling his pluralist alternative into the very source of these attitudes, and so purifying the corrupted strategy at its very origin, can we hope to truly eradicate the potential for abuse. What we gain is a more thoroughgoing approach to prevention of abuse in this field.

To be sure, the Europe of modern nation-states replaced the holders of sovereignty and granted the latter to the people themselves. The fusion of state and religion, too, ceased to be as intensive as it was during Europe's deeper past. But, of course, monism remained regardless of its particular institutional repository, and the divergent religious manifestations can still be observed also in the more modern environment of sovereign nation-states. Differences between European states thus remain, for instance, along the lines of different symbolic endorsements of laic versus religious foundations underlying the central tenets of their constitutions, such as fundamental rights and principles. These are different expressions of sovereignty of a particular state *demos* on these matters as embodied in its particular constitution. Through the symbolism of such preambles, which capture the nations' identities and deepest values,[72] some state constitutions thus entrench a strictly laic approach to understanding of their constitutional foundations. While reading the preamble of the French constitution, Weiler explains, "you will seek in vain for whatever mention of religion or transcendence."[73] Indeed, "[t]his preamble is exaltedly laic, as it is grounded in the historic anticlericalism of the French revolution. Article 1 of the French constitution explicitly proclaims France as an 'independent, laic, democratic and social republic'."[74] However, some other states do not shy away from reference to "God" (Germany) or even "the Holy Trinity" (Ireland) in their constitution's preamble, Weiler writes, and observes how others

[70] Cf Weiler (n 5) at 117–18, where he discusses religious boundaries while continuing to use the same passage as the one from his discussion on nationhood, saying that prevention of the most egregious forms of abuse of the "other" is "the easy part" and that we should deal with these things at the deeper level.

[71] Weiler (n 11) at 60. Cf Weiler (n 5) at 118.

[72] Weiler (n 5) at 34–5, 39.

[73] Weiler (n 5) at 39.

[74] Weiler (n 5) at 39.

go even further. "Part of the European constitutional tradition are also those member states" whose constitutions provide "a national, official, and institutionalised state church."[75] Such is the case for the Greek, Maltese, and Danish constitutions, for instance.

While these various states are all generally understood as respecting freedom of religion as well as freedom from religion, their different constitutional endorsements of religious and/or laic foundations for their fundamental constitutional tenets entail distinct consequences in positive constitutional law, as Weiler correctly acknowledges.[76] This is because those symbolic characterizations of identity serve as a deeper normative ground to which judges and other constitutional interpreters often turn when deciding hard cases.[77] These different symbolic constitutional foundations then represent the concrete building of monist boundaries along religious lines by each state and its *demos* within the Europe of sovereign nation-states.

It may well be the case that the boundary abuses flowing from monism are less egregious now than before. However, there is plentiful evidence that the potential for an actuality of abuse is still present in the modern day.[78] Weiler welcomes the new European strategy in its attempt to tame the monist potential for abuse within the nation-states in the name of some essential humanity. He firmly believes that the European constitution should contribute its added value to, and deal with, these boundaries so as not to leave them entirely within the domain of states and in the hands of their single ultimate sources of constitutional authority.[79] However, Weiler also maintains that this added value, this taming of the opposing source, should not be such as simply to melt these boundaries in the name of boundless essential humanity between the European peoples.

So what, then, is that added value that according to Weiler the new Europe and its constitution should contribute in this field? It is, again, best sought in the more nuanced approach of his substantive pluralism. According to this, neither of the opposed monist strategies represents the best approach to dealing with these issues. On the one hand, a nation-state sovereign's will should not be seen as representing the ultimate source of constitutional authority in its territory, so as to be left entirely free to follow exclusively its own choice where these differences prevail. Conversely, the new Europe and its constitution should likewise not be understood as replacing the ultimate source of constitutional authority with its own that would—in the name of essential humanity within one united *demos* on the European scale—melt these constitutionally recognized religious boundaries between the different peoples into a supposedly "neutral" laic state of Europe. The constitution of such a state would now render these boundaries constitutionally irrelevant, at least within the domain of federal EU law if not the entire domain

[75] Weiler (n 5) at 40. [76] Weiler (n 5) at 54. [77] Weiler (n 5) at 54.

[78] Not only is it the case that one can point to continuing instances of terror and bloodshed associated with religious boundaries in the Europe of today. The improper approach to boundaries in this field might in the long run well be a source of a more modern type of conflict, as recent developments after 11 September 2001 seem to remind.

[79] Weiler (n 5) at 38–9.

of constitutional law. This, too, would, according to Weiler, constitute subtle mistreatment of "the other", by mistakenly assuming that the proper response to the differences between religious and laic understandings of constitutional foundations is to "melt" them. This would, he argues, not respect the religious dimension, since while assuming neutrality between laic and religious value, it actually endorses "laicity" itself.[80] Not to acknowledge the Judeo-Christian heritage as part of the value-identity underlying Europe's constitution is thus "not a demonstration of neutrality," for Weiler, but rather "a Jacobin attitude"[81] and "a Jacobin ambush".[82] In his view such a strategy would be a false understanding of essential humanity. Weiler believes, moreover, that it would also replace nation-state monism with the opposing monism of a European superstate, thereby simply transferring the potential for abuse into an even more powerful entity. Instead of adopting either the first or the second of these two ultimate sources of constitutional authority, the new Europe should not, Weiler implies, endorse the ultimate dominance of either one over the other. Clearly, we could say that the two should be understood as heterarchically coexisting at the same level so that they would be able to tame one another and thereby bring out their respective valuable dimensions, while rejecting those that are corrupted.

The statal monism thus "tames" the unsound understanding of "essential humanity"—the mistaken "neutrality" that melts the essentially human categories of laic as well as religious constitutional foundations—from the European monism. It thereby transforms it to a richer and more plural understanding of essential humanity. This is the understanding that recognizes both of these distinct, albeit substantially overlapping, constitutional foundations—the laic and religious—as themselves being indispensable parts of essential humanity, and so requires inclusion of them *both* in the meta-constitutional substance of a truly plural European constitution. The sound value deriving from such essential humanity is the humility associated with religious boundaries. It requires our difference in this respect to be recognized as indispensable, while also demanding that each should reach across difference in accepting the still-different other as accepting himself. As with nationality, then, it is this humility that is so different from the melting-pot type of arrogance, as Weiler would have it, either in the form of imposing exclusively laic or exclusively religious constitutional foundations for Europe. Such a refined understanding of essential humanity, he writes, "is wholly European: it does not mean exercise of 'neutrality' in the sense of exclusion of both options, but a tolerant pluralism the essence of which is that it includes both."[83]

Just as with nationality, the process of taming—here too—works also in the opposite direction. The European monism itself tames both coexisting dimensions,

[80] Weiler (n 5) at 44–5.

[81] J. Weiler, the opening presentation lecture on his book, *Christian Europe* (Rimini, September 2003) <http://www.zenit.org/english/visualizza.phtml?sid=41077> accessed 20 September 2013.

[82] J. Weiler, "Faith in the Agnostic State," interview in *Tablet* (26 March 2004) <http://www.tabletmag.com/jewish-arts-and-culture/books/763/faith-in-the-agnostic-state> accessed 16 October 2013.

[83] Weiler (n 5) at 46.

the laic and religious tradition respectively, requiring that they both become congruent with its sound value of humility.

Thus, not everything from the Judeo-Christian heritage of Europe can be understood as reaching to the sound pluralist foundations of Europe's constitutionalism, and so as comprising part of the constitutional identity that Europe should properly assume. History also reminds us of *that* dark side of heritage: of its corruption into an exclusivist ethos that contributed to religious wars in Europe, to all sorts of domination of "the other" that was often justified in the name of Christian values, and to the instrumentalization of authentic religious beliefs by those who were currently pursuing power and authority.[84] To such exclusivist strategies one could add other instances in which the tradition's ethos was perverted and used even against the socially, economically, or otherwise disadvantaged non-members of the collective religious identity.[85] Such an exclusivist dimension of the Judeo-Christian tradition is excluded by the process of taming as being corrupted because not congruent with the sound understanding of essential humanity. It is contrary to Weiler's demand for humility in this area, according to which the only sound objective of the religious "I" is to accept and actually protect "the other," and especially the weaker other, as myself. "The other" is to be accorded human dignity in his "otherness."[86]

While the exclusivist part in the Judeo-Christian tradition must therefore be excluded, Weiler clearly also points to what he sees as the sound part from this tradition. It is precisely the part emphasizing human equality and dignity, freedom, respect for reason and human rights,[87] while grounding those in a religious foundation. According to the latter, these are inviolable fundamentals that "flow from the understanding that man was created in the image of God... and was so accorded inviolable equality and dignity [along with] independence and freedom."[88] This particular religious grounding, Weiler further explains, provides a specific emphasis within the various nuances of liberal tradition, which is, he argues, "specifically European."[89] It primarily emphasizes the specifically understood human dignity that determines an ethical order within the confines of which freedom then also has its place.[90] This is distinct from being primarily focused on the expansion of freedom independently of the confines of the ethical order deriving from the religious foundation and its specifically understood human dignity. Or as Weiler further explains:

[84] Menéndez (n 28) at 20. [85] Menéndez (n 28) at 20–1.

[86] To the extent that Menéndez (see n 28) fails to see this key normative requirement of Weiler's pluralism he is, in my view, misreading the latter. Weiler's pluralism emphatically demands exclusion—through the described taming with the coexisting laic source—of all the mentioned abuses and, what is more, of the subtlest monist potential itself in this field that could lead to them. This is meant internally (among Europeans) as well as externally (in relation to non-Europeans). The process of pluralist taming between the two *coexisting* sources is the core of Weiler's pluralism, yet it does not find its place within Menéndez's account of that theory. Instead, Weiler's pluralism seems to me to be depicted by Menéndez, in effect, as if it were entrenching only one source, which is typical of monism and indeed characteristic of Europe's abusive past.

[87] Weiler (n 5) at 49–50. [88] Weiler (n 5) at 49–50.

[89] Weiler (n 5) at 50. [90] Weiler (n 5) at 50.

Just as it is at the symbolic so there is also at the practical level an important difference between emphasizing freedom in the American and dignity in the European understanding of human rights. Genesis gives priority to dignity, referring to the man and woman as beings created in the image of God. According to the religious view of the World, freedom is not without confines and has to be an integral part of the ethical order.[91]

It is in this way that Weiler's sound constitutional building block originating from religion should be perceived. Instead of "being timid of and turning its back to modernity," the refined Judeo-Christian tradition, Weiler explains, also starts "emphasizing the value of reason, of science and technology, of welfare that can be brought by a free market, and of democracy in the domain of politics. Above all, it puts the notion of choice—this essential element of modernity—into the heart of religious and human sensibility."[92] This does not mean that it also readopts the "pathologies of modernity"[93] and its "epistemological and value relativism" that rejects any belief in objective truth and leads to "a strange freedom without any content."[94] The refined Judeo-Christian tradition transcends those pathologies through its belief in, and emphasis on, that specific understanding of human dignity. Weiler explains that at the same time it recognizes the limits of choice and is "aware of its moral duties by being humble before transcendental truths . . . [F]rom its focus there never escapes the fact that in the center there remain a human being, family, human communities, and their responsibilities that belong to their dignity and are one of the primary vehicles through which their love is expressed."[95] The refined content of the religious constitutional foundations is thus a "human modernity"[96] instead of the "pathological modernity."[97]

In a similar fashion it is necessary, according to Weiler's pluralism, for the purely laic tradition to be modified before it can become part of Europe's meta-constitution. It too must be congruent with the correct understanding of essential humanity. It must adopt humility in relation to the religious "other" and be modified so as to be willing to accommodate the contrary religious dimensions. The "Jacobin" laic aggressiveness against religion therefore has no place in Weiler's pluralist meta-constitution and hence in Europe's objectively valid constitutional identity. But the taming should, at the same time, retain the sound core of the laic tradition, which has its foundations more broadly in the "humanist and Enlightenment tradition, Kantian and neo-Kantian."[98] Equality of persons and their dignity, freedom, respect for reason and human rights, have laic foundations for the non-religious, Weiler notes, and observes that this is a different source for these values, which are, as we have seen above, also a sound part of the European religious tradition. Weiler concludes that the laic tradition thus modified should have a place, along with the similarly modified Judeo-Christian tradition, in the common meta-constitution of Europe, and should so be seen as part of its external, objectively valid constitutional identity.

[91] Weiler (n 5) at 50. [92] Weiler (n 5) at 150. [93] Weiler (n 5) at 57.
[94] Weiler (n 5) at 148. [95] Weiler (n 5) at 151. [96] Weiler (n 5) at 151.
[97] Weiler (n 5) at 57. [98] Weiler (n 5) at 49.

But crucially, Weiler also acknowledges that there is no perfect match between these modified versions of the laic and religious foundations:

> In the way in which fundamental rights are determined and conceptualised, and with respect to issues of solidarity, or "community", there exist important differences between the Judeo-Christian and laic tradition.[99]

These foundational differences, Weiler further acknowledges, will sometimes necessarily be evident at the level of positive law.[100] His response, however, is that this, too, is part of Europe's constitutional pluralism under which constitutional interpreters are required to build a further balanced synthesis of the refined substantive meta-constitutional building blocks. "A European judge," he writes, "has a difficult task (difficult and yet a gratifying one), to build a synthesis of fundamental rights that should in a particular way express this European pluralism."[101]

As was the case with national boundaries, so here too we see that Weiler's balanced and modified ethical blocks within the laic and religious tradition truly deserve the label "building blocks" of a European constitution. They are regarded by Weiler as foundational substantive components of the European constitution and the more concrete balancing as between them will hence be undertaken by those—whether they be judges, academics, or others—who interpret the European constitution further.

Weiler rejects the view that such substantive pluralism is a Trojan horse in favor of those who affirm the values of the Judeo-Christian tradition and who would in this way be better off in the future constitutional development of Europe. It would be such a deceit, Weiler argues, only if the alternative of the wholly laic Europe would indeed work and be the neutral option between the two poles. But for Weiler this is fallacious. Such an approach would be no more neutral than one that purported to rest the European constitution on religious foundations. Hence, the only real plurality we can have here, in his view, is one that recognizes equally both the laic and religious dimension and balances them carefully in the preceding manner. Seen in this light, to include into Europe's meta-constitutional substance the refined building block of Judeo-Christian value-tradition—along with the refined lay one—should be understood as "welcoming Helena" rather than letting in a "Trojan horse."[102] Weiler therefore concludes that it would mean enrichment in the spirit of true pluralism.

It is, moreover, important to understand that Weiler appears primarily to require such a substantive pluralist balance "only" within the EU. He sees these building blocks as the meta-constitutional substance for Europe but recognizes a certain sphere of autonomy to the individual member states' constitutions. "If the French or Italian constituent constitutional authority wishes its constitutional order to be interpreted in the light of the noble humanist tradition," Weiler thus writes, "then this choice is entirely acceptable."[103] But he does not regard this as neutral and

[99] Weiler (n 5) at 56.
[100] Weiler (n 5) at 56.
[101] Weiler (n 5) at 56.
[102] Weiler (n 5) at 56.
[103] Weiler (n 5) at 56.

reaffirms his view that "such a choice is not appropriate for —Europe."[104] For, "the European judge does not have the luxury enjoyed by his nation-state colleagues who in this sense have to deal with a uniform constitutional symbolism." Contrary to those judges, "a European judge interpreting a European constitution must respect the different symbolisms that are in some sense contrary to each other."[105]

This does not mean that the member states' monistic practice is not affected by the new Europe's pluralist meta-constitutional substance. It is, and there are two reasons for this. Firstly, the EU sphere will, of course, penetrate into what used to be the exclusive domain of each nation-state under the old monism. To this degree the member states and their constitutions, together with those who adjudicate thereon, are clearly affected by the pluralism that imbues the EU's meta-constitution. It should, moreover, be acknowledged that Weiler's substantive pluralism is connected to his proposal regarding the dilemma of "who decides who decides," by which he requires that this question, too, be approached in the spirit of pluralism and mutual balance that rejects a one-sided monist "diktat." This is discussed later in this chapter.[106] Secondly, there is the spill-over effect, which would spread the new pluralist spirit even into fully internal domains. The process is the same as the one meant to work in relation to non-Europeans.[107]

1.4 Concluding the explication

The preceding analysis therefore reveals several building blocks representing Weiler's normatively superior, pluralist conception of Europe's meta-constitution. These building blocks reveal Weiler's more concrete understanding of the abstract notion of heterarchy of sources of constitutional authority, and so the more tangible meaning of his constitutional pluralism. It can therefore be concluded that for Weiler the abstract notion of constitutional heterarchy, which connotes the idea of there being two or more sources of constitutional authority of which none is ultimately superior, but equally powerful and coexisting at the same level with the other(s), has to be understood as the reconciliation of the opposing substantive values contained in each of the opposing monist sources. This is an external inter-systemic balance that is not supposed to lean towards either of the monist poles, but to represent a particular kind of mutual recognition, or tolerance, that is substantively elaborated. The particular substantive building blocks, which arise out of such a mutual taming and reconciliation, are thus precisely the meaning of Weiler's heterarchy when seen from a less abstract perspective. They are the substantive content of Weiler's "constitutional tolerance."

In addition to the substantive determinations, there is also a sphere where the content of constitutional tolerance is not elaborated substantively and externally by Weiler, but is left in its abstract form as a general interpretive rule; that is, one that exhorts the Union and member-state officials themselves to use the particular

[104] Weiler (n 5) at 56. [105] Weiler (n 5) at 56. [106] See pp. 94–6.

[107] See p. 90, following. I am indebted to Joseph Weiler for our exchanges and his comments on this reading of his theory that reaffirms my understanding (NYU, New York, September 2006).

normative spirit of constitutional tolerance in their further reconciliations through their everyday decision-making. This general spirit is to become prevalent in the "sphere of public administration," as Weiler explains: "in the habits and practices it instils in the purveyors of public power in European polities, from the most mundane to the most august."[108] Or in "policy-setting forums," where "a similar discipline will become routine":

> In myriad areas—whether a local council or parliament itself—every norm will be subject to an unofficial European impact study. So many policies in the public realm can no longer be adopted without examining their consonance with the interest of others, the interest of Europe.[109]

The same will hold for the judicial sphere: "Think, too, of the judicial function, ranging from the neighbourhood *giudice conciliatore* to the highest jurisdictions: willy-nilly, European law, the interest of others, is part of the judicial normative matrix."[110] And the process of everyday decision-making in the spirit of the interpretive rule of constitutional tolerance will take place "also at Community level":[111]

> Think of the European judge or the European public official who must understand that, in the peculiar constitutional compact of Europe, his decision will take effect only if obeyed by national court, if executed faithfully by a national public official with whom he belongs to a national administration which claims from them a particularly strong form of loyalty and habit. This, too, will instil a measure of caution and tolerance.[112]

What is more, it is hoped that the new general spirit of constitutional tolerance will spill over to non-Europeans as well:

> This is critical, because in the daily practices which I am extolling, the public official is invited and habituated to deal with a very distinct "other", but to treat him or her as if he/she was his own. One should not be starry-eyed or overly naïve; but the hope and expectation is that there will be a spillover effect, a gradual habitation to various forms of tolerance and with it gradual change in the ethos of public administration which can be extended to Europeans and non-Europeans alike.[113]

In addition to the substantive building blocks and the general interpretive requirement there is one further specific conclusion that reinforces the pluralist character of the proposal. This is the fact that, as touched on earlier, this pluralist arrangement, while not concealing its claim of external normative superiority as the best meta-constitution of Europe, is something that is not imposed on any of the actors. On the contrary, it is proposed, and is so in any of its arrangement's parts.[114] In this sense Weiler refers, as we saw, to his distinction between the pluralist Europe, where nations are invited to obey by the peoples of Europe, and the still monist

[108] Weiler (n 4) at 21. [109] Weiler (n 4) at 22. [110] Weiler (n 4) at 22.
[111] Weiler (n 4) at 22. [112] Weiler (n 4) at 22. [113] Weiler (n 4) at 23.
[114] Weiler discusses this important feature of his pluralism with respect to both, the building blocks associated with national boundaries (Weiler (n 4) at 21; see also p. 81) as well as those associated with religious boundaries (Weiler (n 5) at 121–2). The same applies also to the more general interpretive content of his constitutional tolerance, as just elaborated; the same pluralist strategy is also employed by MacCormick (see Chapter 1, pp. 24–5).

Canada, where Quebeçois are obliged to obey by the people of Canada.[115] In Europe "acceptance and subordination are voluntary" and thus "they constitute an act of true liberty and emancipation [ie true pluralism] from collective self-arrogance and constitutional fetishism: a high expression of Constitutional Tolerance."[116]

Weiler's theory of pluralism thus explicated could have far reaching normative consequences. Throughout Europe's history, and that of political thought, we have understood constitutional authority, as well as law and political power stemming from it, in monistic terms. Their ultimate *locus* was always said to rest in some ultimate source of authority, in the sovereign, whoever that happened to be during a particular historical era throughout Europe's past. Our political theory—from Bodin, Hobbes, and Rousseau, to Kant, Bentham, Austin, Dicey, and finally Kelsen and related thinkers—testifies of this monist line of thought. Moreover, the criterion of such an ultimate source of political power and its constitutional authority has normally been understood in Schmittian terms: as the one that prevails in the extreme situation, that is, in the case of conflict between alleged sovereigns. This monist understanding, as we saw above, contributed towards the egregious boundary abuses that can be observed throughout Europe's history.

Weiler's constitutional pluralism seems to be a break with this persistent line of monist thought. He re-examines the very substantive values that led to abuse and readjusts them so as to render this less likely for the future. He rejects the monist pursuit of such substantive values, together with the previously prevalent attitude of those who held such values towards those who differed in that respect. His conception of constitutional heterarchy is designed to diminish the most subtle potential for abuse that, in the long run, sooner or later leads to the egregious one: as is evident from our recurring history. On this reading it is therefore a theory which, by reaching far back into Europe's past, deals with the traditional arrangement of the source of political and legal authority that is at the same time also the source of the recurrent abuse. The theory proposes an alternative arrangement of the plurality of coexistent and specifically substantively determined sources of authority in order to renew the old arrangement ethically and thus get rid of its potential for abuse at its very source. This is a vision that seeks to correct no less than the path taken by our entire traditional political theory thus far, which has been characteristically monist from its beginnings.

2. Situating the Theory

Having explicated Weiler's understanding of constitutional heterarchy, his constitutional pluralism, we are now in position to make further use of our Ariadne's Thread and situate the theory correctly on the map of the pluralist labyrinth. While the central preoccupation of the theory is not to work out the details within the

[115] Weiler (n 4) at 21. [116] Weiler (n 4) at 21.

most abstract theoretical discourse, we saw that the theory does inescapably imply some general pluralist position within that discourse. It explicitly rejects to explain and determine Europe normatively in some monist terms that would imply an exclusive ultimate source of constitutional authority on a given nation-state territory or the territory of Europe as a whole. The theory instead assumes that there are heterarchically related sources of constitutional authority in Europe, which means that they are each already autonomously rooted and coexist as equally important over some shared territorial space. Since Weiler's primary focus is not on the details within this most foundational level of the pluralist discourse, it is not instantly clear what more precisely his understanding of pluralism at this level does look like—whether it is more like that of MacCormick, where the heterarchical coexistence at the foundational level is understood in terms of the substantive territorial overlap,[117] or whether is it more like that of Walker, where the foundational overlap is procedurally understood,[118] or perhaps something different altogether. Having said that, however, it is possible to infer back from our explication of Weiler's substantive elaboration of heterararchy, which goes beyond the mere foundational discourse and is the primary focus of Weiler's theory, that Weiler's heterarchy at the most foundational level too could not but imply some sort of substantive concessions and would thus roughly be a variant of MacCormick's substantive overlap. This seems to be the best reading of his conception. This is not only because Weiler himself has recently made it explicit that for him the mere procedural concessions at the foundational level are not enough for the two confronting sources to lead to his particular substantive vision of constitutionalism for Europe that he considers superior.[119] It is also because, without at least some of his substantive refinement doing some work already at the deepest foundational level, Weiler could not really eradicate, as he claims to do, the abusive monist potential from as deep as its "very source."

Any further potential debate as to what exact variant of substantive overlap Weiler might endorse at the foundational level can be left open at this stage. What is more important now is to notice further, following Ariadne's Thread, that his primary contribution to the pluralist discourse appears within one of the remaining three pluralist discourses. Weiler primarily works within the discourse of the *what* and constructs a meaning of pluralism with reference to that particular sector and its context. This whole new sector of the labyrinth has not yet been encountered with either of the pluralists examined thus far. It clearly goes beyond the mere foundational level of the discourse as defined by our decoding tool and most characteristically represented by MacCormick's work. In its focus beyond the foundational level, Weiler's sector of the labyrinth is, however, also nowhere near Walker's non-foundational sector. Indeed, the sphere of the *what* is in the very opposite direction of the sphere of the *how*. That is, unlike Walker's epistemic pluralism, Weiler's substantive pluralism to a significant degree understands the notion of constitutional heterarchy to be about the proper substance (or content) as

[117] See Chapter 1, pp. 22–4.
[118] See Chapter 1, p. 22; Chapter 2, pp. 38–40.
[119] Weiler (n 24) at 13–18.

opposed to the mere *form* of constitutional discourse. To this extent it does not deal with the question of the *how* of the common constitutional discourse. The *how* attempts in a radical way to avoid external substantive arbitration between a range of different substantive self-determinations of constitutional identity by various constitutional orders in disagreement. These inevitably involve only internally valid, objectively incommensurable understandings, and so epistemic pluralism leaves it to the orders to determine the proper constitutional identities for themselves. By contrast, substantive pluralism directly engages exactly in the discourse concerning the right external determinations of the common substantive constitutional identity and argues, as elaborated earlier, for a particular substantive meaning of pluralism with reference to that kind of issue.

The distinct orientations between the two approaches, one primarily being concerned with the sphere of the *how*, the other with the *what*, are important. This is why the concrete meaning of heterarchy in epistemic pluralism amounts strictly only to the minimal procedural requirements at the level of second-order constitutional discourse[120] that are joined on the first-order level by a further but deliberately unspecified exhortation to reflexive mutual reconciliation.[121] And this is why the elaborated meaning of heterarchy in substantive pluralism, by contrast, amounts primarily to positing a much thicker meta-constitutional substance: the particular substantive building blocks which penetrate both the second as well as first-order level of the constitutional discourse and are considered to be the objectively (inter-systemically) valid and balanced external determination of the common constitutional identity. It is only after these substantive building blocks are determined that Weiler's substantive pluralism also briefly enters the discourse of the *how* and suggests a particular normative exhortation for further reconciliation through the process of interpretation by the actors themselves. And even this exhortation to reconciliation in the spirit of mutual recognition (his particular understanding of tolerance) is more specifically determined in his substantive pluralism than it is in Walker's epistemic pluralism. The latter is deliberately left open, since it is considered inappropriate to impose one sacrosanct form of mutual reconciliation.

It can be concluded that the two versions of constitutional pluralism, while both speaking abstractly of the heterarchical coexistence of constitutional authorities and thus of pluralism, really understand its meaning in very different, even opposing ways. To be certain, to the general common question that they both deal with, the issue of the best common conception of constitutionalism for Europe, they both respond with a constitutional pluralist conception. They both reject monism and endorse the abstract understanding of heterarchy. But when they answer the further pressing question of what this pluralism (heterarchy) really means, substantive pluralism answers with a proposal from the sphere of the *what*, which is precisely what the epistemic pluralist's further understanding of heterarchy prohibits. The contrast between the two positions can thus be starkly represented. Epistemic

[120] Pp. 34–7. [121] Pp. 43–6.

pluralism remains only within the sphere of the *how* and regards any impositions on the actors from the sphere of the *what* as unjustifiable; as monism. By way of contrast, for the substantive pluralist a proper understanding of constitutional heterarchy, of pluralism, cannot be had in the first place without the pluralist elaboration within the sphere of the *what*, so that any attempt at constructing pluralism within the sphere of the *how* alone is bound to result in a conception that is not pluralist in the soundest sense possible and, to this extent, is not pluralist at all.

This stark difference between both understandings of pluralism is reflected even in that single applicative pluralist discourse with which both authors *do* jointly engage. Like Walker's, Weiler's theory also deals with the first theme, of *who*, as defined by our decoding tool. As in Walker's case, Weiler's pluralist proposal regarding the dilemma of "who decides who decides" is closely related to his broader conception of constitutional pluralism. In this light, Weiler starts by explaining that "[t]he constitutional discourse in Europe must be conceived as a conversation of many actors in a constitutional interpretive community, rather than a hierarchical structure with the ECJ at the top."[122] He posits that "a feature of neo-constitutionalism in this case would be that the jurisdictional line (or lines) should be a matter of constitutional conversation, not a constitutional *diktat*."[123] And Weiler does not have in mind only a formal meaning of conversation after which, then, either a national or EU institution could still reserve the last say to itself. He criticizes in this sense, for instance, the approach of the German Constitutional Court, which recognized that decisions have to be taken in cooperation with the ECJ but within that conversation then still reserved the last word to itself. This way, "[a] European *diktat*," Weiler writes, "is simply replaced by a national one."[124]

Therefore, in an attempt to avoid either the national or EU one-sided diktat as regards the issue of "who decides who decides," Weiler proposes firstly the creation of a special Constitutional Council. This would have jurisdiction only over issues of competence and would, crucially, be composed in a way that recognizes the equal status of each of the two orders. On the one hand, it would be composed of "sitting members of the constitutional courts or their equivalents in the Member States."[125] In this way the national orders would be responsible for deciding about competence issues. On the other hand, they would be thus deciding jointly, under majority rule, and the EU would additionally be represented by the president of the ECJ who would preside over the Constitutional Council. In this way the EU order would also be, no less than the national ones, responsible for deciding about competence issues. The argument seems to imply that the coequal status of both orders, and their respective coequal roles as to the issue of *who* decides, would thereby be recognized in such a Council as fully as at all possible. All of the parties—those of the EU and

[122] N Weiler (n 1) at 322; J. Weiler, "The European Union Belongs to Its Citizens: Three Immodest Proposals" (1997) 22 EL Rev 150, 156.

[123] Weiler (n 122) at 156. [124] Weiler (n 122) at 156. [125] Weiler (n 122) at 156.

member states—would correspondingly also have the power to start proceedings before the Council, and no single member state would have a veto power.[126]

Secondly—and although this point has not been explicitly argued—his theory necessarily implies that such an institution, too, would be bound to take fully into account in its decision-making the sound building blocks that represent Weiler's substantive constitutional pluralism; the substantive part of his constitutional tolerance. It is inherent in the substantive nature of these meta-constitutional blocks that they have normative implications also for the proper determination of jurisdictional disputes.[127]

Thirdly, in the areas where the refined substantive building blocks of the common European constitution could not point to a jurisdictional right answer, his specific *interpretive* dimension within his constitutional tolerance would, it seems, take over the role of the normative guide.[128]

This approach, Weiler believes, is perhaps the best way to "square the circle."[129] It avoids jurisdictional diktat by any single constitutional order or its institution, be it national or the EU, and comes closest to a true pluralist conversation over competences that would actually shape views, as opposed to ending with a self-indulgent monist diktat.[130] Through such a common Constitutional Council, pluralistically conceived, any conflict between the two coequal constitutional orders could easily be resolved, and any potential serious impasse avoided. And these resolutions would originate from the institutional arrangement based on the genuine pluralist respect that fully retains the equal and self-standing status of both orders.

Such a proposal and meaning of pluralism within the theme of the *who* differs starkly from Walker's answer to the same dilemma and *his* own meaning of pluralism within this particular pluralist discourse. As it was observed, inside this particular discourse Walker declares that we have pluralism only when the institutional question is left open. For the epistemic pluralist, Weiler's proposal for the Constitutional Council is thus inappropriate and clearly monist: it imposes a final decision-making authority where, by nature of things, it cannot provide such an external (inter-systemically valid) solution, but can at best only provide a third, equally incommensurable internal answer to the dilemma.[131] By contrast, for Weiler the proposal to leave the answer to the question of *who* as radically unconstrained as it is under epistemic pluralism, seriously undermines one of the very preconditions for a responsible cohabitation of equals under true pluralism.[132] Being unable to help secure and preserve his prior substantive construction of

[126] Weiler (n 122) at 156.

[127] This reading was endorsed by Weiler in our exchanges on this point (NYU, New York, September 2006). I am indebted to him.

[128] Discussion with Weiler (see n 127).

[129] Weiler (n 1) at 322; Weiler (n 122). Discussion with Weiler (see n 127).

[130] Weiler (n 1) at 323.

[131] N. Walker, "Sovereignty and Differentiated Integration of the European Union" (1998) 4 ELJ 355, 387; cf the remark in N. Walker, "All Dressed Up" (2001) 21 OJLS 563, 570, fn 19.

[132] Weiler (n 24) at 14–17.

pluralism, such an open solution is, for Weiler, thus inevitably a non-pluralist step in the direction of one or the other of substantive monisms.[133]

3. Towards the Assessment

3.1 The cluster of values

In the assessment section of Chapter 2 we saw that epistemic pluralism entrenches only one value as the priority and ultimate value on the externally valid meta-constitutional level: just the very thinly defined Eigenvalue of reciprocal equal respect. No other value can be regarded as externally correct under epistemic pluralism, either with respect to the second or first-order constitutional claims. Hence, I used the term "*ascetic* version of *mere* reciprocity" to connote this particular Eigenvalue underlying epistemic pluralism.[134] What is behind such a thin meta-constitutional external minimum is Walker's assumption about why we (should) get into (constitutional) politics in the first place: in order to resolve our differences in a way that does not externally privilege one or more subjects in relation to others. It is also implicitly assumed that to entrench the ascetic mere reciprocity alone at the external level is, by default, to secure the highest degree of non-privileging, and thereby to accord maximum equal respect, with its corollary of autonomy. This is the foundation for the view that it is this conception of pluralism, as determined by such a thin external meta-constitutional value, that is clearly the most pluralist.

It is clear that Weiler's theory is considerably thicker and more substantive at the meta-constitutional level. It embodies a variety of building blocks (values) that are understood as the very representation of the "life of decency" of which he speaks in connection with Europe's constitutionalism.[135] There is in substantive pluralism thus no single priority Eigenvalue that would relegate others to a lower level of constitutional priority. Rather, there is a cluster of several different externally valid values that all coexist at the same meta-constitutional level of priority and together underpin the theory of substantive pluralism. For Weiler, constitutional politics is ultimately thus not simply about solving our differences, and even less about solving solely through some version of *mere* reciprocity as the only externally valid component of constitutionalism. The thicker substantive blocks represent, for Weiler, the ultimate external truth of the decent life as the end in itself of the European constitutional project.

It is, however, crucial to understand that, according to Weiler's view, this does not mean that these substantive building blocks embodying a vision of the decent life, thereby compromise values of equal respect and autonomy. On the contrary,

133 Weiler (n 24) at 14–17.

134 The attribute "mere" referred to the fact that reciprocity was the single value entrenched at the externally valid meta-constitutional level, and the term "ascetic" was meant to denote its particularly thin (proceduralized) version as it appears in epistemic pluralism. See Chapter 2, p. 60.

135 Pp. 76–7.

he implies that the external validity of these values is necessary to enhance the values of equal respect and autonomy to the highest degree possible. But how, more precisely, is that so?

Firstly, it might be thought that the strategy of privileging such a thicker set of substantive content by declaring it externally (inter-systemically) correct at the meta-constitutional level runs contrary to the decent bounds of *equal respect* for the Other.[136] This is because in the modern day such a bold and open constitutional identification of external truth seems to appear offensive: the Other might feel "wounded, offended, humiliated"[137] by it. Indeed, "from the point of view of the postmodern multicultural sensibility any attempt at elevating such a [thick substantive] content to the level of external truth appears ridiculous."[138] " 'Even if it is true, at least keep it for yourself; why insult the Others?' "[139] So what almost instinctively appears to be the more equal-respect-friendly strategy is that of endorsing "epistemological scepticism and [its] relativisation of truth characteristic for postmodernity."[140] That "seems as an attractive way to constitute the relationship: there is no real [ie external] truth, everyone has his or her own. Hence, let us live together in a full unity [of this kind]!"[141] This is indeed exemplified by Walker's epistemic pluralism, which requires suspension of propositions about external validity, and hence the subsequent entrenchment at the externally valid meta-constitutional level of only this minimal procedural rule itself. The deep assumption, underlying his proposal, was precisely that this preserved the highest degree of equal respect as the single and ultimate Eigenvalue of epistemic pluralism.[142] The implication was that those contested propositions that claimed only internal validity stood a better chance of being seen to fall within the bounds of a decent respect for the differing views of others than did propositions of openly external validity over which there was no higher level of disagreement.[143]

Yet, "we cannot stop at such an immediate instinctive reaction," Weiler writes generally of such approaches.[144] He reminds us that to assert one's external (inter-systemic, interpersonal) truth is also to constitute one's identity.[145] And this is extremely important, he cautions. It eventually requires founding the relationship between the I and the Other on the open undisguised truth, which becomes a precondition for the true equal respect. Weiler explains how only an uncompromising statement about the truth of the I enables full recognition of that identity. Only that truly constitutes the I. At the same time it is crucial to understand, Weiler continues, that it is only such a constituting of the true I that inevitably also draws the line and discovers the Other in his/her genuine Otherness. That is, it also

[136] This is relevant both, in the interpersonal as well as inter-systemic sense of dealing with the "other": for constitutional discourse between Europeans themselves as well as between Europeans and non-Europeans, and for constitutional discourse between the different European states as well as between Europe and its relation with the rest of the world. Thanks to Joseph Weiler for a clarifying exchange on this point (see n 127).

[137] Weiler (n 5) at 106. [138] Weiler (n 5) at 106. [139] Weiler (n 5) at 106.

[140] Weiler (n 5) at 108. [141] Weiler (n 5) at 108.

[142] See Chapter 2, pp. 57–60. [143] See Chapter 2, pp. 36–7 and n 29.

[144] Weiler (n 5) at 106. [145] Weiler (n 5) at 106.

constitutes him/her as the *true* Other—either in the individual or collective sense—and recognizes that Otherness and its identity in its authentic uniqueness. The true I and the true Other not "only happen to exist within social reality; from an ontological point of view they are necessary and condition the very existence of one another."[146] The uncompromisingly external assertion of truth is thus actually precisely what constitutes the I and the Other. It is a necessary precondition, in Weiler's view, to any true equal respect. Indeed, the Other may wonder how someone who is not strong and open enough to genuinely declare, and thus respect, the truth of his/her own deepest beliefs could possibly be able truly to respect the beliefs of the Other, which are often radically different from his/her own.[147] Any respect of this kind, the argument seems to imply, would neither be truly genuine nor truly full. We have thus just exposed here Weiler's key assumption, which is contrary to Walker's, that the external truth of his substantive building blocks at the meta-level enables rather than diminishes the highest degree of equal respect. "At the end it turns out that it is precisely the uncompromising proposition of truth... that represents the most careful way for assuring respect of an identity, of the uniqueness of the I and the uniqueness of the Other."[148]

Secondly, Weiler assumes that such pluralism also facilitates realization of *autonomy* to the highest degree. He acknowledges that the objective truth of his substantive building blocks is ultimately grounded in the transcendental domain. For him, their sound dimensions are the very representation in the constitutional domain of the idea that we are all born in the image of God and that, hence, one shall love the "other", in his *otherness*, as one loves oneself.[149] A different interpretation would be a misrepresentation of his view.[150] However, if the substantive building blocks are ultimately grounded in such transcendental truth, this might be thought to cut against the autonomy of those who feel that this is being imposed upon them at the meta-constitutional level. It might therefore seem that something thinner would allow more space for the value of autonomy, as exemplified once

146 Weiler (n 5) at 106–7.

147 Weiler (n 5) at 107: "How would he who has no respect for his own identity be able to have it even in relation to that of my own?"

148 Weiler (n 5) at 108.

149 The key command from Leviticus, on which Weiler ultimately rests his whole conception of constitutional pluralism, provides: "But the stranger that dwelleth with you shall be unto you as one born among you, and thou shalt love him as thyself; for ye were strangers in the land of Egypt: I am the Lord your God." It is also telling in this sense that Weiler's title of his monograph, *The Constitution of Europe*, as initially proposed to the publisher, was *In the Image of God*. I am indebted to Joseph Weiler for sharing this further insight, and for a discussion on this point of the very ultimate justification underlying his building blocks and so his particular "decent life" as the end of Europe's constitutionalism (see n 127).

150 Indeed, it may even be questioned how far Weiler personally believes that there is a *sufficiently strong* secular equivalent that he keeps adding to the theistic underpinning. Cf J. Waldron, *God, Locke and Equality: Christian Foundations in Locke's Political Thought* (Cambridge: Cambridge University Press, 2002). Weiler seems to be adding the phrase "and the secular equivalent" in order that *those who thought* there was such a sufficiently strong underpinning could freely endorse *it*. I am indebted to Joseph Weiler for a discussion on this point that led to this explication of his position as described (see n 127).

again by Walker's epistemic pluralism. So how, one might ask, does substantive pluralism not compromise but enhance autonomy?

The first part of Weiler's answer begins by his explanations that the transcendental truth in which, in his view, the particular building blocks are grounded, is proposed rather than imposed ultimately. While he asserts the uncompromising validity of the particular building blocks, and does not ultimately subscribe to the secular alternative,[151] he nevertheless adds the latter and considers it externally valid in the constitutional domain. This is precisely because his metaphysical justification itself teaches that the very nature of its own external truth is that it allows for a refusal of itself. It is this position that fully explains his ongoing parallel endorsement in his texts of the alternative laic foundation as regards religious boundaries, or of the secular equivalent to the particular metaphysical vision that refines pluralistically national boundaries. It is this that explains also the possible rejection of the entire pluralist arrangement and exit from a pluralist Europe. For Weiler, this necessary freedom to "say no even to God," this "truth about the truth itself," is of "immense preciousness."[152] It is only by having this freedom that a human being truly becomes an autonomous being.[153]

Nevertheless, to have the choice to say "no" is a degree of autonomy which is, according to Weiler, *not yet the highest* realization of autonomy, though it is its necessary precondition. This is where the second part of his answer to how autonomy is enhanced by substantive pluralism begins. Weiler believes that it is to have the choice to say "no," but nonetheless to choose to accept the external valid ultimate truth as deriving from God, which opens doors to an even higher degree of autonomy. A fully autonomous submission, he explains, has the capacity to generate the highest attainable autonomy when

> obedience and submission are to a transcendent authority which is not of this world. In that very act of submission is encapsulated an emancipation and liberation from any authority of this world. By enslaving oneself to an authority outside of this world, one declares an independence of, and refusal to submit—in the ultimate sense—to, any authority of this world.[154]

Weiler attempts to illustrate this paradox of submission[155] by exemplifying how—even though there is in "kosher laws, Sabbath laws and the laws of purity in sexual relations" nothing to be explained for the purely rational idea of autonomy—the notion of autonomy as understood by the religious is wholly and inescapably dependent on some such submission. "By abstaining from eating everything that one fancies, one liberates oneself from that powerful part of our physical existence."[156] Similarly, "[b]y arranging life so as not to work on the Sabbath, one subjugates the even more powerful call of career and the workplace." By "refraining

151 See text at n 150.

152 Weiler (n 5) at 109–11, 119–22; exchange with J. Weiler (n 127).

153 Weiler (n 5) and exchange with him (n 127). For more on this concept of (individual and collective) autonomy, see Weiler's work in progress, *The Genesis of Our Civilisation: Five Essays on the Book of Genesis*.

154 Weiler (n 4) at 4.

155 Weiler (n 4) at 4.

156 Weiler (n 4) at 14.

from sexual abandon, even if loving, even if within wedlock, one asserts a measure of independence even over that exquisite part of our lives too."[157] The same paradox serves to explain why in the political context autonomy can be enhanced to the maximum extent only if the open acceptance of the *transcendentally* grounded building blocks that, for Weiler, form the moral/spiritual essence of European constitutionalism, is also available. An autonomous individual can say "no" to those transcendental values, but submitting oneself to them openly, to the religious individual, represents reaching a higher degree of autonomy, while the non-religious are free to follow their own non-transcendental variant so that the greater degree of autonomy in society is also to be understood in the sense that there is the appropriate choice for *both* of the groups. For Weiler, citizens of Europe should have the possibility of attaining such a higher degree of autonomy, in both senses described, openly. It is for this reason that he argues, in his, *Christian Europe*, that Europe should intensify its spiritual dimension[158] also in the constitutional domain, instead of excluding such values, as duly refined in the preceding sense, from its meta-constitution.

On this reading, the carefully balanced, substantive blocks are thus not understood as a relative limitation of autonomy but as the very realization of it. For Weiler the highest degree of autonomy is not only about having choice, but also in part about what one does with that choice.[159] In a similar vein we have seen that, for him, these substantive blocks do not compromise the value of equal respect, but facilitate its enhancement to the highest degree, albeit without imposition.

It can be concluded that our identification of the meta-constitutional values underlying Weiler's substantive pluralism reveals a very different picture from that depicted by epistemic pluralism. For advocates of the latter theory, it is only the *mere* procedurally defined reciprocity that is entrenched as externally valid at the meta-constitutional level. Except for the ascetic version of equal respect and autonomy, all other values are relegated to a lower rank of constitutional priority. The picture under substantive pluralism is, by way of contrast, that there are several different substantive values entrenched at the meta-level, which form a coherent whole together with the more substantively understood values of autonomy and equal respect. The substantive values constituted by the building blocks are inseparably bound up with those of autonomy and equal respect in the manner discussed.[160] The consequence is that there is a cluster of externally valid and mutually dependent values underlying substantive pluralism, as opposed to a single externally valid priority Eigenvalue underpinning epistemic pluralism.

Clearly, epistemic and substantive pluralism rely on some very different assumptions. Epistemic pluralism sees the ultimate purpose of (constitutional) politics as providing a framework for resolving our different views in a way that does not externally privilege any of them. This presumes that its Eigenvalue, which is the

[157] Weiler (n 4) at 14–15.
[158] Weiler (n 5), Part Three entitled "'The New Things'...! European Spirituality", 125–51.
[159] I am indebted to Joseph Weiler for the insight into this point (see n 127).
[160] Exchange with Weiler, n 127.

mere procedurally defined reciprocity, is the only externally valid value. It also presumes that this self-evidently assures the highest degree of neutrality and so the highest degree of equal respect and autonomy. This assumption is taken for granted as uncontroversial. We can now see that Weiler's substantive pluralism is premised upon significantly different underlying assumptions of the highest equal respect and autonomy. This goes in hand with his different understanding of the ultimate goal of European constitutionalism. The latter is above all in securing the decent life, as realized through the substantive values which constitute Weiler's building blocks, and which are for him ultimately grounded in transcendental justification. Whether or not this equally controversial approach can succeed (the question is further addressed in Chapter 8), it is internally coherent. It also engages in an argument against its competing accounts on the deeper ethical/moral level and does not close itself off from that orientation. This is different from the current default strategy as assumed under epistemic pluralism, even though the latter might just as well be refined so as to open itself and then attempt to defend its own different assumption on openly ethical/moral grounds. Having prepared both theories for the inter-theoretical assessment, we shall return to the different underlying assumptions in Walker's and Weiler's work in Chapter 8.

4

Interpretive and Participative Pluralism

1. Explaining the Theory

1.1 Its basis and orientation

Miguel Maduro is another author who deals with the question concerning the best conception of constitutionalism in Europe. He explicitly rejects the traditional—monist—variant as the only right or superior version of this concept, and instead declares himself to be the follower of the pluralist alternative. Like the three authors before him—MacCormick, Walker, and Weiler—he approves of MacCormick's abstract general notion of heterarchically coexisting constitutional authorities in Europe (those of the nation-states and the EU) of which neither is the ultimate or superior (source of) authority over the other. The analysis will nonetheless show that the actual version of constitutional pluralism Maduro proposes is unlike any one of those examined thus far. While briefly endorsing no more than the most abstract version of the pluralist idea just mentioned, Maduro does not then focus primarily on the more extensive explication of such theoretical foundations themselves. It can be discerned from various parts of his scholarship that his focus is rather on how pluralism might operate in practice—how it dictates both (1) a different type of constitutional interpretation (EU law included) in any of Europe's constitutional orders, and (2) a different way of defining participation and representation in such orders under the new pluralist framework. From this more practical orientation it is then possible to observe in retrospect the emergence of another particular version of constitutional heterarchy.

Maduro works under the proposition that there is a diversity of voices coming from different constitutional actors in Europe (explanatory pluralism), not only as with regards to the dilemma of final decision-making authority, as he remarks, but also as to constitutional issues in general.[1] He does not differentiate between second and first-order constitutional claims, and maintains that these different and often conflicting voices *ought not* to be understood as in a hierarchical relationship *inter se* (normative pluralism).[2] He suggests that we need to discover how to manage the non-hierarchical relationship between them so as to gain from that diversity, without at the same time generating conflicts that ultimately could destroy those legal orders

[1] M. Maduro, "Contrapunctual Law: Europe's Constitutional Pluralism in Action" in N. Walker (ed.), *Sovereignty in Transition* (Oxford: Hart Publishing, 2003) 501.

[2] Maduro (n 1) at 522–3.

and the values they nourish.[3] For Maduro, it is a common European legal order that should be understood as integrating—in a specific, non-hierarchical way—these voices and claims from both national and EU constitutionalism.[4]

A particular synthesis of Maduro's several contributions on the topic of European constitutionalism, as will be attempted in this chapter, allows one to observe how this common European legal order—or better, Europe's common meta-constitutionalism—comprises two main pluralistic dimensions. The first is concerned with a set of principles ("framework principles")[5] that derive from his version of interpretive pluralism and is examined in subsection 1.2. The other is a specific participation/representation-enhancing dimension to this meta-constitutional order that springs from what I will characterize as Maduro's "participative pluralism." This one is analysed in subsection 1.3. We will see that both pluralist dimensions, though distinct, are also linked to each other in a specific way. They are complementary and should be seen as together representing Maduro's comprehensive conception of constitutional pluralism. It will also be observed how such a conception belongs to the theme of the *how*, rather than the *what*, as delineated by our Ariadne's Thread at the inception of the mapping analysis (section 2). Maduro's particular conception within this sector of the pluralist labyrinth will then further determine also his position as regards the *who*, that is, his conception of pluralism with respect to the narrower issue of "who decides who decides," which will also be discussed in section 2 of this chapter. All this will be followed by section 3 and its general intra-theoretical assessment of Maduro's version of pluralism (and of some other versions that fall within his genre) with a view to preparing the theory for the inter-theoretical assessment in Chapter 8.

1.2 Interpretive pluralism

The framework principles leading to Maduro's version of interpretive pluralism are about determining the common basis for discourse among the various constitutional actors in Europe. They function as rules of interpretation. "For pluralism to be viable in a context of a coherent legal order," Maduro thus writes, "there must be a common basis for discourse." He explains that "[s]uch a basis is a set of principles shared by all the participants that, while respecting their competing claims of authority, guarantees the coherence and integrity of the European legal order."[6] This commitment is voluntary, but still, if constitutional pluralism is to succeed, all constitutional actors in Europe must commit themselves to these principles. In this sense, the framework principles may still be presented as a limit to pluralism. However, Maduro's position is that this particular limit to pluralism is necessary in order to allow pluralism the largest possible remit.[7]

The first such common rule (or "framework principle") is the requirement that the relationship between constitutional actors in Europe be understood in particular pluralist terms. Every constitutional order must respect the identity of the other

3 Maduro (n 1) at 523–4.
4 Maduro (n 1) at 524.
5 Maduro (n 1) at 524, 529.
6 Maduro (n 1) at 524.
7 Maduro (n 1) at 524.

legal orders. For Maduro, this means that it must be for every order itself to determine its own identity, but this must not be affirmed in a manner that challenges either the identity of the other legal orders, or the pluralist ethos itself.[8] Thus, "[i]dentity is lost if it is not self-determined," while at the same time "such self-determination should not dispute the self-determined identity of the other legal orders."[9] This requires that in the process of reasoning and decision-making, constitutional actors take each other into account and adjust to each other's different but equally legitimate claims.[10]

But how exactly could identity be fully self-determined and, by this very act, not also dispute and challenge the other identities that seem clearly contrary to it? In other words, what exactly is meant, under Maduro's conception, by "taking into account" and "adjusting to" each other's identities? This can be made clearer after analysing two further interpretive rules (framework principles) that his conception introduces.

The second interpretive rule is the requirement that every constitutional actor who engages in the process of interpretation be "obliged to reason and justify its decision in the context of a coherent and integrated legal order."[11] Maduro believes that even in a plural situation of competing constitutional claims it is possible to have a coherent legal order, but only as long as all the participants share the same commitment to such a coherent order, which entails adjusting their competing views in accordance with some minimal set of discourse principles.[12] Hence, one such principle, he says, must be to submit one's claims to the requirement of a coherent construction of the common order.[13] Maduro emphasizes that this coherence must be assured both vertically as well as horizontally. "When national courts apply EU law," in other words, "they must do so in such a manner as to make those decisions fit the decision taken by the European Court of Justice [vertical] but also other national courts [horizontal]."[14] The latter requirement of horizontal coherence is seen as crucial because such direct exchange between national courts does not appear to be current practice of the courts in different member states.[15] For Maduro this is problematic as it opens the door to fragmentation of the European constitutional order.[16]

The requirement of coherence is to prevent, or at least reduce, the potential for erosion of European law by national deviations from it. It seems that in the same way some universalized argumentation and justification would also need to be employed by European constitutional interpreters.[17] We can see that the idea of coherence implies at least the basic form of universalization. The latter functions as

[8] Maduro (n 1) at 526.

[9] Maduro (n 1) at 526. See also M. Maduro, "European Constitution: What if This is as Good as It Gets?" in J. Weiler and M. Wind (eds), *European Constitutionalism Beyond the State* (Cambridge: Cambridge University Press, 2003) 99.

[10] Maduro (n 1) at 526.

[11] M. Maduro, "The Heteronyms of European Law" (1999) 5 ELJ 160, 167; cf Maduro (n 1) at 533.

[12] Maduro (n 1) at 527.

[13] Maduro (n 1) at 527.

[14] Maduro (n 1) at 528.

[15] Maduro (n 1) at 529.

[16] Maduro (n 1) at 529.

[17] Maduro (n 1) at 524.

a constraint on constitutional interpreters and comes in the form of a refined interpretive question. The right question is no longer what would be the best decision for a particular constitutional order (identity) itself. It is rather that of which decision would be the best one for *all* of the European constitutional orders (identities)—national as well as supranational, and in the vertical as well as horizontal sense. That is, the answer to the new interpretive question will need to be in the spirit of the Golden Rule ("do unto others as you would have them do unto you"), and not in the light of a mere self-centered or partial perspective of any particular constitutional order.

The universalization requirement may be necessary to attain the desired end, but is not sufficient to attain the desired end under which self-determination of an identity does not at the same time challenge or dispute other identities that oppose it. It seems that each time I engage in the inquiry over the question of what is best for us all, I could still be challenging aspects of other constitutional identities with which I disagreed. At least, there is nothing in the basic requirement of universalization, as inherent in coherence, that prevents me from concluding—from the perspective of what is good for us all—that certain opposing views are wrong. To be sure, I will be constrained in a way that I was not before by views emanating from within other systems, and they might well shape my own position at least to a degree. However, this does not alter the fact that other constitutional identities can still be challenged and disputed by my own inquiry into them. The point is not just one of theoretical concern, since under the regime of such a still relatively open interpretive constraint one could still dispute other identities to a *significant* degree. "Do unto others as you would have them do unto you" does not necessarily rule out the universalization of those norms that seem acceptable to a radical but always coherent "consistent fanatic," to give R. M. Hare's example.[18]

On my reading, Maduro does attempt to close this gap. He seems to imply a further requirement of a stricter degree of universalization than that implicit in the concept of coherence. While coherence is described by Maduro as the second of the common rules of the discourse, he treats the principle of universalizability as the third and special one of these rules, while also describing it as the "further framework principle":[19]

> any judicial body (national or European) should be obliged to reason and justify its decisions in the context of a coherent and integrated European legal order. However, for that to be possible and in order to satisfy the requirement of equality in the competing determinations of EU law, any national decisions on EU law should be argued in "universal" terms . . . Such decisions must be grounded in a doctrine that could be applied by any other national court in similar situations. If national courts become aware that the decisions they take will become part of European law as interpreted by the "community" of European and national courts, they will internalise in their decisions the consequences for future cases in other

[18] R. Hare, *Freedom and Reason* (Oxford: Oxford University Press, 1965) ch 9. Cf R. Forst, *Contexts of Justice: Political Philosophy beyond Liberalism and Communitarianism*, tr. J. Farrell (Berkeley, CA: University of California Press, 2002) 195.

[19] Maduro (n 1) at 529.

national courts and the system as a whole. This will prevent national courts from using the autonomy of their legal systems as a form of evasion and free-riding and will engage the different national courts and the ECJ in a true discourse and coherent construction of the EU legal order.[20]

Although this language could probably be interpreted in different ways, it nevertheless seems to imply a degree of universalization higher than the basic one. If the universalization Maduro has in mind really is a "further framework principle,"[21] and one that could prevent erosion of EU law, which is, as we have seen, still left significantly unconstrained even under the regime of basic universalization, then this must mean acceptance of a kind of *inter-subjective* type of universalization.[22]

This is only possible through an even more specific and refined interpretive question. None of the constitutional systems is called to dispute (second-guess) self-determinations by other such regimes as declared by each of those regimes themselves, but must treat all such self-determined declarations as simply given positions from which to inquire what could be the best common answer for us from the point of view of all *these unquestioned* positions. The even-more refined interpretive question thus becomes: given my position, and given the different position(s) of the other side(s), which I am not called to question and second-guess, what would be the best common decision to be adopted *for all* of us and as seen from the *actual point of view of each of us*? The idea is that my answer to that question, while not challenging and disputing the equally legitimate identities of others, at the same time also represents a special accommodation from my side. It is an answer that the other sides could hypothetically also accommodate, since it would be reasoned for our community from the point of view of each of the *unchallenged* and *undisputed* identities.[23] Only under such type of universalization, which leaves determination of identity wholly to its own identity holder, might we conclude that the identities still remain *self*-determined, but also *accommodated inter se*. Only the inter-subjective reading of Maduro's principle of universalization thus seems reconcilable with his particular understanding of the first framework principle (ie the requirement of pluralism itself) under which identity must be at the same time both self-determined, because otherwise lost, and not unadjusted to others, because otherwise it would dispute the self-determinations of identities by those others.[24]

Of course, Maduro recognizes that even under this type of universalization, national deviations are still possible. However, the point is that decisions would be

[20] Maduro (n 1) at 529–30.

[21] Maduro (n 1) at 529. Maduro also characterizes it as "another principle," ie the principle *in addition* to the principle of coherence which he defines first (see Maduro (n 1) at 529).

[22] Cf J. Habermas, *The Inclusion of the Other: Studies in Political Theory* (3rd edn, Cambridge, MA: The MIT Press, 2001) 31.

[23] Reasons produced by this type of inter-subjective interpretive thinking are said to be reasons that are justified *between* subjects of a universal and coherent order, as opposed to reasons that justify *themselves* in the context of a coherent order under "just" basic universalization. In contrast to the latter, the inter-subjectively recognized reasons are said to be "reasons we can share" (Forst (n 18) at 194).

[24] I am indebted to Miguel Maduro for a discussion that enabled me to confirm and elaborate this point—that it is this particular *inter-subjective* reading of universalization that captures his idea most accurately (ECJ, Luxembourg, June 2006).

incomparably more inclusive than under a system without such universalization,[25] and the degree of inclusiveness would be such as to prevent erosion of the EU legal order.[26]

What remains puzzling is that while Maduro applies his principle of coherence explicitly to both the European as well as national order,[27] he only speaks of the national judicial bodies when explaining his further principle of universalizability.[28] On the face of it, this would mean that, while the national constitutional actors are required to act according to the inter-subjective universalization, the European ones would in their interpretations need to apply only the basic type of universalization implicit in Maduro's principle of coherence. Indeed, when further explaining what universalization means, he curiously continues to speak only of national courts. Perhaps it is just coincidence that the European actors are not mentioned in this context. But perhaps, and despite, the lack of Maduro's explicit explanation, this indeed means that the different types of universalization are required for both types of constitutional actors while this distinction is yet to be explained by a specific argument.[29]

One way or the other, Maduro's theory is a typical example of what I shall characterize as "interpretive pluralism." Interpretive pluralism is a theory concerned with the search for the right interpretive question which constitutional actors need to ask themselves in their process of constitutional interpretation if they are to make decisions correctly and legitimately. Such an interpretive formula is meant to apply throughout all different issues that arise, and the theory does not engage in more direct substantive argument as to the best answers to such specific issues. Engagement in the more substantive domain is left to the interpreters, and thus the constitutional identity-holders themselves, provided that they pose the right type of interpretive question.

It is in this sense that Maduro's interpretive pluralism then obviously differs from the substantive pluralism of Joseph Weiler. While in Maduro the identity holders themselves need to be understood as determining their own identities, in Weiler's theory it is Weiler himself who—to a considerably greater degree—enters the discourse over the more proper substantive dimensions to national and European constitutional identities. To be sure, interpretive pluralism is, of course, also substantive in its basic and general normative premise prescribing that the "other" be respected and his view taken into account. Nevertheless, while including that abstract pluralist premise, it is substantive, not interpretive, pluralism that also engages in a much more comprehensive further discourse on the level of the direct

[25] Maduro (n 9) at 99–100. [26] Maduro (n 9) at 99–100.

[27] Maduro (n 1) at 529–30. [28] Maduro (n 1) at 529–30.

[29] My initial dilemma on this point has been resolved. It is actually more of a coincidence that Maduro did not include the EU courts in his discussion of the principle of universalizability. When writing that part of the article I understand that the immediate issue he had in view was the problem of erosion of EU law coming from the horizontal side of the various national courts providing different interpretations of EU law. However, his statements about the universalizability requirement between the national actors should nonetheless be read as applying to the EU side and its actors as well. I am indebted to Miguel Maduro for this clarification (see n 24).

external determination, with regard to the right content (the *what*) of constitutional identities. That is its very goal and orientation. By contrast, interpretive pluralism "only" engages in a discourse as to which are the right *types* of questions to be asked by an interpreter when dealing with issues of rightness and truth. It does so with a goal of answering a slightly different research question—that of *how* to construct a framework that would in some best way enable the constitutional identity holders to *themselves* determine that content of their constitutional identities. Interpretive pluralism thus, to a significant degree, diverts from the more substantive discourse and its corresponding external determination of the right constitutional identities. That is *its* very orientation. To borrow Frank Michelman's characterizations, interpretive pluralism is dealing more with a "test property" than with a "target property."[30] Weiler's substantive pluralism, by contrast, works to a much greater degree on the level of the target property itself, when he himself engages in defining the "true"[31] and more "authentic"[32] parts of Europe's heterarchical constitutional identities. It is in this sense in which it could be said that substantive pluralism is more substantive than interpretive pluralism. But, of course, the distinction here is a matter of degree.[33]

This serves to confirm that Maduro's interpretive pluralism works within the sphere of the *how* of constitutional discourse, as one of the three distinct spheres of pluralism delineated by our decoding tool. It does not itself enter into the substantive sphere of the *what* of that discourse, nor does it directly deal with the question of who decides who decides, which was characterized as the sphere of the *who*.[34]

1.3 Participative pluralism

The framework principles described in the previous subsection are rules of interpretation. They are meant to facilitate the proper horizontal as well as vertical constitutional discourse across Europe, and so constitute part of the common basis of that discourse. In addition to those interpretive principles, Maduro seems also to assume another dimension that needs to be considered for that discourse to be meaningful, and to achieve its purpose. This dimension, too, would impact upon the common basis of the pluralist discourse, that is, Europe's meta-constitutionalism as understood by Maduro, and is indeed central to his pluralist vision.

This dimension concerns improvements of democratic processes. More precisely, it is about enhancing participation and representation by the common constitutional discourse. I would argue that Maduro's recent scholarship implicitly

[30] F. Michelman, "Dilemmas of Belonging: Moral Truth, Human Rights, and Why We Might Not Want a Representative Judiciary" (2000) 47 UCLA Law Review 1221, 1244.

[31] J. Weiler, *The Constitution of Europe* (Cambridge: Cambridge University Press, 1999) 343.

[32] Weiler (n 31) at 343. [33] Michelman (n 30) at fn 68.

[34] But this is not to say that Maduro's theory does not deal with the question of who decides who decides. As we will observe in section 2 of this chapter, Maduro's interpretive pluralism indirectly determines also his view with respect to that question.

links this dimension to his theory of constitutional pluralism.[35] It is in this democratic added value that his conception of constitutional pluralism must ultimately be grounded: "precisely in here . . . we can find the basis for the legitimacy of Europe's claim to independent political authority and to be a community of open and undetermined political goals."[36] Maduro argues that there are at least three spheres in which European constitutionalism could and should enhance representation and participation across Europe.

Firstly, the existence and further development of European constitutionalism could enhance our representation and participation in the *transnational European sphere*. National democracies no longer control many decision-making processes, which, however, have serious impact on life within a national polity, but take place in spheres beyond its borders.[37] One of the legitimacy deficits, Maduro notes, has to do with the fact that the EU order tends to be mainly the domain of an elite.[38] He explains, for instance, that "the transaction and information costs involved in EU law litigation tend to promote the participation of a particular, elite group of litigants in the construction of EU law."[39] "These litigants," he complains, "often coincide with multi-national companies and are supported by cross-national legal strategies while, for example, national court involvement in this litigation does not benefit from the same cross-national perspective or coordination."[40] There is also the question of whether "all national courts participate in an equal manner and [whether] they all have equal bargaining power."[41] Or is it instead that "the European Court of Justice develops privileged partners for dialogue," which would correspond to "a democratic deficit in European legal discourse"?[42] National constitutionalism is unable by itself to cure such legitimacy deficits that occur in the transnational sphere while significantly affecting life within its own borders. And yet, it seems that in these processes that escape national democracies, the modern citizen must have a voice too, and an equal one, if democracy is to be taken seriously. The pluralist constitutional discourse that Maduro envisions therefore needs to be such as to promote the broadest and most equal participation possible. Specific transnational channels for democracy must be cleared, and new channels must be created. These would constitutionalize a more inclusive and fair participation and representation at the transnational level. And since this goes beyond the reach and capacity of mere national constitutionalism, it is precisely European constitutionalism—in its meta-pluralist dimension—that can actually help here

[35] "But this constitutional pluralism must not simply be about regulating the question of ultimate authority between national and EU constitutions. It must be grounded on a particular understanding of the value to be derived from this plurality of constitutional sources and of the relationship between EU and national political communities" (M. Maduro, "How Constitutional Can the European Union Be? The Tension between Intergovernmentalism and Constitutionalism in the European Union" in J. Weiler and C. Eisgruber (eds), *Altneuland: The EU Constitution in a Contextual Perspective* (2004) Jean Monnet Working Paper No 5/04, 27). Cf Maduro (n 1) at 527.

[36] M. Maduro, "Where to Look for Legitimacy?" in E. Eriksen et al. (eds), *Constitution Making and Democratic Legitimacy* (2002) Arena Working Paper No 5/2002, 106.

[37] Maduro (n 36) at 107; cf Maduro (n 35) at 28; Maduro (n 9) at 83.

[38] Maduro (n 1) at 527. [39] Maduro (n 1) at 527. [40] Maduro (n 1) at 527.

[41] Maduro (n 1) at 527. [42] Maduro (n 1) at 527.

and bring added value to democratic deliberative inclusiveness. Or so the argument seems to imply.

Secondly, not only in the transnational sphere, but also in the sphere *between national democracies*, European constitutionalism can and should enhance representation and participation. "[I]t has always been true," Maduro writes, "that national democracy excludes from participation and representation in the national political processes many interests which are affected by its decisions."[43] That is, there is a degree of discrepancy between "the democratic polities in which one participates and the democratic polities that affect us."[44] Correspondingly, national democracies cannot legitimize the different decision-making processes of other national democracies that affect our lives, and also "cannot cope with our desire to be involved in different polities."[45] So within this sphere, too, we can observe the deficit in participation and representation under the current regime of national democracies and their traditional, monistic understanding of constitutionalism.[46] For Maduro, this is not compatible with "the claims of the modern citizen to have a voice in any polity that affects him or her and even to have a choice between different polities."[47]

Once more it is believed that European constitutionalism—if understood through the common pluralist conception proposed as best for the new Europe—can and should bring the added democratic value in this sphere as well. One result of such a plural constitutional conception could be, for instance, that we would "no longer [be] prisoners of our original polity" and would instead be able to "choose to live among a variety of polities."[48] Maduro argues that such a right to choose among polities is "a new form of democratic participation" introduced by his pluralist conception.[49] In this sense he refers to direct enhancement by EU law of constitutional rights of participation in any national polity in which one chooses to reside.[50] Moreover, EU law indirectly provides us also with constitutional rights of enhanced representation of our interests affected by other national polities: "many of the rights granted by EC market integration rules and the principle of non-discrimination on the basis of nationality can be conceived as such."[51] Here, Maduro specifically refers to his particular construction of EU economic law, which "should be conceived of as providing the European citizen not only with economic rights but with political rights to have their interests taken into account in non-domestic national political processes."[52] These novel features of the pluralist understanding of constitutionalism, he concludes, "promote the constitutional ideals of full representation and participation" within the second sphere.[53]

[43] Maduro (n 36) at 107; Maduro (n 35) at 28; Maduro (n 9) at 83.
[44] Maduro (n 36) at 107; Maduro (n 35) at 28; Maduro (n 9) at 83.
[45] Maduro (n 36) at 107; Maduro (n 35) at 28; Maduro (n 9) at 83.
[46] Maduro (n 36) at 108; Maduro (n 9) at 85.
[47] Maduro (n 36) at 107; cf Maduro (n 35) at 28–9.
[48] Maduro (n 9) at 85.
[49] Maduro (n 36) at 108.
[50] Maduro (n 36) at 108.
[51] Maduro (n 9) at 85.
[52] Maduro (n 9) at 85. Cf M. Maduro, "We the Court: The European Court of Justice and the European Economic Constitution (Oxford: Hart Publishing, 1998) 169–73.
[53] Maduro (n 9) at 85.

Thirdly, Maduro believes that further legitimation for the EU's independent constitutional authority, and thus for the corresponding conception of pluralism, lies in the EU's ability to enhance representation and participation also in fully *internal national contexts.*[54] He contends that "even if the national polity is the only jurisdiction taken into account in measuring democracy, there is a democratic added value arising from European integration."[55] This is because even within national democracies there are malfunctions that cannot just be ignored.[56] Maduro exemplifies this theme by three related points that should, in his view, be made about modern democratic processes of parliamentary representation. Firstly, while appearing highly democratic on the surface, the traditional parliamentary political processes "may be captured by small concentrated interests" of a controlling national interest group, at the expense of "a dormant national majority."[57] Secondly, collective decision-making frequently takes place outside the formal political processes.[58] Thirdly, true representation and participation is actually dependant on variables far more complex than the mere mechanism of political participation through elections.[59] The key conclusion Maduro draws from all this is that in some cases, national political processes have become captives of particular interests, values, and assumptions that are *unduly* taken for granted.[60] "Economic protectionism and the frequent 'hijacking' of the powerful concept of national interest" serve as two examples of what Maduro has in mind when speaking of such an undue limiting of the "truly deliberative character of national democracies."[61]

According to this view, there are several concrete ways in which European constitutionalism can—and should—improve representation and participation in this fully internal sphere. It could do so especially by creating conditions for the "inclusion of foreign interests in the national political processes," which would "in many cases lead to the satisfaction of dispersed national interests that were previously under-represented in that national process."[62] This would raise the voice of the unduly suppressed domestic interests, as well as bring some that were previously wholly excluded from public discourse processes back into the domain of public deliberation, thus "correcting biases of the national political processes."[63] As a consequence, we would get a broader and more active representation of domestic interests. Indeed, it is European constitutionalism that can provide, for example through its offering of another channel for constitutional litigation that can be used by individuals, this "new form of voice" within domestic political processes.[64]

Moreover, the existence of EU constitutional authority provides for certain overarching constitutional rules regulating "inter-dependence and competition among States" within an economically integrating Europe.[65] Such a regulation of

[54] Maduro (n 36) at 109 in connection to 106. [55] Maduro (n 36) at 109.
[56] Maduro (n 36) at 107; cf Maduro (n 25) at 29; Maduro (n 9) at 93.
[57] Maduro (n 35) at 29; cf Maduro (n 36) at 109; Maduro (n 9) at 93–4.
[58] Maduro (n 35) at 29. [59] Maduro (n 35) at 29.
[60] Maduro (n 36) at 107; cf Maduro (n 9) at 93–4.
[61] Maduro (n 36) at 107–8; cf Maduro (n 35) at 29, and Maduro (n 9) at 93–4.
[62] Maduro (n 36) at 109. [63] Maduro (n 9) at 94; Maduro (n 36) at 109.
[64] Maduro (n 9) at 94. [65] Maduro (n 36) at 109.

interstate competition by the EU "should be used to prevent negative externalities (cross-national transfer of costs derived from national policy choices) that affect the accountability in national political processes."[66] This would similarly enhance true representation/participation within national democracies. And the same types of rules could also increase "national comparative information" as another channel through which EU constitutionalism should perfect national democratic processes.[67] In a similar way, the open method of coordination should be understood "as a new form of competition among States that can improve national deliberations on particular policies."[68]

After surveying, in addition, Maduro's idea of enhancing participation/representation in Europe, we are now in a position to constructively pull together the comprehensive picture of his constitutional pluralism. Recall Maduro's assertion that we need to discover how to manage the non-hierarchical relationship between the constitutional orders in Europe, so as to gain from that diversity without at the same time generating conflicts that could ultimately destroy those legal orders and the values they nourish.[69] We saw that it was the common European legal order that should, according to Maduro, be understood as integrating in the heterarchical pluralist way the validity claims of both national and EU constitutional law.[70] Based on the preceding analysis it can now be seen that this common European legal order—Maduro's meta-constitutionalism for Europe—has two main pluralistic dimensions, which determine the more concrete meaning of Maduro's constitutional heterarchy.[71] The first was the set of interpretive meta-principles that led to Maduro's version of "interpretive pluralism." The other dimension is the participation/representation enhancing aspect of this meta-constitutional order, and I characterize it as "participative pluralism." They both come from different parts of Maduro's scholarship, but should be combined here into this comprehensive vision of his pluralism.[72]

Participative pluralism, which concerns enhancing participation/representation, determines the normative course of this pluralism. In addition to the inclusive rules of interpretive pluralism, this normative compass thus cannot but itself become another necessary part of Maduro's common constitutional discourse. It is only on such a combined common meta-basis, or "framework"[73] as he calls it, that we can then engage in the construction of constitutional identities; argue for, and propose different substantive constitutional views. But it is not necessary that we agree on more:

> We only have to agree on having the debate and how we are going to have it. In other words, we must agree to discuss different conceptions of the common good relevant at the European level and we must accept a common framework for that discussion. It is here that deliberative constitutionalism becomes relevant.[74]

[66] Maduro (n 36) at 109. [67] Maduro (n 36) at 109. [68] Maduro (n 36) at 110.
[69] See pp. 102–3. [70] Pp. 103–4. [71] Pp. 102–3.
[72] I am indebted to Miguel Maduro for an exchange that helped clarify my reading of his conception on this point (see n 24).
[73] Maduro (n 35) at 53. [74] Maduro (n 35) at 53.

The key characteristic to note is the inherent link between the two pluralist dimensions. Interpretive pluralism would not seem to make much sense to Maduro without being set within the proper normative direction that participative pluralism sets. Even if constitutional actors played by the required interpretive rules, the discourse would be skewed and not really pluralist if there were significant deficiencies in the channels of enhanced participation and representation. Equally, under Maduro's conception, participative pluralism would also make little sense if by attempting to perfect participatory conditions, the actors did not play by the specific pluralism-enabling interpretive rules described under interpretive pluralism. A proper understanding of Maduro's constitutional pluralism thus indeed requires us to see that the two dimensions are integral parts of the common, comprehensive pluralist conception.

Yet, things cannot be so simple as they sound *in abstracto*. There is a dilemma here: this relationship between the two components of the common meta-framework leaves open the puzzle of which one prevails in case of conflict between the two. Is it interpretive pluralism with its rules of inter-subjective interpretation that should be given priority? Or should the more concrete participative minima, or some thereof, prevail, even if inter-subjective reasoning does not lead to them, as might possibly be the case? To resolve this dilemma, Maduro would explain that it is the enhanced participation and representation that is the ultimate purpose of his pluralism; the interpretive rules should, by contrast, be seen as a mechanism that best promotes this normative goal.[75] However, he would also insist that it is not that any of the participative/representational minima can be prescribed directly by the theory; that would represent too great an external intrusion and would unduly compromise his vision of true pluralism. They could only be reached through the use of the interpretive mechanism.[76] The hope is that by directly prescribing at the meta-level (external validity) merely the interpretive rules coupled with just the *general* requirement of taking into account the element of participation, the actors would then by themselves gradually come to adopt *some* sufficient set of participative minima as constituting a meaningful conception of constitutional pluralism under this theory. The examples described above about how pluralism could enhance participation are thus correctly to be understood precisely as mere *possible examples* to which such pluralism *could potentially* lead, and not as parts of the pluralist meta-constitutional framework itself. However, insofar as the interpretive mechanism does not then actually lead to some such enhanced minima of enhanced participation/representation, Maduro's pluralism does not have another solution to offer. He refuses to prescribe his normative content directly and thus to override the framework of interpretive rules.[77]

This is the entire version of Maduro's constitutional pluralism. It is grounded, as its author writes, "on a particular understanding of normative value to be derived from this plurality of constitutional sources and of the relationship between EU and

[75] I am indebted to Miguel Maduro for the exchanges that enabled me to elaborate on this point and the following two aspects of the theory (see n 24).

[76] Interview (see n 24).

[77] Interview (see n 24).

national political communities."[78] The particular normative value is the improved degree of democracy that such constitutional pluralism might be able to bring with respect to the three forms of democratic deficit as they appear in monistic statal constitutionalism. It is the "democratic added value" understood as a more fully inclusive discursive process among equals that has also the capacity for mutual correction of each constitutional actor's malfunctions.[79] While the latter, too, flows from the arrangement, it cannot be secured without participatory pluralism's conditions of truly free and open membership, or without the inclusive rules of interpretive pluralism.

2. Situating the Theory

We have seen how Maduro's interpretive pluralism, working within the sphere of the *how*, clearly differs from Weiler's substantive pluralism and its sphere of the *what*.[80] A similar observation could be made of Maduro's participative pluralism. Although this pluralist dimension might at first glance remind one of substantive pluralism as defined earlier in Weiler's proposal, it is actually distinct from the latter in an important sense.[81] To be sure, the *general* normative premise of enhancing broader participation and representation is substantive in nature, as are also the anticipated concrete democratic enhancements. However, even if Maduro's interpretive pluralism would indeed lead to the latter, this type of normative "substance" is still conceived exclusively in instrumental terms. It is understood solely as a means that would enable conditions in which the actors would then be in a position freely and on truly equal terms to *themselves* engage in substantive determinations of ends. Maduro insists on understanding the coexisting constitutional entities (the EU included)[82] in Europe emphatically as communities of "open and undetermined political goals."[83]

He is quite explicit in explaining how his proposed common conception of constitutionalism should be understood in these exclusively instrumental terms. When describing one of the presuppositions of his project, and specifically of his proposal for enhancement of participation and representation, he writes:

> The third assumption is probably the most contentious one . . . My view is that the broader goals of political communities derive from the co-ordination and satisfaction of individual preferences as judged by individuals themselves.[84]

[78] Maduro (n 35) at 28.

[79] Maduro (n 35) at 28; Maduro (n 9) at 80.

[80] Pp. 107–8.

[81] The following is in addition to the point that participative pluralism obviously differs from Weiler's substantive pluralism by not directly proposing itself as the best normative solution, but only doing so indirectly—via the mechanism of interpretive pluralism. See earlier at p. 113.

[82] Maduro (n 36) at 106; cf Walker's discussion of Maduro's point that the EU ought to be seen as a community of open and undetermined political goals, in N. Walker (ed.), *Sovereignty in Transition* (Oxford: Hart Publishing, 2003) 22, fn 53.

[83] Maduro (n 36) at 106.

[84] Maduro (n 9) at 80.

Maduro explains that he assumes so "even at the epistemological level," and continues:

In my view, not only outcomes but also processes are to be measured in terms of individual representation and participation. As a consequence, the democratic character of the political form of organization of the polity is not assessed [in Maduro's project] on the basis of whether its results meet the interests of individuals (which would always be measured by criteria independent of the individuals' preferences) but on whether such process grants effective representation and participation to all affected individuals.[85]

In contrast with this rhetoric, a great deal of Weiler's substance seems to be meant as an *end in itself*, and not as exclusively instrumental. Recall, for instance, how before launching the discussion of his substantive proposal, Weiler writes:

Democracy, dear friend, is not the end. It is but a means... The end is to live a life of decency, to honour our creation in the image of God, or the secular equivalent. A democracy, when all is said and done, is as good or bad as the people who belong to it. A democracy of vile people will be vile.[86]

What this "decency" actually means for Europe, according to Weiler, is then explicated in his discussion and proposal for the particular substantive building blocks and values behind them. Weiler's substantive proposal regarding the latter goes well beyond discussions of democracy understood in the narrower sense (full participation and representation within a political process), and engages directly in the discourse over particular substantive ends themselves. To a considerable extent this discourse is directly concerned with the "target property." By contrast, Maduro's participative pluralism remains exclusively at the level of the "test property" and reserves the discourse on direct substantive goals to the participants themselves. He would understand any such direct substantive proposals, coming from himself and going beyond the instrumental enhancement of equal participation and representation, as inevitably "measured by criteria independent of individuals' preferences" because not measured "by individuals themselves."[87]

It can clearly be concluded that not only the interpretive pluralist dimension but also the participative one—and so Maduro's whole conception of constitutional pluralism—works within the sphere of the *how* as discerned by Ariadne's Thread. The conception represents an attempt to build a framework theory at the level that would avoid the theory's own arbitration between different and opposing substantive *self*-determinations of constitutional identities by various constitutional orders and their actors. It thus deals with a different question—the *how* of the common constitutional discourse—from that of the more directly substantive discourse within the sphere of the *what*. Despite referring to the same term, Maduro's pluralism, which is primarily situated within its own sector of the labyrinth, thus

[85] Maduro (n 9) at 80.

[86] J. Weiler, "Europe: The Case against the Case of Statehood" (1998) 4 ELJ 43, 60; cf his, "In Defence of the Status Quo: Europe's Constitutional *Sonderweg*" in J. Weiler and M. Wind (eds), *European Constitutionalism beyond the State* (Cambridge: Cambridge University Press, 2003) 18.

[87] Maduro (n 9) at 80.

inevitably represents a significantly different concept than does the meaning of pluralism from, say, Weiler's sector of the *what*. Moreover, Maduro's meaning of the term, as presented so far, is also not yet the same as are those still other meanings of pluralism that deal with the theme of who decides who decides, the theme of the *who*.

The meaning of pluralism that is most closely compatible with Maduro's use of the term is that of Walker's epistemic pluralism. The theme of *how* is the same general theme within which Walker's meaning of pluralism is also situated. The *how*-type of common framework of constitutional discourse under interpretive/participative pluralism is nonetheless slightly thicker than that from epistemic pluralism. It does not entail only to ascetic mere reciprocity. The latter, as we saw, avoids external positing of any sacrosanct specific right interpretive question, be it at the second or first-order discourse level; it considers such a move as unduly stifling the full fluidity of the discourse. But Maduro's pluralism, while avoiding direct substantive discourse, does construct the right type of question to be asked in constitutional interpretation; hence the label of "interpretive pluralism." The distinction in relative thickness becomes even more obvious when we add the necessary participative dimension to Maduro's pluralism. The externally valid interpretive rules are thus joined by another general requirement of the actors to take into account the factor of participation/representation within the alternatives they consider. As we shall see later in this chapter, these differences between the two versions of constitutional pluralism lead to different particular versions of the Eigenvalue underlying both proposals.

Although the primary goal of Maduro's version of constitutional pluralism is the broad one (ie his contribution within the sphere of *how*), he too, like Walker and Weiler before him, also deals with the narrower issue of "who decides who decides." While Maduro's meaning of pluralism within this sphere of the *who* is clearly a different concept than his primary concept of pluralism from the sphere of the *how*, it is indirectly shaped by the latter.

Concomitant with Walker, and unlike Weiler, Maduro at first glance seems to propose that we have pluralism in this domain only when the question of "who decides who decides" remains open.[88] He believes that only by leaving the question open will we be able to fulfill, to the highest degree possible, the normative goal of mutual self-limitations and adjustments between systems.[89] In defending this claim he first reminds us that the concept of constitutionalism plays an important limiting role, and that this is also so within the traditional nation-state setting. However, Maduro maintains that within the latter we have not been able to achieve full realization of this goal, since the traditional understanding of constitutionalism "tends to concentrate power in a final authority through its hierarchical organisation."[90] And it is this very deficiency, Maduro concludes, that we now have a chance to correct in the new European constitutional context.[91]

[88] Maduro (n 1) at 522. [89] Maduro (n 1) at 522. [90] Maduro (n 1) at 522.

[91] Or in Maduro's own words: "In a multi-level or federal system it is the vertical or federal conception of constitutionalism (as a form of limited government at the State and federal level) that requires the issue of 'who decides who decides' to be left unsolved. Of course, all constitutional systems

This particular proposal for "leaving the question open" has been made at many places in Maduro's works,[92] including briefly in the central part of his, "Contrapunctual Law," where his broader notion of pluralism is primarily discussed. However, what appears puzzling is that at the end of the same work, Maduro then proposes something that is difficult to square with this position.

At the end of "Contrapunctual Law," after elaborating his broad theory of interpretive and participative pluralism, Maduro says he will "highlight the normative power of this model of constitutional pluralism in addressing some of the most pressing issues in the current European constitutional debate," one of which is the dilemma of "who decides who decides."[93] The core of his proposal is the following:

> In the first place, as stated above, I believe that any judicial body (national or European) would be obliged to reason and justify its decisions in the context of a coherent and integrated EU legal order. Secondly, both European and national legal orders must create the necessary mechanisms to adjust to the claims of authority of the other legal orders . . . In fact, I would argue that their [ie national courts'] claim of ultimate authority should only be exercised in the event of a systemic conflict arising between the European legal order and the integrity of the national constitution. In that case, national constitutional courts could still affirm their ultimate authority either at a moment of constitutional ratification or by creating a situation of constitutional exit. In the latter case, the constitutional conflict could be established by a national constitutional court in a specific case but would have to be of such importance as to affect the entire constitutional relationship between the European Union and the Member State and, therefore, to raise the issue of exit. Only such an understanding of national constitutional authority by national constitutional courts is capable of respecting the principles of contrapunctual law highlighted. In the exchange of this adjustment of the national constitutional claims of authority to the claim of authority of EU law, the European Court of Justice ought to recognise an enhanced role for national courts and national constitutionalism in the interpretation and application of EU law.[94]

It seems that according to this proposal, the national courts would have the final say in those cases that would cross the line just described. At the same time, in all other cases, the European Court of Justice would have the final say. So, could it be that, after all, Maduro is proposing just another division of the final authority? If this is the case, then it is contrary to his earlier and often-stated position that the "open question should be left open." If, however, Maduro sees his proposed division of the final authority as merely his own internal view within a range of possible interpretations, that is, if he recognizes that that arrangement is just one among many possible reasonable *interpretations* which must surely *all* be treated as legitimate, even if he internally happens to disagree with them, then he encounters another kind of problem. Namely, Maduro writes exactly the contrary: that "*only such* an

have historically developed forms of allocating the final authority as a way of preventing conflicts and guaranteeing that constitutional resolutions are accepted by all. But what if what makes the European legal order unique is that the open question should remain open?" (Maduro (n 1) at 522–3).

92 Maduro (n 11) at 166: "I prefer the Neil MacCormick's legal pluralism which leaves the open question open"; Maduro (n 9) at 97: "that requires the decision of 'who decides who decides' to be left open. The open question should be left open"; cf Maduro (n 1) at 522–3.

93 Maduro (n 1) at 531.

94 Maduro (n 1) at 533–4.

understanding of national constitutional authority by national constitutional courts [ie the division of final authority as he has just proposed] is capable of respecting the principles of contrapunctual law highlighted."[95]

It seems, therefore, that Maduro would either need to adjust his view concerning this latter proposal on "who decides who decides," and see it as just one among many equally reasonable and legitimate interpretations under the principles of contrapunctual law,[96] or else, his former position on this issue, which posited that the open question be left open, would need to be revised. It would then acknowledge that what is eventually proposed is just another, although specific, distribution of final authority. Under this option he would acknowledge that what he means by pluralism within the theme of the *who* is that the question of who decides is actually not left open. Both of these positions, as they now stand, however, do not seem to fit.

Given this challenge, the following seems to be the most coherent reading of Maduro's proposal.[97] The final decision-making authority is distributed between the European and member-state courts according to the nature of the conflict described above. Only in those *systemic* conflicts when the member-states are also prepared to raise the issue and risk of exit do the member-state courts have the final authority. In all other conflicts they have to defer to the final authority of the ECJ. The question of *who* is thus *not* "left open" in the conventional sense of the term, or as some other pluralists, such as Walker, have used that same term. However, the question *is* left open in a different and limited sense. It is still understood that it is for each of the two courts in conflict to interpret the boundary with *equal* authority—to decide whether a given case *does or does not constitute a conflict of systemic proportion*. This, too, is different from monism within the theme of the *who*. When read in this manner, Maduro's unique pluralist position is therefore different from the "radical pluralism" as endorsed at one point by Neil MacCormick,[98] according to which the confronting institutions are given no further rules to solve the conflict.[99] It also contradicts Walker's epistemic pluralism, which similarly maintains that we leave the question more radically open.[100] The difference comes from the rationale that only such a more intense normative limitation of conflict, as proposed by Maduro's particular normative divide, avoids sufficiently the risk of making pluralism non-viable. Indeed, Maduro's leaving of

[95] Maduro (n 1) at 534 (emphasis added).

[96] Of course, in this case his proposed division of final authority ceases to be part of his proposed pluralist proposal which national (and European) courts are meant to follow, and merely becomes one of the many possible and legitimate interpretations which these courts need not necessarily adopt and follow. That is, they might have their own internal views on this issue that would need to be treated by Maduro as equally legitimate and correct interpretations under the regime of principles of constitutional pluralism. And if the courts are not meant to necessarily follow Maduro's own interpretation, then his claim about presenting the "normative power of this model of constitutional pluralism in addressing some of the most pressing issues," loses its weight. That seems to go as part of the "price" of adjusting Maduro's conception in this way.

[97] I am indebted to Maduro for the exchanges that led to the elaboration of this point (see n 24).

[98] See pp. 187–9. But see also MacCormick's change of mind at a later point (pp. 188–9).

[99] See pp. 187–9.

[100] See pp. 51–3.

the *who* question open cannot be understood in the way this same phrase has been used by others. At the same time, it is also not the same as the meaning of pluralism that Weiler has in mind when he is working within the theme of the *who*. We saw that he envisions the resolution of conflict through the common institution explicitly entrusted with the final decision-making authority in jurisdictional conflict, where this institution is strictly pluralistically conceived so that it preserves equality and self-standing status of the confronting orders and is thus, in yet another sense, also unlike the situation under monism.

3. Towards the Assessment

Enhancing and securing equal participation and representation—the "added democratic value" that is said to underlie Maduro's normative theory—is actually Maduro's own version of the Eigenvalue of reciprocal equal respect and autonomy. We saw how there were no other externally valid building blocks in Maduro's conception of pluralism beyond the deliberately open meaning of the participative dimension and the mere instrumental rules of interpretation. Indeed, Maduro insisted that, if any substantive end was further elaborated and required by the theory itself, this would improperly interfere with his requirement of leaving constitutional communities to be entities of "open and undetermined political goals."[101] It would be improperly to propose something measured by criteria independent of the actors' own preferences because those would be measured not by the actors themselves.[102] There is thus no cluster of values within Maduro's vision of the meta-constitution for Europe. What seems to be ultimately underlying both participative and interpretive pluralism, is the one Eigenvalue of equal respect and its corresponding autonomy of the actors involved.[103]

Although there is in this an obvious general similarity with Walker's approach, this particular version of the Eigenvalue of equal respect is slightly different from that underlying epistemic pluralism. The difference corresponds to the difference in each theory's common external (inter-systemic) arrangement. Firstly, there is the participative dimension in Maduro's pluralism that points to a specific normative direction. Only if the actors gradually come to establish a sufficient set of relatively thick participative minima does Maduro's normative pluralism really succeed. It is implicit in this conception that the highest degree of equal respect and autonomy is reflected in the full participation and representation as envisioned by the normative goal. This meaning of the Eigenvalue is thicker than that of epistemic pluralism. Epistemic pluralism regards the highest equal respect and autonomy as being constituted by that theory's much thinner external minima of pluralism that

[101] Maduro (n 36) at 107. [102] Maduro (n 9) at 80.

[103] I am grateful to Miguel Maduro for an exchange that helped clarify my reading of his theory on this point (see n 24).

do not normatively limit themselves to the specific narrower goal of enhancing participation.

Secondly, the interpretive pluralist dimension in Maduro's conception also contributes its own part to this difference. We saw that, aiming at the highest possible degree of equal respect and autonomy between the actors within constitutional discourse, Maduro's interpretive pluralism then prescribes the *right type* of interpretive question to be asked in constitutional discourse. It is the use of this inter-subjective mechanism that is, in combination with the participative dimension previously mentioned, understood by Maduro as realizing the highest degree of equal respect and autonomy. This particular version of reciprocal equal respect is clearly different from that found in the Eigenvalue of epistemic pluralism which, by way of contrast, holds that the prescription of a particular kind of right interpretive question would already be too thick an external imposition on what should be a more open agonistic negotiation. On that view the sacrosanct question would unduly stifle the specifically agonistic type of debate which, as epistemic pluralism assumes, is the condition securing the highest possible degree of reciprocal equal respect and autonomy.

It can be concluded that Maduro's Eigenvalue of reciprocal equal respect is not the radically thin variant of mere reciprocity, such as the ascetic mere reciprocity of epistemic pluralism. His is a slightly more demanding, thicker version of mere reciprocity as the single priority value entrenched at the meta-constitutional level of Europe. It is based on the assumption that entrenchment of this slightly thicker meta-substratum corresponds to the highest realization of equal respect and autonomy. Only such an Eigenvalue constitutes the proper meaning of constitutional pluralism, according to Maduro's vision of the concept.

The reason for the two slightly different Eigenvalues behind Walker and Maduro's pluralisms seems to lie in the somewhat different orientations of the two projects. The specific normative orientation of Maduro's constitutional pluralism is enhancement of participation and representation (democracy), which he sees as the ultimate goal of Europe's constitutionalism. And he understands that this kind of goal—fully inclusive democracy—cannot be achieved solely by enhancing the scope of inclusion, but also requires that the participating subjects take into account the different impact that decisions might have on differently situated subjects. His focus is thus emphatically also on the intensity of inclusion.[104] But while Walker's project is clearly also related to participation/representation, his immediate goal and orientation is more on the even broader quest of redeeming constitutionalism from disagreement: that is, on finding the most neutral framework for as large a universe

[104] I am grateful to Miguel Maduro for this point. I understand that the emphasis on the "intensity of inclusion" is critical for understanding the particular content of his value of equal respect underpinning his pluralism. Without giving the element of intensity considerable significance it is not possible, on this reading, to develop the highest degree of the value of equal respect/autonomy and its corresponding state of fullest participation/representation that he has in mind. See n 24.

of existing claims as possible, which would not arbitrate between them beyond mere agonistic reciprocity. This means that such an agonic freedom would—more often than other similar approaches[105]—sacrifice the value of seemingly more reasonable claims for the sake of an agonic neutrality to all.[106] To be sure, both Walker and Maduro's variants of equal respect and autonomy are not only about widening the scope of inclusion for different subjects and their interests/claims but also about enhancing intensity of inclusion between the participants. They both require reciprocal treatment between the included subjects and their interests as opposed to some completely anarchical state of "negotiation" between them. Still, the difference is that Maduro's understanding of the highest realization of this value amounts to a thicker degree of external determination in relation to both the intensity of reciprocal inclusion as well as its scope.

Prioritization of this particular Eigenvalue at the meta-constitutional level also differs from Weiler's strategy. At this externally valid level where Maduro reserves the space for his particular version of the Eigenvalue of reciprocal equal respect, Weiler has, as we saw, a cluster of different values that he considers indispensable for any right conception of constitutional pluralism. This cluster of values flows from Weiler's own different understanding of the goal of his pluralist project and of Europe's constitutionalism as such. He has written several times that enhancement of democracy involving participation and representation cannot be enough: a "democracy of vile people will be vile"[107] even if it has participation and representation enhanced to the highest possible degree. Indeed, we saw that the goal of Weiler's pluralist project is not only to enhance democracy narrowly understood, but above all to determine the thicker substantive building blocks as representing the ultimate external truth of the decent life as the end in itself of European constitutionalism and of any superior conception of constitutional pluralism. Only such a substantive approach can, in Weiler's view, truly realize the highest degree of equal respect/autonomy as one of the values of the meta-level.[108]

Analysis reveals that Maduro's conception is controversial from the perspective of these alternative pluralist proposals. Its point of departure from the other two theories is its particular underlying Eigenvalue on which it is based. In this respect it is important to note that at this level the theory does not currently attempt to defend its superiority against the contending alternatives. This leads to the conclusion that, while the theory is elaborated and coherent, it is not yet defended in relation to its decisive underlying assumptions.[109] One who aims at establishing inter-theoretical superiority of this theory, will, at some stage, have to try to justify

[105] See pp. 47–8.

[106] Maduro, by contrast, wants to stress emphatically that the normative orientation underlying his conception and project of constitutional pluralism is to be understood as an openly biased, not a neutral one. I am indebted to him for this point. See n 24.

[107] Weiler (n 86) at 60.

[108] See pp. 92–3 and 96–101.

[109] One reason for this might be that—as I said in the Introduction—the pluralist authors seem to assume, generally, that their theories are much more similar, and mutually corroborating, than the mapping analysis shows them to be.

the superiority of its Eigenvalue in relation to the other two corresponding alternatives. This will be considered more fully in Chapter 8.

What has been explored so far refers specifically to Maduro's particular contribution to pluralism. But there is also a more general point that ought to be made concerning the rest of the sub-branch to which his theory belongs. Maduro's conception belongs to the group of interpretative pluralists. There are other authors, like Samantha Besson, Massimo La Torre, Mattias Kumm, and others, whose theories, or particular parts thereof, also belong to this same general group. Maduro, however, has come the furthest in my view; the other proposals seem inferior in that they share an even more profound difficulty of this group. That is, their principled understanding of pluralism in interpretive terms has not been elaborated to the level of sufficient concreteness so that it could be meaningfully assessed in light of the alternative proposals. I shall explain this in more detail after first having considered some of these contributions.

Samantha Besson has argued that according to the "European integrity principle," which she develops, "each jurisdiction or legislature in Europe, be it European or national, would have to do more than just speak with a single voice in its own legal order."[110] Namely, "it would have to try to do so in a way that is representative of the entire European political community's expressed legal views, thus revealing the true sense of constituting such a community in the face of diversity in Europe."[111] While having "this aim in mind" each authority would have to "take into account past laws and decisions of the other European and national authorities and try to adjust its own laws and decisions so as to make them fit with the former as much as possible."[112] With this, "it would confirm that it is one of the many national and European authorities to create and apply the law of complex and pluralist but single European legal order."[113] Understood in this way, the principle of European integrity would "ensure that European integration amounts to a truly dynamic and cooperative project in which dialog and mutual learning receive a central role in constituting a European political community."[114]

Although Besson does not develop it, she has in mind some form of reciprocal foundations, as she writes:

> This model of constitutional control builds upon judicial conversation [citing Weiler and Trachtman], but goes further than what is usually understood by these terms, as it results in true *cooperative constitutional control.* This may be done mainly through a form of mutual or reciprocal interpretation and justification. One sometimes also speaks of a "polycentered mode of judicial decision-making."[115]

While working on his own theory, which is primarily about the narrower question of "who decides who decides" (our sphere of *who*),[116] Mattias Kumm also touches

[110] S. Besson, "From European Integration to European Integrity: Should European Law Speak with Just One Voice?" (2004) 10 ELJ 257, 259.

[111] Besson (n 110) at 259.

[112] Besson (n 110) at 259.

[113] Besson (n 110) at 259.

[114] Besson (n 110) at 259.

[115] Besson (n 110) at 278.

[116] See Chapter 5, pp. 147–9.

on the broader sphere of the *how* and proposes the following elements of interpretive pluralism:

Additionally, the Court's handling of this standard must meet the *universalizability test*: It must exercise its review in a way that is compatible with other Member States Courts engaging in a comparable practice of review without undermining the coherence of the European Legal Order. The [German Federal Constitutional Court] is not the only court that plays the role of a subsidiary guardian of the European Legal Order. It is part of a community of interpreters and needs to take into account the different interpretive traditions in the community and the possibility of reasonable disagreement between them.[117]

Massimo La Torre, who made one of the earliest contributions to the topic, is also brief in his definition of interpretive pluralism. Still, one cannot miss the abstract interpretive pluralist dimension in that short definition. According to La Torre, pluralism in the new Europe is thus

to be meant... as a normative criterion which recommends that the judge (and the citizen) do not direct themselves solely to *one* source of law when in search of a regulation for a case. Legal pluralism would here mean a multiplication and differentiation of the sources of law or—said differently—of the various arguments which justify a certain course of action or a specific legal decision. Pluralism in this concept is moreover a criterion which implies the recommendation of a *comparative evaluation* of prescriptions and values and their interpretations according to a general rule of *integrity*. Rules receive their meaning from their reference to other ones.[118]

Now, the problem, in my view, with these and other principled proposals of interpretive pluralism is that they do not make it sufficiently clear which of the various stages or variations of universalization they actually propose. This renders any meaningful assessment difficult and problematic for the following reason.

When building the stages of universalization, the first stage is one at which all we have is fully idiosyncratic reasoning with no universalization at all. It means, for example, that a constitutional interpreter acts as an agent defending an idiosyncratic national tradition against the European Union. Such an interpreter would reject anything that comes from the EU and is contrary to the national tradition within which she or he interprets; the interpreter accepts only what comes from the EU, but is *not* contrary to the idiosyncratic national tradition and its exclusively self-centered perspective.

Stage two already involves subjective universalization.[119] Variants of the Golden Rule can be interpreted as: you do take into account also the interests of the EU, but only as judged by yourself. That is, you impose on the EU only those decisions which you yourself would like, or would not mind, to see imposed on you by the EU. This is sometimes called "subjective universalization":[120] although you take

[117] M. Kumm, "Who is the Final Arbiter of Constitutionality in Europe? Three Conceptions of the Relationship between the German Federal Court and the European Court of Justice" (1999) 36 CML Rev 351, 381.

[118] M. La Torre, "Legal Pluralism as Evolutionary Achievement of Community Law" (1999) 12 Ratio Juris 182, 193.

[119] Forst (n 18) at 195.

[120] Forst (n 18) at 195.

into account the interests of the "other", there still is a degree of idiosyncracy present in your judgment when you engage in such universalization. This is because you still universalize only from the first-person-singular perspective. Thus, the Golden Rule, "do unto others as you would have them do unto you," does not rule out those interpretations and decisions that would be perfectly acceptable to, for example R. M. Hare's "consistent fanatic."[121]

Stage three is usually characterized as "inter-subjective universalization."[122] Some scholars criticize the second stage as not taking the "other" into account to a sufficient degree.[123] According to this view the principle of universalization needs to be understood neither from the standpoint of the first-person singular (the Golden Rule; cf Singer;[124] Hare[125]), nor perhaps from the "impersonal" standpoint of a third-person singular (cf Nagel[126]), but from the standpoint of the first-person-*plural*.[127] In this way, it is argued, inter-subjective types of reasons respect the second-person-singular views to the same degree as they respect our own, first-person-singular ones. They do not evaluate (universalize) the former from the subjective perception of the latter, but rather start building (universalizing) an at least hypothetical agreement (eg decision; standard) from the strict assumption that both of the actual views, the first-person singular and second-person singular, are *equally valid*. It is in this sense that the universalizing assessment is conducted from the perspective of a first-person plural rather than a first-person singular. The result is that the eventual decision (ie the counterfactual, but allegedly the only agreeable common standard), if so based on inter-subjectively universalized reasons, would be quite different from that based on subjectively universalized grounds of stage two.

Which of these versions of universalization are proposed by the many interpretive pluralists in Europe who argue that one side should "take into account" the other? This is not, in my view, clear from the relevant literature, even though it is crucial. For if one assumes the second version of universalization as underpinning one's proposal for interpretive pluralism, then such a theory does not exclude the possibility of a "consistent fanatic" on either the national or the European side. In such a case either could use the interpretive rule of "taking the other into account" in a way that would leave little actual, meaningful pluralism.

But if the version of universalization were the third, then other problems would apply to such a theory. For example, such a theory would introduce an artificial ethical formula that would be supposed to work in all ethical contexts and to which the theory would always give precedence over the more authentic, primary ethical views of the subjects involved in the discourse. By imposing such an artificial ethical formula "for all seasons," the theory might exclude many of the now cherished

121 Forst (n 18) at 195; Hare (n 18) ch 9.

122 Habermas (n 22) at 31; Forst (n 18) at 195.

123 See, eg J. Habermas, *Moral Consciousness and Communicative Action*, tr. C. Lenhardt and W. Nicholson (Cambridge, MA: The MIT Press, 1990) 43–115; J. Habermas, *Between Facts and Norms: Contributions to a Discourse Theory of Law and Democracy*, tr. W. Rehg (Cambridge, MA: The MIT Press, 1996); Forst (n 18) at 195.

124 M. Singer, *Generalization in Ethics* (2nd edn, New York, NY: Atheneum, 1971).

125 Hare (n 18) ch 9; and his, *Moral Thinking* (Oxford: Oxford University Press, 1981).

126 T. Nagel, *The View from Nowhere* (Oxford: Oxford University Press, 1986).

127 Forst (n 18) at 195.

values associated with our primary beliefs. To a degree this seems paradoxically to cut against the idea of pluralism which, as many feel, ought to be more sensitive to the respect of plurality of ethical values in their very different ethical contexts than is perhaps assumed by the artificial inter-subjective formula.[128]

Of course, the interpretive pluralism of the European authors could also be situated somewhere in between the second and third version of universalization; indeed, the various degrees or even nuances of universalization might vary from context to context. But this would not avoid the problem. On the contrary, this is really where the shared difficulty of these proposals becomes most problematic; that is, any of these unelaborated interpretive proposals could in theory imply any among the whole variety of options in between the second and third versions of universalization. It is simply impossible to know, without having that elaborated and clarified by the respective authors, which exact variation of universalization they have in mind and so what exact kind of interpretive pluralism is proposed by each of those contributions. Without knowing this, it is not possible to describe accurately the pluralism that these authors consider to be optimal, and hence this renders serious assessment against alternative pluralist conceptions mute.

I conclude that while proposals within the group of interpretive pluralism are not sufficiently elaborated for a meaningful (be it intra or inter-theoretical) assessment, the particular proposal by Maduro, which does go further and transcends this difficulty, is sufficiently defined to enable such a further assessment. Moreover, it can be further concluded that, if constructively construed the way it has been at some of the key points above, the conception is internally coherent. While it thus passes the muster of the intra-theoretical analysis, it should be further concluded that the theory does not yet win its (underlying Eigenvalue's) superiority in a full-blown ethical discourse against alternative plural visions concerning the best constitutionalism for Europe, but rather posits it in a presumptive move. This version of pluralism too, like those examined before it, thus calls for that further—*inter*-theoretical—assessment, which will be explored in Chapter 8.

[128] For a detailed account of problems with this (basically Maduro's) approach to constitutional pluralism, see Chapter 8, section 2.

5

Institutional Pluralism

1. Explaining the Theory

1.1 The framework

Mattias Kumm is another author who uses the abstract language of constitutional pluralism and considers the latter to be the opposite of constitutional monism. He too explicitly claims that it would be wrong in the new circumstances for Europe to follow the traditional monist course,[1] and instead insists that the new constitutionalism in Europe ought to pursue the pluralist path.[2] While assigning himself to the camp of constitutional pluralists, the question remains what exactly is it that *he* has in mind when he uses that term pluralism. In order to make this sufficiently clear we again need to dig deeper and well beyond the author's mere abstract rhetorical account. There we encounter yet another surprise; Kumm's work understands the term almost exclusively in the sense of the question of *who* should have the authority (jurisdiction) to decide, and the further question of *who* should have the *final* authority (the final say when both have the jurisdiction) to decide. His meaning of pluralism is therefore a concept that appears almost entirely just within the specific theme of the *who* as defined by our Ariadne's Thread.[3] Inside that theme, Kumm's is another unique version of pluralism.

Underlying Kumm's conception of constitutional pluralism are three sets of partially conflicting values. The first set represents the values behind what he labels the "principle of expanding the Rule of Law."[4] It is explained that "[t]his principle aspires to the uniform application of supranational laws providing for the predictability and regularity associated with the Rule of Law and extending it to the supranational level."[5] The materialization of this goal "was the normative argument underlying the ECJ's European monist position."[6] The values behind the principle

[1] M. Kumm, "Who is the Final Arbiter of Constitutionality in Europe? Three Conceptions of the Relationship between the German Federal Constitutional Court and the European Court of Justice" (1999) 36 CML Rev 351, 375, 384.

[2] M. Kumm, "The Jurisprudence of Constitutional Conflict: Constitutional Supremacy in Europe before and after the Constitutional Treaty" (2005) ELJ 262, 266–7, 301; Kumm (n 1) at 375, 384.

[3] P. 11.

[4] Kumm (n 1) at 375.

[5] Kumm (n 1) at 375–6.

[6] Kumm (n 1) at 376.

of expanding the rule of law are thus those that commit supranational as well as national players in Europe to pursue a course of integration aimed at establishing a united Europe. This principle and the values behind it are realized to a higher degree, Kumm explains, when the member states' courts do not have the authority (jurisdiction) to subject EU law to constitutional review, but when such jurisdiction is only in the hands of the European courts.[7] Similarly, the principle is also realized to a higher degree when the ECJ has the *final* authority (not the sole authority but at least the final one) in questions of constitutionality on the European level.[8]

The second set of values is the one behind Kumm's principle of "Liberal-Democratic Governance" or, as he also puts it, "the principle of democratic legitimacy."[9] These are types of values that are generally seen as situated at the opposite end than the first set of values, which they confront. According to Kumm, the principle of democratic legitimacy thus "accommodates legitimate national sensibilities regarding protection of substantive ideals of individual rights and democratic self-determination against encroachment by illegitimate forms of supranational legislation." And if the first principle addressed the legitimate concerns of the European monist position, this one corresponds to the "sensibilities underlying the national statist conception, for which there are defensible grounds."[10]

Parallel to the confronting sets of values and their corresponding principles there is an additional value or principle, namely, the principle of "Constitutional Fit."[11] It is said to reflect the pluralist understanding of constitutionalism in Europe, and requires that judges dealing with constitutional conflict do not look solely to their respective national constitution or exclusively to a constitution of the EU when choosing the right rules for resolution of a conflict.[12] They must instead seek guidance from both of these sources: "The task of national courts is to construct an adequate relationship between the national and the European legal order on the basis of the best interpretation of the principles underlying them both."[13] In this light, "[t]he right conflict rule or set of rules for a national judge to adopt is the one that is best calculated to produce the best solutions to realise the ideals underlying legal practice in the European Union and its Member States."[14] Examples of the right pluralist interpretive question are thus the following: "what is the best understanding of the relationship between national and European constitutions, given the normative commitments underlying legal practice in Europe, seen as a whole?";[15] "what is the interpretation of the relationship between national

[7] Kumm (n 1) at 378. [8] Kumm (n 1) at 382.

[9] Kumm (n 1) at 376; Kumm (n 2) at 294; M. Kumm, "Who Is the Final Arbiter?" (1998) Jean Monnet Working Paper No 10/98, 23.

[10] Kumm (n 1) at 376. [11] Kumm (n 1) at 375.

[12] Kumm (n 1) at 375; Kumm (n 2) at 286. [13] Kumm (n 2) at 286.

[14] Kumm (n 2) at 286. [15] Kumm (n 2) at 287.

constitutions and the EU constitution that *best fits and justifies legal practices in the European Union, seen as a whole?*"; "what makes national and European constitutional practices in Europe appear in their best light?"[16]

These three sets of principles (values) that underlie Kumm's pluralist proposal are said to provide the "normative framework for the assessment of any set of doctrines dealing with the question of the relationship between the ECJ and the Courts of the Member States."[17] Kumm's general and abstract normative claim posits that the best set of doctrines dealing with the relationship between the ECJ and the courts of the member states is the one that realizes his three underlying principles, or values, to the maximum possible extent, all things considered.[18] Crucially, Kumm's scholarship does engage in further specification of the meaning of this highly abstract and general normative framework. In drawing parts of his work together we shall be able to observe, in what follows, what his version of constitutional pluralism really means and looks like. Subsections 1.2 and 1.3 thus start by analysing, through the prism of our interest in pluralism, his earliest work on the issue of conflicts between the courts in Europe. Once the basic contours of Kumm's pluralist conception thus emerge, we will move on to begin unfolding a more comprehensive picture of the conception (subsection 1.4). The latter will develop from the analysis and evaluation of some of Kumm's later work, which will be merged in a particular way with the earlier one. After thus joining the various parts of his scholarship into a more complete conception of his pluralism, we will be able to determine its specific place on the map of the pluralist labyrinth—that is the subject of section 2. The latter is then followed by a section that concludes with an intra-theoretical assessment of this version of pluralism.

1.2 Who has the authority?

There are two different stages through which Kumm elaborates his pluralist conception. In the first, he deals with the question of who—the ECJ or the highest courts of the member states—should have the authority to decide on constitutionality of EU law. This is not yet the question of who has the *final* authority, with which he will deal in the second stage, but only the question of who has the authority—jurisdiction—to start deciding in such cases.

According to Kumm there should be a general presumption under which the member states' courts do not have the requisite jurisdiction to subject EU law to constitutional scrutiny.[19] This follows from the principle of the expansion of the rule of law that presupposes the European legal order as an autonomous, supreme body of law within a certain sphere.[20] However, Kumm also posits that there may be warranted reasons of sufficient weight to rebut the general presumption, and

[16] Kumm (n 2) at 286.
[17] Kumm (n 1) at 376.
[18] Kumm (n 1) at 376.
[19] Kumm (n 1) at 378.
[20] Kumm (n 1) at 377–8.

explains that this is where his principle of democratic legitimacy steps in. Hence the following balance of jurisdictional authority that is proposed:

> If the legal practices on the European level as reviewed by the ECJ do not provide sufficient guarantees *that fundamental principles of the constitution* are protected, the extension of jurisdiction to European legislative acts can be justified: German courts and other authorities are implicated in the application of European Law in Germany. They are bound by the fundamental principles the German Constitution espouses. This includes the fundamental principles underlying the catalogue of basic rights (Art. 1-19 GG) as well as the principle of democracy (Art. 20 Sect. 2 GG). *If the legal practices on the European level, and in particular the practice of review by the ECJ, do not provide sufficient guarantees that these principles are generally respected to a sufficient degree, then jurisdiction should be asserted in the areas where such danger persists.*[21]

This means that under Kumm's version of constitutional pluralism (at one place he labels it "Liberal Legal Pluralism"[22]) it is possible and correct that the ECJ and a member state court both have the reviewing jurisdiction in a certain set of same issues. I will call this the situation of institutional or—to simplify—judicial overlap. The above-defined domain in which such an overlap is proposed—when the fundamental constitutional principles are at stake *and* when the ECJ does not provide sufficient guarantees for their general protection at the EU level—is what Kumm understands as his general model. The standard of "sufficient guarantees" appears in this relatively more general form in Kumm's 1999 article,[23] and was further explained in his contributions from 2004[24] and 2005.[25] According to those explanations, a national court should assert jurisdiction to review EU law only in those areas of fundamental constitutional principles where there exist "*persistent structural deficiencies*"[26] at the EU level. Such "structural deficiencies" are, in Kumm's view, the best applicative meaning of his standard of "sufficient guarantees."[27]

[21] Kumm (n 1) at 378. Kumm's article focused on the relation between the ECJ and the German Federal Constitutional Court. There seems to be no reasons, however, why one could not take his proposal to hold generally for the relation between the ECJ and last-resort constitutional interpreter of any member state. That is what I understand the proposal was also meant to include. My text thus speaks of the relation in general terms.

[22] Kumm (n 9) at 22, 23.

[23] The work I am referring to actually first appeared in 1998 as a Jean Monnet Working Paper (see n 9) and was then published in the CML Rev (see n 1). The content, or at least terminology, changed slightly between both versions, and at some places the older variant matters for the purposes of the analysis here. Hence my occasional reference to the older work.

[24] M. Kumm and V. Comella, "The Future of Constitutional Conflict in the European Union: Constitutional Supremacy after the Constitutional Treaty" in J. Weiler and C. Eisgruber (eds), *Altneuland: The EU Constitution in a Contextual Perspective* (2004) Jean Monnet Working Paper No 5/04.

[25] Kumm (n 2).

[26] Kumm and Comella (n 24) at 12.

[27] The test of "sufficient guarantees" is more open than the more specific "structural deficiencies" test. That is, "structural deficiencies" spells out in more specific terms what Kumm believes is, on application, the best concretization of the more general model of "sufficient guarantees." Importantly, he understands that there may be some reasonable disagreement about which test to use to operationalize the general approach, while agreeing on the general approach. This clarifies the relationship between these two different standards as set in his proposals from 1998 and 2004/05 respectively. I am indebted to Mattias Kumm for his clarification on this point. Email correspondence, August 2005.

In his 1999 article, Kumm explained that there were "two areas, where such an assertion of jurisdiction could be considered."[28] Then in his later contributions (from 2004 and 2005) he added a third area while at the same time arguing that if the draft Constitutional Treaty is adopted, the first two areas lose their potential for conflict and should practically fall within the jurisdiction of the ECJ alone. In light of the later ratification failure of the draft Constitutional Treaty, I shall first deal with Kumm's proposal regarding the first two areas, which was elaborated in 1998 and so not under the assumption that the Constitutional Treaty would be adopted. Following that, Kumm's later proposed adjustments in the light of the draft Treaty, together with his opening of the mentioned third area of overlapping jurisdiction, are presented and assessed from the current new circumstances.

The first fundamental constitutional area in which Kumm proposes that a national court can assert its jurisdiction along with the jurisdiction of the ECJ is that when some interpretation of EU law implicates fundamental rights. He assumes that what counts as "sufficient guarantees" that the level of fundamental rights protection would be sufficient at the EU level is subject to interpretation within reasonable bounds. Kumm explicitly refers to one such possible interpretation, namely, the standard elaborated by the German FCC in *Solange II*. He describes it is as "a reasonable" application of his more general standard,[29] while further referring to two features of this application. Firstly, in its assessment whether the standard of sufficient guarantees has been breached, the member state court must not focus on the individual case, "but on the general practice of rights adjudication on the European level."[30] Secondly, the standard of protection of those rights must be "essentially comparable" to the standard of basic rights protection within the national constitutional regime and practice.[31] Kumm concludes that, when in the member state court's view the standard is breached, it can assert its own jurisdiction. This would then be the kind of jurisdiction over an issue in which the ECJ asserts and rightfully has its own jurisdiction as well.

The standard from *Solange II* should be understood as just one among possible reasonable applications of Kumm's more general standard of "sufficient guarantees." It was mentioned that Kumm himself later, in his 2004/05 contributions, implied that we should assess "sufficient guarantees" in terms of "persistent structural deficiencies" on the EU level. In his view the latter is the best among the reasonable applications of the general standard.[32] That said, one should note that this application is not entirely the same as the application introduced by *Solange II*. Under that application the assessment is not merely about some "structural deficiencies" but rather, or also, about substantive standards of protection themselves. As is implied in Kumm's own brief mention of that case, the national court applying *Solange II* is not, for instance, simply to look into whether "the replication

[28] Kumm (n 1) at 378.

[29] "Here the standard formulated in the '*Solange II*' decision seems a reasonable one" (Kumm (n 1) at 378).

[30] Kumm (n 1) at 378.

[31] Kumm (n 1) at 378.

[32] See n 27.

of the basic rights catalogue" exists at the EU level, but will investigate further into the actual "standards" of protection that need to be "essentially comparable" to the national ones.[33] More generally, we know that *Solange II*, to which he refers, could hardly be read as requiring only the comparison of mere *structural* mechanisms (the *structural* standard) that need to be generally comparable to the national level of protection. The very point of that case is about the concern for the same level of *substantive* standards of protection, whereby such a substantive level of protection is assessed generally, not in a particular case at hand. If this is so, then Kumm's own preferred application (the assessment of mere "structural deficiencies") is a slightly different applicative proposal than the more substantive one under *Solange II*. That said, he seems to consider both of these applications reasonable and sees both as agreeing on his own general model of "sufficient guarantees." This reading of Kumm also differs from Christoph Schmid's critical observation of Kumm's proposal, namely, that the later merely amounts to a "faithful restatement of the jurisprudence of the German Federal Constitutional Court."[34]

The second area in which, according to Kumm, the member state court could assert its jurisdiction is the area of "legislative jurisdiction."[35] Kumm explains that "the fundamental principle here protected is the integrity of the practice of political self-determination [ie democracy] on a national level," and adds that this principle is "violated if legislation is enacted on the European level concerning subject matters for which there is no reasonable jurisdictional base."[36] He further suggests that in determining the latter violation (ie determining its own jurisdiction in addition to that of the ECJ) "the *court* could use the same approach it has used concerning basic rights jurisdiction: *It has jurisdiction only to the extent that there are no sufficient safeguards instituted on the European level to prevent an unjustified usurpation of legislative power.*"[37] When in its own judgment this standard is breached, the member state court should, as Kumm concludes, assert its own jurisdiction. As under the fundamental rights above, so here this would also be the jurisdiction in addition to the one exercised by the ECJ. Here too, we would have judicial overlap.

1.3 Who has the *final* authority?

The question of who should have the authority to decide, that is the jurisdiction and competence to decide, is thus settled. This completes the first stage of Kumm's pluralist proposal. Before us is the second stage with its question of the *final* authority. For even when the jurisdiction of the member state court is determined in addition to that of the ECJ, this does not yet by itself settle also the further

33 Kumm (n 1) at 378.

34 C. Schmid, "The Neglected Conciliation Approach to the 'Final Arbiter' Conflict: A Critical Comment on Kumm, 'Who is the Final Arbiter of Constitutionality in Europe' in this Review" (1999) 36 CML Rev 509, 509.

35 Kumm (n 1) at 379. 36 Kumm (n 1) at 379. 37 Kumm (n 1) at 379.

question of who should have the *final* say (ie final authority) whenever the two courts with jurisdiction come up with different outcomes in their respective substantive rulings. Kumm makes his proposal here as well.

He sets up a test that draws the divide between the sphere in which the ECJ should have the final authority and the sphere in which the member state court should have this sort of authority. The test is presented as "the most appropriate standard of review" that the member state court should exercise in its substantive ruling, that is, after it has determined that it does have jurisdiction.[38]

The test is two-pronged. In order that it is the member state court (and not the ECJ) that eventually has the final say about a piece of EU law, the violation of either fundamental rights or legislative jurisdiction (only here the member state court has the jurisdiction to assess the validity of EU law) must meet both parts of the test. In the member state court's judgment it must, *firstly*, be a violation of EU law, including, but not limited to, the EU fundamental rights and principles as they appear under the EU legal order. *Secondly*, the violation must also represent a breach of national constitutional principle. It must either be a violation of the basic rights or of the principle of democracy under the member state legal order.

Regarding the first part, that is, the question of the violation of EU law, things work similarly as they did with the first-stage question of "who decides." As was the case there, so here the member state court should, as Kumm posits, proceed under the presumption that the ECJ is the primary arbiter of the EU legal order. The same principle of expanding the rule of law to the European level is, again, underlying this presumption. Kumm explains that this means that "the court [ie the member state court] will not pass judgment without the ECJ having pronounced itself on the issue" and that, after that pronouncement, the level of scrutiny by the member state court should be low (the standard of "*manifest and grave*," "*Evidenzkontrolle*").[39] This should hold for both areas of the court's potential review, the fundamental rights as protected on the European level, as well legislative jurisdiction of the European level.

To this Kumm then also adds the following interpretive requirement: in its application of the standard, of the final authority divide, the court "must meet the *universalizability* test." This means that "[i]t must exercise its review in a way that is compatible with other Member States Courts engaging in a comparable practice of review" and to do so "without undermining the coherence of the European Legal Order."[40] The member state court ought not act as if it were "the only court that plays the role of a subsidiary guardian of the European Legal Order."[41] It must instead operate as "part of a community of interpreters and [thus] needs to take into account the different interpretive traditions in the community and the possibility of reasonable disagreement between them."[42]

[38] Kumm (n 1) at 380.
[39] Kumm (n 1) at 381.
[40] Kumm (n 1) at 381.
[41] Kumm (n 1) at 381.
[42] Kumm (n 1) at 381.

After finding the breach of fundamental rights or legislative jurisdiction on the level of EU legal order, the member state court does not yet have the final authority in the case. The holder of that authority is still the ECJ, unless in addition to the first, the member state court also finds a breach of the *second* part of the test. As already noted, this second part of the test requires that, in addition to the violation of the EU legal order, the member state court also finds that such a violation is severe enough to constitute also a violation, of either basic rights or the principle of democracy, at the level of the national constitutional order. For it should not be, as Kumm explains, that any breach of EU law as detected by the member state court (ie the breach of the principle of expanding the rule of law as the member state court understands it) should in and of itself count also as a sufficient violation of the national constitution. This is so, again, due to Kumm's "strong presumption that a 'united Europe' (the realization of the Rule of Law at the European level) is best served by allowing the ECJ to assume its role as the final arbiter of constitutionality on the European level."[43] Therefore, even if, in the member state court's own judgment, the EJC decides a case poorly, mistakenly, and in the way that intrudes slightly on the member state's constitution, that will by itself sometimes not be enough to warrant disobedience of the ECJ's judgment by the member state court. "Considerations of unity and coherence," Kumm concludes, "generally have greater weight."[44]

But when, then, *does* the breach of EU law suffice to constitute also a breach of the national constitutional principles, of either basic rights, or the principle of democracy? Kumm's answer to this key question for both areas is rather simple: whenever the intrusion on the national constitutional principles is *disproportionately* grave.

As to the area of basic constitutional rights he thus explicitly writes: "When assessing whether a measure constituting a *prima facie* violation of basic rights is justified," the member state court "applies a proportionality test."[45] This "involves balancing the individual's interests against the collective goods or competing rights that the provision reviewed aims to promote,"[46] while doing so against the correct benchmarks constituting Kumm's version of the universalized interpretive approach. So "[f]or national laws, the significance of these collective goods and competing rights are assessed before the backdrop of the national community's collective self-understanding," whereas "[f]or European laws . . . the relevant frame of reference must be the European community's self-understanding."[47] It is only a balanced interpretation that takes equally into account both these aspects that

[43] Kumm (n 1) at 382. [44] Kumm (n 1) at 382.
[45] Kumm (n 1) at 383. [46] Kumm (n 1) at 383.
[47] Kumm (n 1) at 383. At this point Kumm refers to Habermas, which seems to signal what he actually does not explicate, namely, that the interpretive rule is meant to establish the specific *intersubjective* kind of universalization as opposed to some other form of it. On the other hand, the particular invocation to Habermas could well be understood also in the more general sense—as to a representative of the general strand of public rationality.

seems sufficient for Kumm. The significance of this interpretive rule is that the member state court, "even when adjudicating national basic rights" can no longer perceive itself only as the actor in service of its own national interest, as "*just* guardian of (unchanging) national values embodied in constitutional principles." Now its reasoning is and must be "deeply influenced by the fact that Germany is a member of the European legal community."[48] By taking into account the European along with the national self-understanding, the court is thus also "inevitably contributing to the process of developing a normatively appropriate understanding of the Communities' interests."[49] The idea behind Kumm's addition of this interpretive rule is clearly that, in this way, also his third of the three framework principles underlying his conception of pluralism—the principle of constitutional fit[50]—is now properly respected by the pluralist divide he is constructing. The pluralist symmetry in the balance between the first and second of those principles is only truly secured through the third framework principle.

As for the area of legislative jurisdiction, the following is when the breach at the EU level is sufficient to constitute also a breach of the member state principle of democracy: "There is no constitutionally sufficient basis for legislation enacted on the European level if the loss of democratic self-determination incurred by the transfer of legislative power is not offset by good reasons justifying the Community's action."[51] Again, in applying this version of the disproportionality test, the pluralist interpretive rule has to be followed here as well: "the weight of the interests involved at the Community level must be assessed with reference to the European Communities self-understanding."[52]

The critical part of Kumm's proposal, therefore, amounts to the following final divide. When the member state court will find that what it believes (while the ECJ disagrees) is a breach of the EU law does *not* violate the principle of proportionality, as explained, then *it will be the ECJ who will have the final constitutional authority in the disputed case.* This will hold so for the EU as well as the member state legal orders. Conversely, when the member state court finds that such proportionality has been breached, it is itself who will have the last word in the disputed case over constitutionality of the EU law. In such a case, the ECJ may continue to resist, but "[s]ince it can be expected that national authorities will, in case of conflict, feel bound by the decision of their respective national court rather than the ECJ, [here] *the Member States appear to be the final arbiters of constitutionality in Europe, for all practical purposes.*"[53]

This is then the whole divide that determines *who*, the national or European institution, should have the *final* decision-making authority, and when so. If that is truly the case, what should one then do with the following and central part of

[48] Kumm (n 1) at 383. [49] Kumm (n 1) at 383. [50] See pp. 127–8.
[51] Kumm (n 1) at 384 (the emphasis of the whole sentence omitted).
[52] Kumm (n 1) at 384. [53] Kumm (n 1) at 384.

Kumm's explanation, taken from his conclusion: "Who is, under this approach, the final arbiter of constitutionality in Europe? This paper does not answer that question. Instead it provides good reasons to stop asking it and address the underlying concerns by redirecting the question."[54]

I believe such a statement is misleading to an extent. After all, we have seen that Kumm's approach *does* actually deal with and, indeed, answers the question over the institutional *who* of the decision-making authority, as well as of such *final* authority. However, there is one sense in which the statement could also not be misleading. In that case, the term "final authority" would need to be understood in a broader sense, one that is separated from the just mentioned and very distinct meaning behind the same phrase that Kumm seems to use too uniformly. Namely, it is true that the two institutions would each have their accorded final authorities only *within* their own respective orders. Neither of those orders would thus have some ultimate Final Authority over both orders, seen ultimately as representing one and the same superior order grounded in *one and single source* of ultimate foundational authority (monism).[55] In this broader sense of the term "Final Authority," Kumm's proposal could indeed be seen as leaving the question over *who* has *that kind* of Final Authority somewhat "unanswered," (although to say that neither of the orders/institutions is in the position of representing such a Final Authority is also to answer the question). Kumm states: "The reason why it [ie Kumm's proposal] refuses to answer the question is that *within a pluralist framework, it does not make sense to speak of a [F]inal [A]rbiter of constitutionality in Europe.* In the approach outlined here the ECJ is conceived as the final arbiter of constitutionality at the level of the European Legal Order and the member state Constitutional Courts are conceived as the final arbiters of constitutionality at the national level."[56] Indeed, the broader meaning of Kumm's term "Final Authority" as implied in this conclusion is different from the same term as used continuously throughout his work. The "Final Authority" now refers to the foundational discourse and so to the deepest sector of the labyrinth that deals with the sources of authority of both orders. The "final authority" used throughout his text, however, referred to the distribution of the final decision-making authority between the European and member state institutions within the different and much narrower discourse of the *who*. For our purposes here, Kumm's brief mention of the "Final Authority" in the conclusion, and his corresponding endorsement of pluralism at that foundational level, is important: it proves that Kumm's pluralism within his discourse of the *who* is indeed a species of constitutional pluralism—it is understood to be grounded in some, though unelaborated, *foundation* of constitutional pluralism instead of monism.

[54] Kumm (n 1) at 384.

[55] The distinction in capital letters between "final authority" and "Final Authority" is mine (not Kumm's) and is introduced in order to help us distinguish between both very different meanings of the same semantic term.

[56] Kumm (n 1) at 384.

1.4 Later developments

As already mentioned in this chapter, the explicated conception is the initial version of Kumm's pluralism. Kumm later had more to say on the topic. The most substantial further refinements thus came from his consideration of the impact that the changed circumstances of the proposed, but later unsuccessful, draft Constitutional Treaty could potentially have for constitutional conflict in Europe and thus for his initial theory itself.[57] The fact that the ratification of the Constitutional Treaty has not been successful does not, however, make Kumm's latest refinements mute in their entirety. As we know, some of the relevant changes that the Constitutional Treaty envisioned were then nonetheless adopted substantively unchanged in the new Lisbon Treaty. Moreover, some of the adjustments that Kumm introduced seem to be applicable irrespective of the reforms and the failure of the Constitutional Treaty. Furthermore, in the case of those changes which due to the failure of the Constitutional Treaty have not yet occurred, it remains useful to observe how aspects of Kumm's version of pluralism might change in some not-too-distant future. From the perspective of the broader theoretical aims of this book, it is likewise appropriate to examine all of these further refinements and to do so with a view of constructing the more comprehensive and current picture of Kumm's version of constitutional pluralism.

In his latest contributions, one of the articles he co-authored with Victor Comella, Kumm argues that under the regime of the new Constitutional Treaty the likelihood of a constitutional conflict in the two areas—fundamental rights and legislative jurisdiction—would be abolished. This would supposedly occur due to these three groups of factors: (1) the explicit entrenchment of the supremacy clause as it appears in the Constitutional Treaty, (2) the nature of the ratification process, and (3) the structural reforms in the European Union, brought mostly by the Constitutional Treaty.

1.4.1 The supremacy clause

Kumm and Comella argue that for the first time the Constitutional Treaty now actually codifies (in its Article I-6) the supremacy clause, and that this strengthens the case for the supremacy of EU law. Firstly, the supremacy of EU law has so far been based on judicial doctrine, precedents of the ECJ. However, when it is entrenched as part of the Treaty (legislative act) this by itself implies "greater legitimacy and authority then interpretive decisions by courts."[58] Secondly, they argue that "if the Member States have collectively acquiesced to anything" with

[57] There are two articles comprising this later work. Kumm and Comella (n 24); Kumm (n 2).
[58] Kumm and Comella (n 24) at 6.

respect to the judicial doctrine of supremacy of EU law, "they are more likely to have acquiesced to a 'legally open' situation in which the ECJ has claimed supremacy for EU law while some national courts continue to insist on the evaluation of the ECJ's supremacy claim in light of national constitutional commitments." But now the explicit entrenchment in the Constitutional Treaty does make a difference in this sense, which, as the authors imply, gives the principle of supremacy of the EU law further weight.[59] Based on these two arguments, Kumm and Comella conclude that a likely consequence of the explicit entrenchment is that national courts will be less willing than they have been thus far to refuse to apply EU law on national constitutional grounds.[60]

At the same time, however, the authors seem to undermine their own claim when they acknowledge, I believe correctly, that such an entrenched supremacy clause might nevertheless still leave enough interpretive space to allow for the continuity of some conflicts.[61]

Firstly, they acknowledge that the way the supremacy clause is written does not seem to affect the issue of *Kompetenz-Kompetenz*:

> the clause establishes the primacy of the "Constitution and law adopted by the institutions of the Union *in exercising competences conferred on it*." This suggests that secondary EC legislation has primacy only to the extent that the Union has acted within its sphere of competences. But the supremacy clause does not by itself say who should settle the question whether EC legislation is or is not *ultra vires*.[62]

The potential for conflict with respect to the *ultra vires* claims therefore seems to remain. Or more precisely, the wording of the new supremacy clause does little to reduce it.

Secondly, the authors also acknowledge the ambiguity of the phrase "shall have primacy over the law of the Member States," that is, the ambiguity around the actual meaning of the supremacy clause.[63] They first note that "[t]echnically . . . the national Constitution is part of the 'law' of a Member State" but are correct then to add that, "since the deepest controversy has never concerned the primacy of EU law over national legislation, but its primacy over national Constitutions, it is striking that the clause does not explicitly say that the EU law trumps the Constitutions of the Member States."[64] While the US Constitution, stating that it is the "supreme Law of the Land" and that "the Judges in every State shall be bound thereby, anything in the Constitution or Laws of any State to the Contrary notwithstanding," is clear in this respect, the new European supremacy clause is ambiguous. It

[59] Kumm and Comella (n 24) at 7.

[60] Kumm and Comella (n 24) at 7.

[61] Kumm and Comella (n 24) at 7.

[62] Kumm and Comella (n 24) at 7–8.

[63] This point was made soon after the Convention's proposal for the Constitutional Treaty came out. See P. Craig, "What Constitution Does Europe Need? The House that Giscard Built: Constitutional Rooms with a View" (2003) The Federal Trust for Education and Research Online Paper No 26/03: "This [ie the ambiguous phrase] could be interpreted to mean, following the jurisprudence of the ECJ, that supremacy operates over all national law, including provisions in a national constitution. It could alternatively be read so as to accord primacy to EU law over national law, primary and secondary legislation, but not the national constitution itself."

[64] Kumm and Comella (n 24) at 8.

seems, therefore, that if the primacy of EU law would not extend to national constitutions themselves, the written supremacy clause would, again, hardly add much to reduce the potential for conflict.

Thirdly, with respect to the interpretation of the supremacy clause the authors also mention the relation between Article 6, paragraph 3 and Article I-5 of the Constitutional Treaty. While the first reiterates that the Union shall respect national identities, the second introduces a more specific novelty in this respect: it provides that "*the fundamental constitutional structures* of Member States are an integral part of the national identity to be respected. The new Art. I-5 can plausibly be read to authorize domestic courts to set aside secondary EU law when it disrespects national constitutional identities *as a matter of EU law*."[65] This too, therefore, diminishes the weight of Kumm and Comella's first claim that the entrenched supremacy clause, written as it is in the Constitutional Treaty, actually reduces the potential for conflict. If we follow their third point, it seems that it might even enhance it.

1.4.2 The nature of the ratification process

According to the traditional view, Kumm and Comella write, the supremacy of EU law would not be controversial when constitutionally entrenched through a procedure that could be taken to express the will of a European *demos*. While acknowledging that the adoption of the Constitutional Treaty can probably not be interpreted as such an act by the European "pouvoir constituant," the authors nonetheless argue that certain specific features of the ratification process do have implications for reducing the potential for constitutional conflicts.[66]

Firstly, Kumm and Comella note that in some jurisdictions the ratification of the Constitutional Treaty may "coincide with the amendment of the national Constitution."[67] This, they explain, would "explicitly recognize the primacy of EU Law *as a matter of national constitutional law*." They might even incorporate some explicit rule such as the one saying that "nothing in this Constitution shall be interpreted to preclude the effective enforcement of EU law."[68] The practical effect of such an amendment, the authors argue, would then be to eliminate conflict for as long as it was not revoked.[69] This conclusion nonetheless sounds too bold. The immediate problem of the argument is that it is not too realistic to expect that many states would adopt amendments of this kind: indeed, there will probably be no such states at all. Realistically speaking, the authors' expectation that the potential for conflict will be reduced in this particular way thus carries little weight.

Secondly, Kumm and Comella argue that "the ratification decision may well qualify as an act of the national 'pouvoir constituant', in some countries," while explaining that some structural factors, such as providing citizens with a direct say in the ratification process, have an important role to play in that the ratification

65 Kumm and Comella (n 24) at 8.
66 Kumm and Comella (n 24) at 10–11.
67 Kumm and Comella (n 24) at 11.
68 Kumm and Comella (n 24) at 11.
69 Kumm and Comella (n 24) at 11.

qualifies as an act of the national pouvoir constituant.[70] The authors conclude that in such cases domestic courts would be less likely to invoke the member states' constitutions as the ground for setting aside EU law.

Finally, as a third reason for the conflict-eliminating effects of the nature of the ratification process, Kumm and Comella cite the quality of this process. They state that "the authority of EU law could be strengthened by the quality of the ratification procedure seen as a whole in Europe" while at the same time acknowledging that "that would depend on the degree of public participation in each state, and on the extent to which the debates in the different states are linked to each other."[71]

Despite their initial optimistic rhetoric, the authors themselves later nonetheless seem to acknowledge that the supremacy clause and the nature of the ratification process alone are unlikely to present "conclusive reasons" for all domestic courts to accept supremacy of EU law in the two critical constitutional areas, the fundamental rights and legislative jurisdiction.[72] Indeed, taking into account also the several additional critical observations that we were able to identify at various parts of the argument it would be more accurate to conclude that the potential for conflict would scarcely be reduced at all. The courts that now refuse to accept the supremacy of EU law over their constitutions would very likely continue to do so even after the Constitutional Treaty's explicit mention of the supremacy clause and despite the factor of the ratification process.

Being at least implicitly aware of this remaining potential for conflict, Kumm and Comella still want temporarily to keep in place the particular jurisdictional divide between the two orders. It is the one already mentioned above with respect to Kumm's initial proposal:

> We now suggest this: It is legitimate for national courts to continue to assert jurisdiction to review EU Law on constitutional grounds, but only if and to the extent that such review addresses and is targeted towards *remedying persistent structural deficiencies* on the EU level. National constitutions should be read in light of a strong interpretive principle according to which nothing in the national constitutional provision prevents the enforcement of EU law, unless national constitutional provisions address or compensate for structural deficiencies on the level of the EU.[73]

1.4.3 The structural reforms in the EU

Soon after reiterating Kumm's jurisdictional divide, in the standard of "structural deficiencies," the authors then introduce the third and decisive innovation of the Constitutional Treaty. This third innovation eliminates, they argue, the structural deficiencies of the EU level in the areas of fundamental rights and legislative jurisdiction, thereby settling the potential for conflict. We should thus no longer

[70] Kumm and Comella (n 24) at 11.
[71] Kumm and Comella (n 24) at 11.
[72] Kumm and Comella (n 24) at 12.
[73] Kumm and Comella (n 24) at 12 (except for the highlighted phrase the emphasis of the whole para is omitted). Cf p. 129 this chapter.

have judicial overlap in both these areas. However, the authors at the same time introduce a third and new area of conflict: that concerning specific national constitutional identity. They argue that in this newly exposed area of conflict the structural deficiencies are not cured even after introducing reforms like those envisioned by the Constitutional Treaty. Before engaging in the analysis of this new area of conflict we should first take a closer look at the exact justification for the claim that the Constitutional Treaty settles conflict in the two traditional areas.

As to the jurisdictional boundaries, the authors argue that the Constitutional Treaty provides some innovations which, "seen as a whole, may well provide the kind of structural guarantees that national courts have reason to deem sufficient." They are sufficient to guarantee that the EU institutions would not unduly misinterpret the boundaries," so that from now on the national courts "should refuse to address questions of competence when asked to do so by litigants."[74] The main structural innovation that the authors mention is the requirement that "[n]ational Parliaments are to be informed of EU legislative proposals, so that they can express their informed opinion that the proposed legislation does not comply with the principle of subsidiarity."[75] They are referring to the new provisions in the Constitutional Treaty (and the Lisbon Treaty) requiring that, in the case that a qualified minority of the national parliaments rejects it, the Commission must examine its initial proposal again. This could produce a thorough record of relevant reasons which, or so the authors argue, "could form the basis for the ECJ to engage in a meaningful assessment whether concerns relating to subsidiarity were given the appropriate weight."[76] Kumm and Comella admit that whether this particular procedure would be a sufficient safeguard in practice is yet to be seen, but nonetheless conclude that it has the potential to significantly reduce the possibility of conflict, so much so that "[u]nder these circumstances, national courts should be hesitant to review EU law on jurisdictional grounds."[77]

As for the area of fundamental rights, the authors argue that the "structural deficiencies" of the EU level are also no longer an issue. Noting that this was a cause for concern, including their own, they nonetheless now observe that it has been widely believed since the 1980s that the ECJ is providing a level of fundamental rights protection that is essentially equivalent to that afforded by national courts under their respective constitutions. The authors add that the inclusion of the Charter of Fundamental Rights in the Constitutional Treaty is likely to have a positive impact on the level of protection of rights in the EU as well.[78] If the EU ratifies the European Convention on Human Rights, they further remind, this will provide "an additional institutional layer of protection." For all these reasons they

[74] Kumm and Comella (n 24) at 12. [75] Kumm and Comella (n 24) at 13.

[76] Kumm and Comella (n 24) at 13.

[77] Kumm and Comella (n 24) at 13. Cf Kumm (n 2) at 296: "after the ratification of the draft Constitutional Treaty it will be difficult to sustain the claim that national courts should second-guess assessments made by other political actors and the Court of Justice concerning competencies and subsidiarity."

[78] "[R]ights are more visible now; they will be invoked more often, probably, and the ECJ cannot be oblivious to their gravitational pull" (Kumm and Comella (n 24) at 14).

argue that "there is no longer a reason for national courts to substitute their assessment for that of the ECJ interpreting the EU's Charter of fundamental rights."[79] The potential for conflict and judicial overlap in this area is thus no longer present. Or so the authors conclude.

This justification for the settled conflict in the area of fundamental rights and legislative jurisdiction will be assessed together with an assessment of the proposal for opening the third (new) area of conflict.[80] We should now first add the latter to the analysis.

1.4.4 Specific national constitutional identity

Kumm introduces the new area only in his most recent contributions,[81] and argues that we should have judicial overlap in this area because the "structural deficiencies" here remain significant and persistent even under the improved regime of the Constitutional Treaty. It is explained that "beyond the abstract provisions concerning fundamental rights and the principle of democratic self-government giving constitutional significance to jurisdictional boundaries, constitutions contain a host of other provisions that can conflict with EU law."[82] Kumm gives examples such as the explicit Irish constitutional rule protecting the life of the unborn,[83] the similarly specific provision of the Greek constitution providing that only higher education provided by public institutions could be recognized,[84] or the German express constitutional rule that limits military service to men.[85] The third area of legitimate conflict is thus about this kind of specific national constitutional commitments that reflect a specific national constitutional identity as enshrined in the form of *specific constitutional rules.*[86]

This slight shift in the proposal obviously requires some answer to the question as to the special structural deficiencies in this particular area that supposedly justify the intervention of national courts and thus require judicial overlap. Kumm and Comella tell us that "democratic deficit" still persists at the European level, and that it would continue to persist even if some regime like the one envisioned by the draft Constitutional Treaty were introduced. This is because the latter, as they claim, does not make sufficient progress with respect to this particular case of structural deficiencies. It "does not in fact strengthen directly representative institutions on the EU level, and even if it had, it is clear that the development of a practice that would be democratically meaningful would take time."[87] There is for instance "the lack of a European public sphere," no "sufficiently thick European identity," nor other crucial means through which we could, any time soon, get rid of this deficit.[88]

79 Kumm and Comella (n 24) at 14.

80 Section 3, this chapter.

81 Kumm and Comella (n 24) at 16–18; Kumm (n 2) at 296–8.

82 Kumm (n 2) at 297.

83 Irish Constitution, Art 40 III no 3.

84 Greek Constitution, Art 16.

85 German Basic Law, Art 12.

86 Kumm (n 2) at 297.

87 Kumm and Comella (n 24) at 16.

88 Kumm (n 2) at 300. Or as Kumm explains in some greater detail: "For so long as (a) the national community has not explicitly committed itself to EU law as the supreme law of the land *and* (b)

For this reason, Kumm and Commella argue, the specific constitutional rules at the national level possess a relatively higher democratic quality than decisions adopted by the EU level. They could plausibly be assigned directly to the will of the people itself.[89] Both authors thus conclude that it is because of this particular structural deficiency of the European level—the relatively greater "democratic deficit"—that we should continue to have national courts intervene in this new, third area of conflict. Of course, given the structure of Kumm's basic conception we know that, at this point, this only suggests judicial overlap in this domain: a license by Kumm and Comella to the national constitutional courts to decide on issues from this area along with the ECJ pronouncing on the same issues.

The theory settles the question of authority, the issue of "who decides." But how about the question of the *final* authority, the issue of "who decides who decides" when the answers by these courts in this particular area diverge? Should it remain open, as we have seen was the case under epistemic pluralism? Kumm and Comella do not believe so. Under their theory the conflicting claims should not just be raised one over another. They instead propose a particular refined version of Kumm's old divide, one that would in a supposedly most balanced way settle the issue:

> Given the—perhaps inevitable—comparative democratic weakness of the European legislative process, we suggest that *Member States should have the possibility to override the EU legislation by national constitutional legislation, when they deem that questions of fundamental importance for the national community are at stake. When a national community, following the procedure set out in its respective Constitution, decides to entrench a specific rule, the implications of which in a particular case are clear (that is, the constitutional provision does not allow for reasonable interpretive disagreement as applied to a particular case), then national courts should respect that choice.* They ought to apply the national Constitution and set aside EU Law, if necessary.[90]

It is important to understand that this divide of the *final* decision-making authority should be respected also by *both* constitutional sites and their courts, and thus also by the EJC: "I propose that *the guarantee of the constitutional identities of Member States in the Constitutional Treaty should be interpreted by the Court of Justice to authorise national courts to set aside EU law on certain limited grounds that derive from*

European institutions have not established a political process with elections and directly representative institutions at its heart and remain dependant on national democratic processes for its legitimation *and* (c) a European public sphere, European civil society and a European identity as the sociological prerequisites of a meaningful democratic process have not yet developed to a sufficient degree, a blanket rule requiring national courts to set aside national constitutional provision is incompatible with respect to democratic legitimacy and the institutional role of courts in constitutional democracies" (Kumm (n 2) at 297).

[89] Crucially, the requirement of specificity of a constitutional rule is meant to help to assure that constitutional ruling by a national court in such a case "can in fact be plausibly attributed to" an act by "the people" and not to the court's own interpretive balancing like in cases of abstract constitutional provisions (Kumm (n 2) at 298). See more on this at pp. 144–5 and 156–7.

[90] Kumm and Comella (n 24) at 16; cf Kumm (n 2) at 298.

the national Constitutions (such as those suggested: when specific rule-like commitments pertaining to fundamental constitutional commitments are at stake)."[91] While this is not to say that the ECJ does not have the authority also to decide in this area ("[t]he Court of Justice would also be able to contribute its views on the interpretation of the national constitutional principles at stake"),[92] it does mean that it would need to recognize that "the ultimate authority on the interpretation of the national constitutional provision would remain with the national court."[93]

Let us take a closer look at the new version of the divide. *Firstly*, it is proposed that the ultimate decision-making authority be divided between the two institutional sides according to the criterion of "*questions of fundamental importance for the national community*."[94] In another article, Kumm uses the language of "national commitments" that are "constitutionally essential."[95] As a matter of practical reality, the final interpretation of this standard seems to be in the hands of the national constitutional courts.[96] If in an individual case the ECJ has a different interpretation of this standard, it is equally free to pronounce it through its own decision within the context of the judicial overlap, but this nevertheless does not result in the ECJ having the final say as a matter of practical reality since EU law does not get enforced in this case.[97]

Secondly, the next element of the divide requires that the entrenched constitutional provision is clear and specific. Both authors explain that this would reduce dramatically the risk of endangering the critical value of the uniform enforcement of EU law. In one of his own later contributions Kumm also adds that the "clear and specific" test has the purpose of "ensuring that the specific national constitutional norm . . . *has in fact been legislated by the constitutional legislator*."[98] It "seeks to ensure that the substantive constitutional judgement can in fact be plausibly attributed to a specific act of 'the people' rather than the fact that constitutional court has been granted sweeping powers to interpret unclear or abstract

[91] Kumm (n 2) at 303; cf Kumm and Comella (n 24) at 19. [92] Kumm (n 2) at 303.

[93] Kumm (n 2) at 303; Kumm and Comella (n 24) at 19.

[94] Kumm and Comella (n 24) at 16. [95] Kumm (n 2) at 297–8.

[96] "Even if a constitutional norm is clear and specific, it need not be a constitutional essential. A close analysis of the legislative history and public function of the German constitutional provision generally prohibiting women from serving in the armed forces, for example, was most likely to lead to the conclusion that it does not qualify as an essential constitutional moment. Its legislative history is thin, the principle it embodies is unclear, and it has not played any significant role whatsoever in German public and political life. Had the case come up before the Federal Constitutional Court it would have responded correctly by setting it aside and apply EU law instead." Kumm goes on to say that the Irish protection of the right of the unborn "most likely qualifies" as a constitutional commitment that the highest national courts ought not to set aside, while reporting that the Greek provision about the public monopoly in higher education is "a difficult case." Kumm (n 2) at 300.

[97] Cf Kumm (n 2) at 303: "where the enforcement of EU law is at stake."

[98] Kumm (n 2) at 298.

constitutional clauses."[99] I will later argue in section 3 that this cannot succeed quite as envisioned since, as the previous paragraph indicates, the national courts will not be able to avoid reasonable interpretive disagreement that pervades these constitutional provisions precisely through questions such as whether or not some provision is "fundamentally important," or "specific enough."[100]

It seems that prima facie assessment of whether we are dealing with "clear and specific" constitutional norms would already need to be part of the first—"who decides"—stage of inquiry by a national constitutional court. To determine that a case at hand is about the third area of conflict, the national court would need to distinguish it from, say, *abstract* constitutional provisions belonging to Kumm's area of "fundamental rights" (the second area). Such abstract provisions are subject to reasonable interpretive pluralism. But sometimes the provision prima facie falls within the third area—and if specific and about national constitutional identity, it would belong here even if it were about a specific fundamental right, I understand. In that case the national court may decide on the issue along with the ECJ (judicial overlap). The second stage then seems to be the deeper, no more just prima facie, assessment of whether the rule in question could be considered sufficiently clear and specific so as to warrant national derogation from EU law. This is already about "who decides who decides," the final authority. As with the first element of the divide ("questions of fundamental constitutional commitments"), so here it seems to be up to the national court to finally determine whether the rule meets this second element. When the court is interpreting a *national constitutional provision*, which is the case here, Kumm and Comella conclude that while the ECJ could pronounce on the issue, "the ultimate authority on the interpretation of the national constitutional provision would remain with the national court."[101]

As noted, the authors introduce the requirement of specificity also in order to "reduce dramatically" the risk of endangering the key framework value of the uniform enforcement of EU law. But what more precisely do Kumm and Comella mean by the *specificity* of the constitutional rule? They explain that for the purposes of their proposal we need not indulge in a philosophical discussion of the meaning of specificity. Neither do they engage in a discussion about the need for relative narrowness of the substantive scope of the rule that is to be considered specific.[102] Nothing like that means specificity as defined by the two authors. Instead, they operationalize specificity in "institutional" terms.[103] It thus means the following:

> a constitutional rule is specific in a particular context if it can be plausibly said that its application does not require an independent interpretive judgement by the court. The relevant normative judgement in the particular case has to be fairly attributable to the

[99] Kumm (n 2) at 298. [100] Pp. 155–6.

[101] Kumm (n 2) at 303; Kumm and Comella (n 24) at 19.

[102] The substantive standard of "fundamental importance to the national community" also cannot help here. It is quite an open standard, and under conditions of reasonable interpretive disagreement such a standard could cover a wide rather than narrow substantive range.

[103] Kumm and Comella (n 24) at 16.

constitutional legislator, not to the court . . . If it is clear in a particular case that a specific substantive decision has been made by the constitutional legislator, national courts have to honor that decision. (Possible examples are the Irish Constitution's protection of the fetus, or the Greek Constitution's commitment to a public monopoly on higher education).[104]

And the proposal also explains what should *not* be understood as a specific constitutional rule:

If, in contrast, the constitutional legislator in effect authorizes courts to engage in open-ended inquiries about the concrete implications of abstract principles (requiring courts, for example, to apply some version of proportionality test, as in the case with regard to most, though not all constitutional rights), national courts may *not* disapply EU law on the grounds of their understanding of those principles.[105]

Yet it seems doubtful that the second element as defined by the theory could really dramatically reduce the threat to uniform application of EU law. This is so because specificity, as the authors describe it, is not a synonym for narrowness. That is, a rule can be very specific in that, for instance, its boundaries are clear and the courts may apply it without any reasonable interpretive disagreement as to its meaning. It can, however, at the same time have a very wide scope. Kumm and Comella do not introduce the requirement of substantive or other kind of narrowness as an additional rule in their theory. Without such an additional requirement it could scarcely be claimed that the threat to uniform application of EU law could not be severe under their theory. On the other hand, introducing such a requirement of sufficient narrowness automatically brings to the theory an additional element that would need to be interpreted by courts.[106] If so, the inevitable interpretive disagreement that would arise between national courts and the European ones concerning the question of appropriate degree of narrowness required would, now also through this route,[107] undermine the theory's ambition. It could not be claimed that it has built a category of constitutional rules that can have their applicative meaning assigned directly to democracy (ie the people) and not to interpretations by the courts. It seems that at this point the proposal encounters the difficult position in which it is doomed if it does define the additional requirement of narrowness as well as doomed if it does not.

Thirdly, the authors also propose three straightforwardly procedural elements that, together with the described two, constitute the entire divide. The first of them has already been implied in the discussion thus far: the political community must deem its interests justifying non-compliance with EU law fundamental enough that it incorporates them in the national *constitution*. This must happen either at the time of constitutional enactment or as a later constitutional amendment. The proposal thus in effect suggests that, no matter how fundamental some interests

[104] Kumm and Comella (n 24) at 16–17. [105] Kumm and Comella (n 24) at 17.

[106] Recall the note above explaining that the question of what is and is not of "fundamental" constitutional significance to national community is already one such element (see p. 144).

[107] I have already indicated that the same problems also arise from the first element of the divide, namely, the question of what is or is not "fundamentally important" for a particular member state and its national constitutional identity.

might seem, if they do not take the constitutional form, the national courts are not justified to follow them at the expense of EU law.[108]

Moreover, there also seems to be a more general problematic aspect to the idea that derogation from EU law should be possible through specific constitutional amendments. Some states have very undemanding amendment procedures, others quite demanding ones. Kumm and Comella's proposal might therefore work as an incentive for some states to change their amending procedures. This way the proposal could put severe pressures on uniform application of EU law, for there is nothing in the theory that prevents radically changing the level of amendment procedure in order at some point intentionally to defend national interests against EU law. On the other hand, if such a strategic behavior were somehow discouraged and perhaps even successfully tamed, this would put states with different amending procedures in a radically unequal position as to the normative opportunity for preserving their fundamental national commitments. Moreover, there are, as we know, constitutions that are very thick. These have numerous specific constitutional rules inscribed in their texts, while others, that are significantly thinner, consist mostly of abstract provisions. Does the theory's requirement of a specific constitutional rule thus not end up granting some of the member states wide opportunities to defend, through their courts, their national interests and derogate from EU law while in effect significantly closing off those opportunities from others that prefer constitutional culture of thinner and abstracter constitutions? If so, this formalist approach of the proposal does not seem to take sufficiently into account the reality of, and values behind, some long-established constitutional traditions in Europe. It treats as non-equal and punishes, as it were, those member states whose constitutional cultures imply thinner and more abstract constitutional texts or customs.

The second of the procedural elements requires that, whenever they are faced with such a conflict, the courts of the member states refer to the ECJ. This way the ECJ would not only "have an opportunity . . . to examine how to best interpret the EU provision in light of the possibility of conflict," but it could "also be able to contribute its views on the interpretation of the national constitutional principles at stake."[109] The authors assure that it would still be the national court that would retain the final authority over the interpretation of national constitutional provisions.[110] Yet the point is, they say, that "just as the ECJ may profit from the views of national courts when it decides how to interpret EU Law, so national courts may profit from the ECJ's views when it interprets national constitutional provisions in a context where the enforcement of EU Law is at stake."[111] In other words, such a procedural device may work as an important incentive for developing a useful vertical and horizontal interpretive dialogue between the EU and national courts.[112]

The third procedural element of the divide is the requirement that the highest national court notifies the Commission of its decision. The point here is that the

[108] Kumm and Comella (n 24) at 17.
[109] Kumm and Comella (n 24) at 19.
[110] Kumm and Comella (n 24) at 19.
[111] Kumm and Comella (n 24) at 19.
[112] Kumm and Comella (n 24) at 19.

Commission would in this way be fully aware of the constitutional concerns as elaborated and exposed by the national court.[113] This would enable it then to assess whether it is helpful, or perhaps urgent, to open the issue and seek resolution on the common political level.[114]

This is then, according to Kumm and Comella, the whole refined divide in the new and only remaining legitimate area of conflict. Inside the domain defined by these *five elements*, the national constitutional courts are the final arbiters even when their decisions derogate from EU law as interpreted by the ECJ. They are the final arbiters in the area of "specific and fundamental constitutional commitments," where the content of this standard is procedurally defined. It is what the national level says it is, provided that it satisfies the three further procedural rules. On the other hand, in all other areas of EU law—assuming that the Constitutional Treaty really cures the structural deficiencies in the first two areas of conflict—it is the ECJ which is the final arbiter. This is the case even if its interpretation conflicts with a different constitutional interpretation from the national institutions in these areas.

Yet, as long as something like the reforms under the Constitutional Treaty is not fully adopted, or for some reason is not sufficient to persuade the national courts to give up their claimed jurisdiction, then the first two areas of conflict also remain. In that case, the dividing lines as set for these two areas in Kumm's initial proposal join the divide proposed for the third area. Together they represent the fuller picture of Kumm's conception and meaning of constitutional pluralism.

2. Situating the Theory

Following the decoding tool of Ariadne's Thread, one realizes immediately that the term "constitutional pluralism" has a different primary meaning for Kumm than it has for any of the authors analysed thus far. Unlike those authors, he is working primarily, and almost exclusively, just within the *who* sector of the labyrinth. He constructs the meaning of pluralism with reference to the specific institutional question of that theme: who, the national or European institutions, should have the authority, and final authority, for deciding cases of conflict between their two respective constitutional orders. This gives rise to my label "institutional pluralism." The inevitable result is a different meaning of pluralism from meanings constructed with reference to, say, the substantive-identity question of the *what* or the general interpretive question of the *how*. It is also different from the meanings of pluralism constructed with reference to the deeper issue of the exact nature of the heterarchical relationship (eg procedural versus substantive) at the very foundational level. While the authors examined thus far do, briefly, also say something about the theme of the *who*, those ideas are only their secondary meanings of pluralism. They are either added on top of, or flow from, their primary meanings of pluralism.

[113] Kumm and Comella (n 24) at 19. [114] Kumm and Comella (n 24) at 19.

These are, however, elaborated within one of the other three discourses and with reference to their different topics.

That said, it is important to recall that Kumm's specific conception of pluralism from the discourse of the *who* does also appear to run all the way down to the foundational level. We saw that, although briefly, Kumm did imply that his conception of pluralism is somehow linked to, probably even grounded in, some notion of heterarchy at the foundational level. The notions of the institutional "final authority" (representing the theme of the *who*) and of the deeper "Final Authority" (characteristic of the foundational discourse) that were discussed above with reference to one part of Kumm's text clearly reveal that.[115] That said, it is also clear that Kumm does not really explain that foundational heterarchy in any detail. While just briefly endorsing the most general pluralist rhetoric at that level, he then quickly goes on to show that the meaning of his pluralism is not in the details within that most abstract foundational subject matter, but rather within the subject matter of the *who*. Since Kumm's primary focus is not on any details within the most foundational conception of heterarchy, it is not yet clear what more precisely would his understanding of pluralism at that level look like—whether it would exactly match any of the visions observed thus far, be something similar, or something different altogether. Nor is it clear what, if anything, Kumm would consider to be pluralism within the theme of the *what*, or the *how*. True, he does introduce some interpretive requirements for both the national and European institutions to follow. These are not meant to address, however, the general question of *how*, in order to get things right, to engage in the entire constitutional interpretation across Europe. They instead serve as part of the criterion addressing the narrower pluralist issue of determining which of the two institutions who are in *conflict*, and argue over the disputed *margins* of their constitutional orders, has the (final) authority to decide—the issue of *who*.

Kumm's conception is unique even when compared only to those features in the other authors' conceptions that appear within the same theme of the *who*. In this sense Kumm comes closest to Maduro's general strategy; we saw that Maduro also proposes the distribution of the final decision-making authority according to a specific divide, that of the "conflict of systemic proportion." Yet Kumm's variant is different from the latter proposal in that the particular divide he elaborates is of course not the same. Moreover, Maduro does not primarily work within the theme of the *who*, but only devotes it a few paragraphs, and so his conception within this theme does not come anywhere close to Kumm's in terms of the detail with which he furnishes his own conception.

Nor is the solution of Walker with regards to this theme akin to Kumm's conception. Kumm does not leave the *who* question "open" in the conventional sense of the term that Walker has, and at one point MacCormick had,[116] in mind. The question is rather "open" in the sense that neither the nation-state institutions/orders, nor the European ones/one, enjoy the kind of ultimate Final Authority that we find under monism (the idea of the supreme law of the land).

[115] P. 135.   [116] See Chapter 6, pp. 187–8.

Although this variant of leaving the question "open" is perhaps more similar to Weiler's, rather than Walker's, strategy of ensuring the pluralist openness within the theme of the *who*, it is also not the same as that one. As we saw, within the theme of the *who*, Weiler has in mind the resolution of conflict through the common institution. It is explicitly entrusted with the final decision-making authority in jurisdictional conflicts, but it is at the same time strictly pluralistically conceived so that it preserves equality and self-standing status of the confronting orders. Kumm's variant of leaving the *who* question open does not presuppose such a common institution and also assumes its own unique divide between both sets of institutions, and thus indeed represents yet another unique variant and meaning of pluralism within this specific theme.

3. Assessing the Theory

According to Kumm's latest tentative refinements, the pluralist divide (except for the third, and new, area of conflict) corresponds almost entirely to the boundaries of the EU law domain as interpreted by the ECJ. That said, the question remains whether something like the structural reforms of the Constitutional Treaty, some of those have then been introduced through the Lisbon Treaty, provide sufficient reason for Kumm to believe that the structural deficiencies on the EU level are really resolved. That is, that they are resolved with respect to the first two areas, so that the national courts no longer should claim jurisdiction, nor their final say, in these constitutional areas. Should this be correct, is the general approach to determining the divides in these areas, the approach built round the question of "sufficient guarantees" and its logic of *Solange*, warranted in the first place? And what about the opening of the third area of judicial overlap as envisioned by Kumm—is it supported by logically consistent and persuasive justification? Or should we abandon the idea of this particular category, and its proposed divide, that determines the relationship between the courts in the particular way as they do?

What follows in this concluding section is an intra-theoretical assessment of the main features of Kumm's conception: the three areas and their divides that actually determine the institutional pluralist relationship between the courts. The aim of the assessment is to confirm those features of this particular conception that appear internally coherent and persuasive, as well as to reveal possible logical inconsistencies or other weaknesses within the conception.

3.1 Fundamental rights

It is most realistic to conclude that, in Kumm's conception of pluralism, this area most likely remains within judicial overlap. Some of the key conflict-alleviating features of the new Constitutional Treaty, such as the ratification procedure, have not occurred. Others have, but as some critical observations have already shown thus far, they could hardly work. Nor has the EU yet become party to the European

Convention on Human Rights.[117] With respect to this area it should thus only be reiterated that Kumm's current position cannot but remain the one from his initial proposal. The pluralist divide in that area thus remains the standard of sufficient guarantees, wrapped in the conditional logic of *Solange* but understood procedurally, in terms of comparative structural deficiencies. What is important to keep in mind, and will shortly distinguish the divide in this area from the one in legislative jurisdiction, is that here the European institutions encounter the dilemma of *who* while deciding on issues indisputably within their jurisdiction. That is, they encounter the question in the incidental way while deciding about a fundamental right that is already part of the EU order even though it might also be part of some other order. Bearing in mind this important specificity of the area, Kumm's proposed divide, and the argument behind it, should be considered internally coherent.

3.2 Legislative jurisdictional boundaries

Things seem more problematic with Kumm's proposal in the area of legislative jurisdiction and its dilemma of *Kompetenz-Kompetenz* (KK).[118] It seems to me that to build a solution to the problem of KK around the element of structural deficiencies misses the point. While structural deficiencies, if they exist, could perhaps legitimately play some initial role in one's deliberation on the question, the real problem of the dilemma seems elsewhere. At best, the element of structural deficiencies is not the totality of the KK problem. Indeed, it is when there are no structural deficiencies at either of the levels that the dilemma arises in all its seriousness. It is at that point that we really need an argument as to why this or that side in conflict should be given the final say. To equate the answer to this dilemma fully with the element of structural deficiencies is thus to avoid the core of the dilemma altogether. A proposal that in such circumstances picks the EU side and its Court with an "argument" that this should be so *because there are no longer structural deficiencies at the EU level*, thus seems to do little more than in effect cover a bare choice with a statement that is somewhat misplaced. The choice remains in place while begging the question and leaving the proposal without an argument.

Regardless of whether the structural deficiencies of the EU level do or do not exist, the dilemma of KK persists. Conflict would not be abolished even if the structural deficiencies were cured. As already outlined by some other authors, the new type of division of competences as it appeared in the Constitutional Treaty, or now appears in the Lisbon Treaty, seems to render the national challenges that the

[117] When it does become party to the Convention, it will take several years before the Strasbourg Court can establish a sufficient body of jurisprudence with respect to the issue of potential human rights violations within the EU legal system, against which one could then make the relevant comparison. Be that as it may, this would not remedy the other mentioned factors that seem decisive for this issue.

[118] I use the term *Kompetenz-Kompetenz* here in the narrower sense—to refer to the question of "who decides who decides" in issues of EU legislative competence. That does not also include the similar question of who decides who decides when the courts disagree in the area of fundamental rights.

EU has unduly overstepped its boundaries even "more likely than before."[119] Indeed, it is expected that this disagreement will be both *more frequent* as well as *more radical.* More frequent, because the introduction of additional lines that are equally or even more difficult to discern than those that came before, supports the view that this only creates *more avenues* for potential boundary breaches, and for suspicion from individuals and the national courts about these. More radical, because the stakes will be higher: significantly different consequences now attached to individual categories of competence will contribute towards even more radically different end results emanating from the diverging interpretations at the level of categories. This only seems to offer more reason in the eyes of the national courts to believe that the European institutions are going *too far beyond* the boundaries.

Moreover, such challenges to competence could be accompanied with the claim that another particular feature of the Constitutional Treaty now makes it more difficult than before to argue that the KK should be in the hands of the European institutions and the ECJ. We know of the fierce disagreement from many national courts that have opposed the ECJ's view on this issue. The thrust of their argument is that nothing like that has ever been agreed upon by the national democracies, through a constitutional amendment or via the Treaties themselves, but is instead a mere judicial aberration on the part of the ECJ. Therefore, if the Constitutional Treaty, aware of these persistent challenges, has now *not* used the clear chance that it had to unambiguously settle this issue *in the text* in favor of the ECJ, then those so far persuaded by the national argument would probably see this inaction as reinforcing their position, and not the other way around. While some other *judicial* doctrines have indeed been explicitly reconfirmed now also by such more *democratic* legitimation, such as by being made part of the Constitutional Treaty's text,[120] this has not been the case with the ECJ's doctrine on KK.[121]

This is of course not necessarily to say that the view conferring the KK on European institutions and the ECJ could never succeed unless there is a provision of some European Treaty or Constitution explicitly stipulating so, and/or unless the competences are drawn with such clarity that this prevents serious disagreement regarding their proper interpretation. However, it does mean that one can scarcely solve the KK dilemma by circumventing it, by not getting into such and many other substantive issues involved in the problem. While the element of structural deficiencies of the EU level cannot play the kind of resolving role that Kumm's proposal assigns to it, one might say that it could perhaps nevertheless play at least

119 Craig (n 63) at 9. Weatherill has similarly argued that the Constitutional Treaty's ascription of particular subject-matter areas to each of the heads of competence will actually generate more confusion that it will resolve (S. Weatherill, "Competence" in B. de Witte (ed.), *Ten Reflections on the Constitutional Treaty for Europe* (Florence: EUI, 2003) 45–66).

120 As Kumm and Comella themselves explain at the beginning of their article, such is the judicial doctrine of EU law supremacy excluding the issue of KK (see Kumm and Comella (n 24) at 24).

121 While dealing extensively with competences, Preamble, Part I, Title III ("Union Competences") and in particular its Art I-11 ("Fundamental principles"), do nothing to support the claim of the EU institutions that the power to decide on the ultimate boundaries of the competence is in their hands. Nor is there anything like that in the provision of Art I-29 ("The Court of Justice of the European Union"). See Craig (n 63) at 9.

some part in the deliberation over a possible solution. Yet, even that seems problematic, especially if we take into account the particular way in which Kumm suggests this factor should have a role. It seems that the chosen standard is misplaced in a way that could not apply to this area altogether.

Kumm in his proposal flatly suggested that the same general approach as defined for the fundamental rights area (*Solange*) be used also here in the area of KK: "[The court] could use the same approach it has used concerning basic rights jurisdiction: it *has jurisdiction only to the extent that there are no sufficient guarantees instituted on the European level to prevent unjustified usurpation of legislative power*."[122] As long as there are sufficient guarantees at the EU level, the national courts would choose not to exercise their jurisdiction in issues of competence. We have then also seen that Kumm's "sufficient guarantees" are to be understood and measured procedurally, in terms of whether there are "*structural deficiencies*" on the EU level or not.

This type of approach towards dealing with conflict between the courts does seem to make sense in the area of fundamental rights. The German Federal Constitutional Court had a reason and justification for choosing to build its approach on the logic of *Solange*. Since its founding, and until only very recently, the EU level clearly had a greater degree of structural deficiencies than the national one in that particular area. While the national level had a written fundamental rights catalog binding as law, was bound by the European Convention on Human Rights, and also had a long-established substantive level of rights protection built on years of interpretive tradition, none of this was the case with respect to the EU level. There was no charter of rights on that level and after it came it was not legally binding. Nor was the EU party to the European Convention. Crucially, it also did not have a comparably thorough record of interpretive history on fundamental rights so that the high level of protection could perhaps be guaranteed through that key route. There was thus a reason for the FCC to choose to build a solution in the spirit of *Solange*: a starting *comparative* advantage on the part of the national institutions in this particular area. This would be rooted in this level's greater structural guarantees for the protection of rights just described. Kumm himself understands that the reason for this general approach, which he also adopts, is in just such a *comparative* difference between the two levels. After describing the thorough structural safeguards on the national level, he writes: "If, however, the guarantees afforded by the EU amount to structurally equivalent protections [to those on the national level], then there is no more space for national courts to substitute the EU's judgement on the rights issue with their own."[123]

Kumm's introduction of the same general approach to the area of specific national constitutional commitments also appears warranted.[124] His theory argues that some key structural deficiencies on the EU level result in a relatively greater democratic deficit on that level compared to the national. There we have a

[122] Kumm (n 1) at 379. [123] Kumm (n 2) at 299.

[124] But see subsection 3.3, where I argue that, for some other related reasons, this approach to this area of conflict eventually also cannot succeed.

well-developed civil society, public sphere, clearly articulated national identities, directly representative institutions, etc. Again, if choosing the general *Solange* approach is warranted here, it can be so only for the reason of traditional *comparative* advantages of the national level in this area. Kumm himself thinks there is such a reason, such a justification for the *Solange* approach, present in this area: "*Given the—perhaps inevitable—comparative democratic weakness of the European legislative process*, we suggest that Member States should have the possibility to override the EU legislation"[125] when the constitutional rule is specific and of fundamental importance to the national community. The idea is that, because of this *comparative* advantage, decisions of the national courts on specific constitutional rules could be directly assigned to the will of the people and not to the courts' interpretations. This is different, the argument implies, from the situation in which the *European* courts are given the power to override such constitutional rules (even if with their own specific constitutional rules) in the name of EU law supremacy.

We can see that the very *raison d'etre* for the national courts' adoption of the *Solange* approach in the two discussed areas has thus been rooted in the traditional structural advantages of the national level as compared to the EU level. This is why the national courts have been able to require the European institutions to develop at least the same level of guarantees in these areas, or else insist that the national courts would exercise jurisdiction themselves. In other words, the approach could be justifiably framed in the conditional terms of *Solange* because it protects a certain achieved standard in the practice of procedural democracy or rights protection that is guaranteed by existing comparative structural advantages of the national side. But were the national institutions to lack any comparative advantages in the area of fundamental rights and specific constitutional rules respectively, it seems they could not approach with the *Solange* strategy. In that case they themselves would provide no better alternative from the European institutions in the relevant sense, and would thus lose the very purpose for which such an approach could be selected and justified in the first place.

This is precisely what seems to make Kumm's selection of the same element—"structural deficiencies"—useless in the KK dilemma. By simply copying the approach from the area of fundamental rights and planting it into the area of KK, the proposal ignores the crucial circumstance: there does not seem to have ever been a state of relevant comparative structural advantages of the national courts over the EU ones in the area of policing legislative jurisdictional boundaries. A close reading of Kumm's text confirms that, unlike in the two previous areas, here he does not really engage in a comparative assessment of the structural guarantees at each of the levels. The result is that he actually does not present any comparative difference in the strength of structural guarantees between the two levels in this area. We are not told who is better suited to interpret the competence boundaries correctly.[126] It seems that in connection with this area it would be scarcely possible

[125] Kumm and Comella (n 24) at 16 (emphasis added).

[126] That the current ECJ's procedure does not suffice for building a serious culture of subsidiarity is not such a *comparative* deficiency of the EU level. For there is nothing in the procedure of the national

to speak of some obvious comparative structural advantages, such as found in the two previous areas, existing on the side of the national courts. And this seems to hold true since the very start, since the very founding of the European level. For example, unlike the case with rights, there *is* here the text that binds as law. These are the competence-related provisions of the European Treaty. Moreover, this document is the *same* for both sides so that neither side has any comparative advantage or disadvantage in this structural sense. If there are structural deficiencies associated with the document, as they were in the rights area, then here they apply with equal force to each of the levels and their interpretations of competence boundaries.

It is also scarcely possible to speak of any richer interpretive tradition of the national courts, that is, of the protection of the "achieved level," when it comes to the decisive questions in this area. These are questions, such as what is the correct interpretation of the competence categories and their proper separation as follows from the Constitutional Treaty? Or, what is the correct meaning of the European principle of subsidiarity that determines the limits of the EU competence use? Unlike fundamental rights, these are both relatively new interpretive categories, inextricably bound up with the EU. They have not developed their achieved interpretive tradition independently of, and before, the EU and its interpretive practice. Hence, we could not speak of some prior "achieved level" existing at the national side, and one which the EU would need to pursue as a goal and hopefully reach at some point.

Furthermore, it would also not be justifiable to assign *in advance* to one of the levels, but not to the other, some greater degree of normative bias with respect to particular types of stakes (eg the European versus the national) involved in the competence disputes, and to infer from that about the greater structural deficiencies of that level.[127] Indeed, according to Kumm's own theory, both of the courts are *normatively* required to take potential positions of all the constitutional orders—all national as well as European—equally into account. Recall his requirement that the right interpretive question is not what is best for the European level, or national one, but rather what is the best interpretation seen from the perspective of all these constitutional orders taken as a whole. An *actual* systematic disparity between the outcomes of the national and European institutions, which might well appear despite such a normative framework, could also not by itself already suffice as a proof of greater comparative deficiencies of the European level in this area. A judicial interpretation of competence boundaries that is too narrow would be no less an infringement on the *demoi*'s self-government than would be too expansive.

courts—which is probably even less inclusive of *all* the European *demoi*—that could better guarantee the proper development of such a culture. So, unlike in the two previous areas, here we do not have the needed comparative advantage in order to really justify the adoption of the *Solange* approach by the national courts as proposed by Kumm.

[127] Kumm and Comella write that "European institutions, including the ECJ, have been widely perceived as not taking jurisdictional boundaries seriously" (n 24 at 12). This itself does nothing to corroborate the view that the problem lies in comparatively greater structural deficiencies of the European level and that consequently the national courts' position should be that of the default one.

If all this is correct then the very *raison d'être* justifying the selection of this approach in the area of rights and specific constitutional rules seems to be missing in this third area of conflict. KK is a different type of problem from the previous two. This makes it doubtful that the element of "structural guarantees" could even play a role as *one* of the elements/factors involved in the discourse aimed at constructing the best pluralist solution. And even if this second problem could be avoided, the first and immediate one remains. The element of "structural deficiencies" is not the totality of the KK problem and does not by itself solve much of it. It instead leaves the proposed divide without an argument. The conception scarcely offers any help to the courts who, regardless of the element of structural differences, always inevitably disagree on such issues, and would, under the proposed delineation of competence by the Constitutional Treaty, very likely disagree even more intensely. The intra-theoretical analysis therefore shows that this part of the conception, if it could be retained, would need to be readjusted and supplied by substantive argumentation. Only then could it enter the inter-theoretical confrontation among the coherent, but different proposals on this issue. Some other rationale should fill the gap and replace the factor of "sufficient structural guarantees" as the decisive test in this area.

3.3 Specific constitutional rules

We have already encountered the first problem with this category: that the standards introduced by it cannot escape reasonable interpretative disagreement between the courts. The standard of specificity, if it is really not going to pose any threat to the uniform application of EU law, will need to be understood also in terms of narrowness. What is and is not a sufficiently narrow constitutional rule is, however, an inherently contested issue. It will be up to the courts' interpretation, not the people, to determine its proper application in an individual case at hand. This means not only that the European and national courts could, and would, often disagree. But it means especially that such national court's interpretations could not a priori be guaranteed grater democratic character as compared to the interpretations of the same standards by the ECJ. The same problem accompanies the standard of "fundamentally important" constitutional rule. It is the highest national court that will need to *interpret* what counts as "constitutionally fundamental." Its own interpretation will inevitably be just one out of many possible and conflicting positions within the bounds of reasonable interpretive disagreement.[128] Here, too, automatic application of the standard is therefore not possible, and thus we must realize that it is not really about the "clear will" of the constitutional legislature,

[128] As we have seen, Kumm himself recognized, for instance, how his example with the Greek provision on the public monopoly of higher education is a "close case," and he correctly expressed himself in terms of likelihood ("most likely") that the courts would go one or the other way when it comes to the other two of his examples. There will be a host of controversial cases like these, and much more so than these.

which is what Kumm's proposal of this category assumes and really needs in order to succeed.

Moreover, the requirement that the specific and fundamental derogation from EU law is fine as long as it takes the form of a constitutional amendment, might be too formal. The proposal would thus be fine even with grave and frequent derogations enabled by, say, lowered standards for amendment procedures by a member state. Alternatively, by additionally perhaps discouraging change in amendment procedures, it would foster quite unequal conditions for different member states and their ability to defend their national commitments against the EU law. This formal approach seems to discriminate between different constitutional cultures and their respective citizens that nourish very different—specific and thick as opposed to abstract and principled—concepts of a constitution.

Another problem is the following. The assumption about the automatically higher democratic quality of a specific national constitutional rule as compared to that of the EU law which it confronts, could sometimes not be maintained even if the rule is indisputably specific and fundamental. Imagine a specific constitutional provision providing that voting rights, including at local and municipal elections, are only rights of the nationals. The rule is specific and clear. A national court does not need to interpret it, and it has been enacted by the constitutional legislator; by, for instance, some majority of a parliament. On the other hand, imagine a specific constitutional rule at the European level which is, however, the opposite of the national rule. It requires that all the European citizens have the right to vote and be elected at local and municipal elections. Compatibility of the European rule with democracy is incomparably greater than that of the quite undemocratic national rule in this example, and this is so whether or not we also take into account the process in which one or the other has been adopted.

When it comes to the argument from the democratic process through which the rule has been enacted, Kumm and Comella thus *too generally* assume the greater democratic nature of the nation-state specific constitutional rules. Even though they are probably correct in assuming that the constitution-making process at the national level is generally more representative of the people's will than is that at the EU level, this does not just automatically provide comparatively greater democratic quality of national constitutional rules in *each and every individual* case. There might be individual instances of specific rules enacted at the EU level that would enjoy a similar or higher democratic legitimation as some of the specific constitutional rules at the national level. Indeed, the democratic quality of an individual decision adopted at the European level might be impressive. Citizens of Europe or their interested groups may have participated intensively and with their authentic opinions throughout wide and intensive forums of participation provided for in a given area of EU law.[129] They might have thus almost literally enacted the particular rule by themselves. By contrast, it is at the same time possible that in a case of some specific national provision confronting such a rule, member-state

[129] Cf P. Craig, *EU Administrative Law* (Oxford: Oxford University Press, 2006) at 324–6.

citizens did not participate at all. They were never asked about their views on the issue and the provision instead came out as a result of some factional compromise between party elites in the parliament. It is clear that in such circumstances too, it is scarcely possible to justify the formal categorical approach of the proposal on the ground that the specific national constitutional rules would *always* be the more democratic.

This point is reinforced by the fact that the directly elected European Parliament now has real power since the procedure of co-decision has been introduced.[130] Following the Constitutional Treaty the Lisbon Treaty even further improved that procedure. Kumm and Comella's remark—that the reforms "do . . . not in fact strengthen directly representative institutions on the EU level"[131]—thus seems wrong as a matter of law. By improving the mentioned procedure, the reforms actually did enhance the role of the European Parliament as the direct representative institution in the EU legislative process.

Moreover, the problems with the proposed category could also go beyond the situation in which we have two specific constitutional rules, from the member state and the EU, confronting one another. It could be argued that even when we have a specific constitutional provision at the member state side, and a non-specific rule at the EU side, this does not necessarily imply that an interpretation by a court, in this case the ECJ, would *always* be less democratic than the direct application of the specific rule by the national court. The fact that some provision is enacted by some qualified—for instance, parliamentary—majority does not automatically guarantee greater democratic quality of that provision. Ideally, such a qualified majority indeed enacts a rule that represents an authentic will of the people, but sometimes it can also adopt something that does not have much to do with such a will, or even goes against it.[132] Even though some constitutional rule is adopted through a nationwide referendum, this is not necessarily democratic.[133] Moreover, there are examples of specific constitutional amendments clearly closing off important rights and channels for democracy, like the ones depriving some group of discrete

[130] Craig (n 129) at 108; P. Craig and G. de Búrca, *EU Law: Text, Cases, and Materials* (Oxford: Oxford University Press, 2003) 144–6.

[131] Kumm and Comella (n 24) at 16.

[132] Raz comments in an analogous way arguing that this "all depends on the circumstances." "For example, we may have sufficient reason to believe that the legislature will not even try to establish what [democratic] rights people have, or what restraint it should exercise . . . whereas the courts, who are in charge of enforcing constitutional [democratic] rights, will try honestly to do so . . . In many countries there are ample reasons to suspect that members of the legislature are moved by sectarian interests to such a degree that are not likely even to attempt to establish what [democratic] rights (some) people have. The same consideration may apply to courts as well. But it is possible for them not to apply to courts, even while they apply to the legislature." J. Raz, "Disagreement in Politics" (1998) 43 American Journal of Jurisprudence 25, 46.

[133] Perhaps the most radical demonstration of this point is the constitutional referendum for Anschluss, which won in Germany as well as Austria by a majority of over 99%. In practice the decision endorsed, among others, that potential political dissenters such as social democrats and communists, as well as Jews, were being rounded up and either imprisoned or sent to concentration camps. Within only a few days 70,000 people had been arrested, not to mention the even darker far-reaching legacy of the decision for Anschluss. If anything, this was not democratic.

and insular minority, or other unpopular groups, of their democratic rights.[134] The closest approximation to self-government is not necessarily guaranteed by the specificity of a constitutional rule, but can *sometimes* be realized even better through, say, a court's interpretation of an abstract constitutional provision.[135]

The approach of carving out this particular category of specific and fundamental constitutional rules is problematic for yet another related reason. It suggests that even something which is far more fundamental than Kumm's examples, but which does not happen to be in the form of a *specific* rule, should a priori not be protected by the national constitutional level and its highest court. It should be sacrificed at the expense of some provision of EU law even if the latter were quite insignificant. This is clearly against the doctrines of the Spanish and Italian courts, and the reason for this somewhat anomalous formalist result is again that same unwarranted, exception-less assignment of greater democratic quality to the specific, but not abstract, constitutional rules.

It should be concluded that the general and categorical approach of Kumm's proposal in this area—that when it comes to the specific national constitutional rules it is the national court that should have the final say *because of the greater democratic character that its decision in such cases would automatically enjoy*—cannot be *always* justified. This does not mean that there is no other possible justification for the same or similar category and its divide, or that this one does not hold in some cases. It is only to suggest that the proposition of the relatively greater democratic deficit of the European level cannot serve as such a general justification, warranting the existence of the newly proposed category. Kumm's proposal needs to be internally refined further in order then to engage in the inter-theoretical confrontation with its competing pluralist accounts and argue there for its own superiority.

134 Cf *Romer v Evans* 517 US 620 (1996).

135 A possible general argument for participatory democracy (governed by some version of majority rule) as *always* being the nearest possible approximation to self-determination thus cannot succeed. In a related sense Raz also maintains that often "[a]rguing one's case before a learned and impartial tribunal gives one more power over the determination of one's rights than being one among the multitude in a participatory democracy, with equality of political power" (Raz (n 132) at 45).

PART II

ASSESSMENT

6

Decoding the Branch

1. The Opening Finding

The mapping has focused on contributions that emerged soon after MacCormick's earliest article and have gradually coalesced, MacCormick's conception included, under the common label of constitutional pluralism. Participants in this discourse and observers alike often conveyed the understanding of mutual similarity and corroboration between these proposals under the common label. So it became a general view that the discourse had initiated, and belonged to, a distinctive common enterprise within constitutional theory. The idea of a branch of constitutional pluralism was born: one that claims to have brought a new and normatively superior understanding of the concept of constitutionalism to Europe and to constitutional thought in general. In light of these understandings, part of the aim of this project has been to clarify what it is that constitutional pluralism truly comprises, and then to see whether, when so clarified, it can be understood as representing a unique common branch within constitutional thought. Decoding and explaining some common essence that would need to constitute the branch, if true, is at the core of this quest.

The mapping analysis conducted through the previous chapters is a precondition to reaching this aim of the project. It leads to an opening thesis that may spring to mind while one surveys the terrain. The thesis is that the contributions under the common label of constitutional pluralism might be much more different than it has been generally assumed. Indeed, someone who enters the labyrinth of constitutional pluralism with an interest in getting to know more about the alleged new enterprise can easily be led astray by its seemingly common-sounding general rhetoric, such as the mutual pluralist respect/tolerance as opposed to some monist disregard of the Other, or the non-hierarchical pluralist autonomy of systems instead of their hierarchical monist dependency, and the like. The more one wanders through the maze, however, the more one realizes that the similar-sounding echoes do not necessarily mean that one is reading the labyrinth successfully. There are different meanings behind the same term of heterarchy, of pluralism, and one soon becomes aware that despite the similar rhetoric one must often actually be within wholly different sectors that merely resemble one another, but are in fact distinct, while also frequently leading in wholly opposing directions. The deceptive general echoes that sound so familiar must be concealing very different projects and topics behind their facade.

The mapping analysis as conducted through the preceding chapters thus engaged with this. It was the decoding tool—our Ariadne's Thread—that played the key role in the mapping's clarification. Employing it, we were able simultaneously to distinguish each proposal as we moved through the labyrinth and observed the different understandings of pluralism. Chapter by chapter, the decoding tool reminded us of the particular location, within the maze, of a given version of pluralism under scrutiny. We were able to know how it differed from, and often contradicted, other versions that worked within sometimes wholly different sectors of the maze. With help provided by using Ariadne's Thread, confusion was avoided despite the deceptive common rhetoric. The labyrinth was gradually being mapped using the tool, which uncovered the variety of very different meanings as we moved along. This now enables us to draw conclusions that confirm the opening thesis.

In Chapter 1 we were able to observe that MacCormick's initial proposal actually appears within a discourse that is situated on the level of the deep foundations of systems theory. It operates with the term "pluralism" in some basic sense as it examines at length and on highly theoretical grounds the relationship between systems and their sources of constitutional authority. It cannot itself be characterized as the discourse typical of the subject matter of the *how*, or the *what*, or the *who*. Indeed, it does not focus on the question of a particular right form of the constitutional discourse, on elaborating a set of interpretive discursive rules that the actors would need to follow in order to constitute pluralism. Nor does it engage with the questions of the right external reconciliation of particular substantive identities, resulting in some building blocks like those identified in Weiler's pluralist discourse. Similarly, the conception does not constitute pluralism by a particular solution within the theme of "who decides who decides." As represented in Chapter 1, MacCormick's initial conception of pluralism simply does not enter those types of discourses, but constitutes a separate discourse of its own.

In Chapter 2 we observed that part of Walker's thinking, too, appears within the sector of the foundational discourse. It was then showed, however, that epistemic pluralism centers decisively, and indeed deliberately, also around the further question concerning the best way to avoid the substantive discourse on constitutionalism and constitutional content. It is thus about the search for the best form—the *how*—of constitutional discourse. In this light, its only objectively valid meta-constitutional demand, besides some wholly uncontroversial minima, is to suspend assertions of the objective rightness in second-order constitutional claims, and to negotiate reflexively when within first-order constitutional discourse.

This differs starkly from Weiler's substantive pluralism examined in Chapter 3. That theory is about the direct quest for some objectively valid substantive building blocks and therefore deals with the substantive discourse itself: the *what* of constitutional discourse. The *how* and the *what* represent two different subject matters, two different discourses and their questions, and the two projects that focus on them respectively are two very different things. When they nonetheless can be seen as parts of the same general quest for the best conception of constitutionalism, the orientations of each project differ significantly; so much so that each would understand the other not only as wrong but also as deeply monist. Walker's epistemic pluralism treats as such any proposal that would entrench at the meta-constitutional level anything more than his thin procedural rules. Likewise, the point of Weiler's direct substantive balance is, at its minimum, to condemn as not consistent with the highest possible pluralist respect any other approach that would refuse to endorse, as objectively correct, his thick substantive meta-blocks. The same common-sounding rhetoric of true and highest pluralist respect, in the inter-systemic sense as well as the intra-systemic sense of individuals and groups, indeed appears to cover up not one but two very different projects with two very different and conflicting subject matters and orientations.

In Chapter 4, our tool then helped decode and situate also Maduro's interpretive/participative pluralism. It was observed that this is also a version of the discourse within the theme of the *how*. Interpretive/participative pluralism therefore shares in general the dissimilarities that epistemic pluralism has in relation to substantive pluralism. The latter insists that enhancement of democracy thinly understood—which is the only goal that, according to interpretive/participatory pluralism, the new Europe ought to foster through its meta-constitution—is not yet itself a sufficiently substantive subject-matter. We have seen how Weiler has written many times that mere democracy thus understood is not to be seen as the end of the European project. Hence, he insists that even if one succeeded with the ambition to enhance representation and participation to the fullest extent possible, one would still not be focusing on the right subject matter of substantive ends themselves of the European project. The subject matter of his substantive pluralism and its discourse of the *what*—resulting in the building blocks—is still significantly different from the immediate subject matter of Maduro's pluralism. For this is concerned "only" with enhancement of participation and representation thinly understood, and thus falls within the discourse of the *how* as explained in Chapter 4. Here too, the difference between the subject matters and their distinct questions/discourses can be translated into a considerable degree of opposition between the two projects, their very orientations, and their understandings of pluralism versus monism. This is the case regardless of the deceptive general rhetoric that covers up the opposition here as well. Lastly, even though the opposition is of a lesser degree when interpretive/participatory pluralism is compared to epistemic pluralism, both instances of the discourse of *how*, there are also some crucial distinctions in the understanding of pluralism between these two cognate approaches, as explained in Chapter 4.

Throughout these chapters the decoding tool then separated yet another type of discourse and meaning of pluralism. This one is primarily neither about the question of the right form (the *how*) nor substance (the *what*) of constitutional discourse as a whole. It is instead focused on the narrower question of *who*—either the nation-state or European institutions—should have the final say in areas where interpretations of the two sets of institutions conflict. A particular conception *within this* narrower discourse is, on this view, understood to represent pluralism as opposed to monism. Kumm's understanding of the term "pluralism" primarily in this sense is the most paradigmatic example of this yet another distinct discourse, or subject matter, that appears within the pluralist literature. Moreover, as we saw in Chapters 2–4, the other pluralists themselves sometimes use the same term ("pluralism") regardless of whether they are arguing for a distinctive conception within *this* particular discourse (the *who*), or when they propose conceptions within their primary discourses (be it the *how* or *what*). This often leads to confusion and mistaken comparisons. For, the meaning of pluralism as understood within the discourse of the *who* of constitutional discourse, and the meaning of pluralism as it appears in each of the other two identified discourses, cannot be directly compared. They too, are considerably different things that ought not to be conflated on the basis of confusing common rhetoric that might echo around them. That being said, it is true that, as we saw in Chapters 2–4, the authors who construct their primary conceptions within the discourses of the *how* and *what* sometimes indirectly build from there also their specific conceptions for the discourse of the *who*. Yet, this only makes the division between the pluralists sharper: due to the distinct background projects, these conceptions of pluralism within the discourse of the *who* then differ significantly. This is so much so that, again, their proponents cannot but consider each other as monist when judged from their own individual perspectives. Recall how an epistemic pluralist who leaves fully open the question of "who decides who decides," and indeed understands this as being pluralism as opposed to monism within the discourse of *who*, has to treat substantive pluralism's proposal for the third arbiter—for example, Weiler's Constitutional Council—as a clear monist solution that is no better than the two old monist options.[1] The epistemic pluralist must also treat similarly Maduro's unique version of the detailed and fixed external division of authority between the existing institutions of last resort, which is what his interpretive pluralism in the last analysis suggests. At the same time, these authors would think of epistemic pluralism's radical openness of the question as unduly destabilizing the system and so as, paradoxically, disabling the real pluralism.[2] In this discourse too, there are precisely as many significantly contradicting understandings of pluralism as there are pluralists themselves.

The thesis is confirmed: the contributions that started to appear under the common label of constitutional pluralism are significantly different things. This stands as the opening finding of the project. But the finding does not deserve such a label only for its natural place in the project in the sequential sense. It is "opening" also because its very confirmation opens out a highly relevant further question, even a puzzle, about the pluralist branch. For if it is true, as I argued, that in important respects the different pluralists do not even deal with the same subject matter, the same sets of questions/discourses, and, moreover, if it is also true that when they can be seen as dealing with the same questions their positions often contradict one another to the degree that they would consider each other's proposals as clearly monist when judged by each other's own standards, then what does this mean for constitutional pluralism *as a branch*? That is, could we truly speak of the novel common branch of constitutional pluralism, or do we have here instead no more

[1] Pp. 52 and 95–6.

[2] We saw that was, for instance, Maduro's view of Walker's proposal within the discourse of *who*. On the other hand, he would also understand Weiler's proposal for the EU Constitutional Council as a monist solution.

but a rhetoric masking a group of actually non-familial proposals with no common core that could bring that alleged uniqueness into constitutional thought, Europe, and the world? What, if anything at all, could a common branch in such circumstances possibly be?

In section 2 it will be argued that there may be a way to solve the puzzle through a missing link. Although the latter has neither been singled out, nor really explained by any of the pluralists, it can be extracted already from the basis of MacCormick's initial account of pluralism. Once the link is then added to the picture, the different proposals and their discourses start to fall together and potentially form a common branch. It will be argued, however, that if they are indeed thus to be seen as belonging to the same common branch, then this branch needs to be understood in a particular way which is different from the way that has been assumed by any of the present pluralist proposals. This will provide the first actual clarification of the common essence of the new branch and its exact relation to the various further understandings of constitutional pluralism as proposed by each of the individual authors. This will also complete the explanation of the labyrinth of the pluralist branch as a whole. In section 3 I will then try to show that this particular decoding of the pluralist branch, this full clarification of the labyrinth, can also be confirmed in a particular way. I will argue thus by drawing on relevant parts of MacCormick's scholarship other than his initial article in which he introduced pluralism. This will at the same time develop his initial account (from Chapter 1) further into a more complete conception of his constitutional pluralism.

2. Decoding the Branch

The very existence of the branch is threatened. At the minimum, the latter cannot be taken for granted under these circumstances, and there is a pressing need to solve the puzzle posed by the opening finding.

There are only two options at this stage. Either these strikingly different projects and their subject matters would have to fit together somehow and form a whole: only in this case could they qualify as a branch. Or else we would have to accept that they are altogether too different and just do not coalesce. In this case we would conclude that actually there is no common branch, but a set of different proposals with no common core that could secure the claim of that potential uniqueness of the undertaking by the pluralists as a group.

At first it might seem that the four different types of discourses are too different. Each of them has its own understanding of the features that constitute constitutional pluralism, and these features appear within distinct subject matters, distinct discourses and their opposing orientations. Whatever common-sounding rhetoric there might be among the "pluralists," the indications of a shared view appear to be just that—mere misleading rhetoric covering up what in reality appears to be an empty idea of a new and distinctive common enterprise or even branch.

It might nonetheless be possible, after such a mapping analysis, to start making real progress towards a different conclusion. The first step towards that end is the following. We saw that the decoding tool not only separates the discourses, but also enables constant comparison of the actual differences between them. Observing things from this perspective, one might have noticed that one of the conceptions—namely MacCormick's—may not be in such a relationship of significant dislocation and contradiction to the other three discourses (the *how*, *what*, *who*) as was observed to be the case between the latter themselves. While surely its direct concern is the highly theoretical question that is not dealt with directly by the *how*, *what*, and *who* discourses, it is nonetheless the type of question that could perhaps accommodate those other three discourses and their specific questions. MacCormick's could be the broadest question, the broadest subject matter that could be seen as being in the background of all of the more concrete subject matters of the *how*, *what*, and *who* discourses, respectively.

Although Weiler's substantive pluralism does not deal directly—on the level of the systemic theory—with these questions over the relationship between systems, and despite the fact that he does not explicitly ground his pluralist proposal in such a theoretical basis, we nonetheless investigated whether his substantive pluralism could be read in a way as to endorse such deep foundations. As discussed in Chapter 2, this link between Weiler's substantive pluralist proposal and its potential basis in something like the final version of MacCormick's foundation—that is, the view about the self-standing, heterarchically coexisting constitutional formations and their sources of authority—could indeed be there.[3] True, Weiler's conception must in such a case be interpreted in a particular way—his concrete building blocks would need to be seen as deriving precisely from the ongoing confrontation and balancing at the deepest normative level between the two coexisting sources/orders of constitutional authority, and as the only normatively sound route[4] out of such a confrontation—but the point is that the link with MacCormick's abstract pluralist foundation can in this way clearly be established.[5]

Weiler wrote recently that his conception might differ from MacCormick's in that his own is grounded not so much in legal theory, but in politics and political theory: it does not follow, in his view, that from a mere confrontation between two constitutional systems pluralism (Europe's *Sonderweg*) would necessarily arise.[6] The latter, as Weiler explains, must be normatively required.[7] We have seen, however, in

[3] See Chapter 3, pp. 73–4 and 91–2. See also p. 224, following.

[4] Out of several routes that are also possible, but are considered unsound in his view. Among those are, for instance, the monist option of the sovereign United States of Europe, where the federal level prevails, or all those non-substantive pluralist proposals from other pluralists that Weiler also rejects.

[5] This is the picture that the analysis in Chapter 3 unfolded; see subsections 1.2 and 1.3.

[6] J. Weiler, "Prologue: Global and Plural Constitutionalism—Some Doubts" in G. de Búrca and J. Weiler (eds), *The Worlds of European Constitutionalism* (Cambridge: Cambridge University Press, 2012) 13–14.

[7] Weiler (n 6) at 13–14.

Chapter 1 that, when fully unfolded, MacCormick's pluralist foundation, in addition to whatever starting point it had in non-normative legal theory, also then had a strong normative dimension that was openly rooted in politics and political theory.[8] On a closer reading, MacCormick's conception is, on this point, not at all incompatible with that of Weiler.[9]

Similarly, with his project of interpretive/participative pluralism, Maduro has also not directly focused on the prior theoretical questions about the systemic relationship between the actors. But while centering fully round the question of the proper form of the constitutional discourse in Europe (our question of *how*), he did at the beginning at least open the possibility to interpretation that his proposal, too, should be seen as originating from something like the broader theoretical foundations of the type examined by MacCormick's pluralism. Before starting with his own subject matter Maduro thus briefly wrote that "it has now become usual to highlight how the different national and European perspectives on the notion of the ultimate authority in Europe require a constitutional pluralist conception of the relationship between European and national constitutionalism," and that "it was rare to draw from that any consequences as to the overall interpretation and application of EU law and as to the way we should address its constitutional questions."[10] Insofar as we read the latter part of the quote as announcing the specific orientation of Maduro's pluralist project, then this does enable us to connect his pluralism to the foundational and broader subject matter of MacCormick's type of pluralism (potentially the first part of the quote).

Kumm's is a similar case. While working within the discourse of the *who*, his account of the pluralist conception within that unique discourse did at one point provide a hint that all of that construction within the *who* might ultimately owe its origin to some pluralist conception at a much more foundational level of discourse. This was the point at which we were able to distinguish the two different meanings of authority behind his explanations: the "final authority" and the "Final Authority," where the first was about the issue of "who decides who decides" (Kumm's primary theme of the *who*) and the second about the question of the foundational ultimate authority. To be sure, Kumm did not develop and defend a whole unique conception of pluralism (of heterarchy) also at that foundational level, nor did he repeat

[8] See Chapter1, section 4, especially pp. 26–7, 29, and n 86, where the normative foundational similarity between both conceptions is clearly exposed. For the equally striking applicative normative similarity between both conceptions, compare the discussion of Weiler's building blocks (Chapter 3, subsection 1.3, especially pp. 77–81) with that of MacCormick's very similar substantive normative construction in this chapter, subsection 3.2, at pp. 177–87.

[9] It might well be that MacCormick gradually came to share Weiler's, as we will later see, valid point as a result of their exchanges; see, eg Weiler's remarks about their discussions in his "Prologue: Global and Plural Constitutionalism" (n 6) at 13. Yet it would not be accurate, I think, to assume that MacCormick thought genuine pluralism could arise out of mere confrontation between two constitutional systems without any further pluralist requirement rooted in normative political theory. In my discussions with him of my text on that point (Edinburgh University, December 2006) he explicitly insisted that I leave that part of the text (referred to in the previous note) intact as the preferred reading of his theory.

[10] M. Maduro, "Contrapunctual Law: Europe's Constitutional Pluralism in Action" in N. Walker (ed.), *Sovereignty in Transition* (Oxford: Hart Publishing, 2003) 501.

MacCormick's, or Walker's, pluralist account within that discourse. Yet, the fraction he had on the "Final Authority" does indicate that he too assumes there is something unique, something pluralist as opposed to monist, also at the foundational level and that, again, his own conception owes its origin to that foundational uniqueness.

The clearest case is Walker's epistemic pluralism. The latter, as we saw, not only assumed such a theoretical basis of his pluralism, but to a degree even, like MacCormick, he himself directly engaged in this broader subject matter before going further into the more specific question of *how*, which for him explicitly springs from that broader theoretical level of the pluralist discourse.[11]

That was easy, one might think. We have found it! MacCormick's foundational discourse on pluralism that deals with the broadest subject matter must actually be the underlying theoretical basis from which all the other (previously intermingled) conceptions of pluralism, with their more specific subject matters, originate. One might conclude that, with the help of Ariadne's Thread, the puzzle is solved.

But is that really the case? Can this first step in pointing to the possible common roots in the foundational discourse truly already unravel the puzzle of the branch? Not quite, I believe. For, as we saw already in Chapters 1 and 2, it is even at the level of this potential underlying theoretical basis that at least some different understandings of pluralism differ and contradict one another.[12] Under Walker's epistemic pluralism it was exclusively its particular procedural concessions that were considered as constitutive of pluralism as regards the basis of the pluralist discourse. That, we saw, conflicted with the different understanding in MacCormick's account of pluralism that instead required substantive concessions as the constitutive feature of pluralism on this same level of discourse. It is, moreover, far from clear what exact type of understanding of pluralism on this same, deepest level would be endorsed by the other three authors whose projects do not (yet) directly engage with this, the broadest subject matter at all. Some of them might endorse Walker's understanding, others MacCormick's, not to mention the possibility that they could introduce solutions of their own, as they did on the more specific levels of the pluralist discourse. We see that the puzzle is real. The disagreement already goes all the way down to the roots and threatens there to strike the pluralist branch a fatal blow. If it is even at the level of the roots—the possible deepest foundational basis itself—that we have different and opposing understandings of pluralism, then there is indeed no branch here at all. Rather there is only a set of different and conflicting meanings of pluralism that cannot be made to fit into a whole by any minimum common denominator. The puzzle seems to be coming after us with a vengeance.

The situation might not, at this point, seem too good for the branch, and yet the solution is not too far away. We should now take the second step towards the decoding of the branch. Picking up Ariadne's Thread again, not only were we able to see that the only place where a solution could potentially be sought is

[11] Chapter 1, pp. 22 and 24, and Chapter 2 pp. 38–9 and 50.
[12] Chapter 1, pp. 22–4, and Chapter 2, pp. 38–40, 50.

the foundational discourse and its broadest subject matter. The Thread now also tells us that we need to be careful to compare only certain things: that is, only those conceptions/meanings of pluralism that do make a contribution within *this* particular discourse. To focus here on Weiler's, Maduro's, and Kumm's meanings of pluralism, which mostly appear outside the foundational discourse, while trying to compare those to one another and to the meanings posited by Walker and MacCormick within the foundational discourse, will not help solve the particular puzzle concerning the branch. For this purpose our focus should instead primarily be on MacCormick and Walker who, as we know, assume conceptions of pluralism within this same foundational discourse as the potential basis of all other, more derivative meanings of pluralism. The key would then be to try and see if their two different meanings of pluralism could perhaps be united in what is even some higher abstraction—conception—within this same foundational level, but an abstraction that would still be distinct from monism. That could potentially provide us with a missing link required to solve the puzzle.

There is actually one even deeper possible abstraction of MacCormick's position within the foundational discourse, just as there is for Walker's. Before identifying it we should briefly bring back to mind the exact distinction between both authors as to the meaning of pluralism within this deepest level of discourse. Recall thus that MacCormick's conception of pluralism, of heterarchy, was constituted by what I called "substantive concessions." According to this meaning of pluralism, constitutional authorities of two orders that coexist over the same piece of territory need to have their own roughly equal share of substantive authority over that territory. The division of authority between the EU substantive sphere and the substantive sphere remaining with the member states is the clearest case in point. This, MacCormick implies, is pluralism, or the new condition of heterarchy that makes the idea of sovereignty in Europe (the idea of a single locus of ultimate authority on a given territory) wholly obsolete. The new pluralist Europe is already in the condition of "beyond sovereignty."

Recall now also Walker's conception of pluralism within this deep foundational discourse. His pluralism (heterarchy) is constituted by procedural concessions: his requirement that any of the two orders' claims to a single ultimate authority (sovereignty) over a given shared territory must be recognized, by both orders, as only internally, as opposed to externally, correct. Walker's epistemic pluralism is thus not defined by substantive concessions. We saw in Chapter 2 that to impose anything more on the orders than Walker's requirement of the thin procedural concessions is already understood as being opposite to this meaning of pluralism. As a result, a member state may, according to Wallker's pluralism, continue claiming its ultimate all-purpose authority over the entire substantive domain on its territory, and even expand its de facto power, as long as it concedes that the claim is now true only from the perspective of its own internal *episteme*. And the member state may also openly aspire to making such a result objectively accepted in the future. The same "thin" regime applies also to the EU. This is indeed why, for Walker, the concept of sovereignty is far from being rendered obsolete in the context of pluralism as he understands it.

Each of the authors assumes different types of concessions as being constitutive of pluralism at the foundational level. Each believes that there is no pluralism without *his* particular type of concessions. At this level the two conceptions of pluralism thus still contradict one another significantly. Yet, as mentioned above, it is possible to draw an even higher abstraction from both these two conceptions. This is the very last possible abstraction within this foundational discourse that may still differ from monism. It is the last remaining place, then, to look for a missing link that could potentially decode the whole branch and still keep viable the claim to its uniqueness as a *common* branch that is distinct from monism.

After thus abstracting MacCormick's understanding of pluralist heterarchy even further, we arrive at a slightly different understanding of heterarchy. Such a heterarchy leaves out some of MacCormick's idiosyncrasies—namely, his requirement of substantive concessions—while still retaining some minimal feature that is common to both MacCormick and Walker. In the same way, if we thus abstract Walker's conception of pluralism, and *his* idiosyncratic meaning of heterarchy, we also arrive at that slightly different conception of heterarchy. This new conception leaves out Walker's procedural concessions while retaining that minimal feature that is common to both his and MacCormick's understanding of pluralism.

The abstract common concept—the common feature—at which we thus arrive is exactly what in Chapter 1 I called "heterarchy minimized."[13] It is the thinnest pluralist principle stating merely the following. Firstly, that two or more constitutional orders and their sources coexist over a shared piece of territory as ultimately self-standing and equal, so that now neither, or none, of them is any longer the single ultimately superior order/source of authority over a given territory. Secondly, in the *most abstract general* sense, this thinnest pluralist principle also implies the need for concessions by such overlapping constitutional orders and their sources. It requires that they somehow recognize that they coexist over the shared piece of territory as ultimately self-standing and coequal and, accordingly, adopt *some* concessions that faithfully reflect this. But the minimized understanding of heterarchy remains silent about the more precise meaning, type, and strength, of such concessions. From its perspective, these could be either merely procedural, or substantive, or both; they could also be extremely thin, or relatively thick, made only with respect to a particular level of constitutional discourse, some of such discourses, or all of them.[14] There just need to be some concessions *as such* that faithfully stick to that first half of the minimum pluralist arrangement as posited in the first step.

Thus, a European pluralist who endorses the "minimized understanding of heterarchy" in the European context, and proclaims himself to be a member of the new common branch of the pluralists as opposed to monists, must explain that neither is the European constitution and its source derivative from, and so hierarchically inferior to, the national ones and their sources, nor are the latter

[13] See Chapter 1, pp. 21–2.

[14] We saw throughout the mapping chapters that different pluralists implied very different types of concessions. The following chapters will show how those differences will also prove decisive in the assessment part of the project.

ultimately grounded in, and thus hierarchically subordinated to, some all-European ultimate constitutional authority and its source. Such a pluralist instead posits that there is no longer the ultimate constitutional authority on any of the nation-state's territories, and that the same is true of the European territory as a whole. A nation-state's and the EU's are both coequal and autonomously rooted sources of constitutional authority that are simultaneously coexistent and overlapping over a given shared territory, and are thus heterarchically, as opposed to hierarchically, related. Moreover, such a pluralist must also still require that both types of orders make appropriate changes (concessions) in their old explanatory monistic accounts, which they are no longer free to follow without qualification. But, *crucially*, as long as the concessions do follow the *most abstract* foundational idea of heterarchical equality and self-standing coexistence, our pluralist must refrain from claiming any kind of *particular* variant of these pluralist concessions. None of those could be seen as constituting constitutional pluralism in the sense of the new common branch encompassing all these authors (the alleged "pluralists") while distinguishing them from the monists.

MacCormick and Walker would thus need to concede that some of the features of their respective conceptions of pluralism that they now consider constitutive of pluralism on the foundational level could not actually be seen as such in the sense of the common branch. Their conceptions and meanings of pluralism within this broadest subject matter must be abstracted one level higher than they currently are, so as potentially to meet each other and the rest of the pluralist camp in the heterarchy minimized.

We saw earlier that it is not entirely clear what exactly those authors who work within the *how*, *what*, and *who* discourses, would endorse at the level of this foundational discourse on pluralism. With respect to them, it can now be concluded that, whatever they endorse on that level, they would need to endorse also the most abstract common denominator of heterarchy minimized, or else, jeopardize the existence of the common branch. If all their different proposals and understandings of what constitutes constitutional pluralism are to be seen as currently belonging to such a branch, then they need to understand the common notion of pluralism in this particular way, in a form quite distinct from any of their current conceptions of pluralism. Their current conceptions of pluralism from within the *who*, *how*, *what*, as well as the *foundational discourse* respectively, would need to be seen as applicative visions. On this reading they are all further applicative discourses that spring in several different directions from the common core of the heterarchy minimized as the minimum common denominator that manages to fit together all of these strikingly different and conflicting conceptions into a common novel branch of constitutional thought. Once this is clear it is no longer possible to teach, as so many authors have been doing so far, that, say, MacCormick's proposal within the discourse of the *who* (his move from "radical pluralism" to "pluralism under international law")[15] was the change of paradigm from pluralism back to monism.

[15] See pp. 188–9 and 209–13. Cf also pp. 51–2.

That is, that merely to propose a single ultimate body, or mechanism, for the resolution of "who decides who decides" is to revert back to constitutional monism. Nor is the same challenge possible against someone like Weiler, who proposed the single institution of a Constitutional Council within our discourse of the *who*, or against Maduro or Kumm, who propose respectively their own final lines of reconciliation between conflicting ultimate interpreters. Unlike monism, all of these proposals a priori assume some type of equal concessions on both sides, and the further option of leaving the question of "who decides who decides" fully open, as is suggested by Walker for instance, is simply an example of yet another type of pluralist concessions. This is thus not yet the test of who is a pluralist and who is a monist. Instead, all of these are "merely" applicative solutions within one of the further discourses of pluralism. Each merely assumes a different variant of the unique pluralist concessions within that further applicative theme. None of those concessions, however, is the same as the monist solution according to which one is not a priori bound to introduce the kind of concessions that would respect that foundationally rooted pluralist equality of the ultimately self-standing constitutional systems and their sources. The same could be explained with respect to the discourses of the *how* and *what* as well as of the thicker level of the *foundational* discourse itself. As long as a particular proposal within those applicative discourses assumes some type of equal concessions, of whatever kind, that faithfully reflect the foundational idea of the minimized understanding of heterarchy, the proposal is one of constitutional pluralism as opposed to monism.

This very thin understanding of heterarchy, as the meaning of pluralism according to the branch of constitutional pluralism, is therefore the ultimate missing link by which alone it is possible to decode the branch, identify the common essence, and solve the puzzle of our opening finding. Moreover, by fitting the link to the existing picture, we are also able to fit the different proposals and their discourses together in a specific way, so that they represent various applicative pluralist strands, originating from that common core. This may well open new questions and criticism concerning the branch, or some of the sub-branches within this common branch (an issue with which we will soon engage[16]), but it also does for us the prior important and necessary work of solving the labyrinth of pluralism as a whole.

Even though the missing link was already latent as an unelaborated fragment within MacCormick's thicker initial account of foundational pluralism, it has never been singled out or explicated by any of the pluralists as the minimum common denominator of their shared distinction from the monists. It now becomes clear why it was important to explicitly extract and distinguish it from the rest of MacCormick's understanding of pluralism in Chapter 1.[17] It also reveals why, in the Introduction, when describing MacCormick's path-breaking new route that this book set out to examine, I had to do no more than present this very extracted and highly abstract minimal notion of pluralism. Even though this did not yet do

[16] We will engage with that at length in Chapters 7 and 8.

[17] Chapter 1, pp. 21–2.

full justice to his understanding of pluralism, this strategy had to be followed because to provide anything more than this thinner description would already be to misrepresent the branch. It would be to present pluralism in a way that could not be endorsed by all these authors, seen as a common group sharing a common project.

3. Confirming the Map

The whole map of the branch that assumes this trajectory of the pluralist development from the described abstract minimum to its various applicative discourses can also be confirmed in a particular way. Although thicker than the common pluralist denominator, MacCormick's conception as proposed in that initial short article from 1993 was itself still very abstract. Beyond his substantively constituted conception of heterarchy that implied within itself also that described minimized understanding of heterarchy, there was little flesh in that article that one could put on these bones of constitutional pluralism. MacCormick himself was, however, aware of the highly theoretical nature of his undertaking. He seemed to have understood that, for such a vision to become practical reality, it would need something more: further development and elaboration which would result in the creation of a further "set of principles"[18] emanating from this alternative to monism. Only this would enable the latter to represent something novel in the real world, not just the world of theory. In the concluding stage of his article, MacCormick interestingly wrote:

> The possibility of such developments [ie pluralist developments] in the practical world depends upon their being grasped imaginatively by the people who make the practical world. This depends upon our being able to work out credible and well-supported ideas, both about rules which are valid relative to particular systems, and yet also about common traditions of ideas linking and over-arching different systems and providing an interpretive tradition, a set of principles in light of which to understand in partial community of thought each particular system and secure its compatibility with other partially overlapping systems.[19]

What is intriguing in such a conclusion to the article that inevitably introduced also the minimum core of pluralism, is that it seems as if MacCormick himself anticipated the various strands of the future development that a foundational pluralist conception would be able to lead to. The necessary elaboration of MacCormick's further "set of principles" that would enable us to grasp and differentiate the abstract idea of two self-standing and heterarchical orders in practice could, according to that concluding passage, develop in at least three directions.

Imagine, firstly, that one would think that the abstract idea of heterarchy of constitutional systems and their sources should be operationalized in the direction of principles establishing a particular form of constitutional discourse in Europe.

[18] N. MacCormick, "Beyond the Sovereign State" (1993) 56 ML Rev 1, 18.

[19] MacCormick (n 18) at 18.

Indeed it would be a "set of principles"[20] establishing an "interpretive tradition"[21] that would "secure [a system's] compatibility with other partially overlapping systems,"[22] as MacCormick wrote. On this reading, the principles should establish a proceduralized discursive framework through which each of the two constitutional systems would then by itself determine parts of its own identity. If one proceeded in this direction, one would clearly be elaborating MacCormick's "set of principles" within our theme of the *how*. And indeed, as we have seen, Walker and Maduro can both be understood as working on the "set of principles" in that particular direction. Maduro's interpretive "principles of contrapunctual law," for example, are meant exactly as the operationalization and the clarification of the abstract and minimal underlying understanding that the legal orders are self-standing and in heterarchical relationship.[23] The same case can be made for Walker.[24]

Secondly, imagine that under the further development of the abstract idea of self-standing and heterarchically related legal orders one would understand also a particular substantive determination of parts of each of the self-standing identities. This determination would represent an externally balanced substantive reconciliation between the two systems. Such a particular external reconciliation would also culminate in a "set of principles,"[25] understood as the further elaborations of the abstract pluralist foundation. It would indeed be an elaboration separating what ought to be seen as the "common traditions of ideas linking and over-arching different systems"[26] from those that are to be "valid relative to particular systems,"[27] as MacCormick also wrote. And this particular direction of the operationalization of MacCormick's abstract basis is represented by our substantive theme of the *what*. Recall for instance Weiler's set of principles, his building blocks, which compose the substantive part of his "principle of constitutional tolerance" and represent the core of Europe's overarching common tradition.[28] They are exactly the product of the pluralist redefinition of the old monistic identities that elaborates and separates two types of equally valid and mutually reconciled identities—the common European and the distinctively national.

The third direction in which MacCormick seemed to have inferred the further operationalization of the abstract idea of heterarchy may develop is reflected in our discourse of the *who*. On this reading, MacCormick's further "set of principles" amounts also to specific solutions as to the question of "who decides" in the delicate sphere where the two systems institutionally overlap. These solutions would thus, within their own specific field or subject matter, also explicitly referred to by MacCormick within his initial article, determine what pluralism as distinguished

[20] MacCormick (n 18) at 18. [21] MacCormick (n 18) at 18.
[22] MacCormick (n 18) at 18. [23] Maduro (n 10) at 501; p. 102.
[24] Chapter 2, pp. 50–1. [25] MacCormick (n 18) at 18.
[26] MacCormick (n 18) at 18. [27] MacCormick (n 18) at 18.
[28] Pp. 77–89, in connection with pp. 73–4.

from monism really means in practice. Indeed, they would in their own field "secure compatibility with other partially overlapping systems."[29] His language throughout the initial article likewise signals that he saw the inescapable need for connection between his abstract pluralist basis and this further type of applicative pluralist discourse of the *who*: this was then the first development to occur.[30] Or, as Maduro observed soon after MacCormick's early contribution: "The focus [of the pluralist scholarship preceding his, ie Maduro's, article] tends to be on the issue on *Kompetenz-Kompetenz* and the possibility of conflict between EU law and national constitutions."[31] "The explanation for this," he added, "lies in the fact that such ultimate conflicts of authority are seen as representing the issue of sovereignty: what is the ultimate source of power in the political and legal organisation of society?"[32]

It seems then as if MacCormick himself, after proposing his abstract pluralist conception within the foundational discourse, sensed the various directions of its further development. His language in the concluding paragraph seems to suggest so. But what confirms this reading is also MacCormick's own work that both followed and preceded his path-breaking article and its abstract pluralist minimum. I will conclude the chapter with an analysis that shows how in that work MacCormick actually made his own contribution within each of those further applicative discourses of the *how*, *what*, and *who*. Indeed the following explication should therefore complete the initial account of MacCormick's pluralism from Chapter 1. Although the depth of his own contribution to these three pluralist discourses varies, he did have something to say about each of them. And this realization, together with the observations discussed so far in this section, not only confirms the existence of the branch and the map as a whole, but also reveals that it was Neil MacCormick's initial contribution that for the first time brought, within a part of itself, that common novel seed (the heterarchy minimized) that eventually makes him the "father figure" of the pluralist *branch*, and the rest of the contributions that followed his progeny.

3.1 The theme of "*how*"

Like Weiler, MacCormick said relatively less on the discourse of the *how* than on other discourses within his pluralism. While announcing the general interpretive principle of mutual respect and adjustment between constitutional interpreters from the different and ultimately self-standing orders, he did not go further to build a detailed specific version of the pluralist interpretive question like that derived from Maduro's interpretive pluralism, for instance. Like Weiler's, MacCormick's interpretive principle appears in the general form:

[29] MacCormick (n 18) at 18.
[30] See, eg MacCormick (n 19) at 8.
[31] Maduro (n 10) at 501.
[32] Maduro (n 10) at 501.

The European Court of Justice ought not to reach its interpretive judgments without regard to their potential impact on national constitutions. National courts ought not to interpret laws or constitutions without regard to the resolution of their compatriots to take full part in European Union and European Community.[33]

Yet, if understood in the light of some aspects from MacCormick's general legal theory, the principle does acquire a more specific meaning.[34] His peculiar friendship with both the positive and natural law tradition is well known. It should thus not come as a surprise that MacCormick's position here begins with the view that, in principle, there are right answers to legal questions. According to MacCormick's own words, his position in this sense leans even towards that of Dworkin and Finnis, or is at least somewhere between Alexy's variant of Habermas and Dworkin/Finnis.[35] But while taking this position, MacCormick also emphasizes that, in crystallizing those right answers, interpreters would often reasonably disagree about who got it right. This too must be equally respected so that a high degree of fluidity within the sphere of reasonable disagreement is ensured. Again, this should be in a way that does not threaten the existence of right answers in principle and does presuppose sufficient substantive checks capable of preventing unreasonableness from taking over.[36]

While this position signals that we might be able later to find at least some substantive building blocks (the *what*) in MacCormick's pluralism,[37] it also has consequences for the thinner, more interpretive, sphere of the *how* of the pluralist constitutional discourse. More precisely, the interpretive principle cited earlier should be understood in light of what MacCormick terms "coherence and consequence."[38] In deciding on matters involving domestic constitutional law, a judge of a member state's highest tribunal thus needs genuinely to have in mind what it would be appropriate to decide about the question at hand if she were sitting at the European Court. This is the requirement from coherence. That might lead the judge to a conclusion that the European Court misinterpreted European law. The type of the right-answer thesis that MacCormick endorses has to be open to the possibility that each of these courts might be mistaken about its own law, about its own best answer. It also suggests, however, that we would get closer to the solution by digging deeper. MacCormick believes that this way we should get a more dialogic and fluid process, which would often generate sequences of cases through which either of the courts could be reminded by the other of some neglected consequence for one of the sides that was not taken sufficiently into account by a particular resolution. This is the requirement from consequence. The possibility that other member states, who are not directly implicated in the case, also intervene at the ECJ when the issue at stake is sufficiently important from their

[33] N. MacCormick, "The Maastricht-Urteil: Sovereignty Now" (1995) 1 ELJ 259, 265.

[34] In my attempt to make the following explication I have benefited from exchanges with Neil MacCormick on an earlier draft of this subsection—I am indebted to him (Edinburgh University, 7–8 December 2006).

[35] Interview (see n 34).

[36] Interview (see n 34).

[37] Pp. 177–87, following.

[38] Interview (see n 34).

own perspective should be seen as additionally contributing to this process of coherence and consequence.[39] Such an interpretive strategy, designed to respect fully that pluralist equality of the constitutional orders from the deepest foundation, does both. It itself facilitates the gradual crystallization of the right answers, of some normative substantive building blocks of the pluralist regime, and also serves as the correct interpretive pluralist formula in the sphere where reasonable disagreement does not allow for any such further substantive closure.

3.2 The theme of "*what*"

This closer look at MacCormick's contribution on the theme of the "how" indicates that, for him, the notion of constitutional heterarchy and its implied recognition between coequal orders will also mean something for our discourse on the *what*; that is, for the question of what these orders should clearly change in the *content* of their old meta-constitutional substances and so in their individual constitutional identities. In other words, MacCormick's pluralism differs from the old monism also in the sense of the content, as opposed to the mere form of proper constitutional discourse. This is the question of external redefinition of the orders' substantive identities, a redefinition that would have to be proposed by the theory itself, while being understood as flowing from the new pluralist foundation—the notion of heterarchy—and its abstract requirement of mutual recognition.

This is the variant of applicative understanding of pluralism that we have so far encountered only in Weiler's substantive pluralism. The following analysis of some of MacCormick's less well-known contributions will confirm that, like Weiler, he, too, developed from his abstract pluralist basis further into the discourse of the *what* (substantive pluralism). On the one hand, MacCormick knew that this would have to be about elaboration of a certain "new European identity" (or even actualization of a kind of European *demos*) that would play somewhat the same role within the EU context as national identity (or the identity of the people as a self-aware *demos*) plays in the legitimation of a state.[40] On the other hand, he was also aware that this new and self-standing European identity would require adjusting—indeed, revising—the concept of identity on the nation-state side too.[41] The unqualified and absolutist national identity as we have known it in the circumstances of the

[39] To this I should add that MacCormick's general work provides elements that can be seen as further elaborating his own position on this theme of *how* within European constitutional pluralism. Cf N. MacCormick, *Rhetoric and the Rule of Law: A Theory of Legal Reasoning* (Oxford: Oxford University Press, 2005).

[40] "[T]he claim that the Community is a duly constituted and self-standing order can be held to presuppose or to require the constructing of a new European identity, or even, as Joseph Weiler puts it in this volume, the actualization of a European Demos. Such an identity, such a Demos would play somehow the same role that national identity, or the identity of the people as a self-aware Demos, plays in the legitimation of the institutions of a state" (N. MacCormick, "Liberalism, Nationalism, and the Post-sovereign State" (1996) XLIV Political Studies 553). Cf Chapter 1, pp. 28–9 and n 86.

[41] MacCormick (n 40) at 554; N. MacCormick, "What Place for Nationalism in the Modern World" (1994) 2 Hume Papers on Public Policy, 79.

sovereign states,[42] and thus prior to the introduction of the idea of self-standing heterarchical orders, would now need to become "tamed" in a specific way by the new, self-standing European identity.[43] And the opposite would have to hold as well: the European identity would need to be defined in non-absolutist, universalist terms. It would then be in congruence with the remaining sound parts of the revised concept of national identity. The "set of principles" of which MacCormick spoke in the concluding paragraph from his initial article would in these circumstances thus be the representation of such a particular and externally valid substantive balance. To use the same expression as in Weiler's case, they would be the *substantive building blocks* of the meta-constitution of Europe. These would in a principled way determine both the sound substantive parts of the identity stemming from the European perspective as well as the sound substantive parts of the identities from the perspective of the nation-states.

So what exactly does this version of MacCormick's substantive pluralism look like? As in the case of Weiler, so here, the key initial step is association of different particular substantive identity with each of the sites respectively—the European and member-states'.[44]

Firstly, "[t]he post-revolutionary world, the world of modernity, was the world of the states . . . They were nation states asserting the inalienable sovereignty of a sovereign nation or people."[45] Hence the traditional notion of a nation-state carrying at its core the idea of omnipotent nation-state *demos* as its ultimate source of authority.[46] This kind of understanding of ultimate authority (ie its link with the sovereign nation-state) has led to a particular concept of nationalism, the true substance of which was—as MacCormick explains—most radically and fully revealed in both World Wars.[47] He inherently associates the situation in which

[42] "The nation state has been a sovereign state, and as such has purported to express the sovereignty of the unitary people, the nation, which is the owner of the state" (MacCormick (n 40) at 556). "[T]he idea that the 'nation-state' must have absolute and uncontrollable control of a territory, and all (everyone) that is found within it, necessarily creates incurable tension between those who are defined as belonging and those who are defined as not belonging, or who so define themselves" (MacCormick (n 41) at 93).

[43] "The European Union has brought about a new form of legal and political order in Western Europe. This creates a politics 'beyond sovereign state' . . . This does not abolish nations as politico-cultural communities. It may create space for the flourishing of nationalism tamed—a fully liberal and humanistic nationalism [that is] compatible with universalistic vision of the common humanity of human beings" (MacCormick (n 41) at 79). "This is both a qualified and non-absolutist view of nationalism, perhaps even a revisionist one" (MacCormick (n 40) at 554).

[44] Recall how Weiler associates nation-state monism (traditional statal intercourse "premised on full sovereignty, autonomy, independence") with "relentless maximization of national interest," and how he associates European monism with the overstated variant of the idea of transnational human intercourse—one that unduly suppresses the sound and valuable dimensions in national and other cultural identities (see pp. 70–1).

[45] MacCormick (n 40) at 553.

[46] MacCormick (n 41) at 79; MacCormick (n 40) at 556.

[47] This is the same substantive understanding and identification of the traditional nation-state monism as in Weiler, who describes the pre-EU era as the period of strong nation-states in Europe. Through their constitutions these states defended their full sovereignty, autonomy, independence, and have done so, Weiler emphasizes, more or less through the lens of their *own national interest*, ie the

we have this ultimate self-standing source coupled with the idea of a sovereign state, with the generation of the particular unqualified and "unwelcome" conception of national identity.

Secondly, such identity and the type of nationalism it produces needs—according to MacCormick—to be "tamed"[48] in a specific way by another identity, grounded in its own self-standing source. This second source leads towards a particular "transnational identity"[49] that appears to be significantly, if not wholly, opposite to the first: "universalistic vision of the common humanity of human beings."[50] MacCormick labels the substance of this second identity "liberal universalism,"[51] and understands it as embodying the idea of some essential and universal humanity regardless of boundaries separating us: "Liberal universalization of the right to respect makes fundamentally unacceptable any disparagement of individuals on such grounds as nationality, ethnicity or gender."[52] And just as he inherently associated sovereign nation-states with the generating of some particular vision of national identity, so MacCormick here now links the generation of this other particular vision of identity (ie "liberal universalism") with the idea of European Union and other all-European forms of common human intercourse.[53]

However, this "liberal universalism," which is meant to tame the particular type of national identity characteristic of sovereignty and sovereign nation-state, should also not, according to MacCormick, be instituted in its radical form, which eradicates the concept of national identity in its sound components. One can imagine how it is possible to associate such a radical version of "liberal universalism" with the monist idea of the European superstate. MacCormick fears that the near-absolute blindness to the types of differences generated by the first self-standing source and its identity would lead us to a kind of national and cultural "melting-pot" on a European scale.[54] He argues that this kind of understanding of the content of "liberal universalism" (an overstated version of it) would amount to an unwelcome and improper meaning of European transnational identity.[55] For the

interest of a *particular demos.* See Chapter 3, p. 70; J. Weiler, *The Constitution of Europe* (Cambridge: Cambridge University Press, 1999) 91.

[48] MacCormick (n 41) at 79; cf Weiler who uses the same exact expression to describe the same normative need: the need for "taming [of] reflexes and ethos of the 'sovereign' national state with new modes of discourse and a new discipline of solidarity" (Weiler (n 47) at 93).

[49] MacCormick (n 40) at 565.

[50] MacCormick (n 41) at 79.

[51] MacCormick (n 40) at 565.

[52] MacCormick (n 40) at 555–65.

[53] Like the Council of Europe and similar organizations.

[54] Cf Weiler and his contrasting of the European constitutional-pluralist project to the American monistic alternative: "This conceptualization underscores, perhaps exaggerates, the difference with the American truly radical alternative liberal project of the non-ethno-national polity, and of a state, the republic, the organization of which, and the norms of citizenship behavior within, were central to its value system" (Weiler (n 47) at 339).

[55] What he rejects is the view that liberalism as a concept (and its taming in the case of the new Europe) should be understood as inherently precluding any privileging of national identity among the factors that constitute human identity. That is, the argument that "there seems no reason to select out a sense of national identity as anything particular alongside of one's family membership, of professional

same reason, he criticizes John Rawls's contractarian version of liberalism that builds on a "deeply implausible ['hypothetical'] vision of human society":

> Atomistic or methodological individualistic assumptions cannot but be false. All individuals as they really are fall into the class of "contextual individuals"... The truth about human individuals... is that they—we—are social products, not independent atoms capable of constituting society through a voluntary coming together. We are as much constituted by our society as it is by us... We have a sense of self because of the way we have learned to be ourselves in the contexts in which we have so learned.[56]

The Rawlsian version of liberalism would, on MacCormick's reading,[57] also represent an overstated version of liberalism, that would in the European context also grant undue primacy and dominance to one particular identity (the radically and improperly universalistic) at the expense of the sound and valuable dimensions of the other one (the national).

The position seems to be as follows. MacCormick does not side with this nationalism-free version of "liberal universalism" that the idea of the monist European superstate might be seen to embody. Yet, neither does he agree with maintaining the untamed version of nationalism brought by the sovereign nation-states and their sovereign nations or *demoi*. His is instead a substantively balanced pluralist path, according to which the substance of nationalism is redefined so that it becomes compatible with the refined version of liberal universalism. Each of the substantive identities draws back some of its constituent parts which MacCormick

or religious affiliations, political convictions and loyalties, local identity (city, town, village, rural area), state citizenship, transnational identity (citizen of the European Union, for example)." Even more emphatically he rejects the "doubt whether autonomous individuals would need, or have any truck with, nationalism" at all: "The decisive counter to this doubt is a vital observation by Yael Tamir, namely, a reminder that individuals are necessarily, in her words, 'contextual individuals'. People acquire character and self-consciousness, and a capacity for self-command, only in a specific social setting." At the same time, "the modern state..., the state-as-nation is the primary theatre [ie such context] of political activity and participation. If one very crucial element of individual autonomy is the opportunity of participating as a full and equal member in fora of political self-government, then the primary such forum for the contemporary world is the state." Hence, "[i]t is not theoretical nationalist imaginings, but the fact of political life, that gives national identity a special place in the contextual definition of the contextual individual in her/his character as political animal." MacCormick (n 40) at 565–6.

[56] N. MacCormick, "Is Nationalism Philosophically Credible?" in W. Twinning (ed.), *Issues of Self-Determination* (Aberdeen: Aberdeen University Press, 1991) 13; cf MacCormick (n 41) at 84; *Questioning Sovereignty: Law, State, and Nation in the European Commonwealth* (Oxford: Oxford University Press, 1999) 179–80.

[57] It should be stressed, however, that this is MacCormick's reading of Rawls on this point. Other readings suggest an interpretation of Rawls that is almost diametrically opposed to this one and allows, and even seems to require, MacCormick's own conclusions as explicated in this subsection. See generally, eg F. Michelman, *Brennan and Democracy* (Princeton, NJ: Princeton University Press, 1999) 66–7; and as explicitly then stated by Rawls for the specific case of the European nation-states, in K. Jaklic, *Democracy's Third Coming: Europe as a Route to Humanity's Third Historic Stage of Democracy*, monograph manuscript, forthcoming, currently on file with Harvard University Law Library, and with author, ch XI, section 3 ("Conclusion"), 278–82, referring to Rawls's explanations on this point to Philippe Van Parijs.

considers unsound and incompatible with the other identity, while retaining those which are sound, which the opposing identity must also recognize as such. At the same time, they remain two distinct identities, grounded in their respective self-standing but reconcilable sources of authority.

As was the case with Weiler, we have so far first observed MacCormick's strategy of substantive pluralism from "a distance," as it were. Let us continue following the pattern from Chapter 3 and now ask how his balanced pluralist reconciliation appears when observed from a closer perspective. While rejecting "certain forms of nationalism," the developments of the new Europe and its condition beyond the sovereign state "create space for a new nationalism, an acceptable and even perhaps mandatory nationalism that is intrinsically liberal in character."[58] So which dimensions of nationalism are then to be rejected and which to be made acceptable? "The answer begins," MacCormick writes, "by taking up the basic moral imperative of respect for persons":

> If, as I claim, a sense of nationality is for many people constitutive in part of their sense of identity and even of selfhood, then respect for this aspect of their selfhood is as incumbent as respect for any other, up to a certain point. The key point is, of course, that at which one national self-expression or self-assertion becomes destructive of another.[59]

The crucial substantive elaboration of this standard begins with MaCormick's development of his conception of "civic-cum-personal nationalism."[60] As the name suggests, there are two distinct components constituting this new version of nationalism. Firstly, in principle none but the civic components are considered sound and valuable in the collective sense. The "new nationalism" does not center its forming of the collective national identity round some externally given fact of ethnicity, or some other involuntary component of identity. To explain more fully what is meant by this, let us look at the "civic" and "ethnic" forms of nationalism that MacCormick contrasts. The former, he explains, identifies "the nation in terms of its members" shared allegiance to certain civic institutions.[61] They are "understood in broad terms to include, for example legal norms and institutions, political representative organs, branches of public and local administration, the organization of education" as well as "churches and religious communities in their secular aspect, and other like institutions having an understood territorial location with which they are connected."[62] Such "[t]erritorially located civic institutions can be objects of allegiance, understood as 'ours' by the people over whom they purport to have jurisdiction," and "[a]s civic institutions, they are necessarily of great political significance to the community which, to an extent, they define."[63] "The point of a civic nation," MacCormick crucially concludes, "is that it is in principle open to

[58] MacCormick (n 40) at 562.
[59] MacCormick, "Is Nationalism Philosophically Credible?" (n 56) at 17.
[60] MacCormick (n 40) at 565. [61] MacCormick (n 40) at 562.
[62] MacCormick (n 40) at 562. [63] MacCormick (n 40) at 562.

voluntary membership."[64] "The community defined by allegiance to institutions," that is, "is open to anyone who chooses to dwell in the territory and give allegiance to the institutions" though "[d]eparture to a different place and different allegiances is also possible, and [is] not [considered] traitorous."[65]

MacCormick contrasts this conception with "the conception of nation as racial or ethnic community."[66] Unlike the former, the latter is "defined as the possessor of a distinctive culture, including perhaps a language thought of as special possession of those and only those belonging to the original ethnic community, grounded ultimately in some kind of shared ancestry or genetic bond."[67] And the point here, MacCormick highlights, is that "[n]ationality so defined is necessary and unavoidably given . . . It has no voluntary element nor opening thereto. You either are a member of this nation or not."[68]

While acknowledging that these two distinct conceptions of national identity are "more ideal types than exclusive alternatives"[69] MacCormick also points out that the "all-important differences of emphasis and degree" remain.[70] In this light he maintains that a line between sound and unsound dimensions within nationalism can still be drawn. He argues that the existing distinction between the voluntary and involuntary elements within both conceptions makes it "plainly enough evident that a liberal commitment to individualism and autonomy is one that would restrict its endorsement to the claims of civic nationalism, with only such associated elements of the ethno-historico-cultural as are compatible with personal freedom and autonomy."[71]

Secondly, this sentence hints that in addition to the purely civic, there are also some other components of national identity, the personal as opposed to the collectively pre-given, which will be recognized as sound and proper. As with the civic conception, this also calls for further explanation. By the "personal components" I mean MacCormick's endorsement of those ethno-historico-cultural forms of nationalism that fall with the category of what he describes as "personal nationalism."[72] "The idea of personal nationalism," MacCormick writes, is "an attractive idea that liberates nationalism from anti-individualism" as it rests on the understanding

[64] MacCormick (n 40) at 563.
[65] MacCormick (n 40) at 562.
[66] MacCormick (n 40) at 562.
[67] MacCormick (n 40) at 562.
[68] MacCormick (n 40) at 562.
[69] This is so, MacCormick explains, since "of course, civically identified communities develop cultural practices and institutions around them, and of course there will tend to be more or less long-standing familial and historical associations with given institutions, so that the community of allegiance will easily and naturally perceive itself as also a community of culture and of historical belonging; on the other hand, the community that conceives itself primarily in terms of blood and belonging, ancestral culture and history will also develop its own institutions, and may tacitly acknowledge a kind of adoption of incomers who over time come to accept the institutions" (MacCormick (n 40) at 563).
[70] MacCormick (n 40) at 563.
[71] MacCormick (n 40) at 563.
[72] MacCormick (n 40) at 563.

that "nation states are not entities wholly independent of consciousness."[73] Instead, as MacCormick explains, "they are socially given, but essentially interpretive elements of the possibility of a certain kind of consciousness and self-consciousness."[74] They are "experienced by individuals as persons who know where they are and where they belong and do not belong." So that

> [f]or any country or national, each of us has her or his own conception of it, and our sense of identification is not with some objective "out-there" entity, but rather with our idea or interpretation of the nation developed out of reflection on civic institutions, social institutions, culture and history. Thus there must be as many Englands as there are English people, and though there is a certain communality of thought, they are not all identically the same. Rather, there is at best a partially overlapping consensus of England-ideas from the point of view of those who self-identify as English, and then also, perhaps, from the point of view of self-defined outsiders. England as a nation is not something that externally guarantees the overlapping consensus, but an idea that emerges from it, to the extent that a broad consensus does in fact emerge.[75]

But because such individualistic understanding of national identity "tends to displace an essentially political idea from the domain of politics, or at any rate from the armoury of normative political theory,"[76] MacCormick considers personal nationalism as not by itself apt to represent the entirely proper understanding of nationalism. This is why he adapts it by attaching it to the already-discussed collective dimension of primarily civic nationalism, while joining the two together into his conception of "civic-cum-personal nationalism." Alongside the purely civic parts of national identity, the latter thus fosters around objective civic institutions some elements of an ethno-historico-cultural community that represent "an important corollary of civic nationalism as ideal-type."[77] But MacCormick crucially cautions that under personal nationalism these can only be those cultural elements that are compatible with individualism and autonomy. Only those that "constitute through the self-conceptions of members an always evolving, always diversifying, always contestable, cultural community through the overlapping but also diversifying ideas of those who identify with the civic nation."[78] It is such a "civic-cum-personal" conception of national identity, as MacCormick explains, that is "fully capable—and only capable—of being stated . . . as a universal principle."[79] It alone can be congruent "with the earlier noted and equally universal imperative of equal allowance for equal respect among national identities, just like other identities."[80] This is that equilibrium point at which, in MacCormick's view, one national self-expression or self-assertion does not become destructive of another.

It is here where we also can reveal the external building blocks that represent MacCormick's substantive line of reconciliation between the two types of

[73] MacCormick (n 40) at 563–4.
[74] MacCormick (n 40) at 564.
[75] MacCormick (n 40) at 564.
[76] MacCormick (n 40) at 564.
[77] MacCormick (n 40) at 564.
[78] MacCormick (n 40) at 564.
[79] MacCormick (n 41) at 90.
[80] MacCormick (n 41) at 90.

identities—the national and the overarching European ones. By investigating the values underlying this particular balance, we arrive at similar conclusions to those under Weiler's substantive pluralism. Firstly, MacCormick's endorsement of the sound dimensions in nationalism partially rests in the idea of preservation and nourishment of the richness of difference in human experience and perspective.[81] Clearly, then, one of his sound, externally valid blocks is nationhood in its value of authentic originality. That is similar to one of Weiler's blocks, although we should add that MacCormick has further specified this sound meta-constitutional block as only the civic-cum-personal type of national originality.[82] Secondly, the other sound dimension originating from the national source is that of belongingness. Though MacCormick does not announce that explicitly, he operates with the understanding of nationalism as "belongingness" throughout his argument for the reconciliation of the two sources and their substantive identities. It is thus sufficiently evident that he, too, like Weiler, endorses national belonging, with its virtue of the "shield against existential aloneness," as the other sound building block originating from the old nationalist monist source. Here too, we can be even more specific and point to the particular variant of this block as it appears in MacCormick: it is only the civic-cum-personal type of national belonging that is considered to be a sound meta-constitutional substance.[83]

These two sound and externally valid meta-constitutional blocks, originating from the old nationalist monist perspective, are combined with another block. As we also saw in relation to Weiler, this comes from the opposite perspective. The taming that works in both ways not only refines the national monist source and its substance. It also does so with the European source. Some essential humanity as the substance originating from that source can no longer be understood as boundless, emptied, essential humanity. What is sound and valuable in it is only that understanding of essential humanity that does not eradicate the sound building blocks from nationhood, but rather accepts and treats them as indispensable co-determinants of the refined understanding of essential humanity itself.[84] This building block was specified by Weiler as a special kind of essentially human humility, as opposed to a mistakenly unifying arrogance, with respect to

[81] After referring to his career-long professional experience with numerous of his colleagues and friends—of different nationalities—from all over Europe, MacCormick writes: "It fills me with a sense of the richness of human experience and culture that there are so many variants of the same common human theme and indeed so rewardingly many ways of being European. I hope we can contrive a politics that secures a survivable economy and ecology of us all, enables us to keep peace among ourselves and yet allows for the mutually respectful flourishing of many nationalities" (MacCormick, "Is Nationalism Philosophically Credible?" (n 56) at 18).

[82] My understanding on this point has benefited greatly from discussions with Neil MacCormick (see n 34).

[83] Again, I would not have been able to make this point without the exchanges with Neil MacCormick on a prior draft of this chapter and section. I am indebted to him. See n 34.

[84] Recall how MacCormick explicitly argues against and rejects the too abstract, emptied, types of "liberal universalism" (see pp. 179–80, earlier). Cf the relevant section ("Objections to abstract individualism") in his, *Questioning Sovereignty* (n 56) at 178–82, where he argues this point against "Kant and his contemporary follower John Rawls" (*Questioning Sovereignty* (n 56) at 179).

our difference in national identity. While MacCormick is perhaps less explicit in naming his own equivalent, it is clear from the above analysis that he does endorse *some variant* of that type of refined block of essential humanity.[85]

We see that MacCormick's theory also has a cluster of externally balanced substantive building blocks, and their underlying values, entrenched at Europe's meta-constitutional level. Although there is no explicit elaboration of potential further blocks, MacCormick's theory does seem to be open, indeed sympathetic, to possible additional candidates. He does seem to understand that the concept of constitutional pluralism could perhaps facilitate something similar also in the field of religious boundaries, not just national ones.[86] Moreover, there are still other fields, like that of democracy,[87] in which MacCormick could clearly be interpreted as contributing some further substantive building blocks to the specifically pluralist meta-constitution. All that would not seem to be incompatible with the theory's *general* insistence that we ought to reject conceptions of constitutionalism that do not recognize "flesh-and-blood individuals," but instead prescribe humanity in too abstract terms, "apart from earthly reality."[88]

Be that as it may, there are currently at least the described building blocks present in MacCormick's theory. It is important to understand further that, as was perhaps even more the case with Weiler, these blocks are not meant to be compromising the value of equal respect and autonomy. By contrast, they are understood precisely as the indispensable means enabling the highest realization of this value for those involved in substantive pluralist constitutionalism. Thus, the particular refined dimensions from nationhood, unlike the excluded ones,

> ha[ve] to be considered both justifiable and valuable on rather the same grounds as the simple negative liberties in the list of civil liberties. Some form of collective self-constitution, some kind of active participation in shaping and sustaining the institutions of social or communal government whose aim is to advance liberty and autonomy, seems to be a necessary part of the whole ensemble of conditions in which the autonomy of the contextual individual could be genuinely constituted and upheld. If autonomous individuals require the context of some sort of freedom-enabling society, then the collective autonomy of the society itself seems a part of the necessary context.[89]

The substantive reconciliation between the two identities also draws attention back to our discussion of the deeper ground on which sovereignty was assumed to rest. It clarifies the particular way in which that ground has now been revised. In a particular way it sets limits to national *demos* and its authority on the state territory where it was before considered under its own sovereign authority. Recall how MacCormick explained that "[s]ince the French Revolution, there has been until

[85] As per nn 83 and 84.

[86] As per nn 83 and 84; cf also MacCormick, *Questioning Sovereignty* (n 56) at 123–4, 186.

[87] MacCormick, *Questioning Sovereignty* (n 56) at 134–5 and ch 9; for a further explication of several of MacCormick's building blocks in the field of democracy, see Jaklic (n 57), especially 176–9, and also cf with Chapter 10, pp. 300–16 of this book.

[88] MacCormick, *Questioning Sovereignty* (n 56) at 178.

[89] MacCormick, "Is Nationalism Philosophically Credible" (n 56) at 14–15.

a few years ago an insistence both on the exclusiveness and on the absoluteness of national rights: [n]ation states were sovereign states, and sovereignty had to be absolute."[90] "There was," moreover, "a parallel doctrine of unity."[91] All these features meant that "[f]or every state, there was but one nation, whatever violence this might do to the facts of history or the consciousness and self-respect of minorities."[92] The whole point now is that it is the latter monist understanding and ground that has been adjusted. The previously sovereign authority of a *demos* on its state territory is now limited by another self-standing source to the domain of "acceptable nationalism."[93] According to the new and adjusted ground, "the members of a nation are as such in principle [still] entitled to effective organs of political self-government" within their state (and now also within Europe as a whole).[94] However, they are no longer entitled to the "self-government in the form of a sovereign state" that would lead beyond the confines of the civic-cum-personal conception of nationalism.[95] "Allied to a primarily civic nationalist conception of membership in a nation," this tamed form of self-government, unlike the old one, "seems to me [ie to MacCormick] to be perfectly compatible with one defensible version of liberalism."[96]

Furthermore, this new form of "acceptable nationalism" also brings us back to our discussion of normative pluralism and MacCormick's claim of its normative superiority over the two monistic conceptions. In the light of the reconciliation just presented, we can observe why more precisely the deconstruction of sovereignty in the context of the new Europe "is considered so admirable a project, indeed, achievement" in MacCormick's eyes.[97] "[H]istorically, and to a degree at present, the whole point of acknowledging sovereign states is that they [ie their particular *demos*] should have absolute authority over an exactly demarcated territory."[98] But this seems to MacCormick to create three great dangers. Firstly, in such monist circumstances peace can only be secured "provided there is no intervention by any state in any other[;] that peace, when it is secured, is only a relative peace. . . . such peace has never been a stable peace."[99] In part this has been because, secondly, such a monist situation is also "all too compatible with violations of rights of individuals and minorities within states."[100] Thirdly, all of this is then inescapably associated, as indicated, also with a relatively lower degree of individual autonomy within such a society. And if the cause of these weaknesses lies in "nationalism allied to sovereign statism that is incompatible with liberalism in the condition of the world as we find it," then the new pluralist conception, decoupling this nationalism from sovereignty while also retaining and developing its sound dimensions, appears to be just the right medicine for, and a guardian against, these excesses.[101]

90 MacCormick (n 41) at 90.
91 MacCormick (n 41) at 90.
92 MacCormick (n 41) at 90–1; cf MacCormick, *Questioning Sovereignty* (n 56) at 185–89.
93 MacCormick (n 40) at 566.
94 MacCormick (n 40) at 566.
95 MacCormick (n 40) at 566.
96 MacCormick (n 40) at 566.
97 MacCormick (n 40) at 566.
98 MacCormick (n 40) at 566.
99 MacCormick (n 40) at 566.
100 MacCormick (n 40) at 566.
101 MacCormick (n 40) at 566.

Of course, one might respond by saying that such universal liberal ethics could also work within each and every sovereign (ie monist) nation-state, whereby it would be understood as resting exclusively on this state's own ultimate source of authority. It is also in this monist sense, one might say, that liberal ethics could perform its "taming" function within each sovereign state. But the whole idea underlying MacCormick's reasoning seems to be that such a condition would not be stable: sooner or later it would, as indeed history teaches, lead to this or that degree of dominance by the sovereign. In the long run we would either face domination by a self-defined national identity at the expense of the overarching liberal universal identity, or vice versa. By contrast, where identity is decoupled from sovereignty, but associated instead with the plurality of mutually constraining coexisting authorities grounded as such already at their very foundation, such pluralism acts as an effective and enduring guardian against the abuse of the substantive applicative reconciliation proposed by MacCormick. This then seems to be the valuable normative difference that MacCormick's pluralism could potentially bring to Europe. It can thus be concluded that the protection of stable peace, and the building blocks, together with the pluralistically construed values of freedom, such as the equal respect, autonomy, and rights, that they sustain, are the "variety of ways"[102] in which MacCormick considers his pluralism normatively superior to either of the monist constructions of the new European reality. There is more to be said about MacCormick's substantive pluralist conception within the theme of the *what*,[103] but this should suffice here to conclude that his conception is, and has been from the beginning, one of "substantive pluralism."

3.3 The theme of "*who*"

So far we have seen how MacCormick develops further his abstract theoretical conception of pluralism in the direction of our themes of the *how* and *what*, respectively. But in addition, he also understands the abstract idea of the heterarchical relationship between the orders and their authorities in terms of the question of who decides in the area where the two orders overlap, and, especially, when they offer conflicting interpretations. With his contribution on this issue, MacCormick thus develops further his abstract theoretical conception in the direction of our theme of the *who*.

After elaborating his abstract theoretical conception of pluralism, he notes that there flow implications from this also for the institutional issue of "who decides who decides."[104] "It follows also," MacCormick thus writes, "that the interpretive power of the highest decision-making authorities of the different systems must be, as to each system, ultimate."[105] This means that "[i]t is for the European Court of Justice to interpret in the last resort and in a finally authoritative way the norms of

[102] See pp. 26–7.
[103] Jaklic (n 57), especially 102–11, 144–5, 176–9, and ch XII.
[104] MacCormick (n 33) at 264.
[105] MacCormick (n 33) at 264.

Community law," while equally, "it must be for the highest constitutional tribunal of each Member State to interpret its constitutional and other norms, and hence to interpret the interaction of the validity of EC law with higher level norms of validity in the given state system."[106] In other words, "[i]nterpretive competence-competence is a feature of the highest tribunal of any normative system."[107] MacCormick termed this "radical pluralism"[108]—the situation in which there is no third institution of some third constitutional order that would be above the highest institutions of the two orders and would arbitrate in event of conflict.

This appears similar to the position as later advanced by Walker's epistemic pluralism within the theme of *who*. Just as epistemic pluralism, so also radical pluralism announces that eventually it becomes only a matter of politics (no longer law) to resolve the issue one way or the other.[109] But it was only in his early writings on constitutional pluralism that MacCormick advanced this radical pluralism.[110] In his later 1998 article he seemed to have moved away from this stance.[111] There he introduced another version of pluralism alongside the radical one, namely, "pluralism under international law."[112] MacCormick explains that both of these versions are pluralistic, in the sense that they recognize two sites of constitutional authority in Europe as ultimately self-standing but interactive (ie heterarchical instead of hierarchical) constitutional orders. Both versions also understand that "the interpretive power of the highest decision-making authorities of the different orders must be, as to each order, ultimate."[113] However, the difference between them is that according to "pluralism under international law," "the obligations of international law set conditions upon the validity of state and of Community constitutions and interpretations thereof," and thus can serve as a device for resolving conflicts between "the heterarchical but not hierarchical relations" between the orders.[114] Because this device is not a new self-standing constitutional order that would be ultimately hierarchically superior to the self-standing constitutional orders of the nation-states and the EU, any remaining collisions between the domestic and European courts could be resolved through their having recourse to international law (perhaps even some institution of international law) without thereby destroying the heterarchical nature of pluralism. According to "radical pluralism," by contrast, these "framework" obligations and their potential fora "simply give a third perspective on the relationship in question, a further non-hierarchical interacting system."[115]

[106] MacCormick (n 33) at 264.

[107] MacCormick (n 33) at 264.

[108] N. MacCormick, "Risking Constitutional Collision in Europe?" (1998) 18 OJLS 517, 528.

[109] "If despite this [ie after following the interpretive rule requiring mutual respect and regard for consequences of a decision in the other system] conflicts come into being through judicial decision-making and interpretation, there will necessarily have to be some political action to produce a solution" (MacCormick, *Questioning Sovereignty* (n 56) at 265).

[110] MacCormick (n 18); MacCormick (n 33); cf the discussion in MacCormick, *Questioning Sovereignty* (n 56) at 219–21.

[111] MacCormick (n 108) at 528–30; cf MacCormick, *Questioning Sovereignty* (n 56) at 219–21 and ch 7.

[112] MacCormick (n 108) at 528.

[113] MacCormick (n 108) at 529.

[114] MacCormick (n 108) at 529.

[115] MacCormick (n 108) at 529.

In his 1998 article MacCormick clarified that "the thesis of 'pluralism under international law'" appears to him as being "contextually more persuasive and appropriate."[116] According to this refined view it seems that radical pluralism became problematic for MacCormick not only because it (1) allows the situation in which "the same human beings or corporations are said to have and not have a certain right."[117] I would argue that, on reflection, it became problematic for him also because it (2) does not take into account the reality of the non-constitutional nature of international law.[118] Yet neither of the two problems applies in the case of pluralism under international law. Here we still have the derivative international-law level to resort to in cases of collision between the states and the EU as the only ultimately self-standing orders constituting constitutional pluralism. As will be observed below, many self-styled "pluralists" have later missed the full purpose of MacCormick's adjustment on this point. This ultimately leads them—but not himself—into what seem to be insurmountable difficulties for distinguishing their conceptions from what we have always had under monism.[119]

This proposal differs from that of Walker's epistemic pluralism. Indeed, Walker would consider it as a switch from pluralism to monism.[120] Nor would Maduro endorse this conception; we saw that he had his own distinct proposal within the theme of the *who*. Weiler's proposal for the Constitutional Council is also different. It should thus be concluded that MacCormick's latest account represents yet another unique solution within this particular theme. Before saying anything more on this theme, we first need an inter-theoretical assessment of the deeper levels of these different pluralisms. Only then will it be possible to judge how each of them does or does not fit into the soundest conception of pluralism. This calls for a systematic investigation into the issue over the superior conception of pluralism. The remaining part of this book is largely concerned with this. Having completed the map, and decoded the branch and its ramifications, it is, however, necessary even before engaging with that to consider the criticism that was levied against the very idea of pluralism. We first turn to this.

[116] MacCormick (n 108) at 532.

[117] MacCormick (n 108) at 530.

[118] As we will see in what follows, for constitutional pluralism to really succeed, the inter-systemic conflict needs to be between two ultimately self-standing, and thus *constitutional*, orders. One must realistically threaten to displace the other as the *ultimate* holder of authority over the given territory. Mere derivative legal system is not enough. Yet MacCormick knew that, as of this point, the idea of replacing the nation-state monism with some new kind of democratic "international legal order" that is ultimately not derivative, but self-standing, and thus *directly* grounded in the ultimate authority of some world *demos* (monist constitutionalism), was not realistic. Cf Weiler (n 6); for details of the argument see Chapter 7, pp. 211–12, 219–24; Chapter 8, pp. 249–50; and Chapter 9, pp. 285–94.

[119] See Chapter 7, pp. 211–12, and Chapter 8, pp. 249–50. In any case, even if the second was not among MacCormick's reasons for the adjustment, I show below that the understanding of pluralism as "constitutional pluralism," as opposed to mere pluralism of "legal systems," is necessary for pluralism to succeed in its claim to be a sufficiently distinct conception from that of monism.

[120] Cf N. Walker, "Sovereignty and Differentiated Integration in the European Union" (1998) 4 ELJ 355, 387; Interview with N. Walker (EUI, Florence, 13 January 2006).

7

A True Novelty

Some important recent contributions have expressed doubts as to the propriety of seeing the described group of approaches as pluralist. There are several main lines of this fundamental criticism. Firstly, some argue that despite all their pluralist rhetoric (pluralist versus monist, heterarchical versus hierarchical) these pluralist approaches are, on closer examination, no different from the traditional, monist approach to legal/political ordering, or at least no different from the latter in any interesting way. Secondly, others start with the same point, but then argue that the only existing variant of pluralism still distinct from monism faces insurmountable problems of integrity and is thus unviable in that sense. Thirdly, there are those who find the field, rapidly expanding with many more very different authors who currently claim to be pluralists, just too messy and thus in a sense too vacuous to be able to provide any meaningful conception of pluralism. In what follows, these criticisms are addressed in turn, while the remaining ones are, for structural reasons, identified and answered in Chapters 8–10.[1] It is shown that, after the comprehensive mapping analysis that decodes the whole picture of the common branch and its ramifications, the criticisms appear in a new light and must be rejected. Within itself, constitutional pluralism does carry a sound core idea that is a true novelty within constitutional thought and cannot be dismissed by any of these criticisms. Some slightly different critical concerns that are not quite yet elaborated by these current lines of criticism might nonetheless be able to harm some of the less sound parts within the branch, while leaving its sound core, and the superior conception that will flow from it, intact.

Even though all these criticisms were elaborated before the mapping analysis decoded the whole picture of the common branch and its ramifications, they are nonetheless serious and could not be quickly dismissed through some easy move. This is in part because they could be read, some more explicitly than others, as going against MacCormick's conception. The most abstract part of this, as we now know, holds the central position in the branch as the underlying basis from which the various further versions derive. Thus, if the criticisms extend to MacCormick's most abstract idea—the only possible common denominator of the pluralist theories—and are successful there, this would be fatal also for the rest of the pluralist theories. It would also undermine the idea of the whole new branch of thought that supposedly evolved, as I have argued, from that abstract core.

[1] Chapter 8, pp. 235–51; Chapter 9, pp. 285–94; Chapter 10, pp. 316–23.

1. Not Distinct from Monism?

1.1 The line of criticism

"[P]luralism has suddenly become fashionable," Nicholas Barber writes.[2] "[It] is now common to argue," he explains, that Europe's intermingling legal systems "demand a pluralist interpretation," and that "[i]mplicit within this call is the assumption that pluralism is a novel and controversial way of understanding legal orders; that the classical, state-centred, models of legal systems cannot accommodate this new phenomenon."[3] It is precisely this "remarkable popularity"[4] that serves as the springboard for Barber's critique of the current understandings of pluralism. "Some recent writers," he states of the pluralist camp, "have turned modesty into a vice: 'pluralism' has become so thin a theory that virtually all respectable writers on legal philosophy would endorse their claims."[5] Barber uses Kelsen and Hart, the two typical monists from the world of legal theory,[6] to prove his claim and show that their models can "without too great a stretch"[7] be made too reminiscent of MacCormick's "pluralist"[8] account.

Barber's presentation of MacCormick's model is brief. He explains how MacCormick identifies a "variety of distinct, but connected, legal systems within Europe," "each with its own rule of recognition or *Grundnorm*."[9] To this, the presentation adds that one version of MacCormick's pluralism (radical pluralism) "then asserts that this is the end of the matter," while another (pluralism under international law) states that "international law may provide rules which can help resolve conflicts between these different systems."[10]

The essence of the argument is that MacCormick's interpretation "may not be sufficiently controversial to be described as 'pluralist'."[11] Kelsen and Hart "could, without too great a stretch, endorse either of these two [pluralist] interpretations" since, as Barber explains, in the last analysis these "'pluralist'" interpretations do little more than actually "bring to mind Kelsen's famous claim that international law and domestic law were parts of the same entity."[12] Barber cautions that, as is the case with MacCormick's "pluralism," so Kelsen's monistic model in its latest version, too, became sensitive to the differences in the point of view adopted:[13]

[2] N. Barber, "Legal Pluralism and the European Union" (2006) 12 ELJ 306, 306.

[3] Barber (n 2) at 306.

[4] Barber (n 2) at 306.

[5] Barber (n 2) at 306.

[6] Or, at least, Barber seems to understand them this way (see Barber (n 2) at 306, 307, 317–18, 326).

[7] Barber (n 2) at 326.

[8] Barber (n 2) at 326.

[9] Barber (n 2) at 325–6.

[10] Barber (n 2) at 326.

[11] Barber (n 2) at 326.

[12] Barber (n 2) at 326.

[13] In his initial (1993) article on pluralism MacCormick presented Kelsen's monist model. The model presented was actually Kelsen's initial monist account stating that international law is the ultimate authority for all the state legal systems: it determines their validity while also coordinating and separating them. Kelsen later changed his mind and proposed an adjusted monist model according to which there are two possible monistic readings: the initial one in which international law has the ultimate authority, and the second in which national law enjoys that primacy. For the initial version of Kelsen's monism, see H. Kelsen, *Introduction to the Problems of Legal Theory*, tr. B. and S. Paulson

From the view point of a national system, there was only one legal order, with elements of international law identified by rules of domestic law. From the point of view of international law, there was only one legal order, with elements of domestic law identified by rules of international law.[14]

Barber seems to conclude that if we now stretch this to the relationship between the member states and the EU, we arrive exactly at MacCormick's interpretation of the new European reality. And the story can be repeated with Hart. Indeed, it was he who pointed to the fact that Kelsen's initial monist account,[15] if at all true, was true only from the point of view of international law.[16] From the point of view of the national legal systems, Hart cautioned, the story is reversed: the ultimate authority resides with these systems, and the system of international law is here the one understood as being derivative.[17] Acknowledgement of the two conflicting points of view is thus inevitably also a feature of monism, and so if eventually even the two great monists can be presented as pluralists, then, Barber concludes, "everyone is a pluralist" and "pluralism ceases to be an interesting theory."[18] This is why the described "'pluralist'" readings are *not* "sufficiently controversial," and amount to "little more than the application of traditional [ie monist] models of legal systems to a new factual situation."[19]

Barber finds the key confirmation that his criticism of the current "'pluralist'"[20] readings is warranted in what he describes is the assumption of these readings, namely, that each of the two groups of courts—the national and European—would follow just its own system's highest interpretive authority regardless of its possible obligations under the other, coexisting system and its rule of recognition. By assuming that the judges would unquestioningly follow the ruling of only *their* system's highest interpretive instance, these kinds of readings may, Barber argues, oversimplify a possible *genuine plurality* in the relationship between the legal systems and their overlapping rules of recognition in Europe.[21] This is why he proposes his distinct model, according to which the judges *within* each of the systems must also be "divided, or undecided" as to which of the coexisting rules of recognition to follow. That way it would then supposedly be "more accurate to say" that we have two rules of recognition coexisting in a given system at the same time.[22] Barber's conclusion is therefore that only such a conception might perhaps

(Oxford: Oxford University Press, 1997) 120–5; for the later adjustment, H. Kelsen, *Pure Theory of Law*, tr. M. Knight (Berkeley, CA: University of California Press, 1967) ch 7. For MacCormick's description of the initial account of Kelsen's model, see his, "Beyond the Sovereign State" (1993) 56 ML Rev 1, 8.

14 Barber (n 2) at 326.

15 MacCormick (n 13) at 8–9.

16 H. Hart, "Kelsen's Doctrine of the Unity of Law" in *Essays in Jurisprudence and Philosophy* (Oxford: Oxford University Press, 1983) 309–42; H. Hart, *The Concept of Law* (2nd edn, Oxford: Oxford University Press, 1994) ch 10.

17 Hart, *The Concept of Law* (n 16) ch 10.

18 Barber (n 2) at 306, 326.

19 Barber (n 2) at 306, 326.

20 Barber (n 2) at 326.

21 "The danger of sticking with these readings is that they may over-simplify the split between the German and European systems" (Barber (n 2) at 326). (In his paper, Barber uses Germany as an example confirming his broader point about the relationship between the EU and member states in general).

22 Barber (n 2) at 326.

be properly understood as pluralism. It is only this understanding, he argues, that is sufficiently controversial and distinct from the described monism. Moreover, it is actually only this conception, as he explains, that allows for the existence of the "overlap" between two systems and their rules of recognition. In a footnote to his presentation of MacCormick's position, Barber thus writes: "Intriguingly, MacCormick talks of legal systems 'overlapping' in these pluralist models.... It is unclear what he means by this. Mere recognition of the rules of one legal order by another is not an 'overlap'."[23]

1.2 Response at the foundational level

Could the model of Kelsen and Hart truly be made essentially the same as that of our pluralists? Barber correctly clarified that Kelsen's final understanding was that either the first system ultimately follows from the second or that the second follows from the first. Either international law is the ultimate source, the ultimate *Grundnorm*, of a national system, or the nation-state's *Grundnorm* is the ultimate source of validity also of international law. At first, Kelsen argued otherwise: that monism means only that international law is the ultimate source of authority and validity of the state legal systems.[24] But then came Hart with his counter-argument that this could hold only from one point of view,[25] and in his later work Kelsen, too, adjusted his initial position to the one described, which acknowledges the possible differences in viewpoint.[26] So Barber correctly identifies and operates with Kelsen's final version of monism. At the same time, however, his critique seems to fail to emphasize sufficiently a further key feature of Kelsen's as well as Hart's theory on monism. That is, after acknowledging the possibility of difference in perspectives, Kelsen continued by explaining that his theory can go no further than describe them both and state that *either one or the other* of the two options must be accepted.[27] There is nothing else, Kelsen explicitly argued, for his theory to do. So, in the end, "he who treasures the idea of the sovereignty of his state, because he identifies himself in his increased self-consciousness with the state, will prefer the primacy of the national legal order."[28] By contrast, "[h]e who values the idea of a legal organization of the world, will prefer the primacy of international law."[29] Hart also did not go any further than clarifying that Kelsen's initial account could be read from either one or the other extreme perspective. This is what also MacCormick himself subtly observed about Hart.[30]

23 Barber (n 2) at 326, fn 90. As mentioned, Barber's own model is, by contrast, to be seen as "an account of overlapping legal orders that goes beyond mutual recognition."

24 Kelsen (n 13) at 120–5.

25 Hart, "Kelsen's Doctrine of the Unity of Law" (n 16) at 309–42; *The Concept of Law* (n 16) ch 10.

26 Kelsen (n 13) at 320–47.

27 Kelsen (n 13) at 346: "This science can do no more that describe them both, and state that one or the other reference system must be accepted if the relationship between national and international law is to be determined."

28 Kelsen (n 13) at 346. 29 Kelsen (n 13) at 346.

30 MacCormick writes: "Hart himself rather gives the basis for the argument [ie for MacCormick's pluralist conclusion] than exploits it to the full himself. Despite the pluralistic or polycentric potentialities

For EU and member states, to perform the necessary hypothetical translation of some more general concept of monism to *constitutional monism* and its new polity context of the EU and member states, Kelsen would probably say that either it is the European constitution that is the ultimate source of validity of the national constitutions, or else, each national constitution remains an ultimate source in relation to which the European constitution is subordinate and derivative. With Hart one would similarly need to acknowledge that his hypothetical concept of constitutional "monism" would go no further than identify the two different monistic perspectives on the question of ultimate constitutional authority—the national and European.

Now, once these further features in Kelsen's and Hart's "monist" accounts, which I said Barber's critique may not sufficiently emphasize, are revealed and translated into the European constitutional-polity context, we can see the stark contrast of these "monist" theories with MacCormick's pluralism. True, like Kelsen and Hart, MacCormick acknowledges the difference in perspective. But unlike them, MacCormick goes on and makes the key *further* conclusion: his abstract conception of pluralism[31] is that *neither* of the *constitutional* systems any longer is to be seen as having the ultimate authority (sovereignty), so that *neither* ultimately derives its constitutional authority from the other. This is clearly "*a third*" and unique, pluralist reading of the situation. For Kelsen, as we saw, insisted exactly on the opposite view: that one *either accepts the absolute position of national monism, or the other absolute extreme of European monism.* There is no third option here and it is made explicit by his theory that no other conclusion is open: there are only the two monist views, and one is then simply to pick one of the two extremes. Hart too, as we also observed, did not make any further conclusion from his acknowledgement of the difference in the point of view.[32] But MacCormick's theory, which crucially demands and makes such a further conclusion—the *third* option—thus stands in direct contrast to both of these non-pluralist accounts. His extension is a novelty in both senses. It actually makes and requires such a further conclusion,[33] and this particular conclusion is by its content a pluralist one; one that explicitly requires that we, and the constitutional orders and their institutions, *do not* adopt either of the two monist extremes that Kelsen explicitly considered as the only two available options.

he points to in developing his theory, pluralism remains more a potential than an actual virtue of his own work" (MacCormick (n 13) at 9). At another place MacCormick similarly remarks: "It has to be said though, that however open Hart was conceptually to a more pluralistic approach, most of his legal writing sticks rather firmly within a common law approach, usually in its Anglocentric form. There is a line of thought here awaiting development" (see N. MacCormick, *Questioning Sovereignty: Law, State, and Nation in the European Commonwealth* (Oxford: Oxford University Press, 1999) at 75–6).

[31] That is, the minimum understanding of heterarchy (heterarchy minimized, our missing link) as the minimum common denominator of pluralism appearing within a part of his foundational discourse and underlying all other versions of constitutional pluralism.

[32] Once again, MacCormick describes it as a line of thought the pluralist potentials of which Hart's theory revealed while itself did not exploit. There is "a line of thought here awaiting development," MacCormick wrote. See his, *Questioning Sovereignty* (n 30) at 76.

[33] At least by a legal theoretician, politicians, and citizens. As to the judges, MacCormick is less explicit in his first article, but on my reading of his later contributions this also holds for them to a degree that is decisive for constitutional pluralism to distinguish itself from the monist accounts even in the judicial sense (see n 48).

The real test for pluralism is therefore not in the mere acknowledgement of the different points of view, although one could probably say that neglecting even that (cf Kelsen's initial model) would be a yet more extreme type of monism. The point is instead in the particular pluralist conclusion that a theory does or does not draw further from that. Barber's analysis appears to mistake these two levels and, while it only focuses on the first, it neglects the second and decisive one. This seems to go hand in hand with what I said was Barber's rather brief presentation of MacCormick's position,[34] coupled with his lack of focus on some further key features of Kelsen's and Hart's theory as described.

The key distinctive feature of the "third way," the uniquely pluralist conclusion, is then also operationalized in the further *concessions* that this distinct approach requires from both constitutional orders and their sources. This should not come as a surprise. For, what I have described here as the "third way" is nothing else but what was in the previous chapter already characterized as the heterarchy minimized; that is, the key minimal common denominator that the analysis revealed as being constitutive of the unique pluralist branch. It is that minimal understanding of heterarchy (pluralism) that differs from hierarchy (monism) precisely in holding that both constitutional orders and their sources have to relinquish their traditional absolutist claims and instead *concede* that neither is any longer ultimately superior over the other. This is in order to get things correct both in terms of descriptive reality (explanatory dimension of pluralism) as well as normative desirability (normative dimension of pluralism). They must recognize one another and their respective (sources of) constitutional authorities as both being ultimately self-standing, coequal, and yet simultaneously coexistent over the shared piece of territory (territorial overlap). By definition there can be no such concessions, and no territorial overlap under monism, be it Kelsen's explanatory monism, or any of the normative monisms that exist.

It is precisely such unique pluralist concessions that enable the *territorial overlap* of constitutional orders to exist as another unique and distinctively pluralist phenomenon. The traditional monist world of constitutional states has been one of ultimately exclusive territorial jurisdictions.[35] By adopting the new pluralist concessions, by contrast, there arises a possibility to conceive of self-standing

[34] Recall that Barber's presentation stopped at the point at which it described how MacCormick identifies a "variety of distinct, but connected, legal systems within Europe," "each with its own rule of recognition or *Grundnorm*," and how one version of his pluralism (radical pluralism) "then asserts that this is the end of the matter," while the other ("pluralism under international law") states that "international law may provide rules which can help resolve conflicts between these different systems" (see p. 191). This presentation thus ends before reaching the crucial second level, ie the pluralist conclusions which MacCormick, unlike Kelsen and Hart, draws from that. Also, Barber's phrase "[r]adical pluralism then asserts that this is the end of the matter" appears to give the impression that MacCormick too, like Kelsen and Hart, did not go further to make his distinctive and key conclusion from the point at which his theory acknowledged the difference in perspectives.

[35] Cf MacCormick (n 30) at 191; N. Walker, "Late Sovereignty in the European Union" in N. Walker (ed.), *Sovereignty in Transition* (Oxford: Hart Publishing, 2003) 21–5; "The Idea of Constitutional Pluralism" (2002) 65 ML Rev 317, 345.

constitutional authorities, but without the element of territorial exclusivity.[36] It thus becomes possible to imagine constitutional authority, or "sovereignty," in ultimately non-exclusive terms. This enables the *territorial overlap* between two or more constitutional polities: neither of the constitutional authorities coexisting over a shared territory is ultimately subsumed to the other, so that one is necessarily the derivative while the other is the ultimate constitutional authority of that territory. It is in this distinctive foundational sense that MacCormick uses his characterization of "overlapping" but self-standing constitutional orders in the new pluralist Europe.[37] Barber's remark that it is not clear what MacCormick means by this term, since the "[m]ere recognition of the rules of one legal order by another is not yet an overlap,"[38] seems to neglect this novel possibility. That is, the *territorial non-exclusivity* of self-standing constitutional authorities that enables the unique overlap on the same piece of territory *but for* the described distinctively pluralist principle and its foundational concessions. It is those that the criticism fails to acknowledge, and simply removes from the account, in the first place.

There is yet another meaning of the concept of overlap that normally appears in constitutional pluralism. Since the boundaries of two constitutional systems in a territorial overlap are inherently contested, this means that in the contested areas the decision-making authority will be claimed by institutions of both constitutional orders at the same time. It will also be claimed in a way that would not make one set of those institutions the superior guardian of the overlap. MacCormick speaks of the overlap also in this other sense, and explains that "[p]rovided the same rules are in fact acknowledged as valid in the area of overlap this will not lead to incompatibility or conflict," and that, "of course, there are [also] elaborate arrangements to try to forestall conflict."[39] To distinguish it from the "territorial overlap" as discussed in the previous paragraph, we should describe this one as the "institutional," or simply "judicial overlap."

Unlike the "territorial overlap," "judicial overlap" is no longer part of the foundational and constitutive level of the pluralist branch. As we know by now, the abstract common denominator of the heterarchy minimized, or the "third way," can be seen as being further explained by the different pluralists in three different general directions, which have been characterized as the discourse of the *how*, *what*, and *who*, respectively. From the perspective of the branch, these are thus already applicative discourses on pluralism, and "judicial overlap" is part of one of *these*, namely, the discourse of the *who*. This brings us to the second—applicative—stage at which I want to respond to the criticism.

1.3 Response at the applicative level

It was explained earlier that Barber finds the key confirmation of his criticism in the assumption by the current "pluralist" theories that the judges would

[36] Cf MacCormick (n 30) at 191; Walker, "Late Sovereignty in the European Union" (n 35) at 23; "The Idea of Constitutional Pluralism" (n 35) at 346.

[37] See, eg MacCormick (n 13) at 8–9; "The Maastricht-Urteil: Sovereignty Now" (1995) 1 ELJ 259, 264–5; "Risking Constitutional Collision in Europe?" (1998) 18 OJLS 517, 528, 530.

[38] P. 193.

[39] MacCormick (n 13) at 8; cf "The Maastricht-Urteil" (n 37) at 264–5.

unquestioningly follow the ruling of only *their* system's highest court. This would, in Barber's view, oversimplify a possible actual plurality in the relationship between the legal systems and their overlapping rules of recognition in Europe.[40] The argument is that such an arrangement may in effect be the same as monism. Recall how Barber, for this reason, proposed his "genuine" pluralist model according to which the judges *within* each of the systems must also be "divided, or undecided" as to which of the coexisting rules of recognition (European or national) to follow.[41] This way, he concluded, it would be "more accurate to say" that we have two rules of recognition coexisting at the same time, and that its two systems actually overlap.[42]

The situation, under constitutional pluralism, in which the national courts support one rationale and the European courts endorse a different rationale is exactly the one I have characterized as "judicial overlap."[43] When dealing with it we are within our theme of the *who* as constituted by the overlapping sphere between (judicial) institutions of different orders and its question of what kind of arrangement is to be proposed within such a context as to the subject(s)—the *who*—of the decision-making authority. Now, when Barber considers the simple variant of judicial overlap too close to—if not the same as—the situation under monism, and suggests his own improvement, he in effect makes his own proposal within this particular theme of the *who*. He considers as pluralist only the arrangement which not only leaves the questions of "who decides" and "who decides who decides" to the two highest courts, but additionally requires that lower courts within each of the pluralist systems be "divided and undecided" as to which of the highest instances to follow. We can label this as "judicial double-overlap."

But while this surely could be another variation of pluralism, or a special emphasis of one of its possible features, the "judicial double-overlap" is not a necessary element of constitutional pluralism. Its absence cannot undermine the uniqueness of the pluralist branch and its distinctiveness from monism, as the critique seems to assume. This is so for two reasons.

Firstly, our mapping analysis showed that points about "judicial overlap" or "double-overlap" are points made only within the theme of the *who*. But to make the idea of constitutional pluralism depend just on a point within one of the applicative themes of pluralism is to ignore the key conclusion resulting from the comprehensive mapping of the pluralist theories. The endorsement of the abstract underlying conception of pluralism, itself already distinct from the abstract monist account, has pluralist implications not only for the further theme of the *who*, but—crucially—also for the themes of the *how* and the *what*. So Barber's criticism, doubting whether the ascription of the term pluralism is warranted, takes too narrow a focus of what constitutional pluralism entails.

The mapping has shown how—by endorsing the abstract pluralist conception at its foundation—one strand of the branch argues that constitutional pluralism means mutual recognition of the self-standing constitutional authorities in terms

[40] See pp. 192–3. [41] See p. 192. [42] See p. 192. [43] See p. 196.

of adoption, by both sides, of some special rules of interpretation assuring that the autonomy of the other authority is actually respected on an equal basis. If one accepts this idea as being grounded in the foundational conception of pluralism, and one finds oneself within the specific sphere of the *how* when searching for its actual materialization, then such a pluralist option is bound to follow its unique foundational rule. It is thus distinct from, and an antithesis to, the interpretive options available to a monist within the same sphere. Moreover, the authors from this strand argue that if the pluralist mechanisms within the theme of the *how* are properly elaborated, this significantly diminishes the risk of conflict and so the whole relevance, for constitutional pluralism, of the sphere of the *who*.[44]

Even clearer seems to be the distinction between those pluralists who seek the more concrete realization of the abstract foundational conception of constitutional pluralism through more substantive reconciliation of two constitutional identities, and the monists within the sphere of the *what*. The latter are free to argue for either of the two dominant subordinations of one substantive identity at the expense of the other. The former, however, introduce a whole new substantive constitutional ethics,[45] stemming from the abstract basis of constitutional pluralism and demanding a balanced substantive reconciliation of the two equally weighty sources of values. Indeed, the monistic lack of particular substantive constraint and the balanced preservation of *both* of these sources/values involve clear distinctions between the two approaches within the sphere of the *what*, and this is proposed as the very reason for which this group of pluralists endorses pluralism instead of monism. Without these pluralist distinctions within the sphere of the *what*, constitutional pluralism loses, in the eyes of substantive pluralists, its very normative essence. This is also why for some of these substantive pluralists the theme of the *who*, within which Barber's criticism is situated, is not among the core aspects of constitutional pluralism at all. The "judicial double-overlap" would not add anything pluralistic to, say, Weiler's vision of pluralism within this applicative theme. Any solution that is, within this applicative sphere, more open than his proposal for the common Constitutional Council pluralistically conceived, actually disrupts the greatest degree of pluralism as Weiler envisions it.[46]

This confirms that one who doubted the distinctiveness of constitutional pluralism while being situated within the theme of the *who*, would indeed take too narrow a view of what the branch of constitutional pluralism really entails. One would mistakenly argue against the whole branch—against the idea of constitutional pluralism itself—when one's arguments would merely concern a tiny, and disputed, aspect within one of pluralism's applicative discourses. Within the *who* sector each of the pluralists has a very different applicative solution to offer, and some pluralists even show that it is not needed to have the institutional question unresolved. Yet all of these different applicative solutions within the *who* are perfectly compatible with, and reflect, the core distinctive idea of pluralism, the principle of heterarchy minimized, which appears at a wholly different,

[44] Pp. 52–3 (Walker); pp. 103–4, 104–8, 116–18 (Maduro).

[45] Pp. 77–89 (Weiler); pp. 177–87 (MacCormick).

[46] Pp. 94–6 (Weiler).

foundational, sector of discourse while exerting its distinctive effects from there in several different directions.

Secondly, even if the sphere of the *who* were the only perspective from which to judge pluralism as distinct from monism, the argument for the "judicial double-overlap" as the necessary distinctive feature of pluralism cannot succeed. The decoding of the branch that was enabled by the comprehensive mapping analysis showed that the ordinary pluralist "judicial overlap" is by itself indisputably distinct from monism. We saw that the pluralist version of judicial overlap occurs only within the uniquely pluralist condition of territorial overlap determined by the mutual acceptance at the foundational level of the idea of heterarchy. At the minimum, such an endorsement of the abstract pluralist conception has the following consequence that is different from monism. The national courts in the territorially determined overlap now need to recognize that they can no longer base their claim to jurisdiction or the final say on the external rationale about their constitution's—and its source's—exclusive ultimate authority over a given state territory and so on the assumption of the European constitution's—and its own source's—inevitably derivative, subordinate authority on that territory. Likewise, the European courts cannot ground their own claim of the jurisdiction and the final say on the rationale that it is their constitution and its source that are now the exclusive ultimate authority on the territory of Europe.[47] Justificatory rationales behind judges' decisions on the question of *who* would thus need to be adjusted to at least this minimum degree under the pluralist type of judicial overlap.[48] This in and of itself is indeed already indisputably distinct from the situation under monism.[49] The monist order is free, and even normatively bound, to follow exactly

[47] Because, for instance, a national *demos*'s grant of authority to the national constitution has been subordinated by the European *demos* and its direct grant of ultimate authority to the hierarchically higher and ultimate European constitution.

[48] "The radical pluralist thesis suggests that neither can or should claim all-purpose supremacy over the other. It would therefore be of value for all participants to make this explicit in some way" (MacCormick, "Risking Constitutional Collision in Europe?" (n 37) at 531). When discussing his pluralism under international law, MacCormick similarly remarks: "What that signals in the first instance is that state courts have no right to assume an absolute superiority of state constitution over international good order, including the European dimension of that good order. This is not the same as saying that they must simply defer to whatever the ECJ considers to be mandated by the European constitution" (MacCormick, "Risking Constitutional Collision in Europe?" (n 37) at 531–2). Cf also MacCormick's comment on the *Maastricht* decision of the German Federal Constitutional Court: "So far as the Constitutional Court was denying that sovereignty has passed to organs of the European Community or Union, we may agree with it on the grounds here argued. But so far as it asserted a resultant continuing sovereignty of the German people, we may doubt it . . . it has to be said that the same analysis as requires us to confirm that sovereignty has not been bestowed on European organs requires us at the same time to deny that it is a continuing property of any Member State" (MacCormick, "The Maastricht-Urteil" (n 37) at 265).

[49] Not to mention the even more specific proposals within the theme of the *who* as elaborated by each of the pluralists as examined above; while none of those includes "judicial double-overlap," each is already, and with its own applicative nuance, paradigmatically different from the solution as appears within the discourse of the *who* under monism. (Cf a supreme court as the supreme final interpreter of the law of the land, whose decisions in jurisdictional disputes between the federal and state levels override those of the state courts, and whose justices are also not selected according to the principle of equality between the self-standing federal and state constitutional orders because there is no such

such rationales. It must normally declare, precisely on that basis, its own highest institution as the final arbiter in disputes regarding the boundary of the decision-making authority between such a sovereign order and its subordinate units. Insofar as the courts under pluralism would on occasion nevertheless repeat the monist rhetoric, a situation that might even be understandable,[50] this would, normatively, have to be regarded exactly as that: mere rhetoric and overstatement.[51] Indeed, even inside the narrow perspective of the theme of the *who* alone, it cannot but be concluded that "judicial double-overlap," while perhaps being an applicative feature of some possible variation of constitutional pluralism,[52] is *not* a necessary constitutive element of it. It is not the exact feature separating the pluralist approach from the monist within the discourse of the *who*. It can be concluded that, by focusing on this relatively unimportant feature of constitutional pluralism, Barber's critique misses pluralism's unique distinguishing features at both the foundational level as well as the particular applicative level of the *who*.

This misunderstanding is, however, only one example of a general and commonplace phenomenon in today's very messy discourse on constitutional pluralism, for which the pluralists themselves are largely responsible. With their different meanings of the term, and wholly different levels of the discourse, they often refer to each other for corroboration through some general same-sounding rhetoric, but actually speak past each other and about different, even deeply conflicting, ideas and subject matters. Doing so without a prior systematic analysis of the branch that would first try to make sense of the core common pluralist idea, they have themselves created that confusion about what, if anything, pluralism really means. Nor can the critics of course be expected to solve that puzzle on their behalf. In such circumstances, without a prior comprehensive mapping analysis and its decoding of the labyrinth using something like Ariadne's Thread, one hardly knows what to focus on when making an argument against the very idea of constitutional pluralism.

2. Fails to Respect Integrity?

Another critic, Pavlos Eleftheriadis, has recently waded into these same murky waters, and in a comparable way as Barber did not long before him. His critique faces similar problems. It seems that the core of Barber's critique was conceived at least with some collaborative effort with Eleftheriadis, or perhaps vice versa. In one

ultimately self-standing equality, but the ultimate derivation/subordination, in the relationship between both orders at the foundational level).

[50] "[D]oubtless there are special reasons of constitutional rhetoric that require a German Court to continue asserting the very sovereignty of the people that the German, like the French, Constitution postulates as fundamental to itself. But..." (MacCormick, "The Maastricht-Urteil" (n 37) at 265).

[51] MacCormick, "The Maastricht-Urteil" (n 37) at 265.

[52] But not Barber's since, as we saw above, his conception is not (yet) pluralist in the first place. At the foundational level he understands that it is "*either* this system and its *Grundnorm*, *or* that system and its *Grundnorm*," that is the ultimately superior one (instead of *neither* this one *nor* that one) over a given territory. That is indeed not pluralism, but the monism of Kelsen and Hart.

central aspect both of their critiques are very similar and I recall several years ago their common discussions along these same lines in one of the constitutional theory seminars at Oxford.[53]

Eleftheriadis argues that the idea of pluralism is either not distinct from that of monism or, in the case when it could be seen as distinct, "fails to respect the value of integrity."[54] As such, it is a failed project—even an "unfortunate distraction" in recent constitutional thought.[55] In what follows we first focus on Eleftheriadis's version of the "not distinct" argument. Our response to this critique is then followed by the examination and rejection of his argument about "integrity." Addressing some final additional aspects of this critique then concludes the section.

2.1 Not distinct

Like Barber, Eleftheriadis mistakenly assigns to MacCormick an understanding of "pluralism" that is a substantially incomplete account of his pluralist idea, so that it is not pluralism at all. That is, he presents only the first half of MacCormick's conception: the nation-state and the EU orders are two confronting orders in Europe, each of which has its own *Grundnorm* and its own respective internal hierarchy. Institutions of the first order strictly follow their order's *Grundnorm* while institutions of the second order follow their own.

But Eleftheriadis fails to add and explain the second, and crucial, part of MacCormick's argument: the further conclusion about the need for the particular pluralist mutual recognition and concessions, of heterarchy, between such orders. He simply omits that and instead acts as if MacCormick concluded that such a descriptive account of two internally hierarchical "monisms"[56] already constituted his conception of pluralism. He then continues misrepresenting MacCormick's claim in this way. When collision between both independent orders arises there is thus, according to Eleftheriadis's presentation of MacCormick, simply "no reason to regret the incoherence."[57] Similarly, Eleftheriadis presents MacCormick's statements about this supposedly "not [being] logically embarrassing" because "the answers are from the point of view of different systems" as if such a monist openness itself was already MacCormick's position of pluralism.

We know from analysis of Barber's critique that this is not a correct reading of MacCormick's conception. Such descriptions of the two confronting, self-standing orders are only the first and preparatory step in MacCormick's argument. That position is not yet pluralism and is no different from the monist accounts of Kelsen

[53] At the time I was working towards my D.Phil. on the topic. Listening to those discussions it occurred to me already at that point that I had a different understanding of MacCormick's core idea of pluralism. The need to clarify the dilemma led to my later discussions on this particular point with MacCormick. While the preceding and following account is mine, those exchanges did crucially reaffirm my understanding as to what would be the most proper way in which to think about these issues. I am indebted to Neil MacCormick for that.

[54] P. Eleftheriadis, "Pluralism and Integrity" (2010) 23 Ratio Juris 365–89, 365.

[55] Eleftheriadis (n 54) at 388. [56] Eleftheriadis (n 54) at 373.

[57] Eleftheriadis (n 54) at 372.

and Hart. This is why MacCormick instead concludes further from that basis that we should reject this "either/or" version of Kelsen/Hart's monism. The two orders must instead make the further step and recognize that neither can any longer proceed independently of each other as if it were a monism (two monisms). They instead need to make some accommodating concessions at the foundational as well as the applicative level.

Indeed, MacCormick's conception is concerned *very* much with the danger of collision and explicitly requires such concessions—the "third way" of mutual recognition of their heterarchical relation instead of monist ignorance from each of the orders. This is why, after all, he argues that collision can and should be avoided through such necessary concessions that the orders need to adopt for explanatory as well as normatively good reasons.[58] The fact that, according to his radical pluralism, those concessions are to be reached through the process of mutual accommodation that is inherently political and moral in nature—although occurring through the political as well as highest judicial institutions of both orders[59]—does not change the crucial fact that they are, according to MacCormick's idea of pluralism, emphatically required. It is thus a serious misrepresentation of MacCormick's view to suggest that his conception means that each of the confronting orders must ignore or be free to ignore the other, and follow its own old monist direction, including its monist rationale for the foundational ultimate authority, while thus keeping its old (monist) *Grundnorm* intact. It is likewise a mistake to present, in this same light, his pluralism as positing that there must be simply "no reason to regret the incoherence" resulting from that kind of non-interaction between both orders.[60] The mutually accommodating concessions from both orders that MacCormick normatively requires at all levels, the foundational one as well as that of the *who*, the *how*, and the *what*,[61] are actually meant to remove that collision in practice. He also believed that that would indeed need to happen in order for his pluralist conception to be confirmed in practice. It is thus likewise a misrepresentation to present phrases from what is only the preparatory stage of his argument—such as "not logically embarrassing" because "the answers are from the point of view of different systems"—as if indicating that his pluralism means that there should be no pluralist concessions because each of the orders should absolutely independently pursue its own monist path. To conclude that, according to MacCormick's conception, the two orders "are not actually communicating"[62] is the climax of this same type of misreading of his position.

We see that this actually constructs a straw man conception of "pluralism." After erecting it himself, Eleftheriadis then complains that the straw man does not represent any kind of unique novel conception at all. And MacCormick has to pay the price: explaining that "th[is] result is not a pluralist result,"[63] Eleftheriadis

[58] Chapter 1, pp. 21–4, 25–9, and Chapter 6, whole of section 3.

[59] This process is political in nature because such a mutual accommodation between both orders is inherently pushing beyond the old, monist version of their *Grundnorms* and is inescapably refining those into the new, pluralist kind of *Grundorms*.

[60] Eleftheriadis (n 54) at 372. [61] See n 58. [62] Eleftheriadis (n 54) at 372.

[63] Eleftheriadis (n 54) at 373.

concludes that MacCormick's conception is thus actually no different from monism. It is instead a description of a situation in which we have "two monisms."[64] In his own words Eleftheriadis then in effect repeats Barber's point on Kelsen/Hart's conception of the "either/or" monism. Under this scheme of two mutually isolated monisms, with no further requirement of the pluralist mutual accommodation, *either* one *or* the other is correct—and thus in a sense *both*, depending on which perspective you take and where you happen to start:

> If we are within the national jurisdiction, then the national monism is correct. If we are within the EU jurisdiction and institutions, EU monism is correct. So there are hierarchies in both legal orders. None of them is pluralist. These are two inconsistent hierarchies and we accept them both, depending where we happen to be. This is a surprising affirmation of... monism.[65] ... If we start at a national court, say a challenge against a member state measure that may or may not give rise to a preliminary reference, we are bound by national monism. If we start at the EU level, say an enforcement action of the Commission against a state, we are bound by EU monism. On both sides this is the end of the matter, since they are both instructed to ignore outsiders. This seems to be just simple monism. None of the two legal orders needs to be pluralist for their mutual disrespect to be true.[66]

But we know that this is not MacCormick's conception. We have rejected what was essentially the same point already when responding to Barber's criticism. Barber and Eleftheriadis, who seem to have begat this point together,[67] are thus both subject to the same response that was already elaborated above in the case of Barber. MacCormick's conception is not the "either/or" type of monism, but instead follows the "third way" according to which both orders are required mutually to recognize, in the binding objective (inter-systemic) sense, that *neither* of them can any longer claim what Eleftheriadis's monist orders claim, nor act the way Eleftheriadis's monist orders act.

At the foundational level, any monist order claims that it alone (and its source) is the ultimately superior order (source of authority) on that territory. All other orders (sources) that appear on that same territory are necessarily, by definition, derivative from it. Each of Eleftheriadis's orders (sources) claims so and thus indeed, as he writes, "ignores" and "disrespects" the other.[68] It is either one or the other that is right, depending on your perspective, and so *both* are free to continue claiming this, and acting completely in their respective monist ways. By contrast, MacCormick's "third way" is distinct and unique by virtue of requiring the opposite. According to it, the orders (and their sources) need to make the second, and crucial, step that must follow this first and preparatory step. Namely, they must at the very least adopt the distinct position of heterarchy minimized: *neither* of the orders (sources) can, if it is to get the facts objectively right and things normatively correct, any longer claim that *it* (and its own source) is the ultimately superior order (source of

[64] Eleftheriadis describes this (his first reading of MacCormick's position) as "double monism" ("Pluralism and Integrity" (n 54) at 373).
[65] Eleftheriadis (n 54) at 373. [66] Eleftheriadis (n 54) at 376. [67] See p. 201.
[68] Eleftheriadis (n 54) at 376.

authority) on that same territory, and so that the other order (source) is merely derivative from it. Nor are any of MacCormick's orders (their sources) any longer permitted to act on that old monist rationale. Instead, they must mutually acknowledge to each other, now as a matter of objective validity that is to bind them both, their self-standing and equal authorities, of which neither is any longer the ultimate, over the same territory. They must also do what is needed to coexist as such without failing due to collisions. Correspondingly, they both must accept adopting some mutually accommodating concessions at all levels that would reflect this distinct and practically viable non-monist principle on which they have just converged.

At the applicative levels, neither of the orders is of course permitted to claim, and act on, the old monist rationale either. What we get here is the need to engage in that distinctive mutual accommodation and respect between the orders, rather than in Eleftheriadis's mutual ignorance and disrespect between them. This must reflect the foundational pluralist principle of mutually recognized equality and the self-standing status of both orders, rather than, as Eleftheriadis would have it, the claim by both about the derivative and thus ultimately subordinate and unequal status of the other. Eleftheriadis indeed simply omitted the second, and crucial, distinctive step of the unique pluralist mutual recognition and accommodation at the foundational and all other levels from MacCormick's conception of pluralism. As a result, he launched his unjustified critique against a monist conception—the straw man—that he himself authored. MacCormick's idea of pluralism is indisputably different from the latter, and escapes its challenge, for the same reasons as it escaped the challenge from Barber.

Anyone who wished to observe further the unique implications for the legal doctrine of the distinct pluralist principle, would be best advised simply to revisit the applicative discourses (the *who*, *how*, and *what*) as already discussed above in the chapters that cover the individual authors who make those applicative contributions. In addition to those, some decisive further pluralist implications are developed in Chapters 8–10, following. Here it will suffice to focus briefly, as an example, only on the applicative theme of the *who*. There is of course the paradigmatic monist rationale, (the classic monist foundational principle) that is legitimately used under monism, but is no longer available under pluralism, to justify the final decision-making authority of the highest court of a given order.[69] In addition to this distinctive effect of pluralism within the theme of the *who*, pluralism also rejects the institutional arrangement that is the paradigmatic reflection of the monist foundational principle within this applicative theme and cannot be squared with the pluralist foundational principle. All pluralists examined earlier thus reject the monist solution of conferring *exclusively* on the highest court of one order—*either* on the European Court *or* on the member-state constitutional court—the authority of acting as the final interpretive arbiter over the disagreements concerning the boundary between both orders. It would indeed be hard to justify that this solution best reflects the foundational idea of equality and ultimately non-derivative nature of both orders. There is nothing in such a solution about mutual accommodation according to equal respect between equally self-standing orders.

[69] The point is more fully explained earlier in the response against Barber's critique (pp. 199–200).

At the same time, pluralism is—unlike monism—also correctly open to all those institutional arrangements within the sphere of the *who* that *do* reflect that foundational equality and self-standing (non-derivative) nature of both accommodating orders. Thus, we have those pluralists who prefer to leave the question of *who* more radically open than others. Think of Walker's radically thin approach to accommodation in this area, in epistemic pluralism and its requirement of resolving first-order disagreement through an agonistic mutual respect between equals. Or indeed, consider MacCormick's radical pluralism that similarly does not impose any *specific* criterion, but simply generally requires accommodation according to the pluralist equal recognition. Moreover, we also have those who do engage more elaborate criteria for the distribution of the (final) decision-making authority, but distribute this authority in a balanced way between the highest institutions of both orders. In this way neither of them retains the whole, or even most, of that authority and is thus, unlike under monism, also not in the position of the final arbiter over the boundary disputes. Mattias Kumm and Miguel Maduro are clearly in this group, and we know from our analysis that both of their theories within this applicative theme can and should indeed be seen as perfectly fitting reflections of the distinctive pluralist principle of equals from the foundational level. Furthermore, we have those like Weiler who do vest in one institution the power to interpret all, or most, boundary disputes with final authority. Crucially, however, this is not an institution of either one of the orders under pluralism, nor of some other order beyond them. Instead, the institution is a composition of both orders to an equal degree, carefully designed so as to reflect that equality of both self-standing orders. It is thus merely a distinctively pluralist device to solve conflicts between both orders—rather than a monist imposition from an institution of some third and ultimately superior order—in the manner that does not disturb, but instead reflects the foundational mutual equal respect between both self-standing yet accommodating orders. Indeed, these are all solutions that tend to arise when mutual accommodations in the applicative sphere of the *who* truly respect and follow the pluralist principle from the foundation. This is indisputably different from what naturally tends to arise in an order with the monist foundation: when the power of the final arbiter of the boundary disputes is vested in the highest institution of the one, but not the other, of the ultimately hierarchical orders.[70]

Similar distinctively pluralist effects for the legal doctrine and politics could also be observed for the applicative spheres of the *how* and the *what*. MacCormick's idea of pluralism is indeed different from that of monism.

2.2 The argument from integrity

We saw that failing to construe MacCormick's position fully, Eleftheriadis operates with the monist conception—his own two monisms. By sensing perhaps that this cannot be squared with so much of the explicit language used by MacCormick on

[70] See p. 217 and n 112.

the need for mutual accommodation at all levels, Eleftheriadis seems to realize that he might need to dig deeper. And so he does. He explains that, while this monism is the option that MacCormick seems to have in mind, there is nonetheless also a second possible understanding of MacCormick's thesis. Eleftheriadis presents things strictly, and explicitly, as if there were only these two candidate options for understanding what MacCormick wanted to convey. "MacCormick's analysis," Eleftheriatis asserts, "leaves us with only two"[71] variants of how his thesis could possibly be understood: he either had in mind the first option, which is no pluralism at all, or else, he meant a second option, which is, according to Eleftheriadis, a pluralist conception but, as he then adds, one that faces other fatal problems. What then is, for Eleftheriadis, that second and last option?

"It may be," Eleftheriadis writes, "that when MacCormick says that relations between states and the EU are 'interacting systems of law' without 'an all-purpose superiority of one system over another' . . . he means this: courts may help themselves to either of these two monisms."[72] This is to say, "it is open to them to endorse either a solution derived from national law or a solution derived from EU law."[73] "This would be pluralism proper," since the "national system" now "does not actually take the official monism seriously": instead, "[s]ome days we would be choosing national monism, whereas on other days we choose European monism."[74]

This understanding of pluralism, according to which any domestic or European court, and indeed any public official,[75] should also be able to "choose freely between two rival constitutional frameworks"[76] and sometimes decide according to one monism, while sometimes according to the other monism, is a version of the proposal within the sphere of the *who* that we characterized above as "judicial double-overlap."[77] We observed that this potential variant of pluralism, as first suggested by Barber within that applicative sphere, was not a necessary element of the pluralist conception. This was so neither from the perspective of pluralism as a branch nor from the sole perspective of the applicative theme of the *who*.[78] Moreover, none of the examined pluralists thus far has actually incorporated the element of "judicial double-overlap" into his conception of pluralism. What they instead presuppose is the simple, but already uniquely pluralist,[79] "judicial overlap," wherein each set of institutions—the national and European—follow their own highest court and its pluralistically accommodated jurisprudence and *Grundnorm*. In doing so, however, they recognize the other *Grundnorm*'s part as ultimately self-standing and not as being incorporated through their own part of the self-standing *Grundnorm*.

So far Eleftheriadis's second point is still essentially the same as Barber's and is thus also subject to the same criticisms as already elaborated against this point earlier in this chapter.[80] But the point at which he then departs from Barber is that Eleftheriadis does not consider the "judicial double-overlap" as a potential viable

71 Eleftheriadis (n 54) at 375.
72 Eleftheriadis (n 54) at 373–4.
73 Eleftheriadis (n 54) at 374.
74 Eleftheriadis (n 54) at 374.
75 Eleftheriadis (n 54) at 378.
76 Eleftheriadis (n 54) at 377.
77 See p. 197.
78 See pp. 196–200.
79 See pp. 197–200 and 203–5.
80 Section 1.

path for a pluralist to pursue.[81] Eleftheriadis's unique charge is instead that this kind of pluralism—supposedly the only available pluralist reading of MacCormick—cannot succeed because it fails sufficiently to respect the value of integrity. Under such pluralism,

> [t]here is a disjunction between choosing a national solution or a European solution to a legal question. Ronald Dworkin has spoken of such legal resolutions as "checkerboard laws". Whenever we have conflicting views about abortion, for example, we may say that in odd years we ban abortion and in even years we allow it. This way both sides will be satisfied half of the time. It could be something similar with [MacCormick's] pluralism. Some time the national law wins, whereas others the European law wins. Dworkin has noted how unsatisfactory such solutions are and has proposed that the reason we find them unsatisfactory is that there is virtue in the integrity of a legal order.[82] ... Dworkin argues at length that checkerboard laws violate ... the value of political integrity. ... This ideal requires "governments to speak with one voice, to act in a principled and coherent manner toward all its citizens, to extend to everyone the same substantive standards of justice or fairness it uses for some". He further goes on to explain that integrity is a requirement of a non-utopian society. It applies to persons who live together knowing that they disagree about morality and justice. Even against such a background of disagreement, Dworkin argues, we recognise a separate requirement that we act towards each other with integrity, that is, not capriciously or whimsically. He says that "integrity becomes a political ideal when we make the same demand of the state or community taken to be a moral agent, when we insist that the state act on a single, coherent set of principles even when its citizens are divided about what the right principles of justice and fairness really are".[83]

Even more strongly, what we create by endorsing pluralism in the way Eleftheriadis has come to understand it, is for him "a striking failure"[84] from the point of view of integrity:

> [W]e endorse a constitutional order according to which the state officials (not just judges but also government agents and legislatures) can choose which one of two rival constitutional schemes to follow ... Even if a national court respected the judgment of the Court of Justice and vindicated, say, the claimant over the defendant, the immigration officials down the line in the same case could perhaps choose under the doctrine of constitutional pluralism to endorse a rival reading of the law. They could thus reject the earlier judgment in the name of pluralism ... Under [such pluralism], courts and officials are expected to freely pick and choose which reading of EU law to adopt in each case. Taken at its logical extreme, this unfettered choice will create an almost infinite multiplicity of strands of legal doctrine. Given that a single case turns on, say, three or four issues of EU law (say, discrimination, justifiability, proportionality, and remedies), if there is a choice over each one of them, any court or official may pick and choose and combine the various doctrines at will, according to the available menu. But then the possibilities multiply exponentially. So from two rival lines of precedent we quickly come to have ten or one hundred ... [This is] a striking failure from the point of view of [integrity].[85]

[81] Recall Barber's point about the potential of the "genuine plurality" of this route that has been left unexplored thus far, and the point that by focusing on the monist versions we have neglected this potential route of true pluralism (see pp. 192–3 and 197).

[82] Eleftheriadis (n 54) at 374.

[83] Eleftheriadis (n 54) at 377 (references omitted).

[84] Eleftheriadis (n 54) at 378.

[85] Eleftheriadis (n 54) at 378.

After the comprehensive mapping and decoding analysis, as well as the renewed explication of MacCormick's pluralism as a rejoinder to Barber/Eleftheriadis's first challenge, cited above, the response to the second point also becomes obvious. The value of integrity may well be highly important, but the conception of pluralism that Eleftheriadis accuses of not respecting integrity—the "judicial double-overlap"—is not MacCormick's conception of pluralism. As explained above, none of the pluralists has explicitly required "judicial double-overlap" as a feature of his conception of pluralism, and even less as a necessary feature of pluralism. MacCormick is no exception. Yet nor does he have in mind the first option (two classical, non-accommodating monisms) that Eleftheriadis would primarily assign him.

We have seen that he has in mind the third option, one that Eleftheriadis does not uncover and discuss. Crucially, as we know, that one *does* emphatically and normatively, of course, require accommodations between both orders. It does so at each of the levels: the foundational one, the level of the *how*, the *what*, and the *who*. Indeed, within the sphere of the *who*, which is the one within which Eleftheriadis makes his critique, MacCormick's requirement of accommodations between both orders is satisfied only when the highest courts agree on a *single* first-order solution regarding one and the same section of boundary within the overlap. This must be done in a way that respects the foundational pluralist principle of equality as it flows from the equally non-derivative nature of both orders. Within such a reconciliation, both constitutions and their *Grundnorms* acquire their equal shares. Lower courts and institutions then simply follow such first-order rules regarding the interpretation of boundary that are thus mutually accommodated according to the pluralist foundation. Indeed, with so many of MacCormick's explicit explanations that his pluralism must go hand in hand "with arrangements designed... to prevent incompatibility in areas of overlap,"[86] it is impossible to charge him with the opposite: that his conception is to be understood as if each instance on each side should be free to pick and choose which of the *conflicting* results to pick on a certain day. This is another misreading of MacCormick's clear and explicit language and of his much subtler fuller conception of pluralism. More importantly, bearing this accommodating aspect of MacCormick's full conception in mind, it becomes obvious that there is little room in such a conception for that argument from integrity that Eleftheriadis makes against a wholly different understanding of pluralism, which would require all of the institutions to be free to pick and choose conflicting results. To be sure, it might well happen that, as a matter of practical reality, MacCormick's explicit requirement of mutual accommodation in the area of overlap would not be followed too well in practice; the two highest courts might prove too stubborn, as it were, and violate that normative requirement.[87] But that is, of course, a wholly different practical point, not the one Eleftheriadis makes

[86] MacCormick (n 13) at 16.

[87] Although MacCormick was clear about both, his goal that the conflict should be avoided through this requirement, as well as his expectation that it can be (and also has been) avoided "so far rather successfully" ("Beyond the Sovereign State" (n 13) at 16).

against the conception that has no such conceptual requirement, but instead requires the opposite.

Moreover, even with this other worry, there is certainly no greater room for the integrity argument against MacCormick's conception than there is against those national contexts in which we already see similar processes work well. For instance, we have national systems in which the highest federal court and federal legislature are considered coequal branches of government. Increasingly in the view of many,[88] this is also so when it comes to the most salient issues of constitutional interpretation. Often, only through the process of gradual back-and-forth exchange between equals do such institutions reach a final common agreement on a particular aspect of constitutional interpretation on which they had previously disagreed. If it works within the monist context of one sovereign order, there might well be good reasons to believe that it could work also in the pluralist context between coequal *orders* and their respective highest, but coequal, interpretive institutions.

Finally, and more broadly, the specific pluralist conception of "judicial double-overlap" that Eleftheriadis chooses to attack concerns only one of several applicative spheres—namely the *who*—in which the undisputedly distinct foundational idea of pluralism makes its distinctive contribution. From the perspective of pluralism as a branch, "judicial double-overlap" is thus, as indicated, not a necessary element of the distinct pluralist conception common to the pluralists, but not to the monists. It is therefore wrong in principle to assume that one can do away with the very idea of pluralism (even if focusing just on the legal doctrine, as Eleftheriadis says he does) by simply looking at one, instead of all, of the spheres of its applicative ramification.

It should be concluded that Eleftheriadis errs by assuming that there are "only two"[89] ways in which to understand MacCormick. Both of these he himself constructs: either the option of two non-accommodating orders, which is monism, or the option of "judicial double-overlap," which is, according to him, a non-viable conception of pluralism. Yet MacCormick's conception cannot be understood in either of these two ways. It is instead the third option that Eleftheriadis's analysis overlooks, one that is indisputably pluralist as opposed to monist, while also not subject to Eleftheriadis's challenge from the value of integrity.

2.3 Other aspects

Once MacCormick's idea of pluralism is correctly understood, it is also easier to see the fault of some other charges against his conception. Those are especially common in relation to MacCormick's latest transition, which Eleftheriadis also describes, from "radical pluralism" to his conception of "pluralism under international law."[90] Many have understood this move of MacCormick's simply as a strange reinstitution of monism at another level: now monism under international

[88] See, eg L. Tribe, *American Constitutional Law* (2nd edn, New York: The Foundation Press, 1988) 32–42; F. Michelman, "Living with Judicial Supremacy" (2003) 38 Wake Forest Law Review 579.

[89] Eleftheriadis (n 54) at 375.

[90] Chapter 6, pp. 187–9.

law.[91] Eleftheriadis seems to be slightly more cautious, although he too writes as if this obviously means that "[b]oth national law and EU law are hierarchically subordinate to international law" and that "this brings us close to monism."[92]

It is important, however, to be clear about what that transition really meant. At a later point MacCormick came to believe, perhaps due to the practical worry mentioned above,[93] that the highest interpretive institutions of both orders under pluralism should not, and need not, be entirely unguided in the required process of mutual pluralist accommodation within the area of overlap. Instead, when interpreting their boundary, and reaching that single solution for each segment of the boundary, they should both also make use of the fruitful body of arguments existing in some of the fields of international law, such as international arbitration and conflict resolution.[94] The two courts under constitutional pluralism who are trying to reach a mutually accommodating solution need not, in other words, completely run out of legal argumentation and move fully into politics and moral reasoning. In addition to those, there is obviously also a lot in international law that can, as the argument implies, also be of help in such a mutually accommodating process.

Note, however, that to make a reference to international law is not to say that both constitutional orders and their self-standing sources (their respective peoples) are thereby made ultimately subordinate to the non-constitutional order of international law. By contrast, they remain fully self-standing at the foundational level that is constitutive of pluralism, while in the applicative sphere of the *who* then merely helping themselves with some aspects of argumentation available from the field of international law. International law, in other words, works here merely as an additional practical *device*, along with other potential devices from the fields of politics and morality, for helping settle the boundary conflict with respect to the narrow institutional issue of the *who*. A mere use of a practical device to solve the institutional conflict within the sphere of the *who* is of course not yet the same as saying that you are also giving up your self-standing foundational authority so as to make your order ultimately (foundationally) derivative in relation to the order of international law. Clearly one can just use a device from some other legal system for some purpose (and therefore also not even the whole system as such) without at the same time subsuming one's own to a mere derivative, ultimately non-self-standing, unit of that system. Under our old monist arrangements we had been doing this every day without thereby losing our order's self-standing ultimate authority over its own territory. All the legal systems, including the pluralist constitutional orders, can engage in such borrowing.

[91] See, eg N. Walker, "Sovereignty and Differentiated Integration of the European Union" (1998) 4 ELJ 355, 387; "All Dressed Up" (2001) 21 OJLS 563, 570, fn 19; M. Maduro, "Contrapunctual Law: Europe's Constitutional Pluralism in Action" in N. Walker (ed.), *Sovereignty in Transition* (n 35) at 522–3; "The Heteronyms of European Law" (1999) 5 ELJ 160, 166; "European Constitution: What if This is as Good as It Gets?" in J. Weiler and M. Wind (eds), *European Constitutionalism beyond the State* (Cambridge: Cambridge University Press, 2003); D. Halberstam, "Dialogical Epilogue" in G. de Búrca and J. Weiler (eds), *The Worlds of European Constitutionalism* (Cambridge: Cambridge University Press, 2011) at 288; N. Krisch, *Beyond Constitutionalism: The Pluralist Structure of Postnational Law* (Oxford: Oxford University Press, 2010) at 73.

[92] Eleftheriadis (n 54) at 374.

[93] See pp. 208–9.

[94] Chapter 6, pp. 188–9.

The point that has been so often repeated by critics, that MacCormick's conception of "pluralism under international law" turns both constitutional orders—the national and the European—into ultimately derivative units under monism of international law, neglects this important distinction. Once again, it assigns to MacCormick something that his conception is not. By helping themselves also through their recourse to some aspects of international law, neither of the constitutional orders thereby gives up its own ultimately self-standing nature. Provided that, through this method of resolving conflicts, they follow their pluralist principle from the foundational level, as they clearly could, especially since the rules of international law are themselves saturated with the principle of equality, pluralism remains intact also at the applicative levels, not just the foundational one. The solution under this model for the sphere of the *who* is thus, for instance, yet another applicative variant of the pluralist solution that is distinct from that of monism; such legal, political, and moral reasoning by both orders (their highest courts) does not put either of them (their respective highest courts) in the position of final guardian of their orders' boundary. On this subtler reading of MacCormick's latest variant of pluralism, nor does any institution of international law, or the order of international law itself, become such a final guardian.[95] Arguments from some of the fields within international law are instead merely used as a helpful device, in exactly the same way as those from morality and politics are and ought to be, without thereby in any way interfering with the ultimately self-standing, but not monist, nature of both constitutional orders.

Moreover, the only orders with the *self-standing* authority in this arrangement are both constitutional orders. This is because they alone are the ones that enjoy the *direct link* with the sources that can potentially make any order in a democracy self-standing in the first place: their respective peoples. This feature is at the same time also what makes both orders *constitutional* orders. The order of international law, by contrast, lacks that direct link with some world *demos* or some narrower group of people that it instead only indirectly addresses. Its direct addressees are the states themselves who, in turn, do enjoy that direct link with their peoples and the self-standing (and hence constitutional) authority that comes with it. International order is thus not a self-standing order and also not a constitutional order.

Yet these two features are required in order for any order to compete for the ultimate authority in the first place. Neither constitutional monism nor constitutional pluralism is possible without those two features. Hence, also MacCormick's specific use of the term "constitutional pluralism," and not simply "pluralism of legal systems,"[96] which are so often confusingly conflated in the current literature. In some arrangement in which one of the legal orders is neither a self-standing one,

[95] Although that would of course also not necessarily, already in and of itself, turn the conception into monism. Cf Weiler's proposal of the Constitutional Council.

[96] For this reason, I have been careful throughout this work to use, with reference to pluralism, the term "constitutional orders," not the term "legal systems." The frequent use of the latter in the discourse on MacCormick's path-breaking idea is another route leading to the current state of confusion in the literature on constitutional pluralism, one to which he himself might well have unintentionally contributed a part.

nor a constitutional one, we cannot speak of either constitutional pluralism or constitutional monism. The non-self-standing, non-constitutional, order is always ultimately derivative from the constitutional one. It follows that, even in this sense, international legal order could never be in the position of constitutional monism and the holder of the ultimate self-standing authority with respect to both of our self-standing and constitutional orders. Kelsen's "monism" that does not claim to be constitutional monism, but could at best be monism of a legal system, is therefore a very different concept from that of constitutional monism that MacCormick has in mind. Unlike the latter, Kelsen's monism at the non-translated level of the entire international legal order is not the right concept to compare to constitutional pluralism in the first place.[97] MacCormick's idea and conception of constitutional pluralism is therefore a true novelty also when observed from this angle. Adding international law to the picture, whether in this or that way, could never harm the conception of constitutional pluralism at all.

This distinction between constitutional pluralism/monism and the different concept of simple pluralism/monism of legal systems will, as we will see in due course, become absolutely essential for the practical viability and value of constitutional pluralism. It distinguishes genuine pluralism from some self-styled "pluralist" conception that cannot, in the final analysis, be distinguished from monism.[98] This will be fatal for the mere concept of simple "pluralism of legal systems."[99] The clarification that the distinction exposes in the current context before us about MacCormick's genuine constitutional pluralism, even though it incorporates aspects from international law, is only one aspect of that bigger clarification.

MacCormick's latest variation of his constitutional pluralism, "pluralism under international law," is thus still genuinely pluralist and distinct from monism. The critics are too quick to reach the opposite, somewhat misleadingly obvious conclusion. In a similar way it would be wrong of those who were to assume that this distinct conception could be equated with something that Eleftheriadis defines as "dualism."

As Eleftheriadis defines it, "dualism" is supposed to be the middle position between monism and pluralism. However, from the perspective of our pluralists, it is really just a version of monism. According to Eleftheriadis "dualism" means that legal systems[100] make accommodations. He gives the classical example of a national legal system that accommodates international law, and the national legal system that accommodates foreign law through private international law. Eleftheriadis acknowledges though that, according to "dualism," the national system accommodates international and foreign law through its own ultimate authority

[97] At least not at this historical point, nor in any near future: as long as international order and law do not establish the direct link with its corresponding *demos* that could provide it with that claim to the self-standing, constitutional order.

[98] Chapter 7, section 3.

[99] Chapter 7, section 3; Chapter 8, pp. 249–50; and Chapter 9, section 2.

[100] While engaging in the analysis of MacCormick's constitutional pluralism, Eleftheriadis is one of those who incorrectly operate, in their argumentation, with "legal systems" as opposed to the self-standing constitutional orders alone.

(sovereignty) on that territory. From the perspective of our pluralists, Eleftheriadis's dualism is thus precisely the classical constitutional monism that they have in mind when they use the term "monism."[101] This expansive characterization, by Eleftheriadis, of something as dualism that is actually monism, at the same time pushes himself to reserve the term "monism" for the most extreme, and non-existent, form of monism: that radical form according to which the nation-state then goes on to "entirely ignore"[102] all international law and foreign laws in every sense. As Eleftheriadis admits, "[t]his type of legal nationalism, while logically possible, would render the ordinary contents of private international law and indeed public international law incomprehensible."[103] Yet this is too narrow and uninteresting a conception of monism. It does not exist in practice, and is not what the pluralists have in mind when contrasting their "pluralism" with "monism." What they instead consider "monism" is exactly what Eleftheriadis describes as "dualism": "Most constitutional systems in the world today," he writes, "adopt a version of dualism [since] they recognize the authority of international and foreign law through their own constitutional devices."[104]

This, as we know by now, is not the meaning of "pluralism under international law." According to the latter, the EU constitutional order is not recognized in the national constitutional order in the classical indirect way of monism: via international law and so only by virtue of the nation-state's own ultimate authority on that territory. On the contrary, the nation-state recognizes it as a direct self-standing authority, one that already exists over the same territory independently of the nation-state and with the same degree of direct authority as the nation-state. The national authority recognizes and accommodates it *as such*, and not in the ultimately subordinate sense: by virtue of its own retained ultimate authority. It is thus also mutually recognized that the latter is now lost without the EU gaining it either. This situation is wholly different from monism, that is, from Eleftheriadis's "dualism." The fact that both authorities already are self-standing and mutually recognize each other in *that* sense, while then using some of international law only *ex post* as one of the devices to help them avoid the practical problem of collision, actually escapes that classical indirect (ie "dualist," which is monist) accommodation and instead adopts the pluralist foundational principle right from the start. It makes pluralism under international law a very different concept from dualism that retains that national ultimate authority and explains all the ultimately subordinate systems of law (such as international law and foreign law) through the opposite—that is, monist—foundational principle. To equate these two approaches would be to equate two conceptually opposed understandings.

We have already seen how this conceptual distinction then also reflects itself through important applicative differences between both approaches when it comes to the context of two constitutional orders. Recall the discussion of the theme of the *who* and the different argumentative and institutional right answers that resulted from the pluralist context on the one hand and the monist context of the federal and

[101] See Chapter 6, section 2.
[102] Eleftheriadis (n 54) at 369.
[103] Eleftheriadis (n 54) at 369.
[104] Eleftheriadis (n 54) at 369.

state levels on the other. The same applies to the context of national and international law under Eleftheriadis's dualism versus the context of national and EU law under pluralism.

Eleftheriadis could be read as assuming that, (1) since some accommodation occurs under both these conceptually different approaches, it follows that, (2) there is no difference between a dualist (ie monist) and pluralist accommodation.[105] That would however be incorrect: (2) does not follow from (1). Consider for instance the hypothetical collision between, say, the US Supreme Court (SC) and one of the interpretive/adjudicative institutions of international law (IL). They come into some serious conflict as to the boundary of their orders. The SC thinks that the IL in a given case acted *ultra vires* and thus overstepped the mandate delegated to that institution, and to this area of international law, by the sovereign American people and their Constitution. The IL, on the other hand, happens to disagree. According to the foundational principle, which of the two systems would win the day on US soil? Under dualism the answer is clear: it would be the holder of the ultimate authority on the territory in question. This would be the constitutional order in virtue of which the other system was recognized and accommodated as the ultimately subordinate system within that sovereign territory in the first place. There is indeed no other option under dualism, which is a form of monism. In virtue of its foundational rationale the sovereign order is bound to assert that it is itself, and not the derivative international order, that is the *ultimate* guardian of its boundary. According to dualism (monism), it is the Constitution and the American people that are the ultimate authority (the sovereign) on US territory. Moreover, the right question to interpret and resolve would be the narrower one: whether the IL has followed the mandate given to it by the US that agreed to the relevant international treaty at stake.

All of this is different under constitutional pluralism between the ultimately self-standing EU and nation-state constitutional orders. It is precisely the very monist (ie dualist) rationale, as was already observed above, that is no longer available under such an opposite pluralist foundational principle. Both orders now need to resort to other kinds of arguments. It follows also that in all such boundary collisions, both ultimately self-standing and coequal constitutional orders[106]—that of the nation-state and the EU—need to accommodate each other according

[105] With respect to accommodation between the national and European constitutional orders, Eleftheriadis writes that "there is nothing unusual in this process... Courts always have the task of working out the limits of their own jurisdiction" ("Pluralism and Integrity" (n 54) at 385). Since that occurs also between national and international courts, Eleftheriadis seems to be saying, MacCormick's requirement for accommodation between the national and EU orders is nothing new, and is therefore simply our well-known dualism. The mere existence of accommodation is, however, not the point. It is the whole different type of accommodation—pluralist versus dualist (monist)—that is decisive, in which the very existence of the pluralist principle at the foundational level plays a part.

[106] One might already sense that pluralism itself might never be an option for a constitutional order's relation with international law as the ultimately subordinate system of law, ie the way it is indeed understood under the traditional, dualist understanding. Cf Eleftheriadis: "Most constitutional systems in the world today adopt a version of dualism: they recognise the authority of international law... through their own constitutional devices" ("Pluralism and Integrity" (n 54) at 369). See more at Chapter 7, section 3; Chapter 8, pp. 249–50; and Chapter 9, section 2.

to the foundational requirement of full equality between them. This leads to the well-known result: to one of the several possible pluralist accommodations as proposed by our pluralists within the theme of the *who*. They all clearly followed the foundational requirement of *equal* mutual accommodation in such boundary collisions. They needed to do so, or else pluralism at the applicative level would not exist, while they would thereby be violating their own constitutional principle from the distinctive pluralist foundation. Moreover, the right interpretive question to resolve is no longer whether or not the EU has followed the boundaries of its mandate as delegated to it by the nation-state. The EU is now a self-standing constitutional order. The question is therefore rather *how far* away from the nation-state view it could redefine itself without at the same time unduly compromising the equal self-defining authority of the nation-state constitutional order. This inevitably goes beyond the narrower question over what exactly was delegated. Accommodation under constitutional pluralism is indeed different from that under monism, that is, "dualism."

There are of course also other aspects that make pluralist accommodation unique and need not be considered here in detail. Some of the distinctive ramifications through the sphere of the *how*, and especially also that of the *what*, were already observed above, while more on that crucial distinction is going to follow below. Nonetheless, one general distinction between both conceptually different approaches should nonetheless be mentioned as it is obvious in the selective ("dualism," ie monism) versus relatively unselective (pluralism) accommodation that each of the distinct conceptual approaches assumes. A sovereign nation-state is, according to its monist foundational principle, more or less free as to which individual international treaty to incorporate, or not incorporate, to its own legal system. It can more or less pick and choose according to its own sovereign will. In the case of the pluralist accommodation, however, the non-sovereign nation-state that had recognized the equal self-standing authority over its own nation-state territory to another constitutional order, is of course no longer so free to pick and choose between that order's individual laws. It is precisely due to the distinct pluralist principle that such a state adopted at its new constitutional foundation (at the place of the old "dualist," ie monist one) that it now also needs to accommodate the other self-standing and equal order *qua* such an order,[107] as opposed to picking and choosing at will just some of its laws. Only the former strategy ensures the required normative as well as factual equality of orders coexisting as such over the same territory. As in so many other instances, this is of course a matter of degree; but degrees are decisive.[108]

[107] Even though the content of both orders becomes mutually refined, this does not change the fact that the accommodation must be in relation to the entire order as such.

[108] I would like to end the assessment of Eleftheriadis's critique of MacCormick with a note on remembering Professor MacCormick. To all who knew him he was a remarkable man. I too had the privilege of finding that out for myself in the course of discussing with him my drafts on his idea of constitutional pluralism, which at the time was the topic of my doctoral dissertation. He offered unreserved help with his characteristic attitude of genuine care and enthusiasm that were making students feel as if they too were engaged in some cutting-edge contributions of their own—the attitude

Eleftheriadis concludes his critique by arguing that at least one more version of pluralism, namely Maduro's, attempts to overcome the integrity "problem" by, as Eleftheriadis states, "implicitly endorsing monism."[109] Maduro's principles of contrapunctual law, involving horizontal and vertical coherence and universalization inter-subjectively understood, need to be followed in any interpretation of EU law as some kind of the meta-framework of the *how* of the pluralist constitutional discourse in Europe. It needs to be followed by the European courts, but especially also by the national courts when they interpret EU law in the light of the potential conflict with the national constitutional orders and their identities. Eleftheriadis concedes that this kind of conception appears to establish coherence, thereby satisfying the value of integrity, but argues that this occurs at the price of instituting monism:

> It is easy to see that this is not a doctrine of pluralism at all. It is a doctrine of unity. In exactly the same way as the US Supreme Court oversees the federal jurisdiction under the general principles of coherence imposed by the US constitution, the ECJ will oversee the application of EU law in the various state jurisdictions, under common principles of "horizontal and vertical coherence" whose origins will inevitably be found in the EC treaties and the case law of the European Courts. Maduro's is a monist vision.[110]

There is an obvious response on behalf of Maduro that the assessment overlooks. It consists of two points. Firstly, note that the principles of contrapunctual law legitimize the highest courts of the national orders to bring into their interpretation of EU law also their own national constitutional perspectives. The requirement that they do so in the way that is universalized and coherent with the perspectives of other national constitutional orders and the European constitutional order itself, does not disturb the equal role for those national considerations (to the European ones) to shape the most subtle boundary line between both orders. On the contrary, it precisely ensures that equality as is required by the foundational pluralist principle remains intact. This would have been different if the European perspective was not balanced against the national perspectives, if in their interpretation the courts were to follow exclusively just the common European perspective and construe EU law exclusively just from the perspective of that constitutional order. That might have been monism, but that is not Maduro's proposal. On the contrary, the principles of contrapunctual law require both of these perspectives—each national and the European—to enter the interpretation and have, according to

possessed in academia by the greatest alone. It was in one of his last years that we discussed also the earlier draft of this particular chapter. I know he thought that clarifications concerning his idea made in here clarified some misunderstandings that had started to emerge. He told me so, and the gesture with which he chose to end that meeting has been in its own way one of the incentives behind my persistence to keep on and publish this monograph. He took from the shelf his book, which I still keep, opened the page, and ended the inscription "... with thanks for explaining to me what I really meant." With this updated version of the chapter I merely elaborated the same response to essentially the same kind of critique that I knew he had already rejected long ago. We all are indebted to him.

[109] Here Eleftheriadis writes "monism," not "dualism," which suggests that what he has in mind at this point is even his radical form of monism as defined earlier.

[110] Eleftheriadis (n 54) at 387.

Maduro's explicit requirement of inter-subjectivity as explained in Chapter 4, equal impact on the outcome of the interpretation. This is therefore a strictly symmetrical accommodation between both orders that strictly follows the pluralist principle from the foundation and is exactly the opposite to Eleftheriadis's definition of monism, where the perspective of the other, in this case the national, order is not given that equal status.

Secondly, it seems natural that the ECJ oversees such interpretation *inside* the bounds of EU law. After all, this is the EU law sphere within the new pluralist order. The highest national courts do the same when it comes to the sphere of the national law. That said, we know from our analysis of Maduro's proposal within the theme of the *who*[111] that the ECJ is *not* the ultimate arbiter of the *boundary* between the EU law and national law just as the highest national courts are *not* such ultimate guardians. Instead, we saw in Chapter 4 that Maduro first divides that authority into two halves so that none of the confronting institutions enjoys the monist position of the boundary's ultimate arbiter: in cases of non-systemic conflict the ECJ has the final say, while in cases of systemic conflicts the highest national court has the final say. Moreover, Maduro does not explain which of the two institutions determines what counts as the systemic conflict; that part of the boundary remains fully open even after Maduro's balanced (as opposed to monist) dispersal of final authority between both institutions.

It is obvious from this that, if anything, the ECJ is not put in the position of the ultimate arbiter in conflicts over the orders' boundary. It is precisely not like the US Supreme Court where this is indeed the case in virtue of the recognized supremacy of the federal Constitution over the state Constitutions.[112] The latter monist solution within the sphere of the *who* is a reflection of monism at the foundational level. Maduro's proposal within the theme of the *who* is instead precisely the opposite: the equal dispersal of authority to rule on the boundary between *both*, the nation-state and EU institutions, and in the way that leaves that last part of the conflict entirely open. Such a pluralist approach within the *who* is exactly the reflection of the pluralist foundational principle.

3. Just Too Messy?

The Barber/Eleftheriadis critique of pluralism does not succeed. Yet it might be that what was truly behind this criticism was a sense of a slightly different, though potentially no less crucial, weakness that some but not all of the pluralist proposals face. We will get to the issue of the "bare sub-branches of pluralism" in the next

[111] See Chapter 4, pp. 116–19.

[112] Article VI, Clause 2 of the US Constitution (the Supremacy Clause) declares the federal Constitution as "the supreme law of the land." That is, as the highest form of law in the US constitutional order, requiring that, when a conflict arises between federal law and either the state constitution or state law, state judges must follow the federal constitution ("the judges in every state shall be bound thereby, any thing in the constitution or laws of any state to the contrary notwithstanding").

chapter. In this chapter we are, however, first concerned with a prior question. Responding to the various critiques of the very idea of constitutional pluralism we aim to clarify even further that the concept of constitutional pluralism, as decoded through the mapping analysis, is indeed undeniably distinct from that of constitutional monism. The central preoccupation of this chapter is thus still on the question of what does and what does not count as part of the unique novel branch of pluralism in the first place, and why so. Before proceeding to the further question over the potentially bare sub-branches within such pluralism in the next chapter, which of the particular versions may be better in some sense than others, we still have some remaining work to do with respect to the subject of this chapter.

Many additional scholars have recently come to use the terminology of "pluralism" and are said, or themselves claim, to be pluralists when their proposals could not be squared into the new pluralist branch. It is especially relevant to include this category of "pluralists" in the assessment under this chapter because the problem that such an automatic terminological inclusion gives rise to yet another crucial line of recent criticism. Such an unwarranted lightness of (self-)classifying all sorts of proposals as belonging to constitutional pluralism is partly responsible for the confusion that currently exists in the field. In such conditions it is increasingly hard to see what, if anything, the idea of constitutional pluralism, as distinct from that of monism, might possibly mean.

In this murky situation it seems that even Joseph Weiler, one of the original pluralists, has recently fallen under its spell. By listening to what these other new "pluralists" have been saying, he began to feel that he must then not have been a pluralist in the first place and that, moreover, pluralism is then something whose novelty he does not really see. It appears to him more as a ubiquitous and vacuous rhetoric that just covers the myth of some distinct new concept, from which he now knows he would like explicitly to distance himself.[113]

Yet as we are about to see, this warranted criticism cannot solve the problem using such an escape route. Rather, the path of the clarification leads in the opposite direction. The truth is that these new contributions are wrongly assumed and treated as if they were part of the pluralist branch when they could not possibly be. Their inclusion adds to the mess while indeed making the latter irresolvable. Once this is clarified, and these conceptions are properly disassociated from constitutional pluralism, the picture becomes clear. Unlike these conceptions, it is Weiler's that remains squarely and comfortably within the branch's scope. This reconfirms once more the principled distinctiveness from monism of the concept of pluralism as unveiled by the mapping analysis.

Before explaining his recent critique, Weiler is, however, careful; and rightfully so. He senses that the distinctiveness of constitutional pluralism could perhaps be explained. He would thus *not* like to go ahead and elaborate his criticism "without one [prior] caveat."[114] "It might well be," he writes, "that I am misunderstanding

[113] J. Weiler "Prologue: Global and Plural Constitutionalism—Some Doubts" in de Búrca and Weiler (n 91).

[114] Weiler (n 113) at 15.

Constitutional Pluralism" and that, "in [that] case I still hope my critique will not be dismissed as irrelevant, but at least as useful in mounting a challenge . . . the response to which will help bring clarity to the field."[115]

Weiler's critical claim has two parts. The part that interests us here begins with his own observation about the ubiquity and vacuity of the term "constitutional pluralism."[116] Weiler correctly observes that, on the surface of things, it has become such a magnetic attraction that almost everyone today uses the pluralist rhetoric. The "pandemic" has gone so far that "Constitutional Pluralism," as he writes, "is today the only Membership Card which will guarantee a seat at High Tables of the public law professoriate."[117] More especially, it has recently been "fused" with another pandemic, that of global constitutionalism. The completed ubiquity now makes Weiler wonder: is there anybody out there who is not a constitutional pluralist, anybody who can explain what constitutional pluralism is not? It indeed seems that "when [things are] set up like that, beyond any explanatory power which Constitutional Pluralism may offer," there seems to be little remaining besides the mere vacuous rhetoric: "Pluralist Constitutionalism—good, progressive, tolerant, non-domineering [;] Hierarchical Constitutionalism—bad, regressive, intolerant, domineering."[118]

As to constitutional pluralism in the non-global context, we know that Weiler's criticism is well-placed. It is a response to the multiplicity of different projects and levels of discourse (the sectors of the labyrinth) that we carefully identified and distinguished in our own mapping analysis. Yet the mapping analysis then for the first time cleared this confusing mess in the field. Above all, it then also showed what the branch of constitutional pluralism, as clearly distinct from that of monism, could truly mean. With respect to constitutional pluralism in its traditional European (ie non-global) context, Weiler's challenge is thereby answered precisely by this mapping analysis and its decoding of the branch.

As to the recent attempts to fuse the pluralist idea with the global field, Weiler's challenge remains and is even more important. Here we not only have a complex disarray of very different proposals, but clearly even a situation where some of the leading current proposals could not belong to the branch of constitutional pluralism in the first place. That is so despite the fact that they have been mistakenly assumed to belong to the new branch—indeed, seemingly merely due to the misleading rhetoric of pluralism versus monism. They have been treated as such by others and in a little procrustean way joined to the discourse on constitutional pluralism. This begat that irresolvable confusion and the loss in meaning of any distinctive common understanding of pluralism. It was just a matter of time before somebody—now Weiler—complained of the mess.

Take the "pluralism" of Daniel Halberstam.[119] While explaining that he is applying MacCormick's idea of constitutional pluralism to the global context,

[115] Weiler (n 113) at 15.

[116] Unlike this part of his critique, the other one pertains to the further question over the "bare branches" within pluralism, and is thus addressed in the next chapter.

[117] Weiler (n 113) at 8. [118] Weiler (n 113) at 14.

[119] D. Halberstam, "Local, Global, and Plural Constitutionalism: Europe Meets the World" in Weiler and de Búrca (n 91); "Systems Pluralism and Institutional Pluralism in Constitutional Law:

what he instead does through his direct application to that different context is to inescapably remove from his conception both constitutive dimensions of MacCormick's constitutional pluralism. He ends up with a conception that is neither "constitutional" nor really "pluralism." It does not satisfy two key constitutive features of what the mapping analysis showed was the only possible understanding of the new pluralist branch that is still distinct from constitutional monism.

Firstly, we already saw above that only a constitutional order, as opposed to a legal system, enjoys ultimately self-standing authority. In the democratic era this is because it is only such an order that enjoys the direct link with the people as the source of that ultimately self-standing authority. In the context of the EU this self-standing authority of the EU constitutional order is, according to constitutional pluralism, reflected in its direct link with the people: the claim of the EU to its independent authority grounded directly in the European people(s) themselves, non-obstructed by the indirect mechanism of state responsibility as is known in international law,[120] and further materialized through the directly elected European Parliament, direct applicability of EU laws, and other similar mechanisms. Some mix of the foundational direct authorship claim, the absence of state responsibility, and the existence of democratic mechanisms that make the claim over the direct link with the people themselves realistic, is what makes in our democratic era the EU a constitutional order of its own ultimately self-standing authority. The same is still very much true also with the nation-state.

For constitutional pluralism it is, however, essential that the two confronting orders indeed be such ultimately self-standing constitutional orders. Without the confrontation of *such* orders, there can be no constitutional pluralism in the first place. This is because in the absence of the equally powerful normative and factual claims, the weaker of the orders (and here I should say the mere legal system) is, and in a democratic era also always ought to be, inevitably ultimately subordinated to the other self-standing constitutional order. There is no chance in our era to set things at the foundation of such a non-constitutional confrontation in any other way but the classical monist. Nor is there, as long as the nation-states have at their disposal the doctrine of state responsibility, any factual necessity to do so.[121] By contrast, both of these elements—the normative and factual necessities of pluralism—do, however, exist in Europe in its confrontation between the two ultimately self-standing constitutional orders and their sources.[122]

National, Supranational, and Global Governance" (2001) University of Michigan Law School Public Law and Legal Theory Working Paper Series, Working Paper No 229; "Constitutional Heterarchy: The Centrality of Conflict in the European Union and the United States" (2008) University of Michigan Law School Public Law and Legal Theory Working Paper Series, Working Paper No 111.

[120] Weiler (n 113) at 10–11.

[121] The fact that we may have at one of the applicative levels some mutual accommodations between the institutions of a constitutional order and those of the mere legal order is not of course constitutive of pluralism versus monism. That is the normal way of monism or, indeed as Eleftheriadis would say, "dualism" as we have always known it. See, eg n 105.

[122] For the indispensable role of these elements—the normative and factual necessities of pluralism—in constituting any conception of constitutional pluralism, see Chapter 9, pp. 285–94. Cf Weiler, who observes in a related point that direct applicability without state responsibility is exactly

Even though Halberstam describes his conception as an instance of "constitutional" pluralism as applied to the global sphere between the nation-states and the organizations of the international legal system, it is therefore not possible to accept such a self-characterization. Neither the institutions of the international legal order, nor the latter itself, are self-standing constitutional orders that one needs for the distinct constitutional pluralism to arise and exist in the first place. Halberstam himself describes those institutions as having the "semi-autonomous," as opposed to ultimately self-sanding, authority. The "pluralism" he seems to be talking about might perhaps be some form of pluralism between legal systems. If so, it faces the difficulty that it may not at all be possible to show how any such pluralism of legal systems is ultimately any different from the way the monist states normally interact with other non-constitutional legal systems.[123] Be that as it may, what is clear and relevant for our purpose here is that his conception is not a version of constitutional pluralism. Yet it is only the latter that is, as the mapping analysis has shown, and the assessment will further demonstrate,[124] clearly distinct from that of constitutional monism, and is so all the way down to its very foundation.

Halberstam's slightly misleading use of the term "constitutional" should thus not be misunderstood. The way he understands it is not in line with the traditional use as described above and as used by MacCormick, Weiler, and other members of the branch when focusing on Europe. Attempting to escape a related criticism by Weiler,[125] Halberstam himself made it clear that the way he is using the term is different—merely as a framework under which his legal systems operate.[126] His conception could, as he remarked, do just as well without the "constitutional" while only using the rhetoric of the "legal systems."[127] Incidentally, this reconfirms that the conception Halberstam has in mind is indeed something that could not belong to the novel branch of constitutional pluralism.

Secondly, this same difficulty of the absence of the "constitutional" element in Halberstam's conception also affects the "pluralist" element in his conception. That element within the common denominator of the new pluralist branch cannot but be understood in a particular way. We saw that that denominator ("heterarchy minimized") required that the confronting orders and their sources not only be constitutional, but also mutually recognized as *coequal*, and so all the way to the foundational level. Only that can be pluralism. It is, however, difficult to see how this could be possible under Halberstam's "pluralism." In his vision an ultimately self-standing constitutional order that enjoys the direct link with its

what we have in Europe and exactly what we do not have in international law ("Prologue: Global and Plural Constitutionalism" (n 113) at 10–11). See also his argument as to the normative (democratic) reason why international regimes are not constitutionalisms (Weiler (n 113) at 11–12).

123 Cf the challenge from Eleftheriadis's critique under section 2.3, this chapter.

124 Chapter 8, pp. 249–50; Chapter 9, pp. 285–94; Chapter 10, pp. 295–316.

125 Namely, the criticism that where Halberstam is planting his "flag of constitutional pluralism, is a territory already occupied by the mainstream of both constitutional law and international law" (see J. Weiler, "Dialogic Epilogue" (with D. Halberstam) in de Búrca and Weiler (n 91) at 527).

126 Halberstam (n 125) at 288–90.

127 Halberstam (n 125) at 288–90.

people confronts some semi-autonomous legal order that does not possess such a link.[128] When one of the orders is and ought for democratic reasons to be treated as the ultimate foundational authority from which the other originates as an ultimately subordinate legal system, the required foundational equality between such orders—pluralism—does not exist. We see that Halberstam's conception is indeed neither "constitutional," nor is it "pluralism." Not in the sense in which both of these constitutive elements have been, and could only be, understood by the novel branch of constitutional pluralism.

In a similar vein as Halberstam, Nico Krisch is also regularly placed into the group of constitutional pluralists. This confusion, too, contributes to the irresolvable mess that makes, under the inclusion of everything that merely uses the term "pluralism," the idea of constitutional pluralism no more than vacuous rhetoric. This is so even though in Krisch's case it is yet much more straightforward that his conception does not belong to the branch of constitutional pluralism.[129]

Firstly, unlike Halberstam, Krisch himself makes it explicit that his "pluralism" in the global sphere is not meant to be "constitutional."[130] He understands the latter term in the traditional sense as described above, and thus knows that his conception, as applied to the international domain, cannot claim that kind of status. He even argues that his conception is the opposite of the "constitutional."[131] Yet as the mapping analysis showed, this means that the conception fails to meet this necessary constitutive criterion of constitutional pluralism while thereby also facing the same related problem of distinctiveness as Halberstam does above. The question is how realistic it is to assume that there is some new way of legal ordering (Krisch's "pluralism") in the global sphere of our post-national era, when the nation-states in this era still comfortably retain their constitutional status while the international institutions do not yet acquire their own *direct* legitimation link. At the ultimate foundational level, which does of course impact the applicative ones, they are still the derivative order, and rightfully so.

Secondly, we see again that the lack of the "constitutional" element in one of the confronting orders also then fails to establish the "pluralist" element, of foundational equality as opposed to the monist ultimate subordination, in Krisch's conception. The meaning of the term "pluralism" that Krisch is using is not the one that the proponents of the common pluralist branch need and employ in order to really distinguish their branch from constitutional monism. While we know that this element at the foundational level is decisive for the distinctive novelty of constitutional pluralism to succeed, Krisch makes it explicit at various points in

[128] There is not at this point, and will not be in any near future, some sovereign world *demos* that could offer such a direct link to the system of international law and its institutions. The international legal order instead remains grounded in the states as its direct subjects/addressees.

[129] Although Krisch in his writings relies heavily on MacCormick's conception of pluralism, he interprets the latter in his own way (as mere pluralism of legal systems, which cannot be ultimately distinct from monism) while not explicating that this is actually not what MacCormick understood, or at least could have understood, by "constitutional pluralism." While this is of course a perfectly legitimate interpretive move, invoking the leading constitutional pluralist thereby nonetheless contributes a part to the general misunderstanding about Krisch's own membership in the branch.

[130] Krisch (n 91). [131] Krisch (n 91).

his scholarship that, under his own conception, the several confronting actors are of course not meant to be treated as equals at all.[132] That would indeed be unrealistic to claim in the global sphere where the confrontation is between the various different institutions of the international legal system and the self-standing constitutional orders of the states. Indeed, Krisch is not hiding that he is not a constitutional pluralist. Problems of confusion nonetheless emerge. This is because due to his similar rhetoric others seem to be making wrong conclusions, and because he is also himself referring to Neil MacCormick and others from the pluralist branch—who do keep both those necessary constitutive elements—thereby giving the impression as if his own approach had in common with those something more than just the decorative rhetoric.

Finally, even if we were nonetheless to treat, mistakenly, but for the sake of argument, both Krisch's and Halberstam's proposals as instances of constitutional pluralism, they could not succeed. This is, as will be seen in Chapters 8–10, because precisely in conditions when the confronting orders are not sufficiently constitutionalized and democratic, they lack the sufficient factual and normative challenge to each other. It is this challenge that is unique to constitutional pluralism that provides the necessary "steam," as it were, to get the pluralist process off the ground, and towards the sufficiently superior set of normative ends. Without this challenge, as we will see, the correct (intact) pluralist concessions between the orders would not really follow through the various applicative levels in the way that we need.[133]

Halberstam's and Krisch's attempts at the application of MacCormick's distinctive concept *directly* to the global sphere cannot succeed without thereby doing away with the distinctive concept of constitutional pluralism itself. Their aspiration is nonetheless valid and is in one sense even a step ahead of the current members from the pluralist branch. As will be seen in Chapter 8, to conceive of constitutional pluralism within a limited regional territorial space, such as Europe, similarly does not yet fully abandon monism. To this extent it is still too exclusive of "external others" who find themselves outside the borders of such a pluralist regime. To this extent, Krisch's sense that constitutional pluralism might still be too imposing is certainly warranted.[134] Both Halberstam and Krisch therefore do look in the right direction. It is just that the quick *direct* route they are relying on cannot do this, and even less so under the umbrella of "constitutional pluralism." We will see that there is an *indirect* route through which constitutional pluralism can and should be opened and extended to the global sphere. This will even be necessary in order to preserve constitutional pluralism as a sound approach that is truly distinct from monism and not subject to the critique from the monist exclusion just mentioned.

Once the misclassification of Halberstam and Krisch is clarified, the mess and vacuity of which Weiler spoke in relation to pluralism is also cleared up. This is so

[132] See, eg Krisch (n 91) at 450; also Krisch, "The Case for Pluralism in Postnational Law" in de Búrca and Weiler (n 91) at 432–3.

[133] For more on this crucial role of the pluralist challenge between two constitutionalisms (as opposed to legal systems that lack the latter), see Chapter 8, pp. 249–50; Chapter 9, pp. 285–94; and Chapter 10, pp. 295–316.

[134] Krisch (n 91) ch 2 and, eg 383, 404.

not only with respect to the European context, but also the global. This now completes the full response to Weiler's challenge. The distinctiveness of constitutional pluralism correctly understood is clear and undeniable.

Moreover, this also shows that Weiler's strategy of retraction from constitutional pluralism, on the basis of assuming that these new conceptions must be further representations of MacCormick's idea of constitutional pluralism, is not warranted. Were the mistaken assumption true, and Weiler's conception thus forced into a group of proposals with which it had little or no connection, the value of his conception of constitutional pluralism would indeed be unduly blurred. But the assumption is incorrect. The solution to Weiler's challenge thus also leads away from his retraction. On the basis of the mapping analysis that clarified constitutional pluralism and its principled distinctiveness, we know the following. While those recent proposals for the global context are not instances of constitutional pluralism, as they do not derive from the only possible minimum common denominator of the branch, Weiler's conception clearly does remain in that camp. We have seen[135] why his attempt at distinguishing his conception from MacCormick's at the depth of the minimum common denominator cannot succeed. Weiler wrote that, while MacCormick supposedly grounded his proposal in legal theory, he himself grounded his own in politics and thus normative political theory. As already explained above, however, MacCormick's *legal* level of analysis was merely a reflection of his deeper constitutional pluralism, grounded firmly and emphatically in normative political theory. As parts of both chapters on MacCormick's version of pluralism demonstrate,[136] it cannot be denied, without at least somewhat misreading his scholarship, that that was indeed the case.[137]

While Weiler and MacCormick both comfortably belong to the new pluralist branch and share its common denominator, they nonetheless of course differ to a degree in what each then believes is the best and most valuable way in which to ramify pluralism through the various applicative levels. That difference is, however, a degree of difference between two members of the same family, and it is not, nor could it be, the family of constitutional monism. This way alone could either of these proposals truly work in the first place: the level of application, and the most foundational level of principle, are inseparably connected and inescapably affect each other. Over the long run it is not possible to nourish one, while forgetting and disregarding the other. Both of these authors are constitutional pluralists through and through.[138]

[135] See Chapter 6, pp. 166–7 and nn 8–9, as well as Chapter 3, p. 92. Cf Chapter 10, pp. 320–1.

[136] See Chapter 1, section 4, especially pp. 26–7, 29, and n 86, where the normative foundational similarity between both conceptions is clearly exposed. For the equally striking applicative normative similarity between both conceptions compare the discussion of Weiler's building blocks (Chapter 3, subsection 1.3, especially pp. 77–81) with that of MacCormick's very similar substantive normative construction rooted in normative political theory—Chapter 6, subsection 3.2, pp. 177–87.

[137] In my work I was able to make the connection between both the normative-political and legal dimensions of MacCormick's theory based on my discussions with him on this issue. For those discussions I am indebted to him.

[138] Cf Chapter 10, pp. 320–1.

It can be concluded that the existing fundamental critiques of the very idea of pluralism do not succeed. When properly mapped out and decoded, the branch of constitutional pluralism as such does carry a clear and distinctive principled idea. The latter likewise has a potential to project its uniqueness from the foundation in the several applicative directions and thus to make such an approach operational and distinctive also in practice.

PART III

THE SUPERIOR PATH

8

Within the Branches of Pluralism

In the last two chapters we defined what constitutional pluralism as a branch means, and then defended its distinctiveness against the criticisms of the very idea of constitutional pluralism. That was therefore about the distinctiveness of the branch as such—constitutional pluralism as a whole. Yet as we know, this branch divides into several smaller sub-branches that stem from the common trunk. These different versions of constitutional pluralism all share the principle of constitutional heterarchy, as opposed to hierarchy, at the foundational level. They then, however, go in different directions to explain and reflect that heterarchy at different applicative spheres of the constitutional discourse. Yet it is not that, in doing so, these different versions of constitutional pluralism are all equally sound. Nor do they harbor the same potential for further contribution to Europe and the world. Some of them seem to take a sounder path than others, and the potential of these different visions consequently also varies. I have engaged in individual (internal, *intra*-theoretical) assessments as to the (in)coherence and other individual features of each of these versions already within the mapping analysis. I will now move beyond that and into the *inter*-theoretical assessment that engages the different approaches with each other and at the level of their deepest underpinnings. Such an assessment not only reveals certain remaining weaknesses in these approaches—in some greater than in others—but above all thereby also paves the way towards the superior path, to be then explored in greater detail in the final chapters.

Chapter 8 is divided into three sections. The first draws together some findings from the earlier chapters that set the stage for this further appraisal.

The second section then focuses on the more proceduralized branches: Walker's epistemic pluralism and Maduro's interpretive/participative pluralism. It is argued that, firstly, due to their thinness these approaches lock themselves away, and too quickly, from the key area of inter-theoretical ethical exchange at the level of their underpinnings. Such an exchange would have the ability to expose some decisive weaknesses in these approaches as currently defined.

Secondly, it is thus argued that as far as the discourse of the *what* is concerned, such thinness makes it impossible sufficiently to distinguish these versions of pluralism from monism. To be sure, they are different from monism in the formal sense: they endorse the pluralist as opposed to monist foundation, and adopt their unique pluralist solutions within both formal discourses of the *how* and the *who*. However, both of these are indeed formal discourses. For this reason it could well be that, while fully respecting both of these methodological pluralist dimensions, the regime under such pluralism could in practice still end up endorsing solutions that would not be very different from the monist ones in the decisive sphere of the *what*—the substantive sphere in which our relation to "the other" is truly determined. While different in principle, such versions of pluralism could thus easily end up being insufficiently different from monism in their practical effects within this decisive sphere. Indeed, there is currently little in these approaches that could even prevent Europe from gradually slipping back to the kinds of monist results known too well from its past.

Thirdly, due to the exceptionally thin versions of mutual respect that they simply posit, these approaches are unable to distil, from that richer inter-theoretical discourse that they lock themselves away from, the even sounder conception of mutual respect which alone could remedy these problems as well as secure the long-term legitimacy of the rising pluralist polity. On a closer analysis the types of respect currently implied in both these approaches are insufficiently unconditional, as well as insufficiently universal, to be able to do that work. This deepest foundational weakness goes hand in hand with yet another practical one—that Europe under these approaches is at best still just internally pluralist. In relation to the "external others" who happen to be outside its borders, this polity is still a monist regime. While internally pluralist, externally this is then actually little more than recasting of monism at the higher, European, level.

In the third section the focus then shifts to more substantive versions of pluralism—Weiler's and MacCormick's. It is first argued that the general direction of these branches is sounder. They do not close themselves off from the key area of inter-theoretical ethical exchange, although some minor aspects concerning this issue could be improved.

Secondly, they are also correctly oriented towards the elaboration of some unique substantive pluralist principles, or the substantive "building blocks" of Europe's meta-constitution. These blocks are thus entrenched, together with the conceptions of mutual respect that these approaches imply, at the meta-constitutional level of the discourse. This slightly "thicker" orientation is important since this way alone the distinctiveness of constitutional pluralism is present not only in the formal applicative discourses of the *how* and the *who*, but also in the key discourse of the *what*. It is nonetheless argued that there are some related remaining weaknesses in these approaches that should, in order for pluralism potentially to succeed, be further refined.

Thus, thirdly, it is not entirely clear whether, at their foundations, both substantive conceptions adopt that key universal unconditional type of respect. Yet that is the type of respect that is needed for establishing long-term legitimacy of the regime. It is also needed for securing the regime's fully pluralist nature that opens Europe in a particular way to every bearer of dignity in this world, instead of retaining it for the Europeans alone and thus merely recasting monism vis-à-vis its "external others." While their abstract rhetoric of respect may sound right *in abstracto*, both substantive conceptions still have their pluralism limited to the regional Europe, thereby still casting some doubt as to the type of foundational equal respect they imply. This does not yet as satisfactorily as it should solve those problems from the insufficient distinctiveness of pluralism from monism. Some further substantive refinement is needed at the foundation.

Fourthly, in order for the intact substantive pluralist building blocks to follow from such a pluralist foundation, the latter would also need some further structural improvement. As currently defined, both substantive conceptions still lack a sufficiently powerful substantive-pluralist challenge to the actors, from which alone the intact and distinctively pluralist building blocks could arise.

Finally, such a further improvement of both the substantive pluralist foundation, as well as its building blocks (those too have so far not yet been fully consistent with the truly intact universal unconditional respect), may well pave the way to the soundest, superior conception of pluralism. However, this is not yet to say that such a conception is also superior vis-à-vis all other, non-pluralist approaches. This is so because neither Weiler nor MacCormick have thus far shown what the pluralist conception would mean for the crucial field: for democracy. Yet it is there where this novel approach to constitutional/political ordering has its greatest, perhaps even historic, potential. It is with this that monism simply cannot compete.

Throughout the chapter it will be argued that the current discourse on constitutional pluralism ought to reorient itself away from these identified weaknesses. This will at the same time inevitably begin to carve out the remaining sound path for an improved conception of substantive pluralism, with the latter to be then more fully elaborated in Chapters 9 and 10.

1. Setting the Stage

The mapping analysis showed that all the pluralist theories examined are actually meta-constitutional theories. They are proposals for the ultimate and inherent constitutional content, which is considered externally (inter-systemically) valid and is instituted by the theory itself. It is an antecedent that should be respected and satisfied first, before the actors legitimately begin further discourse about constitutionalism, or about what should properly count as constitutional/unconstitutional. Thus, it is a precondition that even a constitution-maker ought to respect if it is to realize the normatively superior version of constitutionalism and constitution. The meta-constitutional level is one that implies prioritization of certain value(s) and the corresponding subordination to a lower rank of (constitutional) priority of anything not made such a priority. The prioritized meta-constitutional content is a response to the antecedent constitutional question concerning the ultimate purpose of Europe's constitutionalism.

Each assessment section within Chapters 2–6 identified the ultimate value(s) underlying each individual vision of pluralism. The values corresponded to different contents entrenched at the meta-constitutional level by the different theories. We shall now draw these individually identified foundational values together in order to facilitate comparison.

In the assessment of epistemic pluralism in Chapter 2, we saw how Walker entrenches at the meta-level a single value of reciprocal respect. For this reason I named it the Eigenvalue of "mere reciprocity." In addition, it also acquired the adjective "ascetic" mere reciprocity. That was because a *particularly thin* version of this value is being entrenched. Recall that it is the kind of reciprocal respect that requires from the actors to abstain only from asserting the *external* rightness of their second-order claims and, in addition to that, to submit themselves only to an open and unspecified reciprocal negotiation at the first-order level of discourse. What underlies such a thin meta-value is Walker's assumption about why we should get into constitutional politics in the first place: in order to resolve our differences in a way that does not privilege one or more subjects of disagreement over others. It is believed that to entrench only this thin mere reciprocity at the externally valid meta-level is by default to secure the highest degree of non-privileging—of equal respect and its corresponding autonomy—between all the participants and their contesting claims within post-modern constitutional disagreement. This is then the way to redeem concepts of constitutionalism and constitutionality from the formidable challenge of such disagreement. Hence also his view that the conception of pluralism as determined by his thin and single meta-constitutional value is clearly the most pluralist (neutral) one.

In the assessment section of Chapter 4, which examined interpretive and participative pluralism, it was shown that Maduro underpins his theory by his own version of the Eigenvalue of reciprocal respect as the single meta-value. This one is just a slightly thicker version of mere reciprocity. According to this version of pluralism, both levels of constitutional discourse thus need eventually to adopt some enhanced minima of participation and representation that are more thickly and specifically defined than are any of the thin external rules in epistemic pluralism. Only such a thicker participative substratum could truly bring the democratic added value that Maduro sees as the ultimate goal of Europe's constitutionalism. At the same time, the minima are *not* directly prescribed by the theory. It is hoped that they would be achieved indirectly: via the interpretive pluralism as *the only* dimension of Maduro's pluralism that is really entrenched at the meta-level. As we saw in Chapter 4, interpretive pluralism specifies the right type of interpretive question (the inter-subjective type of reciprocity) that needs to be asked at both levels of constitutional discourse, and this is to be employed with the view of achieving hopefully that normative goal of enhancement of participation/representation. To distinguish it from the "ascetic mere reciprocity," we can call this Eigenvalue "inter-subjective mere reciprocity." It is believed that entrenchment of this slightly thicker meta-content, together with the anticipated enhancement of democracy that is expected to result from it, enables the highest realization of the value of reciprocal equal respect and its corollary of autonomy. Hence, it is also this variant of the Eigenvalue that is understood as constituting the most pluralist conception of constitutionalism. Requiring such a content at the meta-constitutional level would be, in the eyes of an epistemic pluralist, already too thick an external imposition on what needs to be a more open agonistic negotiation; it would constitute an undue compromise of the highest degree of reciprocal equal respect and autonomy.

The reason for the two slightly different Eigenvalues underlying epistemic and interpretive/participative pluralism seems to lie in the two slightly different orientations, or meta-goals, of the two theories. The direct normative goal of Maduro's version of constitutional pluralism is enhancement of participation and representation (democracy). This he openly declares as the ultimate purpose of Europe's constitutionalism. He understands that the more truly inclusive democracy cannot be achieved solely by enhancing the scope of inclusion. It must also require that the participating subjects take into account different impacts that decisions might have on differently situated subjects. His focus is thus very much also on the intensity of inclusion.[1] But while Walker's project is clearly also related to participation/representation, his immediate goal and focus is more on the broader quest for redeeming constitutionalism from disagreement: that is, on finding the most neutral framework for as large a universe of existing claims as possible, which would not arbitrate between them beyond mere agonistically open ascetic reciprocity. This means that such an agonic freedom would, more often than other cognate approaches from its family,[2] Maduro's included, sacrifice the need for intensification of inclusion of some for the sake of an agonic kind of neutrality to all. To be sure, both Walker and Maduro's variants of equal respect and autonomy are not only about widening the scope of inclusion for different subjects and their interests/claims. They both are also about enhancing the intensity of inclusion between the included participants and thus require reciprocal treatment between the included subjects and their interests as opposed to some anarchical state of "negotiation" between them. Still, the difference as described is the reason why Maduro's understanding of the highest maximization of this value amounts to a slightly thicker degree of external determination of both the intensity of reciprocal inclusion as well as its scope, while Walker's results in his less specified thinner alternative.

Despite these differences there is also an important commonality between the two meta-contents. In both cases it is still about entrenchment of only one Eigenvalue of equal respect and autonomy at the meta-level, and so "only" about perfecting some truly equal processes within which the actors themselves would then be in position to determine the substantive ends-in-themselves of their individual and collective lives.[3] Maduro thus insists on understanding the coexisting constitutional entities (the EU included) in Europe as communities of "open and undetermined political goals".[4,5] The same is of course true with Walker, who

[1] I am indebted to Miguel Maduro for his clarification on this point (ECJ, Luxembourg, June 2006).

[2] Chapter 2, pp. 47–8.

[3] Collective is meant here to refer also to self-determinations of identities of constitutional systems themselves.

[4] M. Maduro, "Where to Look for Legitimacy?" (2002) in E. Eriksen et al (eds), *Constitution Making and Democratic Legitimacy* (2002) Arena Working Paper No 5/2002, 106.

[5] When describing one of the presuppositions of his project, Maduro also writes: "The third assumption is probably the most contentious one... My view is that the broader goals of political

is even farther away than Maduro from having his theory externally prescribe some ends-in-themselves for the actors within those systems.

In assessing Weiler's thesis in Chapter 3, it was seen that substantive pluralism is relatively different in this respect. Its meta-constitutional content is more substantive. There is in Weiler's version of pluralism no *single* priority Eigenvalue that would relegate others to a lower rank of constitutional priority. Rather he implies a cluster of several different values that all coexist at the external meta-level of priority and together underpin the theory of substantive pluralism. They are the values represented by Weiler's substantive building blocks of Europe's pluralist constitutionalism. They epitomize the "life of decency" of which he speaks in connection to his vision of the normatively superior version of constitutionalism. Under substantive pluralism, constitutionalism is thus ultimately neither simply about solving our differences through some disagreement-redeeming framework, nor only about enhancing representation and participation (democracy). It is above all about determining those substantive building blocks that represent the very grain of the "decent life" as the external end-in-itself that should be realized by Europe's constitutional project.

It is also important to recall that the different meta-values of substantive pluralism do not according to this view compromise the highest realization of the meta-value of reciprocal equal respect and autonomy. On the contrary, according to substantive pluralism the latter value cannot really be understood without those other externally (inter-systemically) valid values. For it is only through them that it attains its true meaning and highest degree of enhancement. The reverse is also the case: the specific values from the building blocks likewise could not be properly understood without this more substantively determined reciprocal equality and autonomy. Indeed, on this view there must be a coherent substantively elaborated cluster of different and mutually enhancing priority values entrenched at the meta-constitutional level instead of a single priority Eigenvalue of mere reciprocity. Only such a relatively thicker substantive approach can, in Weiler's view, attain the most truly pluralist conception of constitutional pluralism.

With his building blocks representing the sound values from nationhood, MacCormick similarly appears to build a cluster of values at the meta-constitutional European level. As in Weiler's case, these blocks are not to be understood independently of the coexisting values of equal respect and autonomy. But the latter also cannot properly exist without those substantive blocks; even at the highly abstract meta-level the true equal respect and autonomy cannot appear in their

communities derive from the co-ordination and satisfaction of individual preferences as judged by individuals themselves... In my view, not only outcomes but also processes are to be measured in terms of individual representation and participation. As a consequence, the democratic character of the political form of organization of the polity is not assessed [in Maduro's project] on the basis of whether its results meet the interests of individuals (which would always be measured by criteria independent of the individuals' preferences) but on whether such process grants effective representation and participation to all affected individuals" (M. Maduro, "European Constitution: What if This is as Good as It Gets?" in J. Weiler and M. Wind (eds), *European Constitutionalism beyond the State* (Cambridge: Cambridge University Press, 2003) 80).

emptied form. MacCormick believes that they should be understood contextually, with those other blocks enhancing their most valuable meaning. While MacCormick's version of substantive constitutional pluralism currently focuses primarily on the building blocks from nationhood, there seems to be an implicit understanding that there could be still further similar blocks arising out of other contexts relevant to pluralism. Traces of this expanding potential of pluralism can be observed at several places throughout MacCormick's work and point to fields such as democracy,[6] religion,[7] and others.[8]

After drawing the underpinnings together we are reminded of how differently these theories understand what should be entrenched as the meta-constitutional content of Europe. We have various different options presented, from mere reciprocity in its ascetic version, and its slightly thicker inter-subjective variant, to Weiler's cluster of different meta-values, and MacCormick's own version of such a substantive strategy. So which of these contents is more correctly entrenched at the *meta*-constitutional level? Which is more properly to be seen as the right ultimate goal of Europe's constitutionalism? Which of these pluralisms is the superior one to adopt and follow? Or is there perhaps another, more advanced option that should be embraced? We need an inter-theoretical exchange between these different approaches, between their underpinnings at the meta-level, in order to make progress towards answering such questions. Let us first focus on the more proceduralized, and thus less substantive, direction that Walker and Maduro take, to be then followed by the more substantive pluralist visions of Weiler and MacCormick.[9]

2. The Proceduralized Branches

There are three fundamental difficulties associated with the exceptional thinness of the Eigenvalue approaches. They are examined in turn through the following three subsections.

2.1 Closing off the area

The theories of epistemic and interpretive/participative pluralism both currently close off the key area of inter-theoretical ethical investigation through which they could be defended in the first place. It is through this same area that one could also uncover some of the remaining weaknesses of these approaches, as well as then

[6] N. MacCormick, *Questioning Sovereignty: Law, State, and Nation in the European Commonwealth* (Oxford: Oxford University Press, 1999) ch 9.

[7] MacCormick (n 6) at 123.

[8] I am indebted to Prof MacCormick for expanding my understanding of this potential within his pluralism (interview, EUI, Edinburgh, 8 December 2006).

[9] As explained earlier (Chapter 4, pp. 107–8 and 114–16), this distinction between a conception that is proceduralized versus the one that is more substantive is inevitably a matter of degree, but a degree that is decisive and warrants the distinction in labels.

point to strategies for fixing those. This is why this "closing off" will be especially problematic. In the case of epistemic pluralism there will be a stronger variant of such a "closing off," one that, as argued in Chapter 2, also threatens to undercut the coherence of the theory. In order to be able to enter the key area, the theory would need to modify some of its tenets. The nature of the closing-off in interpretive/participative pluralism is less strong. While it also currently leaves the key area closed, the theory could still be interpreted in a way that would eventually allow it to enter and argue within the area without actually changing its conclusions. It will be argued that both theories should indeed be adjusted so as to be ready to enter the key area. Such a substantive reorientation of their discourse is unavoidable and will be suggested as the first necessary step towards the theories' sound refinement, to be followed by the rest in the subsequent subsections.

Questions about which constitutional value(s) should be satisfied first, and thus about the ultimate purpose of constitutionalism, are questions about meta-priorities. The latter have their roots in a domain of ethical/moral thinking that deals with deliberation over why some value, within a universe of values, is of such high importance as to be given such priority. One who sought an answer to the questions posed at the end of the previous section would have to engage in such an ethical discourse and explain why this or that particular putative meta-value, and its corresponding goal, is so important and valuable to us as to outweigh the other candidates that compete for such meta-constitutional priority. This is an area in which the selection of the highest goods flows from ethical deliberations of what it is about these goods and about us that makes these the very goods that ultimately outweigh others.

It is perhaps possible to define comprehensively such an area within the field of political philosophy or ethics.[10] However, this is not our endeavor. In our context, the initial relevant part of the area of comparative ethical investigation, one with which we can start, is clearly discernable. It is the inter-theoretical discourse that requires confrontation of the different values underpinning the different pluralisms. The different meta-values and the corresponding meta-goals of Europe's constitutionalism conflict with each other, and we must consider their respective merits in this particular domain of inter-theoretical investigation. We could not avoid entering the domain, as long as the theories are internally coherent and refer to values that are not prima facie unsound, and as long as there is at least a possibility that we would be able, through such an inter-theoretical investigation, to improve our understanding of the superior solutions. The latter will then indeed follow.

Constitutional theories of epistemic and interpretive/participative pluralism, which institute at the meta-constitutional level only one Eigenvalue, assume that

[10] See, eg Taylor's attempt at describing the area by explaining the relationship between what he calls "life goods" and "constitutive goods" (C. Taylor, "Leading a Life" in R. Chang (ed.), *Incomparability, Incompatibility, and Practical Reason* (Cambridge, MA: Harvard University Press, 1997) 173. Cf M. Sandel, *Public Philosophy: Essays on Morality and Politics* (Cambridge, MA: Harvard University Press, 2005).

only one thing is ultimately so important as to be instituted at the meta-constitutional level. But it is characteristic of both of these approaches that, while instituting their respective meta-priorities, they do not enter the domain of ethical thinking from which their priorities inevitably originate. Neither of these two priorities is supported by an actual inter-theoretical justification. They both are instead presumptively instituted. In the case of epistemic pluralism the area is closed by the axiom of epistemic incommensurability that institutes the ascetic mere reciprocity as the single value at the meta-level. In interpretive/participative pluralism such a closure occurs by Maduro's "assumption"[11] that ends-in-themselves of a constitutional regime that are thicker than his intersubjective mere reciprocity must be determined *exclusively* by the actors themselves. This institutes *this* theory's version of inter-subjective mere reciprocity as the only meta-value. On these posited assumptions the theories then build their further framework that must do full justice to the underlying presuppositions. Yet these presuppositions are not to be engaged with other values. By using such a strategy the two theories, as they currently stand, restrict the scope of their constitutional theorizing and appear to deliberately stay out of our key inter-theoretical domain of ethical exchange.

But the exact nature of the "closing off" in the two theories differs. In epistemic pluralism it is particularly strong. The central aim of epistemic pluralism is to redeem constitutionalism from disagreement, or to redeem it in the greatest way possible. Hence, the need to build a meta-framework on the baseline that is self-evidently able to attract lesser disagreement (greater mutual respect and autonomy) between participants and their views than do other potential common baselines. It was observed in Chapter 2 that at first glance the axiom of external incommensurability appears as a self-evidently lesser degree of imposition and privileging between those who disagree, and thus as the baseline that automatically institutes greater equal respect and autonomy than do competing solutions. However, it was further argued in that chapter that on closer examination this "default-superiority" could not succeed. Indeed, it can paradoxically be maintained that the thinner this theory attempts to be, the more controversial and thus imposing it becomes. Epistemic pluralism's strategy of radical thinning, understood as being self-evidently the least imposing, thus undercuts itself. The axiom cannot persist as a *default* presupposition, and yet this is what the theory needs in order to hope to redeem constitutionalism from disagreement.

For these reasons it was also hinted in Chapter 2 that, in order to save itself as a coherent approach, epistemic pluralism would need to ground its defense and potential justification in the very domain of ethical thinking that it now closes off by its axiomatic presupposition. It would need to adopt an understanding of the latter as openly ethical and deeply controversial as opposed to self-evidently axiomatic. Only by thus taking a step backwards would it be able to confront the opposing underlying values of the different pluralisms. By doing so the nature of the project would change, and its orientation shift. The key area of discourse would

[11] See n 5.

become the now closed area of inter-theoretical investigation in which such a priority can only be argued for and potentially justified, and the goal of redeeming constitutionalism from disagreement would need to be abandoned for the quest of the most *justifiably* imposing meta-constitutional arrangement. The project of epistemic pluralism as it currently stands is not such a project.

Maduro's interpretive/participative pluralism also includes a presupposition that closes the key inter-theoretical area while instituting its own version of mere reciprocity—inter-subjective mere reciprocity—as the single meta-value. Whatever the actors who abide by this methodological interpretive formula happen to adopt on this basis is fine and legitimate. Unlike in the case of epistemic pluralism, the point here is not to redeem constitutionalism from disagreement, but to institute the greatest possible degree of representation and participation regardless of how controversial the posited baseline might be in the eyes of those who disagree within constitutional discourse. While it thus also claims to realize the best understanding of equal respect and autonomy, Maduro's theory is not grounded in the idea that it is the least externally imposing and so the least privileging. Still, the key area is nonetheless closed by the theory's presupposition as we are offered no justification for the latter, but only a recognition that it is indeed some kind of a trumping "assumption" that must not be breached. There are two possible variants of the "closing off" implicit in this kind of approach.

Firstly, Maduro could be thinking along similar lines as Habermas, when the later insists on inter-subjective mere reciprocity as the only external meta-value permissibly imposed within a political system of the free and equal. Habermas's theory claims to be able to explain that this standard of his discourse ethic is already binding on us by simply pointing to our commitment to talk to each other the way we do. In effect, "we can bypass altogether reflection on the good."[12] The default superiority of such an approach is supposedly grounded in this pre-theoretical *fact* of such a commitment, as opposed to value. However, even though Habermas argued this point passionately, his theoretical underpinning has been clarified as an obvious value choice in need of ethical justification of its assumed superiority against other rival comprehensive doctrines of which Habermas's is but one.[13] Such a default type of closing off our key area by Maduro's pluralism could thus also scarcely succeed.

Secondly, a potentially more sound reading of Maduro's presupposition, though not one without further problems, would be that which recognizes it as a controversial *value* choice, which is not (yet) further supported. According to this view the theory might perhaps be proven to be ethically superior, but the necessary

[12] I borrow this succinct description of Habermas's strategy from Taylor's account ("Leading a Life" (n 10) at 174).

[13] There is not much to add to John Rawls's persuasive reply to Habermas on this point—see his *Political Liberalism* (New York, NY: Columbia University Press, 1993) section 5, "Reply to Habermas," especially 424–5 and 376–8—except perhaps Frank Michelman's further illumination of Habermas's inescapable ethical value-underpinnings as also being both empirical and contingent (see his, "Morality, Identity, and 'Constitutional Patriotism'" (1999) 76 Denver University Law Rev 1009, 1026–7).

reasoning has not yet been undertaken due to, say, lack of time or purpose to elaborate a grand theory.[14] This type of "closing off" is of course less strong than the one from the default strategies, like that of epistemic pluralism or that by Habermas. Indeed, if Maduro's presupposition were understood in the default sense then this would prevent the theory by virtue of its own axiom from going down to the domain in which the different pluralist proposals and their assumptions diverge. As a result, its claimed superiority could not be defended. But on this second rationale Maduro is free to interpret its presupposition as being in need of such further ethical defense. Yet the fact remains that the theory in its current form does not yet engage in the inter-theoretical ethical defense. Nor have there been any signs over the years of it moving toward that direction. Instead, its methodological axiom at the meta-constitutional level continues to be treated as if it was true by default. This is the case even though it has been argued within liberal thought itself that, without the Habermasian "fact based" type of justification, such a "default superiority" of this particular thin variant of the axiom cannot be taken for granted.[15] It should be concluded that it is essential for Maduro's and Walker's theories to open themselves to the key area, and then actively engage in its more substantive discourse. This is the first step of the substantive reorientation for which I argue. It is one that these most intensely proceduralized branches of pluralism need to take.

2.2 Blurring the distinction from monism

Within the reoriented discourse, all the proposals are of course free to argue for the ultimate superiority of their own meta-contents. It will be argued in this subsection, however, that when both Eigenvalue approaches do open themselves to the key area and attempt to do this, they encounter another, even more serious difficulty. Their strategies of entrenching such mere reciprocity as the single meta-value will be hard to defend ethically within this decisive area of inter-theoretical exchange: due to their radical thinness, these pluralist conceptions can, not in their principle but in their effects, get very close to monism itself, and so inside the decisive dimension of the *what*. That will, by the end of this subsection, lead to the need for yet another—now second—necessary step of substantive reorientation for these radically proceduralized branches. This time it will be the reorientation towards adopting, at the meta-level, some cluster of substantive pluralist principles (the "building blocks" of the pluralist meta-constitution) as opposed to the single and very thin pluralist Eigenvalue alone.

There can be no question that both proceduralized pluralist branches are distinct from monism. They are distinct in adopting the foundational pluralist principle, as

[14] Indeed, this second one would probably make the best candidate-explanation of Maduro's closing-off strategy. I am indebted to Miguel Maduro for sharing his explanations on this point (see n 1).

[15] See, eg F. Michelman, "Morality, Identity, and Constitutional Patriotism" (2001) 17 Ratio Juris 253, 270–1; "Ida's Way: Constructing the Respect-Worthy Governmental System" (2003) 72 Fordham Law Review 345; cf also F. Michelman, "Entrenchment and the Dignity of Legislation," Annual Law and Philosophy Lecture, Columbia University, 2006, Appendix "K". Rawls himself of course famously requires a whole plethora of "constitutional essentials" (his own building blocks) at the meta-constitutional level.

well as in their unique pluralist applications of that principle to the discourses of the *how* and *who*. This was already observed in some detail when addressing the Barber/Eleftheriadis critique. We saw that Eleftheriadis accused Maduro of adopting in his conception the same position for the ECJ as that of the US Supreme Court in the US monist system. Yet it was then explained that this is exactly what cannot be said of Maduro's proposal: unlike in the US monist model, in Maduro's pluralist conception *neither* the ECJ *nor* the nation-state constitutional courts are in the position of the final arbiter of the boundary separating both coexisting constitutional orders. There, that question of *who* is instead left open. It is so in Maduro's own particular way, but one that just as religiously follows, and does full justice to, the pluralist principle from the foundation. This is exactly what the monist applicative solution from the US Supreme Court does not do. The latter's role as the final arbiter of the boundary between the federal and state levels is only compatible with the monist foundational principle that such an arrangement thus reflects and follows within the applicative sphere of the *who*. The same point could be repeated for Walker's own undeniably pluralist solution within the *who*.

It was also observed that the pluralist discourse within the applicative sphere of the *how* was also distinct from the ultimately more one-sided approach within this same applicative discourse under monism. Always to treat both the EU and national perspectives as given, while thereby building an equally accommodating solution from that equal benchmark (Maduro's inter-subjective mere reciprocity), is again one way in which to follow religiously the pluralist principle from the foundation, just as Walker's ascetic mere reciprocity is another. They both are unlike the monist solutions in the sphere of the *how*, where the sovereign order that enjoys the ultimate authority is not of course bound always to treat the view of its subordinate units as self-standing and equal to its own.

Indeed, the procedural branches of pluralism which, after endorsing the distinct pluralist foundation, then focus primarily on the sphere of the *how* and *who* are very different from monism in all these three respects. This uniqueness cannot be denied, as cannot be the distinctiveness of the more substantive approaches.[16] The way it was elaborated,[17] the Barber/Eleftheriadis critique simply had to fail.

There is nonetheless a different problem that, as hinted earlier,[18] those critiques might have sensed, but then failed to elaborate and address in their challenge. This problem concerns only both more radically proceduralized versions of pluralism, and we will see that it does not reach the sounder, more substantive part of the branch. The problem is that, without the pluralist distinction within the *what*, the distinctions within the *how* and the *who* are in a sense still but formal distinctions. True, they are important, and often very much so, especially when appearing in combination with the distinctiveness within the *what*. But when those two are the

[16] The distinctiveness of the substantive approaches is even stronger than that of the procedural ones (see section 3, this chapter).

[17] Against the distinctiveness of the very idea (and thus branch) of pluralism as such.

[18] Chapter 6, p. 172 and Chapter 7, p. 217.

only dimensions of the pluralist conception, it could well happen that, while fully respecting both of their methodological pluralist requirements, the regime under such pluralism would still end up endorsing solutions that would not be much different from the monist ones in the decisive sphere of the *what*—the substantive sphere where our relation to "the other" is ultimately materialized. While different in principle, such versions of pluralism could thus, *in their practical effects and results*, still easily end up being insufficiently different from monism and its own practical results in the key substantive sphere. The practical results under pluralism could well be even worse. It all depends on what kind of content, noble versus corrupt, you happen to have operating under such formal rules, and that we cannot know. Both radically proceduralized versions emphatically insist that that content is not the domain of the theory, but of the actors themselves. Indeed, as far as the content (the *what*) of a regime is concerned, the thinner the pluralism the easier it is for it in its effects to go full circle and return to monism. But of what worth then would be a regime that is formally pluralist as to the *how* and *who*, but whose content—the *what*—is at the same time no less unsound as under some average monism, or more?

Take for instance the conception of nationhood. Under epistemic pluralism the options are quite widely open to the fostering of each actor's own respective vision of nationhood. Imagine then a nation-state in which subjects are very civil, in the epistemic sense, towards one another's self-choice. They do not claim external rightness for their views and are making their first-order constitutional choices only on the basis of the agonistically open-ended reciprocal negotiation towards some middle ground. But when a majority of subjects who fully comply with such a methodological framework happens to have a vision of nationhood that departs radically from that of the minority, the agonistically negotiated middle ground might well then still be one that is tilted far too heavily. Under such a skewed culture of nationhood, that would also be unsound, it cannot, moreover, be ruled out that many would over time happen to acquire an even more skewed vision of nationhood. Under epistemic pluralism, which at the same time keeps things wide open to change, this would gradually lead to further corrective agonistic negotiations. It would thereby be likely to generate an even more deeply tilted, though admittedly still fully open-ended, conception of nationhood, and this circle could continue ad infinitum.

To be sure, at the inter-systemic level such a self-standing actor is now also in a heterarchically relationship with another self-standing actor and its own conception of nationhood. But does this help? One clearly available possibility is that the second actor might well be skewed in a similar way—towards the same, the opposite, or some third vision of nationhood. When they therefore negotiate to find their *inter-systemic* middle ground, their skewed conceptions might well not be corrected, or could even be worsened. In case of the first scenario, where both are tilted in the same direction, but one tilted more than the other, they will indeed likely continue to be skewed even further. Moreover, the inter-systemic pluralist mutual negotiation makes such unsound visions appear "legitimized" and further reinforced, thereby potentially contributing to the deviation. Furthermore, despite the recognized open-ended (epistemically pluralist) nature of the adopted visions, and in part precisely because of it, there is little in the thin epistemic pluralism that could change the course and further escalation of such a process. We see that not only is there no guarantee that such a thin pluralism can, in its substantive effects in the sphere of the *what*, be any different from some average monism. There is also the danger that, after escalation to a certain point, epistemic pluralism might well not have the normative and factual capacity to turn the course backwards and prevent Europe from slipping even further down the old path that it knows all too well. Moreover, when the practical effects within the *what* are the same as those under monism, why keep the formal distinction? Why not slip openly all the way back into a new monism itself? What practical difference, after all, would it make not to do so?

Naturally, things could also not turn out the way as described, but that is exactly the point: under such a thin conception of formal pluralism there is really no way to know.[19] A community in which the actors play by the rules of the epistemically open-ended mere reciprocity might be a description of a very fine community. But it also might be a description of a quite worthless one. Some group, as was the case of Germany, Austria, and Poland during the 1930s, could well meet the thin requirements of the epistemically open agonistic negotiation and its finding of the open-ended middle ground, but still reach degrading results.[20] It is indeed hard to see how such a radically thin conception of pluralism could by itself rule out even a vile regime.

Similar observations could also be made of Maduro's version of pluralism. Here the self-standing orders must be treated as self-defining within the *what*, subject only to the methodological formula of inter-subjective mere reciprocity. In practical terms this means that they treat each others' positions as given. They do not second-guess them, but instead attempt to answer the question what would be the best standard from the perspective of each of those given positions, whatever they happen to be. Again, the difficulty is this. You may have a group of cooperating actors who comply perfectly with this methodological interpretive rule. However, when the content of their self-defined identities happens to be quite radical, perhaps even leaning heavily in the same direction, their inter-subjective middle ground within the *what* could easily be the same as under any average monism, or worse. The mere fact of formal compliance with this thin methodological interpretive formula does not guarantee any distinction from monism in the sphere of the *what*. It is easy to see how this point applies to all sorts of fields within this decisive sphere that materializes our relation with the "other." Besides nationhood, think of, say, religion, social justice, and the related good of self-government (democracy) itself. Two inter-systemic heterarchically actors who both happen to define their approaches in these fields restrictively as to the "other" within

[19] When asked what his conception would mean for the sphere of the *what*, Walker should, consistently with his theory, reply that "part of his answer to that question is exactly that he does not know that answer." I am indebted to him for this point. EUI, Florence, January 2006.

[20] I am grateful to Joseph Weiler for suggesting this particular example concerning the general difficulty elaborated here (NYU, New York, September 2006).

themselves will, after complying perfectly with the inter-subjective formula in their inter-systemic intercourse, keep and thus even further reinforce their restrictive approaches.

When pressed on this point, Maduro's answer is frank. In case the enhancements do not happen to follow he prefers to raise the white flag. In that case, he says, his pluralism does not have any further solution to offer. He refuses to go down the path of making his meta-constitutional level any more substantive than is the inter-subjective methodological formula itself.[21] We saw that Walker adopts a similar stance. This is because both take it for granted that their particular thin understandings of self-choice (the only meta-value entrenched at their meta-levels) are the right understandings of self-choice. Yet any such default assumption for the abstention, in the name of autonomy (self-choice), from further meta-constitutional elaboration would be hard to justify in those contexts in which the relatively thicker external meta-content was exactly about securing the very preconditions to the fully meaningful self-choice. That, remember, is precisely one of the roles of MacCormick's and Weiler's refined building blocks.[22] It would be especially hard to justify this in combination with the fact that such an insistence on the thinner understandings of self-choice could not but miss the opportunity to realize the potential of a great, perhaps even historic, improvement that the idea of constitutional pluralism carries within itself.[23] We will see that substantive pluralism seems to be better positioned to avoid this problem and to unleash that distinctive potential for improvement within the decisive sphere of the *what* while at the same time perfectly keeping its pluralist distinctions also in all other spheres of the discourse.

Note also that some concept of rights could not save both radically proceduralized theories in their current form. In its current form, Maduro's theory does not include a particular body of *concrete* rights as part of the theory's *meta*-level.[24] And quite rightly so, since this would be inconsistent with the rest of its teachings about its thin and single meta-value. Whatever concrete rights the actors end up adopting within their inter-subjective constitutional discourse is up to the actors themselves. Yet the theory does not show what kind of more concrete content of rights the actors under such a discourse would then end up endorsing (at the non-meta level), nor how exactly they would do that. Nor is any such more substantive content of

[21] See Chapter 4, p. 113.

[22] I argue in Chapter 10 that these blocks can be further refined through the lens of individuals' self-rule, so it is there where this inter-theoretical argument attains additional force (see Chapter 10, pp. 300–16, in connection with Chapter 9, pp. 291–2 and Chapter 8, pp. 253–4). Recently, Frank Michelman made a similar point against Waldron's theory and *its* thin version of the single meta-value of mere reciprocity (Michelman (n 15) at 16–22).

[23] See Chapter 10, this book, and K. Jaklic, *Democracy's Third Coming: Europe as a Route to Humanity's Third Historic Stage of Democracy*, monograph manuscript, forthcoming, currently on file with Harvard University Law Library, and with author. In that work I argue that, unlike monism, a sound version of substantive pluralism has the potential gradually, but inevitably, to lead to a further historic leap of democracy.

[24] Nor does it include an element of rights in an abstract form. Even if such an element was meant despite its current absence, this would not make a difference from the perspective of my argument.

rights directly entrenched at the meta-level by Maduro's theory itself. He hopes that the actors would somehow come to adopt some set of rights leading to greater representation and participation: but this is hope, however, and has nothing to do with what is entrenched at the meta-level itself. What is ultimately more important for Maduro is that this level remains as thin as it was initially defined.[25]

Walker's epistemic pluralism presupposes an abstract category of rights.[26] However, he currently does not, and could not, go further to elaborate concrete and independent content of this element as part of the theory's *meta-level*. Here, too, any specific content of this category within a community of members that practise agonistic mere reciprocity, is understood as flowing from precisely this single external meta-value. If the meta-content amounted to much more than this minimum, thus automatically making rights specification less contingent on the community's *own* reciprocally negotiated outcomes, it would interfere with the project's aim of redeeming constitutionalism from disagreement through letting the actors themselves mint the always fluid terms of their open-ended cooperation. Indeed, it is from this agonistic perspective that Walker criticizes Rawls's conception (constitutional essentials as some basic rights plus public reason), and even Waldron's, for still not being wide and contingent enough in relation to the disagreement.[27] To come up with anything more concrete than the ascetic mere reciprocity and the general notion of rights as a product (whatever its content) of such mere reciprocity, would be to engage in the same type of enterprise. It would represent the elaboration of his version of concrete constitutional essentials, which is what Walker criticizes as not taking disagreement seriously enough.[28] Only if rights are kept in the form of a general category, in which case it is possible to keep them above the fray, can epistemic pluralism be consistent with its goal of redeeming constitutionalism from disagreement any better than the non-agonistic alternatives. But if epistemic pluralism has thus to keep the category of rights abstract and tied to *whatever* concreteness is produced in an open-ended discourse under its sole Eigenvalue of ascetic mere reciprocity, then this makes it vulnerable on the grounds I have been expounding in this subsection. It seems that both

[25] Needless to say, Maduro's is not the sole example of this strategy within constitutional philosophy. Habermas, among others, insists on this same point (see, eg J. Habermas, "A Paradoxical Union of Contradictory Principles?" (2004) 4 Political Theory 766).

[26] Establishment of some "conditions and incidents of membership... broadly defined" and of "procedures ['democratic or otherwise'] by which the voice of the membership registers" is among the criteria for constitutionalism under Walker's epistemic pluralism. The rest of these general criteria are: existence of an explicit constitutional discourse, development of an institutional structure, claim to a foundational constitutional authority, development of a jurisdictional scope, the claim to interpretive autonomy, and also endorsement of the axiom of epistemic incommensurability with which such generally defined uncontroversial criteria are consistent. N. Walker, "The Idea of Constitutional Pluralism" (2002) 65 ML Rev 317, 343; see also Chapter 1, p. 35.

[27] N. Walker, "Europe's Constitutional Momentum and the Search for Polity Legitimacy" in J. Weiler and C. Eisgruber (eds), *Altneuland: The EU Constitution in a Contextual Perspective* (2004) Jean Monnet Working Paper No 5/04, 6–7; Walker (n 26) at 335.

[28] Regardless of whether an epistemic pluralist wished otherwise, to pick something like Weiler's and MacCormick's particular sound building blocks from nationhood as externally valid components of the meta-level would be for him to make just such an inconsistent move.

proceduralized theories are eventually—even when adjusted into a theory with an ethical underpinning from within our area—forced to choose between two unpalatable options: to fall short on either logical or ethical grounds.

The only way in which this can be avoided is if the theories, after taking the first step of the substantive reorientation that led away from the logical difficulty, now also take a second step towards the substantivization of their discourse. This second reorientation leads towards the discourse about what kind of a cluster of substantive pluralist principles do we need at the meta-level instead of the single and exceptionally thin pluralist Eigenvalue alone. In order to be sufficiently distinct from monism, as well as to not waste the great potential within the distinct pluralist idea, a sounder conception would thus demonstrate what exact additional pluralist "building blocks" need to be entrenched at the meta level: perhaps directly, but perhaps by showing what more precisely is needed in order for the actors themselves to appropriately substantivize that key level. Yet when both more proceduralized branches were to refine themselves in this way they would have inevitably abandoned some further parts of their current central tenets and would move to the camp of the more substantive branches of constitutional pluralism.

2.3 Insufficient quality of respect?

Before moving on to the more substantive branches we also need to make at least a record here of yet another serious, perhaps even more fundamental, difficulty that flows from the kind of thinness that we find in both proceduralized branches. This concerns the insufficient quality of respect that seems to be inherently built into the very logic of these, and similar, approaches to constructing a legitimate political order.

There are of course a multitude of different answers to the question of what exactly we mean when we say that we should treat each other equally, with equal respect. Consider only three most general directions in which this question is most commonly answered.

Firstly, at one end there is a purely contractarian understanding of equal respect.[29] Besides Hobbes's, David Gauthier's political theory is an example of this.[30] This strand of understanding of what it properly means to treat the other equally teaches that the sole point of social cooperation is mutual advantage.[31] Hence, here you deflect from your primary judgment and treat the other equally according to some common formal standard of compliance (eg follow equal interpretive formula) for the *sole* reason that, in this way, you will receive in return some proper share in the goods of union generated and increased through

[29] Here I echo the discussion in M. Nussbaum, *Frontiers of Justice: Disability, Nationality, Species Membership* (Cambridge, MA: Harvard University Press, 2006) 54.

[30] T. Hobbes, *Leviathan*, C. MacPherson (ed.) (London: Penguin, 1968); D. Gauthier, *Morals by Agreement* (Oxford: Clarendon Press, 1986). See also C. Morris, "Justice, Reason and Moral Standing" in J. Coleman and C. Morris (eds), *Rational Commitment and Social Justice: Essays for Gregory Kavka* (Cambridge: Cambridge University Press, 1998) 186–207; Nussbaum (n 29).

[31] Nussbaum (n 29) at 54.

such a mutual compliance. There is no other condition to your action, no other reason for that equal treatment of the "other," but the maximization of your interest.

Secondly, at the other end there is the purely non-self-interested understanding. The latter would be when you treat the "other" with some purely genuine, warmhearted attitude whereby you take care of the "other" as if the "other" was yourself. Crucially, here the *sole* reason for that somewhat "thicker" attitude is the mere felt duty that you owe this to the "other" as the bearer of dignity. This is a kind of duty that exists and requires such treatment irrespective of whether or not the "other" at the same time also complies with his or her own similar duty. Correctly understood, this duty implies a genuine, unconditional, and uncompromisingly universal respect that is given "for free," as it were, to every existing bearer of dignity and due to his or her mere existence *alone*. Let us call this understanding of equal respect the "intact respect."[32]

Thirdly, in contrast to both these understandings the vision in the middle does not exclude entirely, from what it understands as the proper understanding of equal respect, the element of mutual advantage. Nor does it exclude the requirement that human beings be respected for their human dignity. Unlike either of the other understandings, this variant requires *both* those preconditions. Respect should not be given unless the first *as well as* the second reason for respect are somehow met. You respect the "other" for the sake of the "other's" existence as a bearer of dignity. But if you, too, are not returned that respect and are therefore not ultimately better off from your act of respect (the goods of union), there is, on this understanding, *not yet sufficient* moral reason for you to engage in some kind of equal treatment, be it formal or some more warmhearted, in the first place. Both preconditions must be met. While this is different from pure contractarianism, it is also different from the intact respect. Following Martha Nussbaum, we may call this a "mixed" or "hybrid"[33] answer to what it properly means to treat the "other" with equal respect.[34]

Needless to say, there are also innumerable other variants, sub-variants, and rationales between, as well as within, these three broad general strands of understanding. Different people and actors today hold very different views on this issue.

One characteristic of both strongly proceduralized pluralist branches is that, as a matter of fact, they do not engage in the substantive discourse over which one of these many understandings or rationales ought exactly to be the one that the actors should employ in their discourse. We saw that they both close off that deeper area of the more substantive ethical discourse.

Crucially, we also saw that this goes beyond mere factual observation. There is an explicit assumption that if these thin proceduralized theories were to engage in such a discourse, they would already have engaged themselves in some improper

[32] It is sometimes said that this type of respect is Kantian, though this kind of generalization would not be exactly correct (see Chapter 9, pp. 281–2).

[33] Nussbaum (n 29) at 54.

[34] K. Jaklic, "Liberal Legitimacy and the Question of Respect," Ratio Juris, forthcoming September 2014.

arbitration between the disagreeing actors themselves. We know, after all, that people and actors today, who cannot be described as unreasonable, indeed hold those very different positions on the issue. That being so, both theories also *could not*—not just that they *do not*—decide in favor of one of these rationales, or meanings of equal respect, without thereby cutting against the very point they are trying to make. In Walker's case, only if one does not exclude some of these understandings of equal respect could one truly hope to redeem constitutionalism from disagreement. Or, in Maduro's case, the axiom of non-interference with the actors' own self-definitions would suffer when the theory itself engaged in this substantive discourse and ruled out almost all among the competing substantive understandings of equal respect. To insist axiomatically on some merely methodological procedural formula when you would actually be circumventing it (by ruling out all those who do comply with it but do not share your own thicker substantive understanding of equal respect), would not make sense.

This is why both our theories, instead of engaging in the more substantivized discourse at this point, inevitably take a sharper turn of deflection to the "political"[35] as they understand it. In this way they seemingly remain more impartial between what seem to be conceptions endorsed by reasonable participants in the discourse. That is now even more precisely why both versions of mere reciprocity cannot but be defined so thinly, formally, methodologically alone. The thinner equal respect implicit in them is in one sense—exactly in the sense in which it is thinner—a level beyond most others that it can thus accommodate to a considerable extent. As long as any one actor follows the theories' methodological interpretive requirements, and those alone, it is free to have its own deeper rationale and understanding of equal respect that then inherently also shapes that actor's own self-defined identity. So it is indeed not merely a correct factual observation, but it is also consistent with the very purpose of these theories, that they remain silent on the deeper, more substantive discourse itself, and that they instead treat those views equally as long as those can meet the widely encompassing procedural methodological formulas and their respective thinner, "political" notions of equal respect.

Yet this particular version of the "thinning" strategy, where one does not also engage in the substantive discourse between the different notions of equal respect, does come with a hidden and fundamental cost. What I want to posit here, and will fully explain later,[36] is that only one of these understandings of equal respect—namely, a particular variant of the intact respect—is capable of forming the sound foundation of a legitimate pluralist political order that is still distinct from monism.[37] By contrast, any pluralist conception with the foundation that allows the actors to act according to any, or some, of those lesser qualities of respect is bound to fail on this particular, and several other grounds.

Firstly, those flaws from the "thinness" observed in the previous subsection—the inability to prevent the breeding of the corrupt dimensions in the field of

[35] Rawls (n 13). [36] Chapter 9, section 1.

[37] As will be seen in Chapter 10, it is inherent to this particular respect that it perforce leads to more than a mere methodological formula.

nationality, religion, social justice, etc—can be remedied for constitutional pluralism only by ensuring that the actors themselves adopt the counterfactual ideal of the intact respect at the foundations of their regimes. To adopt any lesser quality of equal respect there, as the actors must perforce be free to do under both more proceduralized branches, is itself a source of skewing any truly sound construction within those mentioned substantive dimensions. This is because, on a closer analysis, any understanding of equal respect that is not fully intact, but rather conditional, in effect then itself contributes to the generating of inequality with respect to "external others," "internal others," as well as the members of the given actor (ie the national *demos*) itself. Nor is any such respect truly universal on a closer analysis, despite its different appearance.

Consider here just one example.[38] Imagine the European nation-states who engage in open agonistic or inter-subjective negotiations with the heterarchically situated EU order and happen to do so on, say, some "mixed" rationale for equal respect. Since they are indeed free to act on such rationales, their constructions within the key substantive domains are in effect inevitably still too self-centered. The actors tend to "get together" in a specific way that may institute some pluralism in the internal domain inside Europe, but turns the latter as a whole into monism in relation to the "external others." This is so because, with these "external others," who are not in a roughly equal position as the members of such a European club, the European actors who endorse the "mixed" type of equal respect do not tend to feel the need to engage precisely for those "others," lack of ability, or willingness, to generate sufficient reciprocal contribution in the first place. The European actors instead primarily cooperate between themselves. Such a Europe is ultimately centered on itself instead of opening itself, and its new potential, in a fully universal manner to the rest of the bearers of dignity outside its borders. While internally pluralist to an extent, from the perspective of the "external others" this inevitably recasts but another form of monism, now at the European level. Inherent in it is thus the partially corrupt, negotiated conception of nationhood, both at the nation-sate and the European levels, that is not as fully compatible as it could be with the truly universal idea of respect. The regime with such a foundation is then itself also one of the sources of inequality. The accumulation of goods is concentrated in the members of the club who can cooperate according to the requirements of the "mixed" conception of respect while the "others" are thereby in effect turned into the secondary recipients of "leftover" justice.[39] Consistently with this respect the members may even insist on the regional requirement for membership, thereby making their substantive dimensions only further corrupt, incompatible with the idea of universal respect and equality between all the bearers of dignity. Vis-à-vis "external others" this is indeed monism even in the fully formal sense. At the same time, such a foundation inevitably also renders the internal version of pluralism not fully sound. Due to the insufficient forms of respect that they cannot but allow from the actors under their methodological pluralisms, neither Walker nor Maduro

[38] The full extended discussion appears in Chapter 9, pp. 270–5.
[39] Nussbaum (n 29) at 18–21, 61–5, 266–8.

has constructed a conception of pluralism that can escape this ultimate challenge from effectively recasting monism itself.

Secondly, the foundation of the particular intact respect that I have in mind, combined with some additional structural features of the new European context, is also the only route though which it is technically possible to generate a sufficiently strong substantive challenge between the heterarchically constitutional orders. This is crucial since, as we will see, it is exactly this strong substantive pluralist challenge alone that is then capable of pushing the confronting actors in the distinctive and fully sound pluralist direction towards the inclusion of every bearer of dignity. That is the direction that is then, internally as well as externally, fully sound in its results within the decisive sphere of the *what*. It is fully compatible with the idea of universal respect and equality between all the bearers of dignity, and is thus also the only one truly distinct from monism and its own partially corrupt results in that same sphere of the *what*. It is, as we will see, characteristic of both more proceduralized branches that, since they must allow the less intact rationales for equal respect, the conflict between both confronting actors does not at all then have the capacity to push the development in this unique and fully sound pluralist direction.[40] Instead, under the more proceduralized branches such a distinctively pluralist project is not even able to get off the ground, as it were. Without the sufficiently strong factual as well as normative incentives inherent only to the substantive challenge,[41] the actors are going to choose the described easier route of the still too self-centered monism in practice, one that is also even formally monist in relation to its "external others."

A related problem with both more proceduralized branches is that their thinness also does not explicitly require that the confronting orders could only be understood as constitutional; that is, as orders with an independent and ultimately self-standing authority grounded in the direct link with their own respective peoples. Of course, both of these theories can easily accommodate this construction of constitutional pluralism, and they do so in the context of the EU and the European nation-states. But the point is that both these theories are also broader. Their thin framework seems to imply that this is but one possible form through which their broader conception of pluralism can be operationalized. There are still others: for instance, the form in which we have "pluralism" between mere legal systems that are distinct from the constitutional orders the way this concept has just been described.[42] Or, both theories also allow for "pluralism" between a constitutional order and a mere legal system.

We have already seen that this kind of broader understanding of pluralism cannot succeed for reasons explained in the case of Halberstam and Krisch.

[40] Chapter 9, pp. 289–94. [41] Chapter 9, pp. 285–94.

[42] This is indeed why Walker presents his epistemic pluralism also as a general systems theory that can apply between all sorts of legal systems (without having that direct link with the people) as opposed to the strictly constitutional ones in the sense just described. Organizations like the WTO could therefore count for him as an actor within some such legal pluralism. Similarly, on some interpretations Maduro has recently argued (the *Kadi* case) that the EU legal order can and should be seen as in a heterarchically relationship with the international legal order.

Not only in the sphere of the *what*, but even in the foundational principle, it is no different from monism. It is but a variant of constitutional monism. Now, what is crucial to add at this point is that, without the confrontation between such ultimately self-standing orders and their peoples as their sources correctly understood (ie the constitutional orders as opposed to some mere legal systems), that key challenge of which we speak here also cannot possibly arise. We will see that in due course, when it will also be observed that without that key structural element even the intact respect could not help get genuine pluralism off the ground. In order to find the sound route for pluralism out of the dangers it is therefore important to note also this additional difficulty with both more proceduralized branches. In order to climb onto one of the green, not one of the bare, branches of pluralism, the distinction between constitutional pluralism and mere "pluralism of legal systems" must be kept sharp.

Thirdly, and back to the intact respect, I have shown elsewhere that it is actually only through the foundation of the intact respect that the project of liberal legitimacy itself—long-term stability of a common regime in circumstances of deep reasonable pluralism—can best succeed.[43] To found a political regime on any other notion of equal respect, including the thinner methodological ones inherent in both proceduralized branches, paradoxically cuts against such a maximum possible approximation to the fulfillment of liberal legitimacy. The argument is explained in the following, where I elaborate and defend the intact foundation as the sound part of the pluralist branch.[44]

Finally, in closer analysis within the substantive discourse between the different understandings of equal respect, we will also see that the subtlest possible strategy of "thinning" a pluralist conception out of our respect for difference actually leads exactly to that *intact*—and not some methodological—type of mutual respect. The fully intact respect will be, in such a conception, not a product of some comprehensive doctrine, but rather itself inherently "political" in nature and thus the best available understanding of the "turn to the political" itself. This kind of notion of equal respect will need to replace at the foundational level any methodological conception of respect as we find it in both more proceduralized pluralisms under scrutiny.

The fundamental difficulty examined in this subsection may appear a little mysterious at this point. But that is why I mentioned that, here, we simply needed to record it. This is in part to complete the picture of difficulties and in part because this one is truly fundamental and thus needs to be recorded, if only briefly, at this point. The whole picture will then fully unfold in Chapter 9, where I argue for the intact notion of respect as the only possible foundation of any sound pluralist conception while contrasting it with the less intact version of respect implicit in the thinner, more methodological variants of equal respect that appear in both more proceduralized branches.

[43] Jaklic (n 34).
[44] Chapter 9, section 1, especially pp. 273–4 as contrasted with pp. 276–82.

The analysis in this subsection clears some of the terrain in our search for the sound path for constitutional pluralism through which the sufficient distinctiveness and potential superiority of this alleged new branch could perhaps be established. After this subsection we know that some of the directions in which to interpret the idea further would not work, but would rather lead us to develop "bare" branches of pluralism. Although we cannot know at this point whether there is a way out of this challenge for the branch as such, we do know that in order for the project at least potentially to succeed the proponents of both more proceduralized branches would need to reorient their current direction and slightly adjust their existing approaches. There is at least a possibility that, by following a more substantive direction, there might be a sound route for leading the idea of constitutional pluralism out of the troubles and into the sufficiently distinct and superior new branch of constitutional thought. In order to make progress and potentially find this out, we need first to clear the remaining terrain and should thus now proceed to the analysis of both currently existing branches that are more substantive in nature. We will see that here it will also not go entirely without difficulties, but that we will be able to make progress towards the aim of carving out the sound, superior path.

3. The Substantive Branches

3.1 Into the opened area

Weiler's substantive pluralism is almost diametrically opposed to the approaches that close off the key area of the inter-theoretical moral/ethical discourse within which the meta-values of our different pluralisms can potentially be defended. Within the post-Enlightenment era, this area has appeared epistemically too soft to many theorists, and the approaches by Walker and Maduro seem to be but examples of this phenomenon from our more specific context of pluralism. Nevertheless, the richer cluster of Weiler's entrenched meta-constitutional values, his substantive building blocks, is not so discursively confined. Weiler understands precisely that it is in this relatively softer area alone where the superiority of his vision could ultimately be established. Instead of closing the area off, he therefore not only leaves it open, but then also enters it.

Weiler's development of his substantive building blocks of pluralism—rooted in a discussion of the most egregious failures of Europe's monist past, as well as the potential of their survival in subtler but embryonic forms—is itself an argument within such an evaluative inter-theoretical discourse. Part of it is a deliberation as to why his refined substantive building blocks ought to be understood as more valuable than the respective Eigenvalues from the alternative pluralist approaches. Thus, recall again how Weiler explicitly argues that democracy, in the thin sense of the mere process, the way he and Maduro understand the concept,[45] is not yet enough.

[45] But see a broader understanding of democracy, one that perforce includes also the self-ruling virtues and thus, among others, also some further refined dimensions from MacCormick's and Weiler's

Even if perfectly enhanced, he basically says, it is not sufficient to secure us from the subtle substantive failures of monism that over the long run tend to lead to an outbreak of egregious abuse. "A democracy of vile persons will be vile," is Weiler's famous line.[46] This implies that the serious dangers of which he speaks can even less be avoided by the even thinner meta-strategy of the mere agonistic framework for negotiation based on the idea of epistemic incommensurability (Walker's ascetic mere reciprocity). At the same time, Weiler also argues why versions of equal respect and autonomy that such Eigenvalues just take for granted cannot actually be understood as the true respect and autonomy. He engages in a defense as to why we are able to achieve the latter precisely through an external recognition of our relatively thicker substantive identity like that proposed through his building blocks, rather than some strategy of greater epistemic relativism.[47] All this is argumentation within the deeper, key area of the inter-theoretical discourse.

Moreover, Weiler eventually even justifies the superiority of his whole conception by an argumentation based on a transcendental view that he understands as the ultimate truth. His substantive building blocks, representing the "decent life" as the end of Europe's constitutionalism the way Weiler envisions it, are ultimately grounded in the command from Leviticus:

> But the stranger that dwelleth with you shall be unto you as one born among you, and thou shalt love him as thyself; for ye were strangers in the land of Egypt: I am the lord your God.[48]

Thus, Weiler's sound building blocks within the field of nationality and religion are understood as the very representation in the constitutional domain of the idea that "we are all born in the image of God,"[49] that one lives decently by respecting the "other", *in his otherness,* as one respects oneself.[50] Indeed, it is from this justification that Weiler draws his "constitutional tolerance" (his blocks) according to which the "other" is not to be required to become like us, in the "come, be one of us" strategy, but to retain his otherness in the external sense while being respected as if he were one of us. Part of the argument, as we saw, is that this enables the highest degree of equal respect and autonomy because it involves not only the freedom to say "no" to the ultimate truth to either accept the coexisting secular alternative, or even reject the pluralist Europe altogether. It also involves the option of having such a freedom but nonetheless to accept that truth. Mere open-ended self-choice, the argument goes, cannot by itself enable the highest degree of genuine self-choice, of true autonomy: the latter inevitably depends also on what one *does* with one's choice.[51]

Furthermore, due to his reference to the specific text, it is possible to say that Weiler selects a very specific conception of equal respect within our key ethical area within which this one and basically all other conceptions of equal respect compete. It is obviously a non-methodological conception the specific content of which is,

substantive building blocks (Chapter 9, p. 292 and Chapter 10, pp. 298–9 and 304–10). For greater detail, see Jaklic (n 23).

46 Chapter 3, p. 76.
47 Chapter 3, pp. 96–100.
48 Chapter 3, pp. 72–3.
49 Chapter 3, pp. 72–3.
50 Chapter 3, pp. 72–3.
51 Chapter 3, p. 100.

moreover, further determined by its openly religious comprehensive doctrine.[52] This is indeed about delving unabashedly into the ethical area closed by both more proceduralized branches.

Weiler's substantive pluralism therefore does take both turns of the substantive reorientation: it enters the inter-theoretical area and then also itself builds a cluster of building blocks at the meta-constitutional level. However, it could be argued that his specific variant of the first reorientation, if understood in a particular way, also has a difficulty of its own. Because some of his substantive pluralism conflicts with rival alternatives we must be interested in learning more precisely how it is that his specific, textually grounded justification (Leviticus) outweighs those alternatives. My understanding is that Professor Weiler would prefer to hint at his ultimate answer[53] while being somewhat reluctant to do much more than that to corroborate his reference to the text.[54] This is in part due to a specific approach to these delicate issues that "Judaism as well as several strands of Islam [unlike Christianity] share."[55] For the first two groups it is sometimes more difficult, if not inappropriate, to argue on ethical grounds when commands are understood to follow from the higher authority. On this view, observing such a rule is not about ethics, but about something else, namely, sanctity. Some read Leviticus as providing that one shall respect the "other" in his otherness as oneself. But that is not how it is written. It states, "respect the other in his otherness as yourself, *I am the Lord, your God.*" The point is that under the theological outlook shared by these two groups the command should be followed not because it would also perhaps have ethical or moral content, but primarily because it is commanded.[56] For Weiler, things at this deep level, but the level which is crucially determinative of his pluralism, are not as much about ethics or morality as they are about sanctity. At the same time he seems to understand that Christianity, for instance, does not have this distinction posited as sharply as Jews and Muslims. "Paul shrugged off this yoke,"[57] Weiler writes, while understanding that the dilemma in Christianity has not been resolved about whether something should be understood as commanded because ethical, or as ethical because being commanded.[58]

[52] Recall the analysis of Weiler's conception on this point (Chapter 3, pp. 86–9 and n 150), where it was also explicated (pp. 86–9) that the religious underpinning of this principle does provide a further unique content.

[53] I am indebted to Joseph Weiler for this clarification (see n 20) cf also his work in progress, *The Genesis of Our Civilisation: Five Essays on the Book of Genesis*, forthcoming; also his *Christian Europe*, J. Weiler, *Krščanska Evropa: Raziskovalna Razprava*, tr. M Ožbolt (Ljubljana: Claritas, 2005), especially Part Three ("'New Things': European Spirituality").

[54] A discussion with Joseph Weiler (see n 20) clarified this point, as well as what follows in the rest of this paragraph and explicates this position. I am indebted to him.

[55] J. Weiler, "In Defence of the Status Quo: Europe's Constitutional *Sonderweg*" in J. Weiler and M. Wind (eds), *European Constitutionalism beyond the State* (Cambridge: Cambridge University Press, 2003) 14.

[56] One can, of course, think of numerous further examples such as that there is nothing ethical about not eating shellfish, or about observing kosher laws, the Sabbath, and the laws of purity in sexual relations, which are examples that Weiler once used in order to make this point (see Weiler (n 55) at 14; also n 53).

[57] Weiler (n 55) and n 53.

[58] This dilemma was already perceived in ancient Greece. Plato's Socrates thus asks Euthyphro: "Is what is holy holy because the gods approve it, or do they approve it because it is holy?" (Plato, *Euthyphro*

While formally it does go into the substantive field, the textual approach within the key area might in some circumstances nonetheless be problematic. It would be so to the extent that it either substantially or wholly closes off, and resists the substantive discussion within our key field by merely referring there to a text, and without arguing for the particular textual solution also from experience and personal sensibilities, theistic or otherwise.[59] The view that "[o]ur commands come from God, and [that so] we can bypass and subordinate the area of personal sensibility," Taylor rightly cautions, likewise carries a "similar containment" as their opposite of the "proceduralist conceptions of morality."[60] Both of the opposite strategies, which assume that we can be spared from making comparative substantive choices, run the risk of being "based on selective blindness."[61] If positions within the field amounted to no more than pointing to a text, it would be to trivialize substantive reorientation as it would not really be to elaborate—which cannot exclude experience *either* way—why it is that one should understand a text and its weight to mean what one takes it to mean. Note that this is not a requirement for secularization of the substantive field: one can use the text-plus-experience in both ways. It is, however, an insistence on a fuller ethical approach that requires a richer fulfillment of the substantive field. It is through this kind of broader approach to the substantive field (one that avoids not only the problems of the Eigenvalue theories but also those of any premature textual closing by the substantive theories) that the substantive reorientation I have in mind is properly understood.[62]

Although not as bold as Weiler's, MacCormick's approach is also one that does not close off the key inter-theoretical area. In his criticism of Kant and Rawls, according to the way he reads them, there is the implicit argument that the area of a comprehensive inter-theoretical exchange, as the only area where we engage seriously enough with our true social contexts, cannot be closed prematurely. Moreover, MacCormick also actually enters the area and argues as to why it is that the more substantive meta-content he assumes is preferable to potential alternatives.

10a). The debate continued during the middle ages. Aquinas, for instance, is thus summarized by John Duns Scotus: "for Thomas, what is commanded is not good merely because it is commanded, but commanded because it is good in itself" (J. D. Scotus, *Duns Scotus on the Will and Morality*, tr. A. Wolter (Washington, DC: CUAP, 1986) 273.

59 I should add that I do not see Weiler's approach as wholly or even substantially closing off the substantive discourse (though at the *deepest* and still determinative level he does retain the described strategy). On the contrary, there is probably more of the substantive discourse in his theory that in any other of the pluralist theories. One could see it as being present in the valuable building blocks themselves and their underlying argumentation. See Chapter 3, sections 1.3 and 2; and Chapter 10, pp. 298–9 and 306. This does not, however, mean that this approach could not improve its substantive dimension even further under the broader strategy proposed here.

60 C. Taylor, *Sources of the Self: The Making of the Modern Identity* (Cambridge: Cambridge University Press, 1992) 512. Cf J. Finnis, *Moral Absolutes: Tradition, Revision, and Truth* (Washington, DC: CUAP, 1991) 41.

61 Taylor (n 60) at 520.

62 I must add, though, that my understanding is that Weiler would be the last to disagree to go there, provided that such a further stretch into ethics indeed proved possible (as I show below that it does).

He argues, firstly, that the strategy of instituting some mere methodological reciprocity as the ultimate meta-value over all others ("abstract individualism")[63] must be rejected, because it fails to deal with flesh-and-blood individuals and operates rather with artificial abstractions:

> Notoriously, this categorical imperative of Kant's addresses humans as purely rational moral agents, as "noumenal" or "intelligible" or rational selves, not as sensual-cum-rational creatures that humans actually are. Notoriously, it fails to make contact with the merely phenomenal world of desires, friendship, pleasures or pains. It poses moral demands of an abstract kind, apart from earthly reality. Between abstract universal principles and concrete decisions affecting real people there is often considered to be an unbridgeable gap . . . The proper response . . . is to revise the position in such a way as to ensure that the . . . principles we set up are principles that have to take account of human sense and sentiment. The acceptability or unacceptability of a universal principle depends on our view of its impact on flesh-and-blood individuals . . . We should reject any approach which says or suggests (as, for example both Kant and his contemporary follower John Rawls at least seem to suggest) that ideas about individuals as moral agents have to be formed in abstraction from their flesh-and-blood actuality. Every individual . . . is a "contextual individual".[64]

Secondly, while this clearly signals no methodological closing off by MacCormick (the first step of substantive reorientation), it is also clear that, in his understanding, this less methodological form of respect inevitably must also be represented through some thicker contexts at the meta-level itself. These are his own meta-constitutional building blocks that are both compatible with the principle of universality and at the same time constitutive of a smaller community. The civic-cum-personal national belongingness and civic-cum-personal originality of nationhood are but two examples. In order to fully materialize pluralism, many more of such universally-valid meta-blocks must, according to MacCormick's vision, be elaborated through various substantive fields (democracy, religion, etc) constitutive of the smaller communities. This second step of substantive reorientation (the need for a slightly thicker cluster of blocks at the meta-level) that MacCormick's conception thus also takes, is underpinned by a further justification within the key area. All these are explained as indispensably important social contexts for us in two respects.

Firstly, it is argued that there is no reason why a collective self-constitution of a nation along these refined lines, which is respectful of "the other" nation, is not valuable on the same rationale—that is, securing conditions of liberty and autonomy for every human being as worthy of the same mutual respect—as is the rationale underlying the rest of civil liberties and reciprocity itself:

> some form of democratic self-determination has to be considered both justifiable and valuable on rather the same grounds as the simple negative liberties in the list of civil liberties. Some form of collective self-constitution, some kind of active participation in shaping and sustaining the institutions of social or communal government whose aim is to

[63] MacCormick (n 6) at 178.
[64] MacCormick (n 6) at 178–9 (footnote omitted).

advance liberty and autonomy, seems to be a necessary part of the whole ensemble of conditions in which the autonomy of the contextual individual could be genuinely constituted and upheld. If autonomous individuals require the context of some sort of freedom-enabling society, then the collective autonomy of the society itself seems a part of the necessary context.[65]

Secondly, and similarly to Weiler, only such a cluster of more concrete refined meta-blocks is seen as a sufficient guarantee of a truly stable peace and pluralistically refined rights for the "I" and the "other." Only something like this could make the pluralist difference in terms of the content—of the *what*—of such a rising pluralist regime.[66] Yet this too is understood as enhancing instead of compromising autonomy. Once again, true autonomy (genuine self-choice) is perceived to be not only about having self-choice. It is also in part about some thicker preconditions to the genuine self-choice that make the latter truly compatible with equal autonomy for everyone.[67]

We see that Weiler and MacCormick both sense the problem we encountered with the more proceduralized, thinner branches of pluralism. Due to their thinness the latter may well, in their practical effects, come around full circle and in effect end up endorsing corrupt substantive dimensions in the decisive sphere of the *what*. That threatens to make them insufficiently distinct from monism itself, and so at least in that decisive sphere. We see that both more substantivized branches thus correctly do both: they not only take the first step of the needed substantive reorientation (by not closing the key area and instead engaging into it), but also its second step. A particular cluster of the building blocks at the meta-level is, according to this vision, supposed to guarantee that constitutional pluralism can avoid that problem from excessive thinness. The general orientation is thus indeed correct. It is nonetheless not entirely clear how exactly both substantive branches could, as currently elaborated, bring about that pluralist distinctiveness and superiority. Let us now take a closer look at that and see what, if anything, needs to be improved in order to remove any remaining obstacle from this generally sounder path.

3.2 The foundational respect

The conceptions of respect assumed at the foundations of these theories do look more like variants of that more intact respect mentioned above. MacCormick writes of the need to expose some more genuine sentiment between human beings instead of replacing it with some colder methodology, while Weiler writes even that

[65] MacCormick (n 6) at 164; cf N. MacCormick, "Is Nationalism Philosophically Credible?" in W. Twinning (ed.), *Issues of Self-Determination* (Aberdeen: Aberdeen University Press, 1991) 14–15; the whole text at pp. 12–15 can be seen as a defense of MacCormick's theory against those that operate only with hypothetical mere reciprocity at the meta-constitutional level and which he criticizes as an "untenable kind of 'methodological individualism.'"

[66] Interview, Edinburgh University, 7 December 2006. Cf Chapter 6, pp. 177–85, in connection with pp. 186–7.

[67] It should be added to these arguments that, as we saw earlier, MacCormick would probably be sympathetic to possible extensions of the same type of strategy to some other contexts of belongingness, not just nationhood (see p. 235 and pp. 258–9).

one must "love" the "other" as oneself. Both authors' understandings of equal respect thus do seem different from the more methodological approach to respect. It is not yet entirely clear, however, that they indeed assume that specific version of the intact respect which, as we will see, pluralism truly needs. Whether or not the correct version of respect is assumed could only be known after first engaging in that richer exchange between the possible alternatives within the key area and then an explicit argumentation for the only kind of equal respect that could still potentially redeem the idea of constitutional pluralism.

The difficulty is that, even though some foundational conception of respect might sound right *in abstracto*, it might then still turn out that it supports what is in effect an insufficiently sound upper structure of pluralism. It is indeed fair to say that even these two conceptions of pluralism imply that theirs is the pluralism of the European entity. Inevitably, however, this is still more or less a recast of monism in relation to the "external others". We saw that this is fatal for the attempt to escape the challenge from monism. Moreover, we know that such a recast of the monist idea at the broader level corrupts the internal pluralism, the generated content (the *what*) of which is then by definition also not as fully universal and intact (pluralistically distinct) as it could be and ought to be. *Crucially*, all this inevitably says something back also about the true underpinning conception of respect, and so we see that the mere fact that something might sound right *in abstracto* is not yet necessarily the proof that the correct type of respect is indeed being instituted at the conception's foundation.

At the most abstract level this respect will thus indeed first need to be further elaborated and explained so that we can truly know it is the right variant, one that can do the work pluralism needs. That kind of respect would be able to solve the conception's problem of recasting monism in relation to "external others". Even if little by little, it would need to be able somehow to push Europe away from the regionally confined formation, and to a more unenclosed project that is opened and internally programmed to some kind of gradual inclusion of all. As we will see in what follows, this is indeed the only structure consistent with the truly sound version of the intact respect, while at the same time the only way in which to escape the challenge from monism. It is also the most noble and valuable path for Europe to take. While Weiler and MacCormick might or might not have the right respect in mind, their conceptions of pluralism, as currently defined, still do not take this crucial step towards the only truly sound (pluralistically distinct and universal-respect compatible) way out for constitutional pluralism.

3.3 The foundational challenge

This discussion on the need for improvement, or at least further clarification, of the underlying conception of respect, thus leads us to a further problem. Even if the correct conception of that intact respect was assumed at the foundations, this alone (although necessary) is not yet sufficient to push the actors in the fully sound direction. The thicker pluralist building blocks of substantive pluralism, which would now need to be fully compatible with that intact universality of the underlying respect, would not just emerge from the latter. Even if Weiler's constitutional tolerance (his version of respect) were the right abstract variant of the intact respect, it alone might be insufficiently strong in practice to lead in that highly demanding direction of some fully intact pluralist building blocks. This is part of the reason why even in theory we instead get results such as the merely internally pluralist formation that is still too centered upon itself and thus monist in relation to "external others". In practice, this difficulty of divergence from some ideal foundation only gets worse.

Even if it were fully sound, the foundational respect could thus in practice do little without relying at the same time also on another key element: the key structural feature of the sufficient substantive challenge between the orders that was already mentioned above when considering the weaknesses of the more proceduralized branches. The strong substantive challenge I have in mind is unique to the fully sound conception of substantive pluralism and is currently not yet elaborated and included in both existing variants of this branch. Yet it is only through this particular kind of further device that the actors can then really be moved also in practice. That is, they can be moved so as to follow the sound intact respect from the foundations and themselves elaborate, and adopt, those fully intact pluralist building blocks at the meta-level.[68]

Just as merely leaving the confronting actors with the intact abstract respect at the pluralist foundation cannot yet do,[69] so also the alternative shortcut of directly imposing the thicker sound building blocks themselves on the actors could not work either.[70] Without some kind of sufficient new stimulus (exactly that unique substantive pluralist challenge)[71] there is no realistic chance that the actors would simply agree to give up their current monopolies and instead abide by the imposed sound building blocks that push them to the self-refinement along the fully intact universalist path. Instead, they would only realistically accept following one of the more comfortable, but not fully intact, paths, such as that of the still externally monist and hence also not sufficiently internally pluralist Europe. Without that further key challenge, which has the potential to push things further, substantive pluralism can impose on the actors no more than they themselves are willing to take.

[68] See pp. 285–94, and the whole of Chapter 10.

[69] Something that Weiler seems to assign to MacCormick's conception. See J. Weiler, "Prologue: Global and Pluralist Constitutionalism—Some Doubts" in G. de Búrca and J. Weiler (eds), *The Worlds of European Constitutionalism* (Cambridge: Cambridge University Press, 2011) 13–14, where he argues that the mere conflict between both heterarchically orders (even if under the requirement of some genuine respect) would not lead to the building blocks that he has in mind. Weiler himself says it could easily lead to the situation of the monist superstate, as exemplified by US history.

[70] This is how Weiler's conception is sometimes read. And in this sense it could indeed even be said that he does not (need to) imply any pluralist challenge between both heterarchically orders at the foundational level. When the thicker blocks are imposed directly, you do not need any pluralist foundation in the first place. But the problem is, of course, that such a direct imposition cannot work (exactly for reasons explained in this paragraph).

[71] See pp. 285–94.

It should be concluded that neither the mere substantive challenge without the fully sound foundational respect, nor the latter without this further elaborated substantive challenge, can be enough to redeem the idea of constitutional pluralism from its challenges. Both these key foundational elements will need to be elaborated and incorporated into the conception in a particular way so as to lead to that truly distinct and superior pluralist path. Further refinement along both those lines is thus needed at the foundation of the substantive branch of pluralism.

3.4 Unreleased potential for democracy

Such a further improvement of both the substantive pluralist foundation as well as its building blocks (the latter have also thus far not yet been fully consistent with the truly intact universal unconditional respect) may well pave the way to the soundest, superior conception of pluralism. However, this is by itself not yet to say that such a conception is also superior to all other, non-pluralist approaches. Something more is needed in order to claim this. I maintain elsewhere[72] that the potential for that lies in the field of democracy broadly understood. The claim is that, were one to elaborate the building blocks of such a sound pluralist conception also in that field, it would enable the initiation of a new and further universalized historic improvement of democracy, comparable in its significance only perhaps to democracy's "first coming" in ancient Athens and its "second coming" in the aftermath to the American and French Revolutions.[73] I maintain that this historic opportunity of the unique new (post-sovereign) European context could not be seized and materialized through any conception—pluralist or non-pluralist—other than the sound version of substantive pluralism.

Yet substantive pluralism in its current form does not yet elaborate the building blocks in the field of democracy. This is its next weakness and the main obstacle to presenting it, already in its current form, as the superior vision of Europe's future constitutional development. Indeed, neither Weiler nor MacCormick have thus far shown what the substantive pluralist conception would mean for the crucial field of democracy. Weiler frankly raises "the white flag"[74] to the attempt to elaborate a conception of democracy for the pluralist Europe; among other things, there are those formidable "problems of translation"[75] that he just does not yet know how to resolve. As for MacCormick, his work on pluralism could, no doubt, be seen as contributing to the shaping of some features that will constitute the necessary components of the enhanced pluralist democracy. Think of his suggestion that we

[72] Jaklic (n 23).

[73] Such an enhanced democracy is not understood merely in procedural terms, but instead does not at the same time exclude from its conception some element of the "decent life" as Weiler would have it (the particular respect for each others' dignity that is non-methodological but fully sound). This meaning of democracy is therefore perfectly compatible with the rest of the substantive building blocks in other fields that are necessary components of such an enhanced conception of democracy. See Chapter 9, p. 292 and Chapter 10, pp. 298–9 and 304–10.

[74] J. Weiler, *The Constitution of Europe: "Do the New Clothes Have an Emperor?" and Other Essays on European Integration* (Cambridge: Cambridge University Press, 1999) 279.

[75] Weiler (n 74) at 270.

redefine democracy in Europe according to some benchmark that escapes the statist assumptions about democracy and instead focuses merely on some context-independent principles, such as the many meanings of subsidiarity he sketches.[76] Such contributions are nonetheless still too incremental in nature and thus insufficient for the task ahead. It is one thing, as MacCormick knew, to propose measures that would, to some degree, improve the current democratic situation as to the EU and its institutions.[77] It is quite another to try to show how a new conception of democracy, one that would actually be superior to the traditional monist one, could arise out of the sound substantive pluralism, and to elaborate its new enhanced model. Although he may have sensed, as I think he did,[78] that the latter would perhaps be possible as well, his work, too, does not yet quite present a solution to this task. If the idea of constitutional pluralism is recognized as having a superior status among the competing visions of Europe's further constitutional development, the existing variants of substantive pluralism need to be further refined in this aspect as well.

[76] MacCormick (n 6) at 145–55.

[77] MacCormick (n 6) at 145–55. See also N. MacCormick, *Who's Afraid of a European Constitution?* (Exeter: Imprint Academic, 2005).

[78] During the defense of my doctoral project on constitutional pluralism at Oxford, where Neil MacCormick was my external examiner, he urged me to try and elaborate in the future what I thought constitutional pluralism might mean for democracy. I may have taken the suggestion a little too seriously (although at an examination, you had better promise anything!). After returning to Harvard to complete my other doctoral project in general constitutional theory I changed and reshaped that project into the suggested topic and, a few years later, ended up defending the thesis on democracy's third historic leap via constitutional pluralism. See Jaklic (n 23).

9

The Superior Conception of Pluralism

In the previous chapter the analysis focused on the question of what does not work in the current pluralist theories and in what general direction this ought to be improved. While this already begins to carve out a sound general path of pluralism, the final two chapters take things one crucial step further. They begin to construct this improvement. This leads to the elaboration of the sound conception of constitutional pluralism that is superior among the conceptions of the new branch, as well as to the contours of the superior vision of Europe's future constitutional development.

In what follows, the analysis delves straight into the key inter-theoretical area within which it is argued for a particular version of intact equal respect as the only possible foundation of any sound pluralist conception (section 1). This foundation must then be joined by the key substantive pluralist challenge; that is, the unique pluralist challenge that is both strong enough to be *able to move* the actors towards the elaboration and adoption of the pluralist building blocks, as well as sufficiently sound in order that they elaborate and adopt the *truly sound* set of pluralist building blocks compatible with that intact respect. This key challenge, unique only to this sound version of substantive pluralism, is elaborated in section 2. This sets the stage for the discussion in the last chapter, where it is then observed how such a sound pluralist approach not only further refines the substantive building blocks observed thus far, but above all also leads to the actors' own elaboration of the key further pluralist building blocks in the field of democracy. This completes the picture of the fully sound conception of constitutional pluralism. Through its route Europe opens up no less than the opportunity for humanity to reach a further historic stage of democracy, one that was unattainable thus far throughout our monist age. Such a morally superior conception of constitutional pluralism at the same time avoids all the weaknesses observed above either with the procedural or the current variants of the more substantive branches.

1. Liberal Legitimacy and the Intact Respect*

1.1 Europe and democracy

The argument for a particular variant of the intact equal respect as the only possible foundation of any sound pluralist conception will expose the sound potential of this

* This section is composed of parts of my longer article on the issue of liberal legitimacy and equal respect. The original publication is that by Ratio Juris. K. Jaklic, "Liberal Legitimacy and the Question of Respect", Ratio Juris, forthcoming in the September 2014 issue.

respect. The latter will be distinguished from the less intact versions of respect such as those implicit in the thinner, more methodological, variants of equal respect that appear in both more proceduralized branches. At the same time, we will see that the intact equal respect also goes beyond the inchoate notions of respect implicit in the foundations of both more substantive pluralist branches. Before engaging in that part of the inter-theoretical exchange and potentially making any improvement in the key area we must, however, first set things in context. As noted, the claim of the superior conception is going to be about democracy. Let us then first say a few words about the context of Europe and democracy, which will then naturally lead to our discussion on the concept of equal respect itself while crucially informing the rest of that discussion.

It is conventionally understood that democracy is one of the biggest problems in European integration. The so-called "democratic deficit" is seen as the most serious disease of the new Europe. Some think that it is fatally malignant and that we ought, in order to preserve democracy, to revert to the old context of fully sovereign and democratic nation-states. Others believe that, given the rest of the advantages brought by the EU in this age of globalization, we ought to try to live with it. What unites the various traditional perspectives is the conventional view that the globalizing Europe clearly suffered on democratic grounds, that it continues to do so, and that further strengthening of EU institutions would probably not be the best thing for democratic values.

This is indeed a serious concern, as well as an immense practical problem. On the one hand, the EU institutions and some influential member states are eager to continue the process of integration irrespective of the alleged democratic weaknesses. They refer to other necessities that call for such further development. On the other hand, others protest fiercely. They feel they are being led by elites far removed from the base, and that further strengthening of Europe is thus equal to stealing power from those who are the only ones entitled to it: the people. The failure to ratify the Constitution for Europe as well as the serious problems with the ratification of the Lisbon Treaty and the rising discussions about some member states leaving the EU are among the manifestations of these deeply rooted feelings.

Indeed, the puzzle of democracy in Europe is intricate and has reached a stage at which many think it is hopeless. This is not a good time for democracy. Or, such is the conventional view. In my broader work on democracy, however, I propose a radically different thesis.[1] The argument is that, though currently deep in its democratic deficit, Europe has paradoxically found itself at an unprecedented historic context that opens the possibility of providing the concept of democracy with improvements of historic proportions. I mean proportions that are comparable in their breadth and significance only perhaps to the "first coming"[2] of democracy

[1] K. Jaklic, *Democracy's Third Coming: Europe as a Route to Humanity's Third Historic Stage of Democracy*, monograph manuscript, forthcoming, currently on file with Harvard University Law Library, and with author.

[2] J. Dunn, *Setting the People Free: The Story of Democracy* (London: Atlantic Books, 2005) 23.

to human history in ancient Greece and its "second coming"[3] in the aftermath of the French and American Revolutions. I argue that both traditional views on Europe and democracy are underpinned by their conventional assumptions about democracy and are thus situated within too narrow a perspective. Observed from a deeper and more historical perspective, there may be an elegant solution to the seemingly hopeless puzzle. The elegant way out of the puzzle, it is suggested, ultimately leads to a "third leap" of democracy that originates in Europe as a result of that new post-sovereign (ie pluralist) context that now enables such an improvement for the first time. If true, this not only enables the Old Continent to solve its current weakness, but to actually turn it into a historic solution—one not only for Europe, but potentially for the world and the entire democratic project. Provided that, in this new pluralist context, we enshrine things correctly at the level of Europe's constitutional foundation and its essential constitutional principles, this would then gradually, but inevitably, lead humanity towards the full-blown realization of the third democratic stage. This opportunity for the democratic project thus originates precisely in the idea of pluralism correctly understood.[4]

Any project with the democratic aim of that sort will inevitably have a starting point in some deep foundations. I mean foundations at a level even prior to the needed essential constitutional principles. Such ultimate foundations are just as crucial since they give rise to those essentials in the first place. And here, at this deepest level, we are of course not working on a clean slate. Long before our current constitutional moment, theorists have tirelessly pursued the question of how to construct the best political system. Naturally, among the different groups of approaches there are those that are more promising for this kind of democratic objective than others, as well as those that would not be capable of unleashing such a democratic potential.

At one end there is the wide-ranging group of traditional approaches that do not take sufficiently into account the reality of reasonable pluralism. The latter is a fact about our human condition that only the age of modern democratic society, more than any other era thus far, has managed to reveal in its full force. By ignoring the latter and instead externally (*heteronomously*) prescribing more than the "other" could under such disagreement reasonably endorse, these traditional approaches usually prematurely close off the possibility of a political system that aspires to government by consent. Yet only in the case of maximum possible approximation to the latter type of political system could the ideal of every individual's self-rule, of democracy, be fulfilled to the highest possible degree.

At the other end there are those who seem to have taken the fact of reasonable pluralism too seriously. Their reaction to the revelation of the deep disagreement has been the conclusion that no common government under law (as distinct from that representing mere power) is possible at all, let alone government under the kind of law that would make its divided constituents self-ruling. Those seeking the most promising foundation for their project of seizing the historic opportunity in

[3] Dunn (n 2) 71. [4] Jaklic (n 1).

Europe thus could not fruitfully search at this end either. As the first group of approaches, so also this second one (although each does so for different reasons) in and of itself stifles the great opportunity of the new context and is unable to realize its historic potential. Yet to throw away the opportunity so easily would be, as my work on Europe and this opportunity aspires to show,[5] clearly too great a price for humanity to pay.

There is, however, a group of approaches that is more promising for our democratic project. This group is situated somewhere between both poles. It is the one that takes reasonable pluralism seriously and yet despite this still does not give up the hope that a common political system, to which every constituent could reasonably consent and thus also in a sense turn herself into its author, could nonetheless be conceived of and arise in practice. In other words, the quest is about how the ideal of fully self-ruling individuals could at least be approximated to as much as it is attainable in the imperfect conditions of this world, and about how a potential common system achieving that could possibly last over the long run. These approaches could be described as those being concerned with the quest for liberal legitimacy of a political order, where the term "liberal" should be broadly understood.[6]

It is within this group of approaches alone that one could potentially find the sound foundation for the project of unleashing that democratic potential of the new pluralist context in Europe, the foundation that would not thwart that new opportunity already at an early stage along the lines of the approaches at both opposite ends. Nonetheless, the leading theories in the field of liberal legitimacy—including the pluralist theories examined in this work—are, at this moment, not yet in the position simply to point to the exact foundation that Europe's democratic project truly needs in order to succeed. The crucial element of the foundation that could do the work for us still seems to be missing from the strand. In order to provide the sound foundation for our project, the idea of liberal legitimacy would therefore either need to be slightly further refined or at least clarified to the degree that the element becomes apparent and accepted as an indispensable part of that idea itself.

The missing element concerns a particular quality of equal respect between human beings as the bearers of the kind of dignity that nothing else in this world possesses. It is of course characteristic precisely of the strand of liberal legitimacy that, at its deepest foundations, it inevitably implies some variant of this respect. That was no exception for the examined pluralist theories either; as members of the liberal legitimacy strand broadly understood they too, as we saw, were ultimately,

[5] Jaklic (n 1); for the condensed argument, see Chapter 10, this book.

[6] Note that it is not that only the theories characterized as liberal in the mainstream sense can be included in this group. A wide range of approaches that would initially be thought of as being, say, critical, or sceptical (which would signal the second group described above), could not but, in the last analysis, fall into the intermediate approach of liberal legitimacy broadly understood. For an especially illuminating clarification, see F. Michelman, "A Civilized Man: Morton Horwitz Struggles with 'Fundamental Law'" in D. Hamilton and A. Brophy (eds), *Transformations in American Legal History: Law, Ideology and Methods* (Cambridge, MA: Harvard University Press, 2011).

and quite emphatically so, about equal respect and individual autonomy. Recall here our discussions on their ultimate values, their meta-contents.

Nonetheless, it is too often the case that the quality of respect needed for liberal legitimacy, and in our case the third democratic advancement, to succeed is either not sufficiently elaborated or is even replaced by some insufficient quality of respect under which liberal legitimacy and its further democratic advancement through history cannot succeed in the first place. In what follows, discussion of the central figure of the strand, John Rawls, who seems to have been aware of the difficulty and struggled with it himself, will first help shed some light on this problem that is now only reinforced in the case of pluralism and our examined pluralists in particular. The focus of the analysis will then move to the positive aspect of the argument—towards the elaboration of the fully intact version of equal respect that would meet the required quality. That will clarify why only that kind of equal respect could possibly constitute the sound foundation through which the project of liberal legitimacy and its further advancement of democracy could potentially succeed in the first place. This is the only way in which pluralism could realize the new democratic opportunity of the new European context, and likewise the only way in which it could still escape the challenges as were identified in the previous chapter.

1.2 Rawls and liberal legitimacy

Rawls's theory of liberal legitimacy—his "political liberalism"—is ultimately centered around one core issue, which he terms "the problem of political liberalism." It is the following:

> How is it possible that there may exist over time a stable and just society of free and equal citizens profoundly divided by reasonable though incompatible religious, philosophical, and moral doctrines? Put another way: How is it possible that deeply opposed though reasonable comprehensive doctrines may live together and all affirm the [common] political conception of a constitutional regime?[7]

The element causing the "problem" is the fact of *reasonable* pluralism. Our condition reflects, as Rawls explains, not simply "a pluralism of comprehensive religious, philosophical, and moral doctrines," but "a pluralism of incompatible yet *reasonable* comprehensive doctrines."[8] For a representative of the liberal legitimacy strand this plurality of incompatible yet *reasonable* doctrines is the necessary consequence of "the exercise of human reason within the framework of the free institutions of a constitutional democratic regime."[9] The irresistible conviction by Rawls as the proponent of liberal legitimacy is that this reasonable disagreement cannot but be recognized and respected within a culture of a democratic society. But if that is so, then the interesting problem/question is indeed that of how is it possible, in the circumstances of such respect for all the differing yet reasonable

[7] J. Rawls, *Political Liberalism* (New York, NY: Columbia University Press, 1993) at xx.

[8] Rawls (n 7) at xx (emphasis supplied). [9] Rawls (n 7).

views, that "coercion implicit in any possible practice of legal ordering, of government by law, can possibly be morally appropriate"?[10] How is it possible that in such circumstances there may exist over time such a stable and just common regime?

Long-term stability of a common constitutional regime within the context of reasonable pluralism, characteristic of the culture of democratic society, is therefore the ultimate quest of Rawls's project. More precisely, it is stability understood in moral (just) terms, not simply strategic (*modus vivendi*) ones. The aim is not simply to elaborate a common political conception that would attract agreement in some existing circumstances. Instead it is to elaborate a conception that is also just in the eyes of its free and equal adherents who all affirm the fact of reasonable pluralism as well as the need for a common regime.[11] The point is this: even if existing circumstances in society changed with time, and adherents of a particular comprehensive view got the opportunity to increase their relative power by adopting a conception more favorable for them, they would refrain from doing so and would instead still endorse the old (ie the just) conception. This is how Rawls's notion of moral (just) stability differs from the purely strategic (*modus vivendi*) one.[12]

1.2.1 Solving the problem through deflection and respect

Deflection

What, according to Rawls, is supposed to solve the problem and attract agreement by the would-be adherents to a common constitutional regime? The answer is: a particular new content of the envisioned regime. It is the content which is—in the circumstances of reasonable pluralism—believed to be so persuasive for the holders of all those conflicting but reasonable views that they could not but eventually accept it as morally superior.

This content is reached by a general strategy of deflection into a broader conception of justice. The general idea is that we adjust our primary view about public justice for all, for this is presumably still not sufficiently receptive to the existing difference, and adopt an even broader conception of it that takes more seriously into account the fact of reasonable pluralism and the corresponding need for further deflection in the light of it. We may call this broader—deflected—conception of justice "legitimate justice," or simply "legitimacy."[13]

While belonging to this abstract general strategy, Rawls's particular variant of deflection also has its own distinctive features. These result in a particular content of the common regime that can and should, according to him, be agreed between citizens in circumstances of reasonable disagreement. One possible result is of course

[10] F. Michelman, "Ida's Way: Constructing the Respect-Worthy Governmental System" (2003) 72 Fordham Law Review 345.

[11] F. Micheman, "The Subject of Liberalism" (1994) 46 Stanford Law Review 1807, 1816; Rawls (n 7) at 145–8.

[12] Rawls (n 7) at 148.

[13] F. Michelman, "Faith and Obligation, or What Makes Sandy Sweat?" (2003) 38 Tulsa Law Review 651, 645, fn 19.

his well-known device of the original position that first leads to his two principles of justice. From those then further flow also several constitutional essentials and together with the principles of justice they complete the full picture of the regime.

Respect

This is one possible content of the morally legitimate regime towards which, according to Rawls, the reasonable can and should deflect. Recall, however, that it was moral stability that was considered, quite correctly by Rawls himself, as the problem that liberal legitimacy aims to solve. Why is it then possible that the system of this or similar deflected kind would arise in the first place, and where would the continued stability of such a regime come from? The fact that the regime could only arise via deflection does not yet tell the whole story.

Rawls writes that "those who grow up under just basic institutions [ie institutions flowing from his proposed deflection] acquire a basic sense of justice and a reasoned allegiance to those institutions sufficient to render them stable."[14] This "stability is secured by sufficient motivation of the appropriate kind acquired under just institutions," which assures that citizens "act willingly so as to give one another justice over time."[15] What kind of motivation does Rawls have in mind?

The "motivation of the appropriate kind" is a particular type of reciprocal respect between the free and equal. This respect both underlies the very foundation of Rawls's vision of liberal legitimacy, and thus dictates the particular type of deflection in the first place, as well as then functioning as the very catalyst (the key stimulus) for ensuring that such a cooperation in fact arises and persists over time.

Rawls's would-be citizens are rational and reasonable. They aspire to the common regime. By being rational they know that such a common regime would enhance their good as well as the good of "others" with whom they would end up cooperating. By being reasonable (having not only the capacity for pursuing the good, but also the capacity for justice) they also know that they cannot do other than respect those "others" as being no less free and equal than themselves. The common regime, they know, could only be pursued in the just way, one that gave due respect to those with whom the would-be citizens anticipate cooperation. For Rawls the just way is not mere *modus vivendi*; in fact, that is the unjust way, according to which the would-be citizens need those "others" because of their own selfish interests *alone*. In contrast, the just way for Rawls is when cooperation with the "others" (the anticipated fellow citizens) is sought not solely for one's own sake, but also for the sake of those "others" who ought to be *respected* as free and equal individuals. The would-be citizens, who have the capacity for justice and know that the common regime in the midst of disagreement could arise only through deflection, go ahead and engage in their deflection in precisely *such* a (ie just) spirit. For Rawls, the preferred operationalization of such a just deflection (though by no means the only one possible) is, again, when the would-be cooperators treat each other through the lens of his original position and its veil of ignorance.

[14] Rawls (n 7) at 142. [15] Rawls (n 7) at 142–3.

Now, when they proceed and deflect in this way, something important occurs. The "others" notice that the would-be citizens act as they do (ie deflect from their deeply held comprehensive views and towards the content of the legitimate regime), also for the sake of their (ie the "others'") good. The "others" experience and feel the respect with which they are being treated. This begins to move them. Inevitably they start learning and internalizing that respect themselves. In addition, knowing that this behavior would bring even more benefit, for them as well as those who respected them first, they too begin to be willing to reciprocate in this practice of deflection, of respect. Rawls writes that in this way they become more and more "ready and willing to do their part in those arrangements, provided that they have reasonable assurance that others [ie our 'would-be citizens'] will also do their part."[16] When this practice of deflection on the basis of a particular kind of respect continues so that "persons with evident intention strive to do their part in the just or fair arrangements, citizens tend to develop trust and confidence in them [so that gradually] this trust and confidence becomes stronger and more complete as the success of cooperative arrangements is sustained over a longer time."[17] This is how it is possible for the common system based on legitimacy (deflection on the basis of equal respect) not only to arise, but then also to be sustained over the long run.

Importantly, this "moral psychology," where would-be citizens are mutually "moved" by one another, does not originate, as Rawls makes clear, simply "in the science of human nature."[18] It is not simply a claim about the nature of human beings, of how we are, psychologically speaking. Rather, it is a philosophical argument about political virtues that we must "learn" and adopt ("apply and affirm") in order to realize the "ideal of citizenship" and thereby also enable the project to succeed.[19] Rawls's conception, or more precisely, its underlying variant of respect, requires the education and raising of *this* kind of citizen. It is only then that the project could succeed.

It is important for our argument to note at this point that, in such an ideal of citizenship, there ultimately seem to be two interrelated answers as to why, in the first place, Rawls's conception should raise the kind of citizens who would be deflecting in the described way. It follows from this account that one part of the answer, and so one reason for respect, is simply that the fellow human beings with whom one anticipates cooperating are owed this for being the bearers of dignity who ought to be treated with respect. However, that is not all. It seems likewise to follow from this account that this cooperation is at the same time inevitably *also* about producing and increasing the "goods of union"[20] in which *all* must benefit as judged by the situation prior to the common project. The Rawlsian citizen, or would-be citizen, is willing to engage in the deflection only in so far as "others" also "do their part". Only then could the citizen herself also benefit by getting also *her* share in the increased goods of the common system. Without the others'

16 Rawls (n 7) at 86.
17 Rawls (n 7) at 433.
18 Rawls (n 7) at 86–8.
19 Rawls (n 7) at 87.
20 Michelman (n 10) at 346.

ability or willingness to reciprocate, to cooperate, there would therefore still be insufficient reason for Rawls's citizens to deflect in the first place. The second, and equally vital, motivation for Rawls's "ideal citizen" to deflect is thus the fact (the condition) that she, too, would get something *in return* for her deflecting in the way that gives "others" justice. Indeed, this explains why Rawls keeps adding at numerous places in his text that proviso that his citizens should be willing to deflect according to justice, but only "provided that others also do their part." While each of the two reasons (motivations) is necessary, neither taken alone is sufficient: only together do they provide the whole reason, the "motivation of the appropriate kind," for the deflection. Or so, at least, it is how it appears.

If all is right, only this full account provides us with the complete picture of the version of respect ultimately underlying Rawls's theory. It is a unique variant of reciprocal respect that combines two distinct rationales (conditions), both of which must be met in order to really have the correct picture of Rawls's respect. It is this unique respect that then inescapably also determines the corresponding unique kind of deflection and content (the original position, the two principles of justice and constitutional essentials) of Rawls's vision of a legitimate regime. It is also this particular kind of respect that is supposed to solve the problem of deep modern disagreement so as to make, despite that disagreement, the stability of the common regime and the enjoyment of its goods of union possible over the long run. As Rawls explains, this type of mutual respect that citizens learn through the process of moral psychology, these "very great virtues" that "make a constitutional regime possible," then ultimately outweighs whatever other values conflict with them:

> When these virtues are widespread in a society and sustain its political conception of justice, they constitute a very great public good, part of society's political capital. Thus, the values that conflict with the political conception of justice and its sustaining virtues may be normally outweighed because they come into conflict with the very conditions that make fair social cooperation possible on a footing of mutual respect.[21]

1.2.2 Is Rawls's type of respect insufficient?

The temptation of mutual advantage

In Rawls's project on legitimacy, respect between the bearers of dignity thus indeed plays the central role. Given its full picture as explained above the question arises, however, whether the kind of equal respect that Rawls seems to require is truly of sufficient quality to do the key work he expects from it. It seems to be conditional, and thus still quite self-centered, in the sense that it is given only under the condition that it is also given back.

To be sure, Rawls's respect is not the one that Hobbes's and David Gauthier's (1986) political theory share. These authors teach that the *sole* reason for deflection (kind of "respect") is *mutual advantage*. There is no other condition to your action but the satisfaction of your pure egoistic self-interest. We saw that Rawls departs

[21] Rawls (n 7) at 157.

from this approach in that he clearly requires the first of his preconditions for deflection. At the same time, Rawls's conception does not seem to be an entirely pure version of the intact respect either. The latter would be when the *sole* reason for deflection is the mere moral duty that we owe this to the "other" as the bearer of dignity, a moral duty, then, that exists and requires deflection irrespective of whether or not the "other" at the same time also complies with her own duty. In contrast to this strategy, Rawls's vision does not seem to exclude entirely from its underlying notion of respect the element of mutual advantage. Unlike either of the approaches described, its variant of underlying respect seems, as was seen, to require *both* preconditions. Respect (deflection) should not be given unless the first *as well as* the second reason for respect are met. If you, too, are therefore not ultimately better off from your deflection, from your act of respect, then there is, on this reading of Rawls, *not yet sufficient* moral reason for you to engage in the deflection (respect) in the first place. While this is different from the fully intact respect, it still implies equal respect that is, as will soon become apparent, too conditional to do the work that Rawls (as well as our democratic project) needs from it.

That this is how the foundation of Rawls's theory can be understood seems to be suggested not only by parts of his own text, but also by the fact that some of the leading authors in the field read him this way.[22] I have examined this in detail elsewhere.[23] So let us just note at this point that this kind of respect corresponds more to the methodological strategies of defining respect as observed above in the case of both more procedural variants of constitutional pluralism. At the least, we saw that those methodological strategies willingly accommodate this type of respect when the actors under pluralism choose to act and define themselves according to it. Moreover, even the respect assumed by the substantive branches is not immune from ultimately being an instance of this kind of less than fully intact respect. Recall for instance the fact that those two conceptions too were ultimately confined to Europe alone, making the latter more or less a monist project in relation to the outsiders.

And its fatal trap

The temptation to instil an element of mutual advantage into the notion of respect seems obvious. Yet to surrender to it would be fatal for the project on liberal legitimacy in general as well as our democratic project in particular. To establish and maintain a political system on the foundation of this kind of respect cannot avoid maintaining and even generating certain serious deficiencies in legitimacy and self-rule (democracy). This holds in relation to the system's own people (members of majority and its "internal others") as well as those people who happen to find themselves outside such a system, the "external others."

[22] See my discussion of those authors in Jaklic (n *). Although still others, some of whom have worked as Rawls's personal colleagues, would like to interpret him at all costs (even if subsequent revision of some of his concepts and the explicit language on mutual advantage was needed for that) as following the path of the unconditional respect.

[23] Jaklic (n *).

Firstly, let's consider the "external others." According to such a respect it would be possible, indeed even most natural, that in their forming a common regime people would still get together in this or that monist way. Rawls himself makes it explicit[24] that he is constructing his theory with the context of the sovereign nation-state-type of constitutional democracy in mind, and his parties to the contract are envisioned as getting together in order to establish a common project of this sort. Similarly, all our examined pluralists are content with the self-standing constitutional actors in Europe choosing to establish their pluralist polity in a way that is confined to Europe and thus still externally monist. It follows that implying some element of mutual advantage that the would-be citizens/actors not only get together by their own free will, but inevitably also get to choose freely their contracting parties, their would-be fellow nationals/actors, in the first place. The latter is the assumed pre-theoretical fact precisely under this kind of respect. It is the approach that does not require full justice already at this initial, pre-theoretical stage of inclusion.

In my other work[25] I show in some detail how the idea of organizing democracy in such a monist way,[26] while being noble in some aspects, is unfortunately also highly inadequate in others. For instance, it still cannot prevent the situation in which the bearers of dignity are, on the basis of mere location of their birth, made radically unequal in their basic democratic powers, in their capacity for self-rule. This is so despite the fact that we firmly believe, at the same time, that the ultimate goods of democracy belong to the bearers of dignity simply because they are such, not for any other contingent characteristic, such as birth, race, wealth, success, and failure. I show, moreover, that, by tending to bring together the more privileged actors who benefit more by cooperating with each other than with some weaker "others," this kind of monism itself generates this problem. Consistently with the still too-conditional type of respect on which it is built, such a regime is unable sufficiently to advance the democratic good to members of those other nation-states who happen to be either unable or, as of this point, unwilling to fully cooperate. Nor is this kind of monist regime, in cases when it does happen to share some of these goods, able to do so in the fully genuine spirit. It shares on the basis of its inherent requirement that it, too, needs thereby to be better off, to get something in return for its sharing. Due to its inabilities in relation to "external others," this variant of respect does not seem to be only too conditional, but in effect also insufficiently universal.

These are some examples of the problems that arise in relation to the "external others" when the theory is underpinned by something less than the fully intact equal respect. We need not explore this aspect further at this point.[27] It needs only

[24] Rawls (n 7) at 11; see also his, *A Theory of Justice* (revised edn, Cambridge, MA: Harvard University Press, 1999) 7.

[25] Jaklic (n 1).

[26] Be it nation-state monism, or some internal pluralism that is still monist in relation to "external others" (the model assumed by our pluralists examined earlier).

[27] For a comprehensive analysis of all the "external" democratic deficits arising out of such a foundational respect, see Jaklic (n 1). For a brief summary see Chapter 10, sections 1 and 3.

to be added that some authors from the liberal legitimacy strand have recently themselves begun noticing the difficulty. Without developing the problem's multiple concrete ramifications as to democracy, Nussbaum nonetheless observes, for instance, that the approaches assuming this kind of respect, or those allowing it to freely enter the construction of the regime, err at their very foundations. In effect they create a select privileged group of contracting people or constitutional actors

> as their basic unit. For reasons internal to the structure of such theories, they are bound to do so. Such theories cannot provide adequate approaches to problems of global justice, that is, justice that addresses inequalities between human beings whatever their [place of birth].[28] [The difficulty] concerns the role of nationality or place of birth in influencing people's basic life chances... Both Kant and Rawls do recognize the importance of confronting issues of justice between nations. But the logic of their theories leads them to pose this question at a second stage, and derivatively... Today this... approach, entrenched in the practices of wealthy nations and in our systems of international law, is proving increasingly inadequate to the world in which we live. There are staggering differences between rich and poor nations in all the areas most central to basic life chances... Even the best attempts [by this] tradition to solve these problems... prove insufficient.[29]

Interestingly, in concluding her remarks on this point, Nussbaum, too, seems to sense that any potential solution to the problem could only be found in some higher variant of respect as the more promising basis for the theory. This would require, she writes,

> admitting from the start that the point of the contract is not, and cannot be, mutual advantage among "rough equals." It must be human fellowship, and human respect, in some more expansive sense.[30]

Secondly, problems stemming from such a conditional type of respect inevitably also affect conditions *inside* the sovereign democratic state itself, thereby preventing the fullest possible release of self-rule (democracy) to the monist regime's own citizens as well as its "internal others."

For instance, any theory that comes to construct liberal legitimacy through the monist formation needs of course to concede that, in such circumstances, other groups will also make their own *monist* regimes, be it in the nation-state monist form, or the form of an internally pluralist community that is externally monist. If so, our own group of bearers of dignity, that is, the citizens forming our own monist formation, will perforce be excluded as the ultimate authors and addressees of authority from that other territory and its monist regime. This will be so regardless of how profoundly the decisions of that other regime may happen to affect our citizens' lives. This problem includes both the loss of our citizens' *normative* title to full authorship (itself an inherent part of the fullest possible state of self-rule and

[28] M. Nussbaum, *Frontiers of Justice: Disability, Nationality, Species Membership* (Cambridge, MA: Harvard University Press, 2006) 92–3.

[29] Nussbaum (n 28) at 20–1.

[30] Nussbaum (n 28) at 270.

dignity), as well as the relative obstruction of their *practical* ability to fully engage in things affecting their lives.

Moreover, the conditional respect between citizens of the same monist formation (between the "I" and the "other" inside that state) cannot but, in some crucial circumstances, breed the feeling of self-condemnation, degradation, and resentment in the thus-respected "other," while also impacting destructively on the moral personality of the "I" engaged in such a conditional respect. The problem is most evident when the conditional type of respect is exercised in relation to that kind of "other" who, despite the increased opportunities of the common regime, happens to fall short of her goals in life and finds herself in distress. Concrete examples can of course be drawn from all sorts of contexts, but let us imagine the "other" who, say, has not succeeded in the material sense and instead finds herself in the position of being dependent on others and their social protection. The (self-)affirmation of the "other's" human worth—the healing of her dignity—is at stake in such circumstances. Yet, to condition your respect in such circumstances (your deflection through which you provide the needed social minimum) with the benefit you *too* must *ultimately* receive in return (your share in the goods of union) is not to engage in the fully genuine affirmation of the "other's" human dignity, of her priceless worth irrespective of achievement or failure. A human being senses all too well the difference between being respected due to their priceless humanity alone, or due to that humanity coupled also with returning benefit that inevitably makes genuine respect conditional and thus no longer fully genuine. To give them the respect of this kind is therefore indeed both "destructive to the giver and [even further] degrading to the receiver."[31] This makes the feeling of self-condemnation, resentment, and degradation even deeper. With this failure to heal the "other's" sense of true worth, and thus dignity, citizens of such a state waste the opportunity for generating the highest level of autonomy, the highest state of self-rule (ie democracy).

Thirdly, all the examples observed thus far are instances of more or less direct obstructions to releasing the maximum possible state of self-rule in human society. Be it in relation to the foreign bearers of dignity, or those that are the monist formation's own citizens, the very act of giving such an insufficient conditional respect creates the deficit. In addition to this intrinsic curtailment, there is, however, also a powerful instrumental effect that such a type of equal respect generates. It is here where one can observe not only further obstruction of self-rule (democracy), but also that fatal nature of such a respect for the project on liberal legitimacy itself.

The central issue for liberal legitimacy is, as Rawls himself presented so well, the question of long-term moral stability of the common regime. This is indeed the quest. Yet it is precisely the act of planting the conditional type of respect (be it its stronger or weaker variant) into the foundation of a legitimacy theory, and thus to the foundation of the rising common regime, that ultimately disables this quest. The conditional type of respect and its consequences breed, as it was seen, the sense of unworthiness in those who fall short under such a regime, and it does so for the

[31] C. Taylor, *Sources of the Self: The Making of the Modern Identity* (Cambridge: Cambridge University Press, 1992) 516.

"external others" as well as the formation's own citizens. The "other" feels inferiority, self-condemnation, resentment. Now, it can be argued with force—and by careful analysis of our recurring history—that such a "threatened sense of unworthiness"[32] works not as the force binding human beings together, the effect that Rawls otherwise correctly relied on a respect to achieve. On the contrary, it works as a hidden source for accumulation of political, ideological, religious, nationalistic, and other kinds of extremism. Over a longer period of time crises are inevitable. Golden ages, when the logic of mutual advantage happens to bring enough for everyone, perish. It is then that the subterranean process of ongoing subtle accumulation of such feelings over time proves most fatal. Sooner or later it leads to an outbreak, with war and terrorism being but two most typical examples of the final upshot. The workings of this recurrent phenomenon in the context of Europe are observed in detail in my other work.[33] Those examples are, however, but concrete manifestations of the general phenomenon. Charles Taylor has described it as the rebounded reflex of the felt-inward unworthiness, or "the projection of evil outward." It works in the following way:

> The bad, the failure is now identified with other people or group. My conscience is clear because I oppose them, but what can I do? They stand in the way of universal beneficence; they must be liquidated. This becomes particularly virulent on the extremes of political spectrum, in a way which Dostoyevsky has explored in unparallel depths . . . In our day as in his, many young people are driven to . . . extremism, sometimes by truly terrible conditions, but also by a need to give meaning to their lives. And since meaninglessness is frequently accompanied by a sense of guilt, they sometimes respond to a strong ideology of polarization, in which one recovers a sense of direction as well as purity by lining up in implacable opposition to the forces of darkness. The more implacable, even violent the opposition, the more the polarity is represented as absolute, and the greater the sense of separation from evil and hence purity.[34]

The lower type of respect[35] would thus paradoxically cut against the central goal of his own project—to enable long-term stability of a just regime and of its ever-growing increase in the goods of political union. If Rawls's type of respect is indeed such, then the seed of destruction has been planted into the very roots of his otherwise noble aspiration. The same point applies also to all theories of constitutional pluralism that allow for less than some fully intact respect to enter their foundations, or their more applicative spheres where the pluralist formations are then being constructed. This insufficiently unconditional and insufficiently universal breeding of the substantive building blocks is exactly what ultimately threatens, as observed above, to make them insufficiently distinct from monism in the decisive sphere of the *what* as well as in relation to the "external others." Only some different, higher, type of respect could potentially perhaps still do the work that the project on liberal legitimacy, and its European manifestation through

[32] Taylor (n 31) at 516. [33] Jaklic (n 1).

[34] Taylor (n 31) at 516.

[35] Provided that it truly *is* that respect that Rawls implies. For the complete discussion of the puzzle on this point, see Jaklic (n *).

constitutional pluralism and its historic advancement of democracy, truly needs. In order to avoid the problem of "rebounded reflex" this respect would need to be such as to extend the good of self-rule to the needy "other" "for free," as it were. It would need to be understood that the good belongs to the "other" not because, in addition to being a bearer of dignity, she is also giving something back in return. Rather, it belongs to her exclusively because of her existence as a bearer of dignity *alone*. Precisely some variant of this kind of respect could perhaps still have that needed potential to heal and to glue human beings closer towards common enterprise(s) that could persevere despite crises that are inevitably going to recur and recur.

My personal view is that Rawls himself became aware of the potential problem and actually sensed that only some fully intact variant of respect could do what he needed. This moves me towards the camp of those who think that, despite the clear tension in his theory, Rawls could nonetheless not be best understood through the lens of mutual advantage.[36] Among other indications for that, there is also some interesting textual evidence, which only exacerbates the tension within his theory on this point.[37]

When Rawls most closely describes the process of breeding the needed motivation (that equal respect, that binding glue) that his citizens need to learn, internalize, and employ, he refers to the example of a family while then pointing out that this same phenomenon can, as he believes, also spill over to the level between citizens of a common system:

> The parents, we may suppose, love the child and in time the child comes to love and to trust his parents. How does this change in the child come about? . . . He is made aware that he is appreciated for his own sake by what are to him the imposing and powerful persons in his world. He experiences parental affection as unconditional [*sic*!]; they care for his presence and spontaneous acts, and the pleasure they take in him is not dependent upon disciplined performances that contribute to the well-being of others . . . Gradually, he . . . affirms his self-esteem . . . and connects [his parents] with his sense of his own worth . . . Given that family institutions express their love by caring for his good, then the child, recognizing their evident love of him, comes to love them.[38]

"The second stage covers," Rawls then goes on to explain, "a wide range of cases depending on the association in question," and eventually comes to "include the national community as a whole."[39] In the same way as in the family, he seems to be saying, our attitudes in those wider contexts, too, arise from the fellow citizens' unconditional affirmation of our worth. That is the affirmation that does not pose any additional condition, such as that the granting of it is given under condition of receiving something (the same) in return *as well.*

Note that the affirmation of worth that Rawls describes in the context of the family is clearly unconditional. The parents genuinely love their child and do so irrespective of her actions. If all is well, they indeed love her irrespective of any

36 See n 21. 37 For the whole analysis of the puzzle, see Jaklic (n *).
38 Rawls (n 24) at 405–6, 429. 39 Rawls (n 24) at 409, 433.

achievement or failure whatsoever. They do not ask anything in return either. This "unconditional" affirmation, to use Rawls's term, of the child's worth, and this alone, is what does "the trick." This has the effect that Rawls so badly needs for his own project to succeed. It cannot of course be assumed that if you change this key element, which Rawls himself describes so well, you get the same result as before. Rawls would hardly use the example from the context of the clear unconditional respect, and even less would he explicitly refer to it as "unconditional," unless he assumed that of course he had the same, unconditional type of respect in mind.

As interesting as the question of Rawls's own true intentions may be, it is not, however, decisive for our purposes. It need not be claimed that the correct reading of Rawls is the mixed contractarian or the non-contractarian, and I leave this question, and the obvious tension in his theory, open. For our aim it is enough to acknowledge the critical importance of further improvement, or at least further clarification, on this point for our own project. Without some more sound foundation, the project of liberal legitimacy and thus democracy's third historic advancement could not successfully proceed, nor could those other weaknesses in the existing pluralist theories be cured. The trap of the conditional respect, as we saw, is fatal. We need an improved foundation that would avoid these difficulties. The discussion therefore now turns to that.

1.3 The sound foundation

1.3.1 Agapeistic respect

Traces of the kind of equal respect I have in mind appear early in the history of thought. I would argue that, due to its distinctive quality, the most basic essence of this respect was sensed already in the writings of some ancient Greek philosophers. Although they never developed it as a concept in any systematic way, they clearly sensed its distinctive nature as they came across it in various different topics they discussed.

Aristotle writes in his *Eudemian Ethics* of the special attitude (*agapao*) towards the "other" when one "grieves with someone who grieves not [also] for some ulterior motive" but in a way that is fully genuine, that is like "mothers who grieve with their children," or like "birds that share each other's pain."[40] To act on this principle is different, he observes, from that when "slaves in relation to their masters share their grief" not solely "for their masters' sake," but either solely, or also, "because when in grief they [ie the masters] are harsh."[41] Aristotle then also explains that this same high ideal ("the same principle") "applies also in the case of joy": when one "rejoices for no other reason than because the other is rejoicing."[42]

[40] Aristotle, *Eudemian Ethics*, 1240a (*Perseus Digital Library*) <http://www.perseus.tufts.edu/hopper/text?doc=Perseus:text:1999.01.0050> accessed 22 October 2013. The example with "birds" may appear puzzling to a modern reader, but it makes sense when one realizes that it was widely noted in ancient natural science that a stork would be consumed with the nest in a fire, rather than fly and abandon its mate and offspring.

[41] Aristotle (n 40) at 1240a.

[42] Aristotle (n 40) at 1240a.

This is different from the principle that one rejoices with the "other" who is rejoicing only provided that one, too, has one's own reason to rejoice.

Another instance of this purely genuine attitude towards the "other" is from *Nicomachean Ethics*. There, at one point, Aristotle speaks of the difference between creditor and benefactor. He explains that one difference is that in the case of the creditor we cannot speak of this high genuine respect for his debtor, of wishing him good unconditionally. "With him," Aristotle writes, "it is not a matter of *agapao*," but instead a matter of "wishing his debtor's preservation" also "for the sake of recovering his [ie the creditor's] money."[43] We are told however that this is different from the case of the benefactor, who "feels friendship and *agapao* for the recipient of his bounty even though he [ie the benefactor] is not getting anything out of him and is never likely to do so."[44]

It is interesting that the word Aristotle uses to describe this genuine treating of (wishing good to) the "other" as (to) oneself, is the then very rare word *agapao*. It is not the common *philein* (love), but *agapao*, an ancient Greek version of a much later term, *agape*, known as the kind of love of your "neighbor" that is no lesser that the love you would accord yourself. This same word, *agapao*, is used by Aristotle to name that same attitude from the passage in his *Eudemian Ethics* that was presented first, above. Whether or not this term had any other, and perhaps several connotations, it could clearly be argued, I think, that one of those was very likely this higher, unconditional treating of the "other", of which Aristotle spoke on both occasions when using this extremely rare term instead of the common *philein*.

Aristotle also uses the term when briefly speaking of artists who have an exaggerated "*agapao* for their own handiwork" precisely because they feel as if their artistic products are part of themselves, and thus love them unconditionally, "as parents love their children."[45] This seems to draw on an earlier work by Plato, who, in one of his even more rare uses of the term, wrote the following in his *Republic*: "For just as poets *agapao* their own poems, and fathers their own sons, so men who have made money take this money seriously as their own creation."[46] Similarly telling is Plato's remark in his *Laws*, where he writes that a step-parent shall "show as much *agapao* for the child whom fate has made an orphan as for his own children," and that he shall thus care with unconditional zeal "for the goods of his nursling as much as for his own goods—or rather, more."[47]

It was thus in ancient Greece at the time of Plato that philosophers started to distinguish and expose this genuinely unconditional treating of the "other". It is not surprising that they often associated it with the context of a family; this type of higher respect (treating the "other" as if the "other" was yourself) is highly demanding, and the family is that primary context in which it clearly *can* succeed regardless of wherever else it also could succeed. Yet, as evident from the Greek literature itself,

[43] Aristotle, *Nicomachean Ethics*, 1167b (*Perseus Digital Library*) <http://www.perseus.tufts.edu/hopper/text?doc=Perseus:text:1999.01.0054> accessed 22 October 2013.

[44] Aristotle (n 43) at 1167b.

[45] Aristotle (n 43) at 1167b, in combination with Aristotle (n 40) at 1240a.

[46] Plato, *Republic*, 330b (*Perseus Digital Library*) <http://www.perseus.tufts.edu/hopper/text?doc=Perseus:text:1999.01.0168> accessed 22 October 2013.

[47] Plato, *Laws*, 228a (*Perseus Digital Library*) <http://www.perseus.tufts.edu/hopper/text?doc=Perseus:text:1999.01.0166> accessed 22 October 2013.

this respect is not confined to the context of a family. It should not be equated with all sorts of affective ties, an "exaggerated *agapao*" as one could say with Aristotle, that a family may also nourish in addition to the genuine treating of the "other". Indeed, the term later changed into *agape* and correspondingly also expanded its meaning to include God's love for humanity as such, and human love for God, as well as the authentically self-giving respect for your "neighbor" generally.[48]

I would like to make it explicit at this point that I am using the term in the most inclusive—that is, "political"[49]—sense, one that could not of course be narrowed to any theistic or non-theistic context and source, nor to any specific cultural community context. This distinctive attitude can be supported by many different and even mutually exclusive sources and comprehensive views while, at the same time, fully retaining the independent, that is, "political," character of its distinctive content. At the same time, I want to make it clear that the term's content is different from methodological or otherwise not fully genuine (conditional) reciprocity under which you may act (also) on all sorts of more self-interested rationales when respecting the "other". This is the opposite of the affirmative, fully authentic *agapeistic* respect, which can generally (though very roughly) also be described as fully genuine, freely giving, non-conditional, and non-self-centered.[50]

Agapeistic respect is thus different from either the stronger or the weaker general strands of the non-intact respect described above. According to those, one does not aim to extend and maximize the good (eg the good of self-rule) to the "other" solely because this way one is better off oneself. Nor does one extend and maximize the good to the "other" out of some combination of intrinsic respect for that "other" coupled with the additional condition of *also* receiving something in return, such as your increased share in the enhanced goods of union that flow from the "other's" required ability and willingness to cooperate. Under the *agapeistic* approach the *sole* reason for extending and maximizing the good to the "other" is instead the mere moral duty that we owe this to the "other" because of that "other's" *mere existence alone.* It is the moral duty that exists and requires such an action on our part irrespective of whether or not the "other" is at the same time also able to comply, or complies, with her own duty. We are giving the good "for free," as it were.

Inherent in such a conception of respect, there is of course also a particular understanding of human dignity. It is exactly the conception of dignity that is not associated with any success, achievement, or failure in life; nor with self-perception of such a success/failure; nor with any capability or willingness for cooperation and

48 In the ancient Greek texts it appears as ἀγαπάω (*agapao*) and ἀγάπῶσι (*agaposi*), or in any of their other derivatives. It is only in the *Septuagint* (3rd century BC) when it first appears as ἀγάπη (agape); see for instance Gen 22:2, 24:67, 29:32.

49 Rawls (n 7).

50 Taylor (n 31) at 516–18, 451; see also his, "Leading a Life" in R. Chang (ed.), *Incommensurability, Incomparability, and Practical Reason* (Cambridge, MA: Harvard University Press, 1997); P. Saurette, "Questioning Political Theory: Charles Taylor's Contrarianism" (2004) 5 Political Theory 723, 728–30. Cf also G. Outka, *Agape: An Ethical Analysis* (New Haven, CT: Yale University Press, 1972) and A. Nygren, *Agape and Eros* (Chicago, IL: University of Chicago Press, 1982).

reciprocity; or whatever other similarly contingent feature. Dignity is, on this conception, instead understood as the awareness and recognition of one's priceless and equal worth already in virtue of one's mere existence as a human being. That alone is what entitles one to the higher version of respect.

All sorts of comprehensive views can serve as the deeper rationale for such a conception of dignity as long as they are not incompatible with the overarching sufficient minimum that constitutes the common "political" content of such a notion of dignity. That sufficient minimum is the undeniable recognition that human beings share the feature of rationality and capacity for justice to a greater degree than anything else in this world. It is that *abstract* humanity, as opposed to the biologically determined concrete capacity of concrete individuals, that is present in each human being *qua* human being and is worthy of awe. If individual human beings with disabilities do not possess the ability *in concreto* this is therefore indeed not a problem for such a conception of dignity.[51] They, too, are undeniably human beings and thus instances of the "being" who came to possess these higher capacities. Their mere existence as such bearers of dignity possessing abstract humanity, quite irrespective of their actual biological inability to exercise it in practice, is thus the reason for their equal respect.[52]

The *agapeistic* version of the intact respect, centered round this particular conception of human dignity, implies several specific features that distinguish it from other, less intensive, variants of respect.

Firstly, and as already seen, unlike either of the two insufficiently intact variants, this respect is *unconditional*. Here the extension of the good (eg of self-rule, of democracy) to its addressees is not conditioned along the lines of "provided that others do the same," or through any other benefit that the givers expect in return for fulfilling their own moral duty. The addressees are not required to cooperate, to give something in return in at least some ultimate sense, but are entitled simply due to their being, irrespective of their achievement, success, or failure.

Secondly, this respect is also fully universal. One aspect of this is that it includes every single bearer of dignity in this world as the rightful and equal addressee of such a respect. Under such a foundation a project of a common political formation could thus not be legitimately designed in a way that would give one group of individuals, such as citizens of a given monist formation who happen to reside over a particular geographical region, preference over other bearers of dignity. The ultimate goal of the common project could therefore no longer be to offer authorship and enhancement of the good of such a project only to its current members as the ultimate addressees/authors of such a project. Instead, it could only be to offer inclusion (including authorship), and enhancement of the good, with respect to *every bearer of dignity* as such in this world.

[51] Rawls (n 24) at 443.

[52] I have argued elsewhere against Martha Nussbaum why I think this is the best reading of Rawls on this point (see Jaklic (n *)).

Thirdly, the other universality aspect of *agapeistic* respect is in the fact that every bearer of dignity must now be recognized as the ultimate addressee of democracy *based on her universal humanity*, not on some other feature that she may also possess. According to this conception, the good is not enhanced *by virtue* of the addressee's membership in a given cooperating group (be it ethnic or civic) engaged in that project, such as is the case under the monist formation, but simply because they possess that universally shared characteristic of being human beings, the bearers of dignity.

Fourthly, there is one further distinctive feature of this type of respect. It is actually not its separate feature, but one that follows from the combination of the unconditional and universal features correctly understood. The fact that one respects the "other" (every single "other") solely due to the "other's" existence as a human being, and that existence *alone*, in and of itself implies, when correctly understood, the fully *genuine* type of respect. That is, one is genuinely willing to give the "other" the same respect as one is giving oneself, whereby this standard is *substantively*, as opposed to procedurally, understood. The respect is thus not genuine when one is giving the "other" some lesser quality of respect (eg includes some further condition for respect) *because* one is also *equally* treating oneself with that same lesser quality of respect or is willing to submit oneself to it. This kind of methodological (procedural) understanding of our principle that one ought to respect the "other" as one respects oneself excludes the possibility of genuine respect. The respect implicit in the principle of treating the "other" as yourself can thus be "genuine" only when it is understood in the substantive sense: when the respect that you accord to yourself is the full respect, one that is genuinely warm-hearted and thus never really gives up on yourself. It is this type of respect that you then ought to give to the "other" as well, and that is inherent in the unconditional universal respect correctly (non-methodologically) understood. This is indeed exactly one of its features that the ancient writers themselves were trying to convey by referring to those examples in which it is most easy to see that the respect is truly warm-hearted, truly completely genuine.

The relevance of this fourth feature becomes especially apparent when one considers the case of the "inimical other." When the respect is *thus* genuine your attitude towards such an "other" would, no matter how inimical her acts, never be to seek to return the hostility, nor to become indifferent towards the "other." When you truly *genuinely* respect the "other" for the other's existence as a human being and that existence *alone*, you instead nonetheless continue wishing good, and seek to do good, to such an "other."[53] Regardless of anything, you simply never give up

[53] Note here the difference between the principle of self-defence and the principle of no retribution. The two principles are, as we know, perfectly reconcilable. The principle of never giving up on the "inimical other" so that one keeps wishing good, and seeks to do good, to such a bearer of dignity does not mean that you are not authorized to do all that you can to defend yourself in a way that at the same time also never gives up on the "other." Of course you must, say, resist an attacker on your children instead of submitting them to him. But there is a whole world of difference between this (self-defence) and inferring further that this also authorizes you not only to wish that bad things then happen to the attacker, but that you also actually seek retribution that goes beyond mere reasonably effective self-defence.

on anyone, including the "inimical other." This kind of understanding of the unconditional universal respect is a unique notion of respect at the level of principle and will also tend to have important consequences in practice. This is for instance one of the main rationales behind the decision of the German Constitutional Court to strike down the death penalty, as well as imprisonment without parole, as being unconstitutional. In this context, to destroy the "inimical other's" capacity for self-rule, and thus human dignity, so drastically and irreparably is to "give up on the 'other'." Note, moreover, how the intact understanding of the unconditional universal respect is different from, say, those conceptions of supposedly unconditional universal respect (which are *not* that) that assume that a human being can somehow forfeit his or her human dignity. Along with Aquinas many have assumed—and perhaps even Kant himself did[54]—that one who commits a grave moral wrong simply gives up his human dignity and, as it were, turns himself into a beast ("*in servitutem bestiarum*") at the community's disposal.[55] That, and precisely that, is not possible under the described conditions of the fully genuine variant of the intact respect.

I have shown elsewhere how this particular variant of the intact respect is different from still other classical candidates for the best understanding of the intact respect, such as those by Kant or Habermas.[56] We need not discuss this here. Suffice it to say that even though it is often assumed that the pure non-conditional type of respect must be the Kantian respect, this is correct only to an extent. Even the version of respect underlying Kant's own theory may, the way it was defined, not yet fully qualify as the type of unconditional and genuine universal respect that the proponents of liberal legitimacy and its further democratic advancement through pluralism need to avoid their challenges. Certainly, Kant is clear about the position of human beings as the only rational beings in the world and hence as commanding a kind of respect as bearers of dignity that nothing else does.[57] Yet this does not yet make it clear whether his respect is meant to be fully universal in the sense that it includes also those human beings who are *not* rational, such as the mentally impaired. Nor does his respect seem to be yet fully unconditional and genuine. Kant's conception of dignity implies that one's mere existence as the bearer of dignity does not necessarily prevent others giving up on one in case of, say, severe failure. They can punish one even with capital punishment, a decision to end human dignity, while following the retributive rationale. Indeed, these elements potentially still signal a degree of conditionality and non-genuineness in Kant's underlying notion of respect that is not present in the *agapeistic* respect. They are instances of the mere methodological valuing, as opposed to the warm-hearted recognition of a bearer of dignity due to her existence alone. It was seen that treating the "inimical other" with the attitude of "an eye for an eye" is not just

[54] See the next paragraph.

[55] J. Finnis, *Acquinas: Moral, Political, and Legal Theory* (Oxford: Oxford University Press, 1998) 281.

[56] See n *.

[57] I. Kant, *Grundlegung zur Metaphysik der Sitten* in Berlin Academy (ed.), *Kants Werke* (Berlin: Walter de Gruyter, 1968) 4:435; Taylor (n 50) at 174.

inconsistent with, but even contrary to, the *agapeistic* type of respect. It may be that these kinds of elements in Kant already prompted some of his contemporaries[58] to argue more broadly that his theory, too, was inescapably too egoistic at bottom. This is still a potential standing objection against Kant. Rawls himself was aware of the problem while trying to avoid the objection for his own refined version of the theory.[59] Indeed, it should be concluded that even with Kant things are not entirely clear: his own conception of respect, unlike the *agapeistic* respect, may well not be the fully sound foundation we need.

1.3.2 Deflection through agapeistic respect

Rawls seeks to solve "the problem of political liberalism" by arguing for a deflection into a particular content of a common regime that is underpinned by a particular type of respect. This is also the key element that is supposed to do the work of gradually "moving" people who now come to adjust their final ends and make them compatible with the content of the common regime arising out of such a respect. Yet it was argued that the weakness of this reasoning might be precisely in the type of respect that it assumes. What most of Rawls's interpreters understand this respect to be is of insufficient quality to do the expected work of "moving" people in their ends, as well as failing to "heal" those who fall short under its regime. Instead, it seems to be, paradoxically, that it is this type of insufficient quality of respect that plants the very seed of destruction—its gradual incitement of the "projection of evil outward"—into the project of the regime's long-term stability. The methodological variants of equal respect implicit in both more radically proceduralized branches of pluralism share the same difficulty. To the extent that the respect implicit in both more substantive branches is also not the variant of the intact respect as just elaborated, the same applies to those pluralisms as well.

The project of legitimacy based on *agapeistic* respect is, however, free from this problem. When deflection from your primary end is on the basis of this kind of unconditional valuing of the "other," the respect is experienced by that "other" in the most intense way possible. It is felt as a truly genuine recognition of one's priceless worth irrespective of anything. By deflecting on this basis the "other"

[58] A. Schopenhauer, "Die Grundlage der Moral" in his, *Die beiden Grundprobleme der Ethik* (Frankfurt am Main: Joch Christ Germanische Buchhandlung, 1841) 101.

[59] Rawls acknowledged Schopenhauer's objection against Kant's doctrine of the categorical imperative. When reminded by Joshua Cohen that his (ie Rawls's) previous reply to this criticism had missed the force of Schopenhauer's objection, Rawls's strategy in his Dewey Lecture was *not* to defend Kant on this point. Instead, he set out to show why he thought that his own (ie Rawls's) version of the theory, which refined Kant further in a particular way, would manage to avoid the problem: "You will recall that Schopenhauer maintained that, in arguing for the duty of mutual aid in circumstances of distress . . ., Kant appeals to what rational agents, as finite beings with needs, can consistently will to be universal law. In view of our need for love and sympathy, on at least some occasions, we cannot will a social world in which others are always indifferent to our pleas in such cases. From this Schopenhauer claimed that Kant's view is at bottom egoistic, from which it follows that it is but a disguised form of heteronomy after all. Here I am concerned not to defend Kant against this criticism but to point out why the parallel objection to justice as fairness is incorrect" (J. Rawls, "Kantian Constructivism in Moral Theory" (The John Dewey Lecture) (1980) 9 The Journal of Philosophy 515–72).

knows you are putting her before any other of your own ethical ends. The experience of this purely genuine recognition is the very source of that "moving" effect. At the same time, a human being feels and knows only too well when the respect is not genuine and thus it is indeed only the *agapeistic* respect that could potentially do the work that the project on legitimacy needs in order to succeed. Only by experiencing that could the "others" genuinely be moved in their moral attitudes and begin embracing the respect themselves, so as to refine and make compatible with it also their own primary ends.

Moreover, it is only *agapeistic* respect that truly "heals" when the worth of "the weaker other" is being challenged. Instilling this type of respect into the regime, therefore, avoids accumulation of resentment and thus the potential for the dangerous "rebounded reflex" examined earlier. It subtly avoids the problem of planting into liberal legitimacy the seed of the project's own destruction, thereby bringing into the system the best potential for establishing long-term stability despite disagreement.

Furthermore, only when this kind of respect is assumed in the counterfactual foundation of a regime does it become possible to make progress towards the next historic improvement of democracy through the new European context. Much more is of course needed in order to institute such an advancement through pluralism, as there are other elements that need to be added.[60] The point here, however, is that this is also impossible when this particular uncompromising version of respect is not the one instituted within the counterfactual normative foundation of a rising pluralist regime. Without it, it is not possible for the constitutional actors to open themselves in a fully universal way to the external bearers of dignity, nor to begin constructing the truly distinct pluralist building blocks within their formations.

We will see more on this applicative discourse in what follows, but what is no less important than such further, more applicative effects, no matter how great, is to note at this point the very great political value of the *agapeistic* respect *already* in its most abstract form: as the kind of abstract spirit of particular quality and force. That is the ultimate engine and source of any fully sound application in the first place. It is from this source alone that the whole process of "moving" and "healing," as well as avoiding those other examined democratic deficits, flows in the first place, and does so truly equally, and universally, for all.

Note that the deflection towards this particular spirit of respect at the same time also does not destroy the goods of union. On the contrary, it is the only route through which the unprecedented degree of such goods could potentially be generated over the long run in the first place. It is not, however, the direct route. Unlike the particular spirit itself the pursuit of such goods is not (one of) its end(s) at all. It does not put concerns over increasing these goods before *agapeistic* respect. Instead, it requires thinking away those benefits. It requires submission into *agapeistic* respect regardless of anything, including those benefits. Yet it is precisely for this "submission" that the route to the unprecedented degree of the goods of union is then paradoxically enabled. It is this route that most effectively manages to

60 Jaklic (n 1); see also Chapter 9, section 2 and Chapter 10.

"move" and bring individuals together despite disagreement. It is this route, moreover, that also enables that "healing" and avoids the problem of the "rebounded reflex," thereby enabling long-term stability of the common regime. It is also this route that enables the further advancement of self-rule for all. If all this is correct then it should also be concluded that the unprecedented degree of the goods of union, inherent in those improvements, flow from the unconditional submission as its incidental, but inevitable, consequence. This is then the "given extra" that is added on top of such an unconditional submission, one that is generated precisely because it is genuinely not made into the further condition for respect.

Note, moreover, that under the *agapeistic* respect the disagreement of modern pluralist democratic societies acquires a special status and role. In a conception of legitimacy, where *agapeistic* respect is the very end of the regime *in and of itself*, the problem of deep postmodern disagreement is turned upside down. From being a real problem, it becomes the essential part of the very solution. It could be said that the unprecedented degree of the goods of union is secured precisely *because of* that disagreement. The highest respect, the one that is ultimately responsible for the incidental increase in the goods of union, can only arise in conditions of disagreement. This is because it is under those conditions alone that one is truly challenged with the radically different "other" and yet learns to overcome even that stronger temptation to oppress. One thereby learns the *higher* level of respect precisely in the context of such a profound difference. Disagreement, in other words, is one of the necessary elements for reaching and further spreading the higher, *agapeistic* spirit of respect and all that flows from it.

Indeed, whatever else will have to be at the foundation of the sound conception of constitutional pluralism in order for the latter to succeed, this particular version of the intact respect will also need to be there as the counterfactual normative ideal navigating the sound conception. Once the project of the democratic advancement through liberal legitimacy is placed on this intact foundation it is possible to show how the abstract spirit from this deepest constitutional basis then actually directs that new democratic advancement through pluralism that the new post-sovereign European context now enables for the first time. It is the advancement in relation to the "external others," "internal others," as well as each nation-state *demos* itself—something that, as seen above, a constitutional foundation of some lesser (eg more methodological) respect fails to secure. Such a foundation therefore avoids those difficulties that, as we saw in Chapter 8, the procedural branches of pluralism face due to the problem of insufficient respect. It also remedies the relative inchoateness of both substantive branches on this point that was reinforced by the fact that their conceptions of pluralism too are still confined to Europe that is externally monist.

Establishing the post-sovereign Europe on the sound foundation does, however, have at least the potential to lead to those fully universal democratic enhancements and thus to democracy's "third historic leap."[61] To explain how the latter could be

[61] Jaklic (n 1).

initiated,[62] we first need to continue our construction of the sound conception by adding still other key features to the foundation of such a substantive pluralism that could then really do that work while also avoiding the other remaining challenges to the current versions of the branch.

2. The Sufficient Challenge

Chapter 8 demonstrated that the more proceduralized branches were too thin to be able to project the actors off the ground, as it were. They did not direct them towards the truly sound elaboration of the substantive pluralist building blocks within the sphere of the *what*. This was what brought both of those conceptions in effect too close to monism in that decisive sphere. It was then likewise seen that both more substantive branches, while following a thicker strategy, also lack a proper explanation as to how that strategy could really work. That is, even assuming for the sake of argument that they did imply the truly sound conception of respect at their foundations, we observed that that alone did not yet have the capacity necessarily to lead the actors to adopt the fully sound building blocks for their formations. Nor could it work, as we saw, to pretend as if it was possible to impose *directly* on the actors such fully sound, but relatively thicker, substantive building blocks.

In order for the substantive improvement to follow, the pluralist foundation thus needs to be further improved. It would need to be able to instil a crucial kind of dialectic into the discourse between both coequal actors. This would have the capacity to somehow cause the actors themselves to mutually move each other in the correct way. The foundation needs, in other words, a particular substantive pluralist challenge that is (1) sufficiently strong to ensure that the actors move each other with sufficient and distinctive force, and it also needs to be (2) truly sound to ensure that they move themselves in the direction of adopting the fully sound applicative building blocks. Such a further improved pluralist foundation will project the actors by themselves to elaborate a system of sound substantive building blocks in the field of democracy while at the same time also incorporating and further refining the blocks observed thus far. This will avoid the remaining weaknesses observed above either with the procedural or the current variants of the more substantive branches. What, then, does that sufficient challenge consist of and how does it work?

Speaking in the most general terms, it is a combination of that unique new *factual context* in Europe, the significance of which needs to be more precisely and fully understood, and of some key *normative incentives* that need to be added and are difficult, if not impossible, to reject in the new factual context properly understood. The new context in Europe is unique in that it provides some new

[62] This is the subject of my other monograph, *Democracy's Third Coming* (n 1). It is of a similar length to this one and thus there is no more than outline here, leaving details to that work, which goes beyond the scope of this project.

factual circumstances in which it is possible to realistically conceive a novel and potentially much more democratic (non-monist) type of people's "getting together." We saw earlier that the traditional type of getting together into a sovereign state monopolized territory in the hands of a select group of people (monism), and that this inevitably created some serious deficit in the self-rule of the "external others", internal others, as well as the sovereign *demos* itself.[63] Some alternative factual context that could make the alternative type of getting together, free of such deficit, practically possible, would thus indeed provide a challenge to the traditional model. The potential of such a factual challenge must be explored. Indeed, when the sound normative incentives are then added to such a factual opening, the actors could not but, through their inescapable dialectic process of substantive mutual engagement under the challenge, themselves begin noticing the serious democratic deficits of their traditional models as well as an elegant, newly available way out of them. Being threatened in their own existence, as they are under such a challenge fully understood, the current actors willingly opt for that new and only way out of the troubles that can still preserve their existence and even reinforce them. It does so precisely through their gradual construction of that sound, superior model of the pluralist democracy.

The new factual context consists of two crucial features. Both of them are necessary for the pluralist challenge to work. At the same time, neither of them, nor both together, are sufficient. The unique normative features must be added as well. The latter, however, would likewise be able to do their part only in conditions when the two factual features are also present. These three mutually reinforcing features are thus the components of the unique substantive pluralist challenge. Let us first observe more closely each of them and then, in the final chapter, more concretely the working of the challenge as a whole.

2.1 Factual pluralism

For a long time, the monist nation-state democracy has flourished in Europe. Despite its democratic deficits there has, until recently, been no challenger that could have come even remotely close to breaking the powerful monopoly of this formation. Indeed, this has been the reality of the European factual condition for centuries. In recent decades, however, this historical monopoly of power has changed. With striking speed Europe has managed to reach a degree of integration previously unmatched in its history. It has come to the point at which it realistically claims a self-standing nature of its new political legal order. As some far-sighted thinkers have correctly observed, this integration, if it continues at this pace, would quite inescapably lead to the eventual replacement of the classical European nation-state with that of the European superstate. Indeed, an increasing number of powerful voices are urging Europe down the superstate path.[64] From a perspective

[63] See pp. 270–5.

[64] See, eg G. Morgan, *The Idea of a European Superstate* (Princeton, NJ: Princeton University Press, 2005); F. Mancini, "Europe: The Case for Statehood" (1998) 4 European Law

that is not wholly short-sighted it is thus also clear already at this point that, with this kind of integration and its pace in place, the European nation-state is, for the first time in its history, faced with a serious *factual* challenge to the continued existence of its sovereign monopoly as well as its existence as a nation-state itself. In the past, any idea of all-European democracy could be little more than a utopian dream. Today, it represents an increasingly powerful challenge that could not easily, if at all, be avoided.

There is wide agreement among European thinkers today that it would not reflect reality to explain that the nation-states are currently still the holders of factual ultimate authority in Europe.[65] It would be, as some say, like trying to push the toothpaste back into the tube. Equally mistaken, in their view, would be to describe the situation as if it were Europe that has already won the race for the factual sovereignty over the territory of Europe. As a matter of factual reality, both descriptions are wrong. Europe is currently in a kind of historical state of uncertainty where we have two roughly equally powerful actors. While the pluralists acknowledge this state of factually equipotent "rivals," they do not yet make enough out of their mere descriptions of this kind of coexistence. What is crucial is to look at the issue from a broader historical perspective. This takes into account also the historical trajectory and dynamics (and here, in addition to the remarkable pace of European integration, the American precedent is also highly instructive), which reveal that both actors are, whether they like it or not, already competing with each other for the position of factual ultimate authority in some future arrangement of Europe. The European nation-state is, on a closer look at such a more historical perspective, indeed already under a much more serious challenge than it might appear at first glance. This will be even further reinforced when the sound normative element is added to the factual one. And it is a good thing too, as we will see, that the

Journal 29; J. Fischer, "From Confederation to Federation: Thoughts on the Finality of European Integration" (2000) Federal Trust European Essay No 8; G. Verhofstadt, *De Verenigde Staten van Europa* ("The United States of Europe") (Antwerp: Houtekiet, 2005); also his "Forging 'United States of Europe' is Key to the Future," Statement (November 2005); J. Delors, "Jacques Delors at the College of Europe in Bruges," reprinted in *Europe* Doc No 1,576 (21 October 1989); cf also the related arguments that Europe is inevitably becoming a "superpower," T. Reid, *The United States of Europe: The New Superpower and the End of American Supremacy* (New York, NY: Penguin, 2004); J. Rifkin, *The European Dream: How Europe's Vision of the Future is Quietly Eclipsing the American Dream* (New York, NY: Penguin, 2004). The idea of uniting Europeans under a European state is an old one. See, eg J. Le Goff, *The Birth of* Europe (Oxford: Blackwell, 2005), who shows that the ambition of constructing a Europe dominated by one people and one empire (which he characterizes as "anti-Europe") has kept resurfacing throughout history. It started with Charlemagne as its initiator and then resurfaced with Charles V, Napoleon, and of course Hitler. For the version of the idea as it has developed under the Pan-European movement, see, eg R. Coundenhove-Kalegri, *Pan Europa* (Vienna: Pan-Europe-Verlag, 1923); A. Zurcher, *The Struggle to Unite Europe 1940–58* (New York, NY: New York University Press, 1989); P. Stirk, *European Unity in Context: The Interwar Period* (London: Pinter, 1989). See also the European Federalist Movement: A. Spinelli, "European Union and the Resistance" in G. Ionescu (ed.), *The New Politics of European Integration* (London: Macmillan, 1972); The Union of European Federalists is the NGO currently representing this civic movement.

[65] See, eg N. MacCormick, "Beyond the Sovereign State" (1993) 56 ML Rev 1; J. Weiler, *The Constitution of Europe: "Do the New Clothes Have an Emperor?" and Other Essays on European Integration* (Cambridge: Cambridge University Press, 1999) 269; N. Walker, "The Idea of Constitutional Pluralism" (2002) 65 ML Rev 317, 338.

sufficiently strong factual challenge is finally here. Were this not so, we would be well advised to reinforce it in the coming years of Europe's further development so as to develop it fully and become aware of this more serious version of the challenge.

2.2 The globalizing age

The powerful new challenge to the nation-state arising out of factual pluralism is an important and necessary precondition to the initiation of the process of our democratic advancement. It is, however, far from sufficient to lead to that initiation. After all, although a rare historic phenomenon, factual pluralism is something humanity saw at least once before this particular occasion in Europe, and yet on that previous occasion it did not lead to the development in which we are really interested.

When the US must have been in its own state of uncertainty at some point during the transition from the loose confederation of sovereign states to the mightier sovereign superstate—*e pluribus unum*—the challenge from factual pluralism did not of course direct the actors to the path of some pluralist democracy that would aspire to transcend the monist model and come to include in their getting together any single bearer of dignity on the globe, regardless of his or her territorial distance from the US. On the contrary, out of the American factual pluralism things led to democratic monism, not pluralism, and that was the right step in that historical context.

This is because, firstly, in the age when globalization had not yet taken place, such a global endeavor was simply not possible. It would be completely utopian at the time of the US founding to try to set up a democratic project of such nature, or even think of any such more inclusive democratic model. Secondly, historically, times then were undemocratic and highly unstable. Even the factually dominant monist model of democracy was then itself highly at risk. Unless it was organized into a factually powerful sovereign force, the second coming of democracy would have more than certainly fallen prey to the widely prevalent non-democratic forces and empires of those times. If the democratic experiment (democracy's "second coming") was to survive it had to be in the monist form: through the initiation of democracy in the form of a powerful sovereign territorial state.[66] Judging by the remarkable success of democracy's second coming that this initiated, the work in the "American moment" was done in the best imaginable way.

Yet contexts change. Ours certainly has as well.[67] In our globalizing age, when we are surrounded by a prevalent majority of democratic states and have gradually

[66] Madison himself was well aware of this and explicitly argued so (J. Madison, "Vices of the Political System of the United States" in P. Kurland and R. Lerner (eds), *The Founders' Constitution*, Vol 1, ch 5, "Deficiencies of Confederation," Doc 16 (Chicago: University of Chicago Press, 1987). See also Chapter 10, pp. 320–2.

[67] I show elsewhere (*Democracy's Third Coming*, see n 1) that before the initiation of democracy's second coming the context had also crucially changed, which is what had enabled such an advancement. I argue that our current change of context in the new pluralist Europe is a change of comparable significance that enables preconditions to a new major democratic advancement.

come to internalize democracy as the basis of legitimacy, much more than a monist state may be possible. This is crucially reinforced by the fact that this same globalizing age also seems to enable, for the first time in history, the practical possibility that any corner of earth is reached through some more inclusive type of getting together. It thus likewise enables that a common supranational democratic formation does not any longer need to be built around a regionally confined territory, but can include territories from different parts of the world. All these key circumstances of our own age were completely absent at the time of the "American moment," making anything else but a monist democracy beyond even the wildest imagination. We will see more about this feature in what follows. Suffice to say that the potential of factual pluralism is obviously crucially reinforced precisely after also adding this further dimension to it, that is, the second indispensable feature without which the superior alternative to monism could also never arise.

2.3 The normative incentives

Having both factual components together, as is the case in the unique new European context, the challenge is importantly reinforced. This is nonetheless not yet enough to ensure the triggering of the process that could then actually lead to the fully sound conception. Not only the existing conceptions of pluralism, but even normative monism itself is still one of the options that can be pursued from such a context. Surely we can still insist, even in the context of factual pluralism, that the right thing to do in such circumstances would be to follow one of the traditional ways of getting together. This would be to either revert back to the nation-state model, or lead things toward the superstate model. This would depend on what group of people we considered, for whatever reason, to be the preferred group of our would-be fellow citizens, our fellow members of the sovereign. But clearly, if the getting together is, normatively speaking, going to be allowed to proceed in either of these straightforward monist directions, the potential of the new context is just as clearly left unused. Both models are well known, both are monist, and both therefore also generate those monist democratic deficits. Indeed, according to this option nothing new happens from the new European context after all. The opportunity that the context carries for the sound pluralism and improvement of democracy is wasted.

Nor indeed is normative pluralism,[68] as the alternative strategy to monism, already by itself sufficient to avoid wasting the new opportunity. We saw earlier that none of the currently existing pluralist approaches leads to the fully sound conception of pluralism, nor anywhere near the initiation of democracy's third historic leap. Some of them waste the opportunity for very similar reasons as this

[68] As we know since the very first chapters of the mapping analysis, normative pluralism denotes the position whereby one considers the situation of factual pluralism to be, for some reason, also a good thing, and not solely the right descriptive account of mere factual reality (see, eg MacCormick, (n 65) at 17).

occurs under normative monism.[69] It is only a particular kind of normative pluralism, what I will call the "germ of substantive pluralism," that can (when joined with the other two indispensable components of the challenge) trigger that crucial process leading to the actors' development of the sound substantive pluralism and its third historic leap of democracy.

The germ of substantive pluralism is, like normative monism, a *normative* vision. However, it differs from the latter in its particular vision as to how people and their actors ought to think about getting together in the first place. This refined normative pluralism consists of several elements representing the absolute substantive minimum (hence the "germ" of substantive pluralism) under which the challenge is still able to do its work and lead the actors (the people, their representatives and public officials, and thus their constitutional orders) to adopt the sound conception of pluralism. They are that third component—the normative incentives—through which the challenge becomes complete and sufficient. They are the following.

Firstly, the germ of substantive pluralism normatively requires that the monist actors who happen to find themselves in the context of factual pluralism in the globalizing age do not, as a matter of external truth, simply disregard each other. Internally speaking, each of them can still be fully convinced about the rightness of its own normative monist vision, as well as pursue the latter with openly (nation-state or European) monist intentions and agendas.[70] Nonetheless, according to the germ of substantive pluralism, each of the monist actors under factual pluralism ought at the same time also to recognize that, externally speaking, the other actor, whose opposite monist claim and aspiration are factually no less strongly backed than are its own, is also there. The other actor is likewise claiming the ultimate authority over the same piece of territory that is also claimed in this way by the first actor itself. As required by the germ of substantive pluralism, this external recognition further implies that the coexisting normative claims and visions of the other actor be at least engaged with and considered by the first actor with all sincerity and equally as its own. It is only *after* such a sincere mutual consideration, through which each of the actors aspires to show to the other the superiority of its own normative vision, that either of the actors is then really free to go ahead and impose its vision of getting together also externally: be it the old model of the sovereign nation-state democracy, the new model of the sovereign European superstate democracy, or something else that might instead come up as a result of such a sincere mutual engagement. Note that the described degree of mutual recognition, as is required by the germ of substantive pluralism, is already different from monism. There, from the start, the claim to the actor's own ultimate authority over a given territory is declared to be correct not only in the internal, but also the

[69] Chapter 8.

[70] If the Hartian jargon of "external" and "internal" point of view sounds too theoretical, feel free to simply replace it with the "objectively valid" claims (those about which both parties can agree as being valid for both) and the "merely subjectively valid" claims pursued from the perspective of one party alone. Irrespective of your choice of the preferred jargon, the substance of the point remains the same.

external sense. There is no requirement, under normative monism, to engage with any of its rivals at any of the levels. Note that this first element of the normative incentive is, in the circumstances of factual pluralism, definitely not too demanding for the actors to accept; indeed, it is the most natural and reasonable one to agree on within such new circumstances.

Secondly, the authorities, or actors, that confront each other are not just any kind of authorities. They need to be imagined as having a particular substantive content. They are the agents of essential humanity charged with furthering as much as possible the ideal of essential humanity. This means that the authorities are to be understood not as, say, monarchs, some select group of people (such as ruling class or working class), or some other authority external to the people, or just whatever authority it is that happens to occupy that position of sufficient factual power. The authorities ought to be seen instead as the respective peoples themselves.

Thirdly, that these authorities (their respective peoples) are truly the agents of essential humanity means that they cannot but both also agree with the explanations about essential humanity that follow from the most sound, intact respect elaborated earlier. They thus assume that essential humanity requires that, despite our profound differences, human beings as the bearers of dignity are all each other's equals who deserve respect in the fully universal and unconditional sense as described. All actors thus know they have to accept that their getting together is sounder when it is not only enhancing the good (eg self-rule) of their own respective peoples, but can indeed be justified as somehow being compatible more than other alternatives with exactly that universal and unconditional maximization of the good (eg of self-rule) in relation to the members of every nation who wish to be its equal recipients. Being the bearers of dignity the members of those nations are indeed entitled to be the equal rightful addressees (authors and recipients) of that good's maximization, and are so by virtue of their existence, their equal essential humanity alone as opposed to some morally arbitrary factor such as, say, location of one's birth. It is not that difficult to accept this kind of spirit of respect—this third element of the normative incentives—either. On the contrary, we saw that any alternative would actually imply that "you" think "you" are somehow worthy of greater respect than is the "other" bearer of dignity.

Fourthly, it is likewise not hard to accept a further, and just slightly more applicative, instantiation of this abstract spirit of essential humanity for the field of democracy. I have elsewhere shown that, as far as the good of self-rule (democracy in the broadest sense) is concerned, this kind of intact spirit of respect for essential humanity cannot but mean that the bearers of dignity owe to one another the maximization of three ultimate goods of democracy.[71] They are at the same time irreducible ultimate ends/meanings of democracy. They are also context-independent and thus represent a valid ultimate benchmark for the assessment of any model of democracy through history. They flow from the intact respect and are fairly simple.

[71] Jaklic (n 1), the chapter titled "The Three Ultimate Ends".

The first is the understanding of self-rule in the sense of every individual's capacity to shape with *effective power* things within the domains of her own life. Human beings are the rulers when they have effective power over the collective as well as individual domains of their lives, so that their genuine will can thus rule effectively through those life-domains.

The second ultimate end and meaning of democracy is the idea of self-rule according to which the individual is not excluded from entering the domains of her life, but instead has the gateways wide open so that her chance for *taking part* (participation) in her life is as great as possible. Although different than the first, this second understanding of self-rule as opened participation is also a unique and irreducible end of democracy: regardless of how ineffective the individual will be in ruling the domains of her life (democracy as effective power), she ought to have the gateways for entry wide open simply because this is *her* life.

The third independent meaning of self-rule says that, for the maximum possible self-rule, it cannot yet be enough that the individual rules over the domains of her life, be it through effective power or/and participation, but that she must also be able to rule over *herself*. This meaning of self-rule is thus about a particular type of virtues, or quality of character—the *self-ruling virtues*—of individuals, as exemplified in the well-known Kantian idea of autonomous self-rule that is free from egoistic (*heteronomous*) desires and inclinations. Moreover, it follows from the above argument for *agapeistic* respect as the soundest political conception of respect that the purest variant of self-ruling virtues is fully compatible with this kind of respect. After all, together with the other two ultimate goods of democracy, the good of self-ruling virtues is one of the three more applicative representations of that foundational respect.

For our current purposes, we do not need more than this brief elaboration of the three ultimate ends/meanings of democracy.[72] We should nonetheless add that it could be shown that all other answers as to why democracy can, in the final analysis, be reduced to one or more of these three ultimate ends.[73] Moreover, each of them is to be understood as the representation of the intact respect: we owe each other the offer of the enhancement of these ultimate goods of democracy, and so in the universal and unconditional sense, simply due to that foundational intact respect for each other's existence (as the bearers of dignity) alone. Furthermore, the ends are defined broadly. It cannot be said from this definition that it excludes this or that applicative interpretation within liberalism broadly defined, where the term "broadly" encompasses both opposite poles, and the space in the middle, of the political spectrum in modern democracies. That exclusion is anyway not the point. The point is rather that there will be a severe democratic deficit concerning these ends that both those opposite poles, and the moderates in between them, will clearly agree beyond controversy that it is such a deficit. It is that kind of deficit that the actors will be able through the challenge to

[72] For a full elaboration and defense of the three ultimate ends of democracy, see Jaklic (n 1).
[73] Jaklic (n 1).

both first show to each other and then, in order to escape such a challenge, solve it through their only available refinements that actually embrace the sound conception of pluralism and its democratic enhancement. Thus understood, these ends are indeed not problematic at all. Both actors can easily accept them, and actually cannot but accept them together with the understanding that the model of democracy that enhances them more (as measured from their context-independent universal, genuine, and unconditional benchmark) is more democratic.

The three ends of democracy are the last of the four normative incentives for which the germ of substantive pluralism requires that the actors agree on and bring sincerely into their mutual exchange. There are no more than these four easily acceptable normative incentives representing the slightly more elaborated, but still highly abstract, substantive content of essential humanity. In addition to both factual components, this kind of normative device (the "germ of substantive pluralism") that the actors ought to imagine is the last necessary component of the needed challenge that can trigger the process we seek. Once all these components are in place, each monist authority under factual pluralism is, as follows from the first normative incentive, free to continue arguing why it is that its own monist model is able to realize these ultimate ends of democracy (essential humanity) more than the competing model and thus ought to be chosen for Europe over that other. Yet we will see that by going ahead and mutually confronting each other under the terms of this kind of an intact substantive challenge, the actors will inevitably move each other so as to end up adopting exactly the sound common conception of substantive pluralism and its resulting democratic enhancement.

Before we proceed, note that the germ of substantive pluralism crucially further reinforces the unique challenge that both actors face due to the coalescence of factual pluralism and the globalizing age. Without the germ, as we saw, even monism, as well as the less sound variants of pluralism, are still possible; the first two components of the challenge by themselves are not yet sufficient. Yet just as with those two, so now also this third component of the challenge would not be able to do anything if it was not for its concurrent alignment with the other two. For instance, to require in the context of factual monism that the people who have got together imagine their endeavor through this kind of normative device would not make much sense. It would be inapplicable, an exercise in utopianism. No matter how strong a normative case some (say, the pan-European movement) could make in the past in favor of some alternative arrangement, nothing would have moved the factually unchallenged sovereign nation-state. Nor would it make much sense to try and normatively move the latter during the context of some pre-globalized age; at that point real progress as to democratic ends could not have been better ensured through anything but a powerful sovereign state model. Indeed, it is only when all three components come into alignment at the same time that the challenge becomes sufficiently strong.

These further refinements of the pluralist foundation make the latter still further unique from the rest of the pluralist foundations with which it otherwise of course shares the minimum common denominator. On the one hand, it is thicker than the foundations from Walker's and Maduro's version of pluralism. In those foundations there is nothing more substantive than the ascetic and inter-subjective mere reciprocities; anything else has to be openly left to the actors themselves. On the other hand, in an important sense this foundation is also thinner than Weiler's. Besides the elaborated abstract substantive content, which the actors easily agree to accept, and cannot but accept among equals, there are no further substantive building blocks that the sound conception would impose *directly* on the actors themselves. The fully sound further building blocks cannot, as we know, be imposed directly as they would not be followed in such a way; the actors first need to realize and show each other that that way is their best choice. And so crucially, under the terms of the substantive challenge as constructed here and as accepted by the authors, those further substantive meta-blocks *are* then *inevitably* the products of the actors' own mutually moving dialectic process. Let us then observe more closely how the sound conception of pluralism (its meta-level) gets further constructed through such terms of engagement, through such a pluralist getting together, while thereby making that contribution to the democratic project.

10

Democracy's Third Coming

This final chapter is a condensed account of my broader project on the third historic stage of democracy that can be initiated and then gradually developed precisely (and only) through the sound conception of substantive pluralism. This is the subject of my other monograph,[1] so to offer here more than this condensed picture would go beyond the scope of this project. Such a condensed account of the democratic project must nonetheless be presented. This is because it provides the further distinctive shape of the sound conception of substantive pluralism—the subject of this work—through which democratic advancement proceeds. It is this that will also complete our emerging picture of the superior conception of constitutional pluralism.

1. The Challenge from Europe

How then does the substantive pluralist challenge lead to our desired democratic enhancement? The challenge is powerful. Through it, one actor threatens eventually to replace the other. This can be either by getting rid of the other actor's continued existence in its self-standing form, which would thus turn such an actor into a mere subordinate unit of the superior first actor, or by replacing the other actor altogether. Consistent with the terms of the challenge the European monist camp is able to launch an unprecedentedly powerful normative charge/offensive against the traditional nation-state democratic model. With its regime of the multiple and high sovereign boundaries through the territory of Europe, the nation-state monist model of democracy has inevitably engaged in a considerable degree of exclusion, and thus democratic deficit, with respect to the rightful addressees of the good of effective power, participation, and self-ruling virtues. It is exclusion that the European monist project can alleviate. I have identified and dealt systematically with all the forms of this nation-state monist deficit in the other work,[2] and so here but a few examples will suffice to illustrate the point.

Firstly, regarding the effective power, take for instance the conceptual impossibility of our sovereign nation-state to reach into another sovereign nation-state and

[1] K. Jaklic, *Democracy's Third Coming: Europe as a Route to Humanity's Third Historic Stage of Democracy*, monograph manuscript, forthcoming, currently on file with Harvard University Law Library, and with author.

[2] Jaklic (n 1) chs V, VII, IX, and XI.

secure there for our citizens the appropriate effective power (eg the right to vote) in the process of adopting laws that bind them. This inability of the nation-state model exists irrespective of the fact that those laws might profoundly affect the lives of our citizens. There is also the mirror image version of this deficit. Our sovereign nation-state is conceptually unable to transfer the spheres under its sovereign jurisdiction to some other direct authority (one representing "external others" from another sovereign nation-state) so that those citizens from other nation-states who are affected by our laws could have their effective power over their own lives thereby appropriately enhanced. Recall that[3] there is a twofold democratic loss involved in both these forms of deficit: that of the affected individuals' *normative* title to full authorship (itself an inherent part of the fullest possible state of self-rule and dignity) as well as the relative obstruction of their *practical* ability to fully engage in things affecting their lives. Or, take the example of the more instrumental, but no less inevitable, deficit as it occurs between the sovereign nation-state democracies. Through the self-centered pursuit as is paradigmatic of such a monist world, some sovereign nation-states inevitably manage to secure a relatively greater degree of effective power for their own respective *demoi*. Others come out of the monist competition much less successfully. However, when you are born into one or the other of these states you are therefore already predetermined to have a relatively unequal degree of effective power. This is so due to a morally completely arbitrary factor of the location of birth. The high monist boundaries of the sovereign nation-states then themselves also effectively hinder any sufficient remedy to this aspect of exclusion. Furthermore, no matter how powerful your sovereign nation-state happens to be, it would, other things being equal, never be capable of ensuring the degree of effective power for its citizens than, say, some much mightier political formation could for its own. Think for instance of the capacity of such different formations to affect world politics and all the numerous issues that affect our lives in that sphere.

The deficits are serious and cannot be cured or alleviated by the nation-state monist model of democracy. Yet, remarkably, the proponents of the European monist camp are able to show that, were we instead to gradually organize Europe into a (federal) sovereign superstate under "one person one vote," and with other democratic attributes of such a formation, all these deficits of the traditional nation-state democratic model could disappear. Under the European monist model, the citizens of different nation-states who were previously affected by the laws from other nation-states, but were excluded from their own share in the effective power with respect to those laws, are now suddenly equal authors and addressees of those laws. Moreover, under "one person one vote" across the whole territory of Europe, and in the spheres that affect us all, the serious deficit arising from the fact of mere birth into a weaker, as opposed to stronger, territorial region within Europe, disappears as well. The same is true with respect to the deficit related to the relative

[3] Chapter 9, pp. 272–3.

weakness of the nation-state as compared to, other things being equal, the greater effective power of such a democratic superstate and consequently its citizens.

Secondly, all the examples explored apply to the good of participation as well, and to illustrate the point further we should add here also a few others. Take for instance the problem of the nation-state's reach into the collective domain between the states. Even when the relatively weaker formation of the nation-state can reach effectively into that domain, the access (the system of gateways) that the nation-state can guarantee to its citizens is relatively closed. Under the monist model of sovereign nation-states this domain is governed by international law: by international relations and its process of treaty enactments. From the perspective of individuals, however, this is, by definition a much less direct and open way of norm-making than the process inside the nation-state. There is no direct link between treaties and individuals as it is only their intermediaries—the states—that are direct subjects of international law. They are so despite the fact that it is individuals' lives that are of course ultimately affected in the domains governed by the treaties. Thus, the option of direct access through the system of gateways such as, say, direct initiatives and referenda is here naturally less open than inside the internal sphere of the nation-state. The whole process gravitates towards government's own negotiations, often further delegated to cabinet members from the field of a particular treaty. Even in countries where *post-facto* ratification referenda can sometimes be held, those usually decide only about treaty applicability inside the nation-state territory. This is so despite the fact that these individuals' lives may be profoundly affected by the treaty regime outside their state borders. This substantially diminishes the availability of access to that sphere outside the borders of the nation-state. Nor is there a possibility of direct access when a closed number of other states decide right from the start to enact some treaty regime for themselves alone, such as the forging of the European Communities and several other international initiatives in Europe. The all-European monist alternative, one that replicates the nation-state model and its system of access at the European scale, would of course be able to remedy these deficits of the old democratic model all across the European territory. Just as the nation-state in its own internal domain, so the European superstate provides its direct and openly available access across what is its own internal domain.

Or, consider the right to be elected for a norm-maker in the international sphere. This too is an example of a gateway to reaching what affects your life, that is, a route to accessing your own life itself to which you ought to have access. The norm-makers in the international sphere between the sovereign nation-states are those who negotiate and sign treaties as well as those who later ratify them. As to the negotiation and signing stage, the key positions are extremely scarce: there is normally only one representative from each contracting state. Moreover, these positions are not as directly available to ordinary citizens as, say, legislative offices are. You need first to be appointed as a cabinet member in order then to be a candidate for this kind of post. As to the ratification position, the degree of openness is also not the same as in the case of a legislator in the internal nation-state legislative context. The ratification position normally does not include access to the key part of the legislative prerogative: norm-negotiation. Due to its extreme scarcity the exercise of this prerogative in the inter-statal sphere remains relatively closed to citizens except for a narrow circle of an indirectly selected elite who can be potential candidates. Furthermore, unlike in legislative office, the post in the ratification cannot normally be held *simultaneously* with the negotiation position. Last, but not least, the territorial limitation mentioned with respect to referenda and elections applies to ratification as well. All of these restrictions on the openness of the system of gateways represent participative deficits. The defenders of the nation-state model know that these would be significantly remedied by the monist European state in which many of those inter-statal spheres would become areas of ordinary legislation. That is, they would be subject to legislative offices that are much more widely and directly available to all citizens.

Thirdly, under the nation-state monist model the maximization of self-ruling virtues also tends not to be best served. Inherent in the monist foundation of the sovereign nation-states is the tendency that generates a subtle but dangerous skewing of the fully *agapeistic* virtues. It tends to inculcate a variant of more self-centered types of virtues. These negative effects on virtues are most evident in those substantive areas that constitute the deepest "boundaries" between people, between the "I" and the "other." Nationhood and religion, two aspects that Weiler focused on,[4] are but two most typical examples of this problem that is so well known to Europe and its past regime of the sovereign monist nation-states.

The persistent weakness of such a regime is that, through the inevitable monist competition between the sovereign nation-states that it promotes, it generates the type of spirit too arrogant about the "other," of the one who happens *not* to be part of your sovereign. While inevitably promoting the thinking and action that are too self-centered it then, crucially, tends to make such behavior appear *natural* by appealing to the state's ultimate end of enhancing the good of its sovereign that appears to be required by the monist constitutional foundation itself. In the monist environment of rivalry and competition between the nation-states, this logic is indeed intuitively persuasive. Gradually, more and more members of the sovereign take it for granted and, whatever other consequence this might lead to,[5] it also leads to the shaping of the monist type of "civic virtues" in masses. Europe knows: this process was best revealed precisely by the sovereign nation-state regime that it had developed to the full just prior to the Second World War. Indeed, that monist intercourse was all about "relentless defense and maximization" of each sovereign's own interest that held firmly to the "full sovereignty, autonomy, and independence" of those states.[6] In the given circumstances it was hard to see, and impossible to persuade masses of others who had by then already internalized them, that the monist goals were actually fallacious. The "virtues" typical of the nation-state monism completely took over. The outbreak that followed was but a final result of the gradual and subtler accumulation of the unsound virtues represented in the corrupt boundaries:

[4] Chapter 3, section 1.3.

[5] I showed in the other work that this also has very negative consequences for the good of effective power and participation (see n 1).

[6] J. Weiler, *The Constitution of Europe: "Do the New Clothes Have an Emperor?" and Other Essays on European Integration* (Cambridge: Cambridge University Press, 1999) 91.

in the "coded expressions" of nationhood,[7] in the "unsound forms of nationalism."[8] As correctly shown by Weiler's analysis, other fields, such as religion, similarly represent still further fertile areas through which the subtle skewing of self-ruling virtues and the erection of the corrupt boundaries proceeds under the regime of the monist nation-states.

Conversely, the proponents of the European monist idea are able to say at least something in favor of their own model as to the issue of virtues. Indeed, in some leading interpretations their model has been envisioned precisely to alleviate this deficit. After witnessing one of the most horrific boundary abuses by the old Europe, the founders of the European idea saw the latter as "an antidote to the negative features" of the described type of monistic "statal intercourse."[9] In the name of *essential humanity*—the idea of a *transnational human* intercourse on the *all-European* scale—the federal Europe would lead to the demise of the nation-states' relentless maintenance and intensification of boundaries.[10] Instead of intensifying the corrupt boundaries typical of the monist nation-state regime, this kind of a formation would indeed significantly "melt" those boundaries across the territory of Europe. This invitation to "come, eliminate the boundaries, and be one of us",[11] certainly has a noble core. "[I]t involves", as Weiler himself recognizes, "elimination of prejudice, of the notion that there are boundaries between humans that cannot be eradicated."[12] Even though this European strategy still maintains a monist boundary at the outskirts of its much more inclusive formation, it still gets much closer than the nation-state monist system to the fulfillment of the ideal of essential humanity and its universal respect irrespective of boundaries. It shapes a variant of more universal civic virtues across the whole territory of Europe, despite the different non-monist national boundaries that now need to be refined so as to become compatible with the more universal civic virtues of the federal level.

[7] Weiler (n 6) at 342.

[8] N. MacCormick, "Is Nationalism Philosophically Credible?" in W. Twinning (ed.), *Issues of Self-Determination* (Aberdeen: Aberdeen University Press, 1991); "What Place for Nationalism in the Modern World" (1994) 2 Hume Papers on Public Policy 79; "Liberalism, Nationalism, and the Post-sovereign State" (1996) XLIV Political Studies 553.

[9] Weiler (n 6). For a more detailed explanation of this fact, see, eg J. Weiler, *Christian Europe* 54 (J. Weiler, *Krščanska Evropa: Raziskovalna Razprava*, tr. M Ožbolt (Claritas: Ljubljana, 2005) 89–93); D. Dinan, *Ever Closer Union: An Introduction to European Integration* (3rd edn, London: Lynne Rienner Publishers, 2005).

[10] See all references in n 9; see also J. Weiler, "Does Europe Need a Constitution? Demos, Telos and the German Maastricht Decision" (1995) 1 ELJ 219, 248; cf the speech by Churchill in Zurich in 1946 in which he called for the "United States of Europe" (cited in Dinan (n 9)); Monnet, and other federalists; J. Delors, "Jacques Delors at the College of Europe in Bruges," reprinted in *Europe*, Doc No 1,576 (21 October 1989); J. Fischer, "From Confederation to Federation: Thoughts on the Finality of European Integration," (2000) Federal Trust European Essay No 8; G. Verhofstadt, *De Verenigde Staten van Europa* ("The United States of Europe") (Antwerp: Houtekiet, 2005); also his "Forging 'United States of Europe' is Key to the Future," Statement (November 2005).

[11] J. Weiler, "Europe: The Case against the Case of Statehood" (1998) 4 ELJ 43, 61; "In Defense of Status Quo: Europe's Constitutional *Sonderweg*" in J. Weiler and M. Wind (eds), *European Constitutionalism beyond the State* (Cambridge: Cambridge University Press, 2003) at 19.

[12] Weiler, "Europe: The Case against the Case of Statehood" (n 11) at 61.

The challenge from the European monist project is indeed powerful. Other things being equal, its democratic model comes much closer than does the nation-state monist model to the ideal of essential humanity. A much greater number of the bearers of dignity enjoy the three ultimate goods of democracy to a much more equal and maximized degree. The monist nation-state should, as the natural conclusion suggests, therefore gradually give way to the superior, European monist alternative. And as we know it, for the first time in history the European sovereign nation-state is no longer in a position to just ignore such a powerful moral challenge.

2. Refining the Nation-State

When the normative challenge is set out in this way, as it is under the accepted sound terms of the substantive pluralist challenge, something important occurs. Proponents of the nation-state, who themselves believe in, and endorse, the sound terms of our pluralist challenge, realize that the nation-state basically only has two options. It either must somehow show how it too can achieve an even greater degree of democratization. If it cannot, it has to back away and willingly comply with being consigned to history. Unlike before, the actor of the nation-state and its proponents now know that the normative democratic challenge is both extremely powerful and at the same time it cannot be ignored. The crucial development therefore is that they cannot help but delve into self-reflection. What would they need to do so that a solution for their project might still be found? Thus, reflecting on their own project they soon begin to realize that there is only one last remaining route through which the escape from the European challenge might still be possible.

While certainly more inclusive than the monist nation-state, and thus closer to the ideal of essential humanity, the European superstate is nonetheless still monist. That being so, the defenders of the nation-state realize that it (the nation-state) has the option of opening itself instead to a particular type of integration, of building a common project, that is *not* monist. While this would still retain the self-standing status of the nation-state, it would also require the latter's refinement. That is, a refinement that could show how the nation-state can thereby come even closer than the European monist superstate to the fulfillment of the sound ideal of essential humanity as defined in the intact terms of the challenge.[13] That, as the defenders know, is the only potential way out of the powerful European challenge. If the challenge cannot be rebutted on this ultimate and thus decisive battleground of the intact essential humanity, then they know it could indeed not be rebutted at all, by, for instance, some less intact standard of evaluation. So how does the nation-state refine itself in this way?

[13] Recall that this is the notion of essential humanity about which the actors could not but have accepted that it means that every single bearer of dignity in this world is the rightful and equal addressee of democracy's three ultimate ends, the ends that are also to be accorded to them on the fully universal and unconditional (hence also genuine) basis (see Chapter 9, p. 291). For all the sound terms of the pluralist challenge that the actors could not but have agreed to, see Chapter 9, pp. 286–94.

Firstly, the sovereignty principle at the foundation (the nation-state people as the single ultimate source of authority over the nation-state territory) needs to be changed through the interpretation or text of the refining nation-state constitution. The refining nation-state must thus make it clear that, in the sphere that affects "external others" equally, its previously sovereign territory is now open to inclusion of those "others" that constitute the equally self-standing authority (of which they are both the authors and beneficiaries, that is, its full "addresees") on that same territory. They are offered such inclusion through some coexisting common supranational project that is not limited to the regional Europe, but to which the nation-state now opens itself through such a refinement at the level of its foundational principle. Such more inclusive foundational principle is more able to capture the unconditional universal respect and its ideal of essential humanity than does some monist monopolization of territory under the superstate strategy still underpinned by its monist foundational principle. It also better fulfills those ideals than some monopolization that aspires to be internally pluralist, but is externally still monist, limited to some regional Europe, such as was the case with most of our pluralists examined earlier. What is gained through the foundational refinement is, among others, both the normative title to direct authorship of "external others" in the laws that affect and bind them, as well as the opening of the development of very real practical possibilities to affect, and take part in, previously unattainable domains of their lives.

Secondly, the refined general substantive role that the nation-state that opens itself in this way adopts for itself must now adhere unbendingly to the intact essential humanity. Its ultimate *telos* is now unquestionably to enhance the three ultimate goods of democracy as much and as equally as possible, in relation to every existing bearer of dignity as their rightful addressee, and to engage in that role out of the unconditional and genuine respect. Such a role must, moreover, also be explicitly defined and entrenched as such in the refining nation-state constitution, or at least through its interpretation. Note that the role thus defined is different from all sorts of available substantive roles under monism; its constitutionally entrenched addressees are different, as is the rationale, and we will see that this will have important implications. However, this does not mean that the nation-state is now no longer able in some context to enhance those democratic goods primarily for, say, its own citizens, or the current members of the common project. What it does mean is that in any such remaining context there will need to be a realistic rationale why doing so in that particular context actually enhances in the ultimate sense those goods for their *rightful* final addressees—every existing bearer of dignity. I have elaborated comprehensively on this role, and defended it further, elsewhere;[14] what is explained here suffices for adding this further feature to the rising refined conception of the nation-state.

Thirdly, it follows from such a foundational refinement that the refining nation-state could only open itself to the kind of common project that is engaged in a

[14] Jaklic (n 1).

gradual, but ongoing and open-ended external expansion that is not regionally confined. This actually implies several aspects. Firstly, it means that the only temporary limit to such a project's further enlargement (spread of democracy's three ultimate goods) could be some clear and present threat of thereby destroying the very capacity for even further enlargement. Secondly, the common project could only be such as to continue to strive with equal, if not intensified, commitment for further expansion even when it crosses the outer boundaries of geographical Europe. Citizens of some neighboring countries might be in an even greater need of such an enhancement and equalization concerning self-rule than the citizens of different European states. Under the sound foundation that is consistent with the intact essential humanity, those could not be legitimately excluded due to their mere location. Thirdly, for the same reason the project's expansion could also not be limited to building a coherent territory of neighboring states, but ought to be neutral in this sense and thus offer inclusion on an equal basis to nation-states from very different parts of the world. For a common project that is truly consistent with the intact essential humanity the expansion to states from different parts of the world is simply the same thing as the expansion to neighboring states/regions. While that might not have been technically possible during our monist past, our new globalizing age (also one of the terms from the sound pluralist challenge) enables this more than ever before.

A proof of the viability of such an approach is already to be found in the current EU regime. Thus, we have EU territories with EU citizenship, EU laws, and elections to the European Parliament from territories throughout the world. Examples include the African Reunion, South American French Guiana, and Oceania's New Caledonia. These are of course embryonic illustrations showing that the phenomenon of distant nation-state inclusions under the fully refined common project is surely also possible and ought to become part of regular reality. Indeed, this kind of unbending orientation towards the "external others" is the only one fully compatible with the intact essential humanity. The truly refined nation-state could only consistently open itself to some such a common project. Due to its open-ended and regionally unconfined nature this kind of common project would obviously no longer be Europe, at least not the way we currently understand it.[15]

Fourthly, under such a refinement the nation-state, as we will see, still keeps both its fully self-standing status as well as more than sufficient key applicative "strength mechanisms" that retain, and even further entrench, it in its powerful self-standing form.[16] Knowing this, and knowing also that only by refining itself according to the intact terms of essential humanity will it be able to supersede the European monist alternative and thus save itself, the nation-state becomes willing to gradually transfer the areas affecting all to the common decision-making level of such a common project.

[15] For an excellent and nuanced account of arguments occupying the EU currently with respect to enlargement, see T. Austin, *The End of Europe? Turkey and the Cultural Border of the European Union* (Cambridge, MA: Harvard University Lamont Library, 2012).

[16] For this key aspect of the refinement, see pp. 310–13. With the "strength mechanisms" the nation-state thus remains not only self-standing, but also unexpectedly powerful.

It becomes willing, however, only under condition that the direct authorship link with the affected people themselves is successfully established at the level of such a project. This must be done in the purely principled sense (the direct title to authorship) as well as the applicative sense (authorship exercised through direct elections compatible with one person one vote etc). This alone, as the nation-state defenders know, opens the possibility of equalizing and enhancing the effective power of those who are democracy's rightful addressees even further than does the monist superstate Europe. Only this can escape its challenge.

At the same time, the truly refined nation-state must just as emphatically also insist on retaining under its own jurisdiction the areas primarily affecting its own people, as well as both aspects of their own *direct* authorship link just mentioned. It must also keep some of the key "strength mechanisms" that can continue to ensure that its self-standing status like this is truly retained and its own area of affectedness not improperly encroached upon through the pressures from the common project (those mechanisms are discussed separately later[17]). When the areas primarily and mostly affecting the nation-state people alone are thereby entrenched at the national level, the effective power of the affected citizens is thereby preserved to the maximum possible extent; were the areas transferred to the common project, or gradually encroached upon by it (as tends to occur under monism),[18] the number of decision-makers would increase, and the relative effective power of the truly affected individuals consequently decrease. This is one of those inherent democratic advantages of the nation-state model that only it can provide, and only through keeping the nation-state in its strong and fully self-standing form.[19]

Under its new sound foundation, the refining nation-state is thus not only bound, but gradually also willing, to entrench and follow both aspects of the refinement according to the principle of affectedness. Together they open the possibility of unprecedentedly equalizing and enhancing the effective power for its rightful addressees—the nation-state's own citizens as well as the "external others". Indeed, this strategy enables the remedying of the monist democratic deficit (as to effective power) of the old nation-state model, as well as that of the superstate model, while retaining the self-standing nature of the refined nation-state and further entrenching it in that status.

Through such a refinement the nation-state also enables the curing of the deficit with respect to participation. It conditions such an opening of itself only if it is to the common project with the direct link in the affected people themselves. What was previously the sphere between the sovereign nation-states, governed by international law, would under this model therefore be the domain of ordinary legislation. This opens gateways for participation not only as widely as they are opened under the superstate strategy, but even more so. The non-monist formation of the common project opens access to the affected bearers of dignity beyond the confines

[17] Pp. 310–13.

[18] Jaklic (n 1); cf also V. Ostrom, *The Political Theory of a Compound Republic: Designing the American Experiment* (3rd edn, Lanham, NY: Lexington Books, 2008).

[19] Recall the goal of the refinement as described at p. 300.

of the regional Europe. Moreover, participation is enabled through direct elections, properly managed referenda, the right to be elected a legislator, judge, direct participant in the common discourse of all the affected, the right to be consulted, and numerous other access points or gateways that are never so open and available in the process of international treaty enactments. The latter process, whether in the sphere between sovereign nation-states or that between the European superstate and other sovereign states, is thus removed much more than the pluralist alternative from the affected individuals. Under both variants of monism those spheres are, even though they profoundly concern those individuals' own lives, still basically closed for them.

With respect to the self-ruling virtues, too, the nation-state can refine itself so that it enables eliminating the monist deficit. It is possible for the nation-state to show that certain national boundaries from those substantive fields that determine our relation with the "other", such as that of nationhood and religion, must remain entrenched through the strong self-standing nation-state formation. Those boundaries include within themselves also some indispensable elements without which the third democratic advancement is not attainable at all. To be sure, they cannot remain the same as the boundaries we had in the old model of the monist nation-state. Nor does it suffice that they simply be made compatible with the civic virtues under European monism; that still recasts monism at another level and therefore cannot secure the entirely sound refinement of either the national or the European boundaries. Instead, in its construction of the sound boundaries the refining nation-state must again strictly follow its intact pluralist foundation and the fully sound substantive role that flows from it. This leads to a unique refined conception of national boundaries that are completely consistent with the idea of universal, unconditional, and genuine respect.

According to this refinement, the ultimate goal of maintaining the boundaries of, for instance, nationhood ought thus to be to affirm, to appreciate, the nation-state citizen's worth not as a member of this nation and/or this state, but as a human being. Here the citizen is not protected by virtue of his or her membership in our superior ethnic or civic group (because they are our own flesh and blood, or because they share the common institutions or some glorious history or culture of our national enterprise about which we may rightly feel proud), but only because she is a human being. Taking this view, moreover, the criteria for nationality and citizenship, like birth, common history, shared culture and institutions, only have a formal character: together in some form they function as a mechanism for distribution between different states of the obligation to protect and offer care. The distribution must, however, be just in relation to everyone in this world so that the dignity of each individual is thereby respected equally.

Equally, any nationhood boundary would need to be fully consistent with the unconditional spirit of the sound role. For instance, this approach makes a difference when it comes to the question of "exiting" from nationality, from citizenship. It implies absolute prohibition against the nation-state revoking one's citizenship. "Exit" could only occur voluntarily. That would probably need to be so even if failure on the part of the citizen was severe and occurred against the nation-state itself, such as in the case of treason. Any contrary understanding of nationhood would seem to violate the requirement of offering recognition unconditionally on the basis of one's humanity as the sole reason for recognition, regardless of one's achievements or, indeed, one's failures. It would also be contrary to the genuine quality of the intact respect that requires of the nation-state never to give up on one, even when the "failure" is severe.

To give a further example, this approach also says something about the quality of the nation-state citizen status once inside citizenship. Consistent with its redefined role the nation-state could not, for instance, engage in differentiations between different classes of citizen based on different grounds on which citizenship/nationality is obtained, such as, reservations of some public offices for citizens born (but not those naturalized) in the nation-state. Under such a nationality policy, it could hardly be said that the conception of nationhood that the nation-state maintains through its particular boundary is unconditional, based not on expected contribution/failure, or a relatively greater possibility thereof.[20]

Such a fully intact approach to constructing the boundaries of nationhood also says something about "access" to nationality and to citizenship. It narrows the range of legitimate reasons for denying citizenship. The mere factor of compatibility with the dominant culture becomes irrelevant and needs to be excluded as part of the citizenship test. No longer could such a rejection of individuals from other cultures, who are, for instance, pressing on the nation-state borders out of their profound lack of basic life needs, be legitimately rejected simply by referring to the will of the sovereign national *demos*[21] as not sympathetic—whether explicitly or implicitly—to the idea of a multi-ethnic future,[22] or to the nonconformity with a particular dominant culture of that country's civic conception.[23] The only legitimate reason for denying access in a given case is when this is inescapable in order to preserve the capacity of the state to accomplish, in due course and in an effective way, an even more extensive expansion of the unconditional citizenship. Only this is truly

[20] Note that this is of course the difficulty that tends to develop under monism. Moreover, there may well be under a monist regime those who see, and even criticize, this difficulty, but they are, partly precisely because they are situated within monism, then quite unable to make a difference. Cf R. Kennedy, "A Natural Aristocracy" in W. Eskridge and S. Levinson (eds), *Constitutional Stupidities, Constitutional Tragedies* (New York, NY: New York University Press, 1998) 54–6; see also S. Levinson, *Our Undemocratic Constitution* (Oxford: Oxford University Press, 2006) 150–7.

[21] That is, the majority representing that *demos* and its will.

[22] *The Guardian* (10 May 2009): "The Italian prime minister... has defended his government's decision to return migrants found off its shores to Libya by declaring that his party rejected the idea of a 'multi-ethnic' Italy." We must not blind ourselves that incidents of this sort are not being bred underneath the façade of the modern European nation-state. Take but the most well-known recent example of the French policy over immigration of Romas: "In an unusually forthright attack on a member state, the EU Justice Commissioner, Viviane Reding, compared France's crackdown on Roma immigrants from eastern Europe this summer to the Nazi persecution of gypsies during the Second World War. She said that she 'personally' expected the Commission to start a legal action 'within weeks' against Paris for breaching the letter and the spirit of European law on the free movement of EU citizens" (*The Independent*, 15 September 2011).

[23] For a potential example of certain such aspects, see, eg the current Dutch citizenship test and the trend as such, <http://www.dw.de/dw/article/0,2144,1935900,00.html> accessed 21 September 2013.

consistent with the unconditionality and universality requirements from the refined foundation.

In addition to the examples of the formal refinement that consider access to nationality, formal equality once inside, and exit from it, the refinement also concerns the content, or purpose, of the national boundaries. Under the refined conception national boundaries are inherently about a special type of protection and care. As Weiler already argued, they offer a "social home."[24] This familiar good sometimes referred to by those who defend nation-states,[25] however, undergoes important further refinement when reinterpreted under the new fully sound foundation and its intact respect. This allows it to be understood in an even more specific way.

Here the "social home" consists of one being accepted (ie one's worth is affirmed) by the nation-state due to one's mere existence, regardless of one's achievements, contribution, failure, and not even due to one's membership in the nation. In the sphere of human intercourse outside the nation-state one may fail for some reason, find oneself in distress and need, or considered by others to have failed. One experiences degradation in dignity, one feels excluded. This becomes much more serious when there is no alternative social space where one could be accepted irrespective of one's achievements, by the mere fact that one *is*.[26] By contrast, when there is a nation to which one belongs, ideally one constituting its own state and thus a social haven that is equally powerful in its authority as is the authority of, say, the common project itself (as is the case under pluralism), then an entity like this, provided that it truly exercises its refined role, is indeed able to offer a powerful "shield against existential aloneness," against deprivation of dignity.[27] With it, the failure in one's perception of one's own worth and self-esteem is much less likely to occur. Having *such* a social home one, moreover, also knows one always has a new beginning.[28] Yet "belongingness" is thus not, as Weiler seems to suggest, valuable already in and of itself; rather it is valuable as a means, and to the extent that it really generates that sense of unconditional, genuine, and universal recognition. That is because that sense is related to the fostering of self-ruling (*agapeistic*) virtues, which is the end in itself.[29]

The unconditional and genuine aspects of the described approach are obvious and need no further explanation. The fully sound universal aspect should nonetheless be further specified. Offering this type of social home ought to affirm the individual's value in virtue of her individual humanity as such and not of, say, her membership in a noble entity about which one could feel strong national pride. The unconditional recognition by the nation-state can indeed function as a

[24] Weiler (n 6) at 338.

[25] See a discussion of the main representatives of "liberal nationalism" in Jaklic (n 1) ch XII, subsection "Refining the Nation-State."

[26] Cf Weiler (n 6). [27] Weiler (n 6).

[28] In connection to the latter, recall the discussion of the "genuine" quality of the *agapeistic* recognition: the idea that the giver of such a respect "never gives up on" the other (see pp. 280–3).

[29] On this, see pp. 308–9, in connection with Chapter 9, p. 292.

powerful shield for self-esteem: irrespective of what happens out there, one always is and will remain a member of this equally important entity that recognizes one's priceless worth. Yet, again, nationhood as "belongingness" is not a sound value in itself. It can generate self-esteem on at least two different bases only one of which is truly sound. The first is by virtue of one's recognition as a member of some powerful and/or noble collectivity (be it in a historical, cultural, civic, or even ethnic sense), which fuels the self-esteem. This rationale generates the so-called "collective self-esteem,"[30] assumed also by most of the liberal nationalists, and is not what the redefined conception here can be about; the latter is consistent with monism where different nation-states are free to glorify their own national achievements which tends to lead to differences in collective self-esteem between citizens of different (eg more versus less successful) nation-states. The refined conception must rather rest on the second rationale, one that fosters "individual self-esteem"[31] by implying that the state is morally obliged, simply due to one's humanity, to offer a social home unconditionally. Unlike the selective collective self-esteem, the self-esteem generated in this way is individual and universal: it affirms the pricelessness of an individual as a bearer of dignity, a characteristic that is non-selective, universally valid, and held by each individual severally. Such an individual-oriented self-understanding of the nation-state could also not be understood in an imposing way. It is not that one is somehow chosen—predetermined—to have such a social home. It is rather that everyone must have the choice of having one, that this good must be there for those who are in need of it. This is not inconsistent with one having a choice to exclude oneself from it according to one's own will. As I have argued elsewhere, such a redefinition of nationhood avoids all sorts of serious problems that liberal nationalists have thus far faced (due to their defending nationhood through collective self-esteem), and provides a fully sound basis for a potential successful liberal construction of national boundaries.[32]

This kind of further refinement of the value of belongingness in relation to the nation-state's own citizens (internal refinement) is necessary, but not yet sufficient, for the nation-state to become fully compatible with the intact pluralist foundation and its corresponding sound substantive role. The offering of this good by the nation-state in an unconditional, universal, and genuine way to its citizens is at best only a partial measure. If it is really successfully to surpass the European challenge, such a refining nation-state must still further refine its conception of belongingness also in its relation to "external others". The broader and ultimate goal of its described endeavor must thus become to offer and spread this good, and do so with no lesser intensity, also across the globe to the external bearers of dignity. Here, too, this could be done only via the direct opening of the refining nation-state and its

[30] J. Spinner-Halev and E. Teiss-Morse, "National Identity and Self-Esteem" (2003) 1 Perspectives on Politics (2003) 515–32. These two authors, while themselves in search of a liberal justification for nationalism, lucidly expose the remaining dark side of nationhood implicit in the existing national-liberal accounts by Isaiah Berlin, Will Kymlicka, Joseph Raz, Neil MacCormick, Yael Tamir, Charles Taylor, and other leaders within contemporary "liberal nationalism."

[31] Spinner-Halev and Teiss-Morse (n 30) at 515–32.

[32] Jaklic (n 1) at ch XII.

territory to the common (supranational) pluralist project programmed towards the kind of open-ended enlargement described earlier. Such a project extending well beyond Europe would thus not only be charged with the role of promoting this kind of national self-understanding in the nation-states abroad. It would also itself, through offering them membership in its own coexisting formation, directly offer its own "social home" to every existing bearer of dignity on what for them was previously a closed territory of the sovereign nation-states within which they had no such a "home" at all. This is yet another aspect of the refinement that makes the boundary from nationhood still further distinct from both, the one under monism or the one under some internal "pluralism" that remains limited to Europe and is thus still externally monist. Neither of those conceptions of "belongingness" is fully sound, neither is yet sufficiently pluralist or pluralistically distinct.

The sound common project thus construed would, moreover, also work as a coequal pluralist check against abuses of the nation-state's own sound role. In our imperfect world, instances of failures to treat with genuine recognition always occur. There would thus inevitably be instances when the refined nation-state, too, would happen to act against such intact recognition. However, when this occurs, but there is then also another and no less significant entity offering genuine recognition to its addressee as such, such an entity functions as the irreplaceable additional check against deprivation of individual self-esteem, of dignity. Not only does it thereby itself work as the *direct* shield affirming dignity in that case, but it also functions as an *indirect* shield in the sense that what was previously a sovereign nation-state is no longer as free to act in whatever unrefined way the sovereign will happens to dictate. The factual pressure from the pluralist coexistence of the fundamentally coequal entity, one that is truly oriented toward all and called to guard exactly against the national construction of boundaries that are not fully pluralist, works as an important incentive for the nation-state to comply with its refined role and minimize its own failures in the first place.

Now, it is exactly when, and only when, the nation-state refines its boundaries in all these sound substantive and formal ways as briefly sketched above that it enables unprecedented alleviation of the monist deficit regarding virtues. The refinement is not sound solely because one could not but accept the moral force of the sound new foundation and its underlying respect in the light of which the conception has been refined. Crucially, it is sound because such a fully inclusive and intact arrangement works as a powerful source for breeding the higher type of virtues—the intact respect—in its citizens. In such a case citizens (now also other than just those of Europe) begin to sense the universal unconditional recognition offered through both coexisting formations, which is in effect the recognition by their fellow human beings whom they have irreversibly encountered in the new globalizing age and will continue to do so. They feel accepted regardless of their achievements, due to simply being the bearers of dignity while also experiencing the universal value that is thereby being bestowed on themselves. They come to affirm their individual self-esteem as persons worthy of this kind of higher respect that nothing else in this world enjoys. By experiencing the powerful value of this type of recognition that is able to reach them through the more fully inclusive pluralist regime, they themselves tend to be affected. More and more they feel the need genuinely to begin extending the same privilege to their fellow citizens by whom they are thus respected in the first place. The more the spirit of unconditional recognition is thus spread, the greater the number of citizens who learn the truly intact virtues and the more self-ruling they thereby become.

John Rawls would, I believe, agree that this offers some promise to work as the right strategy for redeeming the nation-state in its role of maintaining national boundaries. For what has just been described for the field of nationhood is actually only a more concrete manifestation (ie manifestation in this particular area of human boundaries) of the phenomenon that he explained more generally. We observed that with his example of how the virtues are being bred through unconditional recognition. The latter was identified and defended as the central element through which the citizens encounter, internalize, and learn to practise the self-ruling virtues in the first place.[33]

It is not just the boundaries from nationhood, but also those from religion, and other fields, that can be refined under pluralism allowing them to function as such indispensable sources of learning and internalizing the self-ruling virtues.[34] I analyse that in detail in my other work and elaborate several such further sound meta-constitutional components of substantive pluralism. Moreover, we saw that the fully sound pluralist arrangement to which the nation-state opens itself also offers and extends the first two ultimate goods of democracy to their rightful addressees on this universally inclusive, unconditional, and genuine basis. That too is itself an additional source of generating such higher virtues fully compatible with the intact equal respect.

Indeed, only if the nation-state truly follows this remaining route of the intact refinement will it really get closer than the monist European superstate to the highest possible maximization of the self-ruling virtues for their rightful addressees. The breeding of the virtues under the European superstate is, no matter how refined, still monist, and thus creates deficit for this good in the internal as well as the external sense.

As to the internal sense, the tendency of the monist rationale for the monopolization of a given territory in the hands of a select group of people inevitably breeds all sorts of understandings that are too self-centered. Even if the boundaries are now of the civic (as opposed to ethnic) kind, it is probably impossible under monism to justify them through any fully sound rationale. Instead, in practice the monist tendency leads, and especially so in the masses, to morally arbitrary justification

[33] Chapter 9, pp. 275–6 in connection to 266–8.

[34] Similarly, note that the value of originality, of which Weiler and MacCormick speak as being another sound building block, also acquires its greatest force when set within the context of nationhood thus refined. This way it is no longer merely about "preservation of species" and of their rich potential, but above all becomes the essential instrument for strengthening—by generating a bond of genuine kinship—the very conditions for learning that spirit of unconditional recognition within a nation. When members of such a nation are not bound up in a sovereign state, but live instead through a constant direct engagement with the members of their common project under pluralism, the further spread of the spirit from its source is most effective.

factors such as those from, say, ownership of the territory, history of collective achievements or their reverence (collective self-esteem), mere fact of birth into a particular place, or the contractual contribution to the common regime or capacity thereof. Unlike some elusive sound justification for monism that in our globalizing age no longer seems to exist, these corrupt civic rationales are openly available, self-evident, highly appealing, and thus most realistic candidates for the people's own perceptions under monism. This breeds less than the intact self-ruling virtues in citizens under the monist superstate.

The external aspect is also clear. Through a monist regime the spread of the fully sound self-ruling virtues (even if they were truly sound, which they are not) fails to reach and directly affect the "external others". The arrangement through which the refining nation-state opens itself to a fully inclusive common project comes, now also with respect to virtues, much closer to the ideal of essential humanity than does the European superstate. It also comes further than some internally "pluralist" Europe that is externally still monist, which similarly keeps its own variant of the unsound boundary that is neither universal nor could it really be, for that reason, appropriately unconditional and genuine.

Another example of the monist deficit besetting any monist model of democracy is the deficit from the "rebounded reflex." This is the deficit that contributes to the lesser overall stability of a regime. I mention it here since it was already referred to above in the discussion on the particular conception of respect as the soundest foundation of liberal legitimacy.[35] This deficit obviously affects the maximization of all three of democracy's ultimate meanings/goods: effective power, participation, and self-ruling virtues. Only the nation-state that is refined as described opens itself to offering these ultimate goods of democracy (including the share in their authorship) to the "external others" on the fully genuine, non-self-centred, basis and irrespective of their location outside some regional Europe. The "others" notice and feel the change. Note thus that this not only includes many more people who are thereby gradually being included as true equals, but also disables the working of the monist rebounded reflex at its very source. Some variant of the self-centred maximization of these goods through one of the monist rationales is no longer available. The monist foundational principle dictating that logic is gone; it has been replaced with the sound pluralist foundation to which the refining nation-state opened itself. With it is gone also the monist source that bred the rebounded reflex in "external others" who felt very clearly that they were unwarrantedly excluded from being our equals, from being just as worthy primary recipients of justice as we are. Other things being equal, a refined regime of greater long-term stability (legitimacy) that becomes available through such a refinement in and of itself enables a greater amount of the democratic goods than a system with lesser stability/legitimacy.

Finally, there is one last aspect of the refinement that must be explored here. For all of this to work the refining nation-state would need, as its defenders know, also

[35] Chapter 9, pp. 273–5 and 283–4.

to make sure that the new common project does not gradually slip into some kind of a regionally confined, monist superstate. After all, according to this refinement a lot of spheres and thus power would end up being transferred to the common project. Moreover, the latter would also get the direct democratic link (in the foundational and applicative sense) with the affected people themselves. While the nation-state would thereby enable the possibility of the unprecedented democratic enhancement, it would also need to be able to protect its own ultimately self-standing status and, with it, also keep all of those indispensable dimensions of such a democratic enhancement that we saw only the nation-state could provide. The refined nation-state must make sure, in other words, not to destroy the substantive pluralist challenge (which will be, as we are going to see, crucial also for triggering the refinement of the European monist strand), but rather to keep it as part of the new refined pluralist arrangement itself. When that challenge is destroyed, the process of inescapable mutual moving of the actors towards the sound pluralist refinements (the nation-state half of which we have just been observing) does not take place in the first place.

The refined nation-state therefore ought to keep within its own half of the jurisdictional divide those additional areas, or mechanisms", that are decisive for maintaining the relative strength of its self-standing formation. By "relative strength" I mean that which could make the nation-states sufficiently powerful for the specific aim of preventing the potential slipping of the common project towards the monist foundation and the monist superstate. The nation-states should thus be entitled to use this lever for the purpose of directing the common project into the open-ended enterprise as described: one that explicitly recognizes the self-standing nature of the refined nation-state (just as that of its own) and is not territorially confined, but instead charged with ongoing enlargement that is actively extending its direct democratic link to more and more remaining external bearers of dignity.

Just as the other sound nation-state dimensions elaborated thus far, these "strength mechanisms" are representations at the applicative level of the pluralist principle from the foundation of the new arrangement. They are clearly able to produce that sufficient effective strength needed for keeping the challenge alive and the common project in check. According to this balance, the common project (cf the current EU) does not possess some key "essential characteristics of statehood"[36] that should be reserved for the nation-states themselves. For instance, unlike the nation-states, the common project should "not have monopoly of legitimate force over [its] territory, but [should] depend... on the states to apply and enforce its laws."[37] Nor should it have some overall "tax raising powers," but should "depend... on the states" in this respect, too.[38] Unlike the nation-states, such a

[36] N. MacCormick, *Who's Afraid of a European Constitution?* (Exeter: Imprint Academic, 2005) 48.
[37] MacCormick (n 36) at 48.
[38] MacCormick (n 36) at 48.

common project should not be allowed to "raise a defense force of its own";[39] that, too, should be the prerogative of the nation-states and their comparably sized territorial units. Nor should it be able to decide by itself whether a common European action employing all (or most) of the nation-states' troops is needed. Since the nation-state monist regime also has not dealt with this issue satisfactorily, which in part contributed to the relative effective-power deficit between citizens of different member states, a unique new solution along the pluralist lines is needed.[40] Moreover, instead of granting it to the common project, the authority to decide with final authority in cases of boundary disputes—the issue of *who*—should be left open so that the nation-state level too retains its coequal role in it. Any one of the several pluralist solutions, as already proposed by the pluralist authors,[41] would fit this applicative scheme; as we saw, they were all different from the monist solution in that they more or less secured the equal say of both self-standing actors in resolving that issue. Finally, the nation-state could legitimately exercise the option of "exit" in any event of grave aberrations, when the common project was clearly and persistently breaking the very central tenets of the new sound pluralist foundation, thereby drifting towards the monist superstate and thus back to the democratic deficit.

Who could reasonably say in the light of this that the common project could not be sufficiently under check by the nation-states? Who could possibly think that, under some regime of this kind, the explicit normative pluralist principle at the foundation (a force of its own) would nonetheless be gradually replaced with some new monist normative foundation? Who could declare that under this regime the nation-states become mere federal units subordinate to their sovereign whole? Who could profess that the common project established through this kind of refinement is a new sovereign superstate? In each of the state-constitutive elements mentioned, such a common project is indeed different from a state. In each of them it would be different from the existing superstates.[42] Conversely, who could say that such a project is a mere subordinate extension of the old sovereign nation-state entity, such as is the case with international organizations? Its authority is *directly* grounded in the affected people themselves, and is so, as was explained above, at

[39] MacCormick (n 36) at 48.

[40] For one way in which this could work without thereby creating deficit (in effect breaching "one person one vote" in issues that affect us equally), see Jaklic (n 1) text to fn 510 in that work.

[41] The crucial distinctive feature of all these pluralist proposals is that, unlike the monist solution, all of them leave the question (ie "which of the self-standing systems ought to have the authority of the final say over interpretation?") *open*. While there are different meanings as to what specifically is meant by the concept of "leaving the question open," none of those pluralist meanings could be considered as resolving that issue in a way that grants the final ultimate authority to decide to one of the competing systems. That is the monist solution alone. Not even the pluralist solution according to which the final decision is entrusted to neither a European nor a nation-state body, but one composed of an equal number of representatives (judges) from both systems, is therefore monist: the final interpretive authority is neither in the hands of the first nor the second coexisting system. Needless to say, those pluralist solutions insisting that there be no such final decision at all are even more obviously non-monist.

[42] MacCormick (n 36) at 48–9.

the foundational level (the individuals affected, not the states, are its direct authors/ addressees) as well as the applicative one (that direct authority is exercised though direct elections according to one person one vote and through a whole system of widely open gateways for participation). The emerging sound version of substantive constitutional pluralism is indeed very different from both of those monist options.

It should be concluded in the end that the nation-state thus refined is able to rebut the European challenge, and to do so in a way that it cannot but welcome. Given the force of that challenge, this kind of refinement is not just the only, but also the greatest, opportunity at its disposal. For through it, the nation-state not only preserves its existence, but even successfully defends itself in the strong form that is not a mere subordinate unit of some mightier sovereign whole. This saves and entrenches it for another era to come and is thus its best defense strategy. At the same time, the redefined nation-state has turned itself from an unsound monist actor into a pluralist actor of the soundest kind. Sovereignty is abandoned, and is so for invincible reasons. In its refined form the nation-state enables the opportunity of enhancing democracy's ends to their rightful addressees (their own citizens included) far beyond anything a European monist superstate ever could.

3. The Challenge Reversed: Refining Europe

The nation-state defenders may rightfully see this as a fully successful refinement. Yet they know that it is also something more, much more. Through this particular kind of refinement the nation-state has not only managed to evade the powerful challenge of the new Europe, but has now *itself* become such a challenge to the European project. The democratic challenge is now turned back with full force, especially on the European monist camp and its superstate model of democracy. In the light of the new opportunity offered by the refined nation-state, it is now actually the European superstate that suffers from a greater democratic deficit. It does not approach as much as possible the ideal of essential humanity, but instead remains a monist formation based on the monist foundation. As such the European sovereign superstate inevitably discards the dimensions from the refined self-standing nation-state that are indispensable for generating the maximum possible democratic advancement. That being so, there is no reason from the perspective of the accepted sound pluralist challenge why the all-European monist project should continue. Now it is *this* project that not only fails to do everything possible for the maximum enhancement of democratic ends to its rightful addressees, but even disables such a maximization for good; once European monism takes over, the opportunity of the new historic context to lead to the next leap of democracy disappears and is wasted. It is indeed the European project that ought to perish. Or so it seems at this point.

This reversed challenge is just as powerful as was the initial one. Its normative aspect is invoked on the same sound ground (that it comes closer to essential humanity) as was the European challenge, and there could indeed hardly be any disagreement that, from the perspective of the intact standard the proponents of

Europe themselves invoked and had accepted with the pluralist challenge, the refined pluralist arrangement would be more democratic. Moreover, the powerful nation-state still exists and would, as we just saw, continue to do so even in its refined form. Just as before, the powerful normative challenge is thus reinforced through factual pluralism. There is no way for the European camp to ignore it.

This time, it is thus the proponents of the European project that have no choice but to delve deeper into self-reflection. In doing so they too begin realizing that there is nonetheless one last remaining route through which their project could, though now in a refined form, still evade the challenge to its existence. While one option is simply to declare defeat, the other is to resort to the same general strategy of deflection from monism (this time European monism) as was adopted by the nation-state and its deflection from its own version of monism. The proponents of the European project know, in other words, that they too need to refine their project in a way that would adhere strictly to the fully sound guiding standard of the intact respect for essential humanity. There is good reason that, through this kind of strategy, they too would be able to point out that their project likewise carries some irreplaceable dimensions for any further historic enhancement of democracy.

The first and unavoidable step of such a refinement is the replacement of the European monist constitutional foundation with the more inclusive common pluralist foundation that was already described above; this implies abandoning the ambition of developing the European project towards a monist superstate. This foundational refinement is then followed also by the more applicative ones that are actually further representations of such a foundational pluralist principle. Among them are the adoption of the principle of open-ended expansion of the European formation, acceptance to divide jurisdiction with the nation-state according to the principle of affectedness, the establishment of both direct electoral authority and opened access for the affected throughout its jurisdictional sphere, the refined approach to maintaining boundaries, recognition of the sound democratic components of the refined nation-state, and so on. Indeed, the refinement that adheres strictly to the sound terms from the pluralist challenge leads the defenders of the European project to adopt precisely the form of the common project to which the refined self-standing nation-state became willing to open itself. While only that has the ability to solve the European monist deficit, we saw that was not exactly a European project, and certainly not so in the regional sense, so this refinement of the European camp is significant.

Yet it is also sound and powerful. Through it, the defenders of the European project are able to show that it is actually *their* project that is in the position of providing the missing half that the refined nation-state also needed, but was unable itself to provide. For, it is not that the refined nation-state, by the very fact of its refinement, already built the superior model of democracy. It only opened itself to accepting some such common project with which together it then would be able to form that superior model free of the monist deficit. The refined nation-state thus only made its own half of the sound building blocks available while the common supranational project alone could then add the other half. It is, after all, true by definition that it is for its people alone (the equal self-standing authority possessing the direct link) to make choices as to their part of the project and then likewise for themselves to lead its further sound pluralist construction. The nation-state can only open itself to it while offering concurrent support and assistance in its building, but it cannot make the choices on behalf of that coexisting self-standing source of authority itself.

Moreover, it is this powerful and fully democratic link, one that directly connects the project to the free will of the individuals themselves (as opposed to their states), that makes the refined European project self-standing and sufficiently strong. This constitutes its own half in the substantive pluralist challenge as the key source of all the refinement. Through this type of a direct link the people of the European project are inevitably united to the sufficient degree that enables that European check. Being recognized as the immediate authors of the European laws, while also exercising their authorship through the fully democratic system of links enabled under such a refinement, these people are in the position to freely form and express their political will at the European level and effectively to choose/replace their own governors according to how faithfully that will is being followed. This in and of itself represents a democratic force that would, as long as it were clearly exercised within the bounds of the sound pluralist constitution and its new foundation, be impossible in a democratic age to ignore.[43]

Yet in such an arrangement there is also something even more powerful about the refined European project. When things are set in this way there is inevitably always lurking in the background also the possibility of extra-constitutional action, of initiating, for example, a common superstate. Given that some key strength-enhancing mechanisms are in the hands of the refined nation-state as described,[44] such tendencies are still relatively tamed under pluralism: just as they ought to be, but not more. Thus, in the event of some nation-state's own persistent and serious encroachment on the sound pluralist constitution of the new model, nothing could really guarantee the nation-state's continued existence any more. The reason the European people had for adhering to the pluralist regime would disappear. With the direct authorship link established (at the foundational and applicative level) for the first time, the people of Europe could potentially choose any future for themselves. No one can really know for which of both actors such a clash might turn out more fatal. What both actors do know is that the rightful addressees of democracy would be worse off either way. And this check is only further reinforced by the fact that the authority over the issue of *who* (who decides who decides) is, under this pluralist arrangement, also not granted either of the two equally self-standing formations.

43 Indeed, some leading intellectual voices have recently reminded us that this alone could well itself be enough in our new age for the self-standing nature of such a common project to survive and thrive. Habermas essentially makes this point, corroborating it with the example of the current EU: "The European Union (EU) provides a convincing example of how higher-order legal norms [a self-standing system within its own sphere] can function in a binding manner even though they are actually backed and implemented by much more powerful member states that are formally subordinate [in what is not their own sphere] to those norms" (J. Habermas, "A Political Constitution for a Pluralist World Society?" (2007) 34 Journal of Chinese Philosophy 334).

44 See pp. 302–3 and 310–13.

Indeed, it is exactly the European project of this form that constitutes that part of the coequal check that had been missing throughout the long monist era dominated by the nation-state monopoly (factual monism) over the concept of democracy and its many forms of serious democratic deficits.

The sound new pluralist foundation indeed requires both halves of the pluralist "check." Insisting that their own described half be retained in the new conception, the proponents of the European project have thus not only disabled the source of the encroaching deficit that their project would otherwise be opened to from the nation-states. They have also distilled another sound and irreplaceable democratic component from their old monist project. Both the proponents of the European project, as well as those of the refined nation-state, thus cannot but also accept and help maintain this irreplaceable element within their new pluralist model.

Just as the refined nation-state, so the refined Europe in this way (and this way alone) manages to defend itself against the challenge. Its proponents not only succeed in preserving their project's existence, but are thus able successfully to defend it in the strong self-standing form, one that does not make it a mere derivative international, or intergovernmental, type of extension of sovereign nation-states. On the other hand, this process of refinement unavoidably persuades them to abandon their monist aspiration and instead turn the European project into a different formation that is pluralist in the soundest possible way. While accepting the clearly irreplaceable nation-state dimensions, the refined European project at the same time also offers to add to the rising new common pluralist conception those missing irreplaceable dimensions that, just as clearly, it and only it could successfully provide. This ensures that the new possibility of enhancing democracy's ends to its rightful addressees far beyond anything seen thus far does not only remain a possibility, but can now also become reality.

4. Full-Blown Substantive Pluralism

Note that the dialectic process underpinned by the unique substantive pluralist challenge has inevitably moved the actors in the direction of discarding the corrupted dimensions while putting together the sound components from each of their old monist projects. The joining of these sound and irreplaceable dimensions forms the cluster of basic principles, or substantive meta-constitutional building blocks, of the newly rising enhanced democracy. This could also be described as the sound full-blown conception of substantive pluralism, which is different from the "germ of substantive pluralism" precisely in that it also includes all these further and fully sound substantive building blocks that the actors under the challenge now come to adopt by themselves. It is the full-blown substantive pluralism that represents the final picture of what it means to "get together" (ie construct or refine a political formation) in a fully legitimate way, one that, unlike the monist type of "getting together," does full justice to every single bearer of dignity in this world as the rightful addressees of democracy's ends.

Moreover, the full-blown substantive pluralism is also different from the not-yet-fully sound conceptions of pluralism that were examined in the previous chapters. Firstly, it is different from both more strongly proceduralized versions of pluralism (Walker's and Maduro's). Not so only in the type of truly equal respect that it assumes at its foundation, but also in the crucial cluster of the substantive building blocks that it develops and entrenches at the meta-constitutional level of its pluralist arrangement. Those can be developed only through the unique substantive pluralist challenge as the key part of such a sound conception of pluralism. This slightly thicker approach is thus the only one sufficient enough to lead to the fully distinct and sound pluralist direction, as well as the only one capable of getting pluralism off the ground and towards the enhanced stage of pluralist democracy.

The procedural pluralisms were too thin to guarantee the pluralist distinctiveness within the decisive sphere of the *what*. This is remedied in the sound substantive pluralism precisely by that unique and intact substantive pluralist challenge that leads to the sufficient cluster of the intact substantive building blocks *themselves* representing that distinctly pluralist orientation within that decisive sphere of the pluralist discourse—the *what*. We have observed that this orientation is, unlike that under monism, fully intact while also wholly different from monism in its effects. Only this kind of approach is indeed strong enough to distinguish the pluralist conception and its results within the *what* from the monist conception and its own results within the same decisive sphere.

The procedural pluralisms were also not universal enough, and this is remedied in the sound conception of substantive pluralism by the intact substantive pluralist challenge. Unlike the procedural pluralisms that still allow the actors to limit their arrangement to Europe, the sounder terms of the substantive pluralist challenge do not permit such a regional confinement. They instead have the unique effect of engaging both actors so that they inevitably lead each other to move towards the fully universal direction characteristic of this substantive pluralist conception alone. Indeed, only a conception of pluralism that is capable of doing this, and doing it in the fully intact pluralist manner, can possibly be sufficiently distinct from monism. Only this kind of conception avoids the problem of ending up being externally monist as was, for instance, still the case with those too-proceduralized versions of pluralism that paid that price due to their excessive thinness.[45]

Secondly, the sound conception of the full-blown substantive pluralism as developed here is at the same time also sufficiently different from the existing variants of substantive pluralism examined in the earlier chapters. Not only does it clarify the only sound conception of equal respect that could possibly underpin the sound conception of substantive pluralism, and nor is it different only in that, by making them fully compatible with such a truly sound foundation, it further refines those substantive blocks from the existing conceptions, or that it develops still many more substantive building blocks also in the crucial field of democracy where the superiority of the pluralist conception can be established. Similarly, the

[45] See Chapter 8, pp. 239–50, especially pp. 248–50.

uniqueness of this pluralist approach is not exhausted by recalling that, here too, it remedies the non-fully universal orientation of the existing substantive conceptions (in as far as they are still limited to Europe, as Weiler's explicitly is) and thus rescues the very idea of pluralism from the challenge of monism. In addition, it is crucial that this conception is different from the existing substantive variants of pluralism also in that it shows how such a fully sound and distinctively pluralist direction can actually occur in the first place.

It does not *directly* require that the actors adopt its fully sound and elaborated (intact-respect-compatible) substantive building blocks. That is not only too imposing, but also cannot work since they would not be willing just like that, and right away, to adopt such a distinct new conception/refinement. The latter is probably in part why Weiler still feels more comfortable limiting his more direct version of substantive pluralism only to Europe, thereby paying the price of giving away the possibility of the fully sound (equal-respect-compatible and pluralistically fully distinct) content of his blocks as well as the related price of remaining monist in relation to "external others". Yet by employing the unique new European factual challenge in the particular way so as to create that key substantive pluralist challenge that both actors can easily accept, and cannot but accept in the unique new European context, the pluralist approach developed here shows how such a sound full-blown substantive pluralism can nonetheless be developed. Through this unique challenge the actors begin to influence and "move" each other so that each by itself gradually, but inevitably, realizes that its only and best choice is to adopt that sound, universal, and pluralistically distinct direction and its intact meta-blocks. This crucial dialectic process that is unavoidable under the uncontroversial and fully sound pluralist challenge is something that only this kind of pluralist approach is able to secure. In this way it is able to construct the sound conception of the full-blown substantive pluralism that saves the pluralist idea from the existing real challenges identified throughout the previous chapters.

With its cluster of sound, substantive building blocks the full-blown substantive pluralism at the same time also represents the sound pluralist meta-constitution that binds constitution makers and constitutional judiciary, as well as all policy makers at other levels of governance, be it nation-state or European. The sound meta-blocks are thus also very concrete constitutional standards that shape everyday public decision-making. By elaborating and accepting such a conception of substantive pluralism at their constitutional foundations, the actors indeed irreversibly constitute the constitutional blueprint of the enhanced conception of democracy—of the constitutional regime that they are now, unlike under the conditions of monism, able to envision and gradually—but inevitably—put into practice. As new as this may sound, they know that such a strategy and its pluralist model of democracy is the only one truly free of all the monist democratic deficits besetting the monist model of democracy.

The alignment of the unique new factual context in Europe and the "germ of substantive pluralism," which together enable the crucial substantive pluralist challenge, is then the key device now making possible the truly legitimate and uniquely pluralist type of getting together that is free from all the monist democratic deficits. Such a device of the substantive pluralist challenge thus has a crucial dual role. It is a kind of telescope that enables the actors to detect and demonstrate to one another the serious monist deficits of their old respective monist models. At the same time it is also a kind of "scaffold"[46] that then itself helps the actors further in their construction of the refinement and alleviation of the deficits all the way to the full-blown substantive pluralism (and beyond) as the pluralist constitution of the new enhanced democratic model. As such it serves the same general function, and occupies the same general place in constitutional thought, as does Rawls's idea of original position, except that Rawls's device was still bound to the monist nation-state or monist superstate, and could—to that extent—not yet have been fully sound, fully consistent with the intact respect for *every* bearer of dignity. It was thus, unlike the pluralist device, not yet in the position to cure the monist democratic deficits. Due to the different—monist—context for which it was elaborated, it was not yet in the position to follow so uncompromisingly the intact respect as the only basis on which liberal legitimacy, and its project of further advancement of democracy, can be still further improved in our post-Westphalian global age.

Finally, consider that the sound conception of full-blown substantive pluralism developed here also disproves one last critical view suggested recently, namely, that constitutional pluralism is actually not a distinctive type of political/legal ordering because it is supposedly no different than, for instance, some visions of American integration (eg its "dual federalist" interpretation[47]), or federal integration of some other states that have been similarly explained.[48] According to these interpretations, too, the argument goes, both formations—the states and the federation—have been considered independent within their own respective spheres of jurisdiction. Europe under constitutional pluralism would therefore really end up being nothing new.

While this critique might well partially affect some of the existing versions of constitutional pluralism, it does not at all apply to the sound conception of substantive pluralism as developed here.

Firstly, the constitutive pluralist principle at the very foundational level has never been clearly and comprehensively defined in the case of the US. (As we will see, it could not even have been defined.) To be sure, the rhetoric of "dual federalism" is full of similar-sounding terminology such as "separate spheres of jurisdiction" of the federal and state levels, "independent authorities within their own spheres," and the like. Yet this does not yet in and of itself say that *both* of these authorities are self-standing in the most *foundational* sense. It could well be that, whether as a matter of fact, normative principle, or both, there is in a federal regime a monist principle at the very foundational level that then supports a structure of two separate spheres of

[46] Cf F. Michelman, "The Subject of Liberalism" (1994) 46 Stanford Law Review 1807, 1820, 1826, ascribing such an equivalent role of a "scaffold" to Rawls's device of the original position.

[47] R. Schütze, *From Dual to Cooperative Federalism: The Changing Structure of European Law* (Oxford: Oxford University Press, 2010).

[48] A. Somek, "Monism: A Tale of the Undead" (2010) University of Iowa Legal Studies Research Paper, 22–3.

jurisdiction and their corresponding independent orders at the more applicative level. Such an applicative "pluralism" is not really constitutional pluralism. Constitutional pluralism is first and foremost defined at the very foundational level itself, whereas this is not necessarily the case with federalism as we have known it thus far. Indeed, as some of the greatest proponents of the Madisonian practice (of the idealized "dualist," "polyarchical," "compound" reading of the American federalism) themselves have shown, the monist principle from the deepest foundation is part of the reason why the US has inevitably drifted away from any true applicative "pluralism" as well.[49] Part of the difference in the US was indeed the lack of a decidedly pluralist theory at the foundational level that would have explained the pluralist difference there, and so through some sufficiently thorough, clear, and comprehensive account that would have also been able to come across realistically (an impossible task in the US context, as we are about to see).

Nor did Madison himself provide such an account at the foundational level. Those European authors who have recently tried to explain him so[50] fail to take into account that the fact of separate origins of the American order, according to which the latter emerged from both the independent state orders and the independent federal order, does not of course yet say anything about the pluralist versus monist foundational principle of the *new* common order. Foundational monism (supporting either applicative "pluralism" or monism) can arise out of one, two, or several independent sources, just as foundational constitutional pluralism, too, can arise out of one, two, or several such sources. To decide the question over constitutional pluralism versus monism, one needs to consider the newly established normative theory of the specific foundational level of the *new* order. Madison's two-sentence observation on the independent sources from which the integration arose[51] does not say anything about this further question. Without an explicit and realistic theory of pluralism explained for the foundational level of the new order, which never existed for the US, neither Madison nor anyone else could be presented as a constitutional pluralist.

Secondly, this goes hand in hand with the following. Not only would it be impossible to claim the same type of integration between the modern US and the full-blown substantive pluralism as elaborated here (neither a federal state nor an international organization),[52] but the way constitutional pluralism has been explained in this book makes it equally impossible to claim that the US *ever* in its history existed as a pluralist formation. Even if one leaves aside the issue whether there has ever been, in US integration history, a clear theoretical definition of the pluralist principle at the foundational level, such an elaboration at that level is not yet necessarily enough to speak of a formation that is pluralist, as opposed to monist, in nature. One of the central lessons of this book has been that, in order to really speak of a meaningful conception of pluralism that is sufficiently distinct from monism, the foundational principle must also be reflected through the

[49] See, eg Ostrom (n 18); cf also Jaklic (n 1) text to fn 413 in that text.
[50] Schütze (n 47) at 23–5. [51] Schütze (n 47) at 23–5. [52] see pp. 312–13.

applicative levels. This did not occur in the US right from the moment of its founding. When you grant such decisive powers as, say, defense, to the federal level, concentrate decision-making in the roles of a powerful federal President and his cabinet, agree to the federal Constitution explicitly declaring to be the "supreme law of the land" that prevails over the state constitutions in case of conflict, have the highest federal court adopt the role of the final arbiter of constitutionality, including as to the boundary between the federation and the states, and the like, the issue is over. The formation you have just created is in effect a typical monist one and it thus also makes no sense at all in circumstances of such factual applicative monism to speak of pluralism at the foundational level. Both levels are inherently joined and cannot be separated: once such a strong factual monism takes over, the foundational level is, whether one likes it or not, already taken away by monism as well.[53] It would take another real instance of factual pluralism—exactly the current new historic context in Europe—to try again and direct things onto the path of constitutional pluralism. When in these new European circumstances the actors then strictly follow the distinct pluralist direction from the foundation also through the applicative levels—the *what*, the *how*, and the *who*—we can speak of constitutional pluralism that is *wholly* distinct from monism also in its effects. This is, again, why the refined conception of full-blown substantive pluralism as defined here is undeniably distinct from the US or indeed any other known form of federalism, which remain monist and have always been such.[54]

Thirdly, nor was the US, at the time of its founding, even if it wanted to, in the position to pursue anything else but monism. As Madison himself knew well, choosing in those times any less "undivided" route than that of forging from the Confederation the sovereign monist Union (*e pluribus unum*) would most likely prove fatal for democracy across America.[55] Indeed, this would have even subjected democracy's "second coming" itself, this remarkable innovation led by America at

[53] To nonetheless explain that, despite monism at the applicative level, things are pluralist at the foundation level is simply daydreaming, ie no more than an unreal thing to say.

[54] Hence some of the recent attempts at criticism along this line (one of them even concluding that "American constitutionalism continues to subscribe to the idea . . . of constitutional pluralism") cannot succeed. Schütze (n 47); also his "Federalism as Constitutional Pluralism: 'A Letter from America'" in M. Avbelj and J. Komárek (eds), *Constitutional Pluralism in the European Union and beyond* (Oxford: Hart Publishing, 2012); D. Kochenov, "From Dual to Cooperative Federalism: The Changing Structure of European Law—Book Review" (2010) 21 EJIL 23–5. Note, moreover, that the regime under the Articles of Confederation, and so prior to establishing the US monism, was no less monist, just that the ultimate source of authority in that case was each sovereign state *demos*. For a more detailed elaboration of the distinction between that monism and Europe's constitutional pluralism, see Jaklic (n 1).

[55] J. Madison, "Vices of the Political System of the United States" in P. Kurland and R. Lerner (eds), *The Founders' Constitution*, Vol 1, ch 5, "Deficiencies of Confederation" Doc 16 (Chicago, IL: The University of Chicago Press, 1987); G. Morgan, *The Idea of a European Superstate* (Princeton, NJ: Princeton University Press, 2005) 140, 147–8; S. Beer, *To Make a Nation: The Rediscovery of American Federalism* (Cambridge, MA: Harvard University Press, 1993); R. Keohane, "Ironies of Sovereignty: The European Union and the United States" (2002) 4 Journal of Common Market Studies 743–65; F. Zakaria, *From Wealth to Power: The Unusual Origins of America's World Role* (Princeton, NJ: Princeton University Press, 1998).

that historic point,[56] to real danger. Unless the Confederation was replaced by the sovereign Union, foreign powers would, as Madison explicitly argued, be able to play one state off against another.[57] That would increase not only the likelihood of conflict and war, but also crucially reinforce the dominant influence from (possibly even accessions to) the leading foreign powers. Since those were of course not democratic, it is clear what this would have meant. Indeed, without entrenching the American democracy into the new ultimately undivided sovereign Union, into the strong monist superstate, the grand opportunity of democracy's "second coming"[58] would have been wasted. The Americans, the Europeans, and the world, might well not enjoy democracy today if it was not for that monist move towards the sovereign US. Moreover, slavery was additional strong reason why pluralism could not have been a viable option for Americans. It took no less than the unprecedentedly powerful monist superstate to truly eradicate this particular evil from every one of its resisting states.[59]

Fourthly, we saw that for pluralism to succeed it is also essential that it includes all the elements of the substantive pluralist challenge. That was of course not the case with the American "dual federalism." This means that instead of being regionally confined to some sovereign-state territory and its select group of people alone, the pluralist conception is fully universally oriented and thus internally programmed for the open-ended and distinctly pluralist inclusion of "external others". While there are still further unique aspects arising for constitutional pluralism out of the sound pluralist challenge, this suffices to conclude that the challenge from federalism (be it in its "dual" or any other existing form) can indeed not apply against the sound conception of constitutional pluralism elaborated in

[56] Recall the concurrent downfall of the French revolution that slipped France back to (the Napoleonian) despotism.

[57] Madison (n 55). Cf Morgan: "[*I*]*nternal sovereignty*... refers to a domestic authority structure that is centralized, undivided, and absolute... There is a range of historical and sociological evidence to suggest that states that lack internal sovereignty have a difficult time... maintaining their freedom from external subordination. There is also plenty of evidence to suggest that states that lack internal sovereignty are at a relative disadvantage when they find themselves in conflict with states that possess more centralized, undivided, and absolute domestic authority structures. To provide just two illustrations of this point: Consider, first, the early difficulties that confronted the Confederate States of America when the Confederacy sought to protect its external sovereignty form attacks by the British, the French, and Indian tribes. It was not just that the American Confederacy found it difficult to raise the necessary funds to support an army and a navy. Lacking a centralized locus of decision making, the member states found it difficult to prevent foreign powers from playing one state off against another. Decades earlier, James Madison had recognized this problem. His pamphlet *Vices of the Political System of the United States* relies very heavily on the foreign policy implications of the United States' domestic authority structure to make his case against the Articles of Confederation and in favor of a new Constitution [based on] internal sovereignty. [The development of] internal sovereignty, as Hendryk Spruyt has argued, was a consequence of something akin to a Darwinian process of selection" (Morgan (n 55) at 140, 147–8).

[58] J. Dunn, *Setting the People Free: The Story of Democracy* (London: Atlantic Books, 2005) 23.

[59] Cf also Keohane (n 55) at 745, who explains that the civil war resolved the issue between unitary and non-unitary sovereignty (two variants of monism) and put any potentially missing piece of the US sovereignty in its place. The argument from slavery as one of the reasons for the monist US was also made by Neil MacCormick in one of our interviews (Edinburgh University, 7–8 December 2006).

this work. Above all, none of those monist federalisms is capable of confronting and solving the problem of the (external and internal) monist deficit that continues to beset those monist formations in the sphere within as well as between themselves. That is something that only a sound and distinctly pluralist conception of pluralism could do.

And it *can* do it, too. One of the central messages of the sound conception of pluralism is that those who truly accept the fundamental tenets that we are each other's equals and ought to organize our life in a way that is based on the maximum possible self-rule and legitimacy for every bearer of dignity, could not but be shaped in the way that this conception describes. Whether you are from the current nation-state camp, the European camp, or are attracted to some intermediate position while not being entirely sure as to what exactly the latter would best amount to, you will tend to follow the path towards the full-blown substantive pluralism. The dialectical exchange from this chapter is meant to create a tension in your mind, and a mirror for you to see your true self in. This is because you do claim that you respect the "other" as your equal while accepting also the other uncontroversial sound terms of the pluralist challenge as elaborated in Chapter 9. It follows that you therefore only have two alternatives. You can either continue holding to the current European situation or any of the monisms, but will need in that case to realize and admit openly that you do not actually recognize those basic tenets of humanity. Because of the dialectic inherent in this conception your hypocrisy will be revealed. Alternatively, you are free to continue to declare that you accept those basic tenets, but will, if being sincere, realize from the dialectical discussion above that you need, in order to really follow those basic tenets, to further refine your applicative vision precisely in the direction of the sound conception of pluralism.

Crucially in this light, these two inescapable alternatives do not reveal themselves only to the citizens, for you and me, and to scholars on democracy and those debating the best future for Europe along those three different paths, but also to public officials, especially those political leaders and judges who remain the key practical actors in the process of shaping the nation-states and the European integration. As long as they declare their adherence to the fundamental tenets mentioned, as practically all of them passionately do, at least publicly, these actors too are now challenged and faced with the described alternative. Or as MacCormick in one of his brief, but subtle visionary statements once put it:

> Most current liberal theories take for granted the legitimacy of states (and frequently denominate them "nation-states"). They then work out elaborate theories of justice in the political sphere that simply take states as the given and obvious units of political discourse and practice, and discuss the special obligations of governments to citizens and of citizens to each other. Nationalism is not a widely favored doctrine, but unargued nationalist or statist ("nation-statist") assumptions in fact lie unexamined behind such theorizing. The hidden assumptions should be taken out of their closet and either brought up to scratch as an acceptable part of liberal political philosophy, or the whole project should be abandoned.[60]

[60] N. MacCormick, *Questioning Sovereignty: Law, State, and Nation in the European Commonwealth* (Oxford: Oxford University Press, 2001) 181.

The role of scholarship is to reveal what is in such a closet, and prompt its emptying, while showing the available route through which the whole project could be saved and even further improved to previously unattainable dimensions. To do more than this, while exposing the practical actors to the very real challenge (both alternatives) described, is not within scholarship's remit; it is neither within its purpose nor reach. The rest is in the hands of the coexisting self-standing constitutional orders—their officials, policy-makers, and peoples—themselves. Throughout history progress has often depended on a comprehension of a newly arisen historic opportunity revealed by scholarship, and the following actions of the "virtuous few" who have recognized and seized it. There is indeed no reason why, now that a unique historic opportunity has opened by our own changed context, we should and can count on anyone else to do just this.

Of course, to establish such a regime at the level of constitutional foundations would only be the beginning of the new democratic model. The same was the case at the time of democracy's "second coming"[61] and its establishment of democratic foundations through the first democratic constitutions of the sovereign-state democratic model (think, for example, of the foundational constitutional tenets of the US).[62] Yet from Europe's sound new pluralist *foundation*, representing the beginning of democracy's "third coming," things would then gradually but inescapably develop further (as they did in the case of the "second coming") until realizing its unprecedented democratic potential to the full. Indeed, provided that we obtain a clear understanding of the idea of the pluralist meta-constitution—its new sound pluralist foundation and its basic building blocks—we are closer to the initiation of democracy's "third coming" than might first meet the eye. For it is the foundational level that is absolutely the key.

Recall the lesson from history. At the "second coming," the enshrinement of the revolutionary (though then still monist) new principle of "We the People," "created equal," as the only source of political authority to the very foundation of the newly emerging regime was what made a decisive difference. It instilled the new democratic egalitarian spirit[63] that inevitably then created a social atmosphere in which the republic could be further transformed into something more:

> The equality that was so crucial to republican citizenship had a permissive significance in America that could [now no longer] be restrained, and ordinary people, whose meanness and need to labour had made them contemptible in the eyes of their superiors from the beginning of history, found in republican equality a powerful justification for their self-esteem and self-assertion. As a consequence, the age-old distinction between leisured gentlemen and common working people, which the revolutionary leaders continued to try to honour, was repeatedly blurred and eventually dissolved.[64]

61 Dunn (n 58) at 23. 62 Dunn (n 58).

63 Cf with the even more inclusive and intact spirit that is, in our own context, inherent in the pluralist foundation.

64 G. Wood, "Democracy and the American Revolution" in J. Dunn (ed.), *Democracy: The Unfinished Journey* (Oxford: Oxford University Press, 2000) 99–100.

More specifically, the new egalitarian atmosphere sparked the unstoppable avalanche of claims to extension of franchise for all. Increasingly the latter was seen as the actual test of the proclaimed ideal that it was "We the People" who ruled in America. The logic of actual representation replaced that of virtual representation: one could not be seen as being represented "unless he had at least the right to vote."[65] Expanding the franchise thus soon "became a major reform in the early Republic,"[66] and by 1825 almost all the states of the federation extended it to the majority of adult male citizens.[67] Naturally, some continued to object to the reforms, but the egalitarian impulse had simply changed the context too overwhelmingly, so that, by this point, even Madison himself, who had previously been against universal suffrage (the feature that distinguished democracy from his republic) was now decidedly in the reformist camp: "[W]here a propertyless majority threatened a propertied minority," this was *no longer*, in his view, "a danger which could appropriately be handled by excluding that majority from the franchise."[68] By then, he came to believe that to keep the majority disenfranchised simply "violates the vital principle of free government, that those who are to be bound by laws ought to have a voice in making them."[69] The extension towards the universal franchise, advanced on the rationale of the new foundation, was the decisive factor that changed the republic into something more—into democracy.

It is the same democratic egalitarian principle from the constitutional foundations that then radiated and served as the source of democratic transformations also in all further key constitutional moments. The virtuous few continuously kept invoking the promise it had made. Take the abolitionists and the words from the Gettysburg Address, take MLK and his civil rights movement, the women's suffrage movement, or any of the innumerable other examples, small or big, past or current. Foundations are indeed decisive. Once things are set rightly there, democracy "then basically only ever expands and never contracts."[70]

This is why it is so crucial also for Europe to establish the correct path of action at the level of its constitutional foundations. This is all the more so since this is the time at which Europe finds itself in a unique new post-sovereign context from which further historic advancement of democracy is possible. We are faced with an opportunity that could and ought to be seized and carried out for the benefit of all humanity. It is our responsibility that it not be wasted. Provided that our constitutions and constitutional interpretations—the European and national—are refined at their foundational levels according to the substantive pluralist foundation and its spirit of the intact (unconditional and universal) equal respect, the third coming is thereby indeed already initiated. Once that is set right, the normative force radiating from such an explicit substantive pluralist foundation will inevitably play its part as well.

[65] Wood (n 64) at 99–100. [66] Wood (n 64) at 101. [67] Wood (n 64) at 101.
[68] Dunn (n 58) at 83.
[69] Dunn (n 58) at 83, citing from D. McCoy, *The Last of the Fathers: James Madison and the Republican Legacy* (Cambridge: Cambridge University Press, 1989) 195.
[70] R. Goodin, "Global Democracy: In the Beginning" (2010) 2 International Theory 175.

Bibliography

A

Albi, A., "Supremacy of EC Law in the New Member States" (2007) 3 European Journal of Constitutional Law 25.

Alter, K., *Establishing the Supremacy of European Law* (Oxford: Oxford University Press, 2001).

Aristotle, *Eudemian Ethics*, Perseus.

—— *Nicomachean Ethics*, Perseus.

Austin, T., "The End of Europe? Turkey and the Cultural Border of the European Union" (Cambridge: Harvard University Lamont Library, 2012), unpublished manuscript.

B

Bacquero Cruz, J., "The Legacy of the Maastricht-Urteil and the Pluralist Movement" 2008) 14 European Law Journal 389.

—— "Legal Pluralism and Institutional Disobedience in the European Union" (2012), at <http://www.peacepalacelibrary.nl/plinklet/index.php?ppn=341449121>.

Barber, N., "Legal Pluralism and the European Union" (2006) 12 European Law Journal 306.

—— *The Constitutional State* (Oxford: Oxford University Press, 2011).

—— "Legal Realism, Pluralism, and their Challengers," (2012) Oxford Legal Studies Research Paper No. 76/2012.

Barents, R., "The Precedence of EU Law from the Perspective of Constitutional Pluralism" (2009) 5 European Constitutional Law Review 241.

Beaud, O., *Théorie de la Fédération* (Paris: Presses Universitaires de France, 2007).

Beck, G., "The Problem of Kompetenz-Kompetenz: A Conflict Between Right and Right in Which There Is No Praetor," (2005) 30 European Law Review 42.

—— "The Lisbon Judgment of the German Constitutional Court, the Primacy of EU Law and the Problem of *Kompetenz-Kompetenz*: A Conflict between Right and Right in Which There is No *Praetor*" (2011) 17 European Law Journal 470.

Bedner, J., Eskridge, N., Ferejohn, J., "A Political Theory of Federalism" in J. Ferejohn, J. Rakove, J. Riley (eds.), *Constitutional Culture and Democratic Rule* (Cambridge: Cambridge University Press, 2001).

Beer, S., *To Make a Nation: The Rediscovery of American Federalism* (Cambridge: Harvard University Press, 1993).

Bessson, S., "From European Integration to European Integrity: Should European Law Speak with Just One Voice?" (2004) 10 European Law Journal 257.

—— "Sovereignty in Conflict" (2004) 8 European Integration Online Papers, No. 15.

—— "The Taming of Sovereignty: Review of Neil Walker (ed.), Sovereignty in Transition," (2005) 3 International Journal of Constitutional Law 147.

—— "The Many European Constitutions and the Future of European Constitutional Theory," (2006) 105 Archiv für Rechts- und Sozialphilosophie Beiheft, Staats- und Verfassungstheorie im Spannungsfeld der Disziplinen 160.

—— "Europe as a Demoi-cratic Polity" (2007) 116 Retfaerd - Nordisk Juridisk Tidsskrift 3.

—— "The Relationship between European and International Law" (2009) 5 European Constitutional Law Review (special edition).

—— "European Legal Pluralism after Kadi" (2009) 5 European Constitutional Law Review 237.

—— "The Truth About Legal Pluralism" (2012) 8 European Constitutional Law Review 354.

Bignami, F., "Rethinking the Legal Foundations of the European Constitutional Order: The Lessons of the New Historical Research," (2013) 28 American University International Law Review 1311.

Von Bogdandy, A., "The European Union as a Human Rights Organization? Human Rights and the Core of the European Union" (2000) 37 Common Market Law Review 1307.

—— "European Union as a Supranational Federation: A Conceptual Attempt in the Light of the Amsterdam Treaty" (2000) 6 Columbia Journal of European Law 27.

—— "Constitutionalism in International Law: Comment on a Proposal from Germany" (2006) 47 Harvard International Law Journal 223.

—— "Overcoming Absolute Primacy: Respect for National Identity Under the Lisbon Treaty" (2011) 48 Common Market Law Review 1417.

de Búrca, G., "Developing Democracy Beyond the State," (2008) 46 Columbia Journal of Transnational Law 102.

—— "The European Court of Justice and the International Legal Order after Kadi," 51 (2010) Harvard International Law Journal 1.

—— "The ECJ and the International Legal Order: A Re-evaluation," in G. de Búrca and J. Weiler (eds.) *The Worlds of European Constitutionalism* (Cambridge: Cambridge University Press, 2011).

—— with J. Weiler (eds.) *The Worlds of European Constitutionalism* (Cambridge: Cambridge University Press, 2011).

—— "The Road Not Taken: The EU as a Global Human Rights Actor," (2011) 105 American Journal of International Law 6.

—— with P. Craig, *European Union Law* (5th, Oxford: Oxford University Press, 2011).

Burgess, M., *Comparative Federalism* (London: Routledge, 2006).

C

Churchill, W., "Speech to the Academic Youth", University of Zurich, 1946.

Claes, M., *The National Courts' Mandate in the European Constitution* (Oxford: Hart Publishing 2006).

Cloot, E., et al. (eds.) *Federalism in the European Union* (Oxford: Hart Publishing, 2012).

Coundenhove-Kalegri, R., *Pan Europa* (Vienna: Pan-Europe-Verlag, 1923).

Craig, P., "Constitutions, Constitutionalism, and the European Union" (2001) 7 European Law Journal 125.

—— "National Courts and Community Law" in J. Hayward and A. Menon (eds.), *Governing Europe* (Oxford: Oxford University Press 2003).

—— with G. de Búrca, *EU Law: Text, Cases, and Materials* (Oxford: Oxford University Press, 2003).

—— "What Constitution Does Europe Need? The House that Giscard Built: Constitutional Rooms with a View" (2003) The Federal Trust Constitutional Online Paper Series

No. 26/03, at <http://ssrn.com/abstract=516784> or <http://dx.doi.org/10.2139/ssrn.516784>.

—— "Sovereignty and the EU: The UK Perspective and Primacy Clauses" in L. Tichy and T. Dumbrovsky (eds.), *Sovereignty and Integration, Paradoxes and Development within Europe Today* (Centre for Comparative Law, Law Faculty of Charles University in Prague, 2010).

—— "The ECJ and Ultra Vires Action: A Conceptual Analysis" (2011) 48 Common Market Law Review 395.

—— "Integration, Democracy and Legitimacy," in P. Craig and G. de Búrca (eds.), *The Evolution of EU Law* (Oxford: Oxford University Press 2011).

—— *Administrative Law* (2nd edn, Oxford: Oxford University Press, 2012).

—— "Competence and Member State Autonomy: Causality, Consequence and Legitimacy" in H. Micklitz and B de Witte (eds.), *The European Court of Justice and the Autonomy of the Member States* (Antwerp: Intersentia 2012).

D

Davies, G., "Constitutional Disagreement in Europe and the Search for Pluralism" (2010) Social Science Research Network, available at <http://papers.ssrn.com/sol3/papers.cfm?abstract_id=1559323>.

Delors, J., "Jacques Delor at the College of Europe in Bruges," speech, reprinted in Europe Doc. No 1, 576 (21 October 1989).

Dickson, J., "How Many Legal Systems? Some Puzzles Regarding the Identity Conditions of, and Relations Between, Legal Systems in the European Union" (2008) 2 Problema 9.

—— "Towards a Theory of European Union Legal Systems," in J. Dickson and P. Eleftheriadis (eds.), *Philosophical Foundations of European Union Law* (Oxford: Oxford University Press 2012).

—— "The Idea of a Legal System: Between the Real and the Ideal," in N. Walker (ed.), *MacCormick's Scotland* (Edinburgh: Edinburgh University Press 2012).

—— with P. Eleftheriadis (eds.), *Philosophical Foundations of European Union Law* (Oxford: Oxford University Press, 2012).

Dinan, D., *Ever Closer Union: An Introduction to European Integration* (3rd, London: Lynne Rienner Publishers, 2005).

Douglas-Scott, S., "Justice and Pluralism in the EU" (2012) 65 Current Legal Problems 83.

Dunn, J., *Setting the People Free: The Story of Democracy* (London: Atlantic Books, 2005).

—— *Democracy: The Unfinished Journey, 508 BC to AD 1993* (Oxford: Oxford University Press, 1994).

Dworkin, R., "Objectivity and Truth: You'd Better Believe It" (1996) 25 Philosophy and Public Affairs 87.

E

Eeckhout, P., "Human Rights and the Autonomy of EU Law: Pluralism or Integration?" (2013) 66 Current Legal Problems 169.

Eleftheriadis, P., "Begging the Constitutional Question" (1998) 36 Journal of Common Market Studies 255.

—— "The Idea of a European Constitution" (2007) Oxford Journal of Legal Studies 1.

—— "Pluralism and Integrity" (2010) 23 Ratio Juris 365.

—— "Law and Sovereignty" (2010) 29 Law and Philosophy 535.
—— with K. Nicolaïdis and J. Weiler, "Foreword: the Changing Landscape of European Constitutionalism" (2011) 9 International Journal of Constitutional Law 673.
—— "The Moral Distinctiveness of the European Union" (2011) 9. International Journal of Constitutional Law 695.
—— with J. Dickson (eds.), *Philosophical Foundations of European Union Law* (Oxford: Oxford University Press, 2012).

F

Finnis, J., *The Fundamentals of Ethics* (Oxford: Clarendon Press, 1983).
—— *Moral Absolutes: Tradition, Revision, and Truth* (Washington: Catholilc University of America Press, 1991).
—— *Acquinas: Moral, Political, and Legal Theory* (Oxford: Oxford University Press, 1998).
Fischer, J., "From Confederation to Federation: Thoughts on the Finality of European Integration" (Federal Trust European Essay No. 8, 2000).
Forst, R., *Contexts of Justice: Political Philosophy beyond Liberalism and Communitarianism* (Berkeley: University of California Press, 2002).
Fossum, J., with Menendez, J., *The Constitution's Gift: A Constitutional Theory for a Democratic European Union* (Plymouth: Rowman and Littlefield Publishing, 2010).
Foucault, M., (A. Sheridan, tr.), *The Order of Things: An Archaeology of the Human Sciences* (New York: Pantheon, 1970).

G

Gauthier, D., *Morals by Agreement* (Oxford: Clarendon Press, 1986).
Van Gerven, W., *The European Union: A Polity of States and Peoples* (Oxford: Hart Publishing, 2005).
Goodin, R., "Global Democracy: In the Beginning" (2010) 2 International Theory 175.
Le Goff, J., *The Birth of Europe* (Oxford: Blackwell, 2005).
Goldoni, M., "Constitutional Pluralism and the Question of the European Common Good" (2012) 18 European Law Journal 385.
Griffiths, J., "What is Legal Pluralism?" (1986) 24 Journal of Legal Pluralism 1.
Grimm, D., "Does Europe Need a Constitution?" (1995) 1 European Law Journal 282.

H

Habermas, J., (C. Lenhardt and W. Nicholsen, tr.), *Moral Consciousness and Communicative Action* (Cambridge: The MIT Press, 1990).
—— (W. Rehg, tr.) *Between Facts and Norms: Contributions to a Discourse Theory of Law and Democracy* (Cambridge: The MIT Press, 1996).
—— The Inclusion of the Other: Studies in Political Theory (3rd, Cambridge: The MIT Press, 2001).
—— "A Paradoxical Union of Contradictory Principles?" (2004) 4 Political Theory 766.
—— *The Divided West* (Cambridge: Polity, 2006).
—— "A Political Constitution for a Pluralist World Society?" (2007) 34 Journal of Chinese Philosophy (2007) 334.

Halberstam, D., "Constitutional Heterarchy: The Centrality of Conflict in the European Union and the United States," in J. Dunoff J and J. Trachtman (eds.) *Ruling The World? Constitutionalism, International Law and Global Governance* (Cambridge: Cambridge University Press, 2009).

—— with C. Möllers, "The German Constitutional Court Says "Ja Zu Deutschland!" (2009) 10 German Law Journal.

—— "Pluralism in *Marbury* and *Van Gend*" in M. Maduro and L. Azoulai (eds.) *The Past and the Future of EU Law: The Classics of EU Law Revisited on the 50th Anniversary of the Rome Treaty* (Oxford: Hart Publishing, 2010).

—— "Systems Pluralism and Institutional Pluralism in Constitutional Law: National, Supranational, and Global Governance" University of Michigan Public Law Working Paper No. 229, 2011, at <http://papers.ssrn.com/sol3/papers.cfm?abstract_id=1758907>.

—— "Local, Global, and Plural Constitutionalism: Europe Meets the World," in G. de Búrca and J. Weiler (eds.) *The Worlds of European Constitutionalism* (Cambridge: Cambridge University Press, 2011).

—— "Dialogic Epilogue" in De Búrca and Weiler (eds.) *The Worlds of European Constitutionalism* (Cambridge: Cambridge University Press, 2011).

—— "Federalism: Theory, Policy, Law," in M. Rosenfeld and A. Sajó (eds.) *The Oxford Handbook of Comparative Constitutional Law* (Oxford: Oxford University Press, 2012).

—— with Maduro M. (eds.), *The Constitutional Challenge in Europe and America: People, Power, and Politics* (Cambridge: Cambridge University Press, forthcoming).

Hare, R., *Freedom and Reason* (Oxford: Oxford University Press, 1965).

—— *Moral Thinking: its Levels, Methods and Point* (Oxford: Oxford University Press, 1981).

Hart, H., "Kelsen's Doctrine of the Unity of Law" in his *Essays in Jurisprudence and Philosophy* (Oxford: Oxford University Press, 1983).

—— *The Concept of Law* (2nd, Oxford: Oxford University Press, 1994).

Hartley, T., *Constitutional Problems of the European Union* (Oxford: Hart Publishing, 1999).

—— "The Constitutional Foundations of the European Union" (2001) 117 LQR 225.

Hobbs, T., (C. MacPherson, ed.), *Leviathan* (London: Penguin, 1968).

I

Isensee, J., "Staat und Verfassung," in J. Isensee and P. Kirchof (eds.), *Handbuch des Staatsrecthts* (Heidelberg: C.F. Müller, 1987).

J

Jaklic, K., "Liberal Legitimacy and the Question of Respect" (2014) 27 Ratio Juris, forthcoming.

—— *Democracy's Third Coming: Europe as a Route to Humanity's Third Historic Stage of Democracy* (Cambridge: Harvard University Law Library, 2011, forthcoming monograph).

Joerges, C., with Ghaleigh N. (eds.), *Darker Legacies of Law in Europe: The Shadow of National Socialism and Fascism over Europe and Its Legal Traditions* (Oxford: Hart Publishing, 2003).

K

Kant, I., "Grundlegung zur Metaphysik der Sitten," in Berlin Academy (ed.), *Kants Werke* (Berlin: Walter de Gruyter, 1968).

—— *Perpetual Peace: Essays on Kant's Cosmopolitan Ideal*, J. Bochman and M. Lutz-Bachmann (eds.) (Cambridge: The MIT Press, 1997).

Kelsen, H., *Das Problem der Souveränität und die Theorie des Völkerrechts: Beitrag zu einer reinen Rechtslehre* (2nd, Tübingen: J.C.B. Mohr, 1928).

—— *Reine Rechtslehre* (2nd, Wien: Österr. Staatsdruckerei, 1960).

—— (M. Knight, tr.) *Pure Theory of Law* (Berkeley: University of California Press, 1967).

—— (B. Litschewski Paulson and S. Paulson, tr.) *Introduction to the Problems of Legal Theory* (Oxford: Oxford University Press, 1997).

Kennedy, R., "A Natural Aristocracy" in W. Eskridge and S. Levinson (eds.), *Constitutional stupidities, Constitutional Tragedies* (New York: New York University Press, 1998).

Keohane, R., "Ironies of Sovereignty: The European Union and the United states" 4 Journal of Common Market Studies (2002) 743.

Kirchof, P., "Der deutsche Staat im Prozes der europäischen Integration," in J. Isensee and P. Kirchof (eds.) *Handbuch des Staatsrecthts* (Heidelberg: C.F. Müller, 1987).

Kochenov, D., "From Dual to Cooperative Federalism: The Changing Structure of European Law—Book Review" (2010) 21 European Journal of International Law.

Komarek, J., "European Constitutionalism and the European Arrest Warrant: In Search of the Limits of Contrapunctual Principles," (2007) 44 *Common Market Law Review* 9.

—— "Institutional Dimension of Constitutional Pluralism," Eric Stein Working Paper No. 3/2010, 2010, and at <http://papers.ssrn.com/sol3/papers.cfm?abstract_id=1575522>.

Kombos, C., "The Esoteric Dimension of Constitutional Pluralism: EU's Internal Constitutional Sub-units and the Non-symbolic Cumulative Constitution," in P. Birkinshaw and M. Varney (eds.), *The European Union Legal Order After Lisbon* (Kluwer Law International, 2010).

Krisch, N., "The Pluralism of Global Administrative Law" (2006) 17 European Journal of International Law 247.

—— "The Open Architecture of European Human Rights Law" (2008) 71 Modern Law Review 183.

—— *Beyond Constitutionalism: The Pluralist Sructure of Postnational Law* (Oxford: Oxford University Press, 2010).

—— "Who is Afraid of Radical Pluralism? Legal Order and Political Stability in the Postnational Space" (2011) 24 Ratio Juris 386.

—— "The Case for Pluralism in Postnational Law," in G. de Búrca and J. Weiler (eds.) *The Worlds of European Constitutionalism* (Cambridge: Cambridge University Press, 2011).

—— "Pluralism's Promise" (2012) 25 Leiden Journal of International Law symposium, at <http://opiniojuris.org/2012/07/06/ljil-symposium-vol-25-2-beyond-constitutionalism-pluralisms-promise/>.

Kumm, M., "Who Is the Final Arbiter" (1998) Jean Monet Working Paper No 10/98

—— "Who Is the Final Arbiter of Constitutionality in Europe? Three Conceptions of the Relationship Between the German Federal Constitutional Court and the European Court of Justice" (1999) 36 CML Rev 351.

—— with V. Comella, "The Future of Constitutional Conflict in the European Union: Constitutional Supremacy after the Constitutional Treaty" (2004) in J Weiler and C Eisgruber (eds), *Altneuland: The EU Constitution in a Contextual Perspective* Jean Monnet Working Paper No 5/04.

—— "The Primacy Clause of the Constitutional Treaty and the Future of Constitutional Conflict in the European Union" (2005) 3 International Journal of Constitutional Law 473.

—— "Rethinking Constitutional Authority: On the Structure and Limits of Constitutional Pluralism," (2012) conference paper.

—— "The Jurisprudence of Constitutional Conflict: Constitutional Supremacy in Europe Before and after the Constitutional Treaty" (2005) 11 European Law Journal 262.

—— "The Cosmopolitan Turn in Constitutionalism: On the Relationship between Constitutionalism in and beyond the State," in J. Dunoff J and J. Trachtman (eds.), *Ruling The World? Constitutionalism, International Law and Global Governance* (Cambridge: Cambridge University Press, 2009).

—— "The Moral Point of Constitutional Pluralism: Defining the Domain of Legitimate Institutional Civil Disobedience and Conscientious Objection," in J. Dickson and P. Eleftheriadis (eds.) *Philosophical Foundations of European Union Law* (Oxford: Oxford University Press, 2012).

L

Laclau, E., with Mouffe C., *Hegemony and Socialist Strategy: Towards a Radical Democratic Politics* (2nd, New York: Verso, 2001).

Lenaerts, K., "Interlocking legal orders in the European Union and Comparative Law," (2003) 52 International and Comparative Law Quarterly 873.

Letsas, G., "Harmonic Law: The Case Against Pluralism" in J. Dickson and P. Eleftheriadis, *Philosophical Foundations of European* Law (Oxford: Oxford University Press, 2012).

Leuprecht, P., "The Execution of Judgments and Decisions" in R. Macdonald et al. (eds.), *The European System for the Protection of Human Rights* (Dordrecht: Kluwer Academic Publishers, 1993).

Levinson, S., *Our Undemocratic Constitution: Where the Constitution Goes Wrong (And How We the People Can Correct It)* (Oxford: Oxford University Press, 2006).

M

Mac Amhlaigh, C., "Questioning Constitutional Pluralism," Edinburgh School of Law Working Paper, No. 2011/17, 2001, at <http://papers.ssrn.com/sol3/papers.cfm?abstract_id=1905053>.

—— "Concepts of Law in Integration Through Law (and the Price of Constitutional Pluralism)" in D. Augenstein (ed.), *Integration Through Law Revisited: the Making of the European Polity* (Aldershot: Ashgate, 2011).

—— "Late Sovereignty in Post-integration Europe: Continuity and Change in a Constitutive Concept" in R. Adler-Nissen and U. Grad (eds.), *European Integration and Post-colonial Sovereignty Games: The EU Overseas Countries and Territories* (London: Routledge, 2013).

MacCormick, N., with Weinberger, O., *An Institutional Theory of Law: New Approaches to Legal Theory* (Berlin: Springer, 1986).

—— "Is Nationalism Philosophically Credible?" in W. Twinning (ed.) *Issues of Self-Determination* (Aberdeen: Aberdeen University Press, 1991).

—— "Beyond the Sovereign State" (1993) 56 Modern L Rev 1.

—— "What Place for Nationalism in the Modern World" (1994) 2 Hume Papers on Public Policy 79.

—— "Sovereignty: Myth and Reality," Scottish Affairs, No. 11, Spring 1995.

—— "The Maastricht-Urteil: Sovereignty Now" (1995) 1 European Law Journal 259.

—— "Liberalism, Nationalism, and the Post-sovereign State" (1996) 44 Political Studies 553.

—— "Democracy, Subsidiarity, and Citizenship in the 'European Commonwealth'" (1997) 16 *Law and Philosophy* 331.

—— (ed.) *Constructing Legal Systems: "European Union" in Legal Theory* (Berlin: Springer, 1997).

—— "Risking Constitutional Collision in Europe?" (1998) 18 Oxford Journal of Legal Studies 517.

—— *Questioning Sovereignty: Law, State and Nation in the European Commonwealth* (Oxford: Oxford University Press, 1999).

—— "Liberal Nationalism and Self-determination" in D. Clark and J. Jones (eds.), *The Rights of Nations – Nations and Nationalism in a Changing World* (Cork: Cork University Press, 1999).

—— "The European Constitutional Convention and the Stateless Nations," *International Relations* 18 (2004) 331.

—— "Questioning Post-sovereignty" (2004) 29 European Law Review 852.

—— *Rhetoric and the Rule of Law: A Theory of Legal Reasoning* (Oxford: Oxford University Press, 2005).

—— *Who's Afraid of a European Constitution?* (Exeter: Imprint Academic, 2005).

Madison, J., "Vices of the Political System of the United States" in P. Kurland and R. Lerner (eds.), *The Founders' Constitution* (Chicago: The University of Chicago Press, 1987).

—— with A. Hamilton and J. Jay, *The Federalist Papers* (L. Goldman, ed., Oxford: Oxford University Press, 2008).

Maduro, M., *We the Court: The European Court of Justice and the European Economic Constitution* (Oxford: Hart Publishing, 1998).

—— "The Heteronyms of European Law" (1999) 5 European Law Journal 160.

—— "Where to Look for Legitimacy?" (2002) in E. Eriksen et al. (eds.) *Constitution Making and Democratic Legitimacy*, Arena Working Paper No. 5/2002.

—— "European Constitution: What If This Is As Good As It Gets?" in J. Weiler and M. Wind (eds.) *European Constitutionalism Beyond the State* (Cambridge: Cambridge University Press, 2003).

—— "Contrapunctual Law: Europe's Constitutional Pluralism in Action" in N. Walker (ed.) *Sovereignty in Transition* (Oxford: Hart Publishing, 2003).

—— "European Constitution: What If This Is As Good As It Gets?" in J. Weiler and M. Wind (eds.), *European Constitutionalism Beyond the State* (Cambridge: Cambridge University Press, 2003).

—— "How Constitutional Can the European Union Be? The Tension Between Intergovernmentalism and Constitutionalism in the European Union" in J. Weiler and C. Eisgruber (eds.) *Altneuland: The EU Constitution in a Contextual Perspective*, Jean Monnet Working Paper 5/04, 2004.

—— "The Importance of Being Called a Constitution: Constitutional Authority and the Authority of Constitutionalism" (2005) 3 Int J Constitutional Law 332.

—— "Interpreting European Law: Judicial Adjudication in a Context of Constitutional Pluralism" (2007) European Journal of Legal Studies 1.

—— "Three Claims of Constitutional Pluralism" (2009) at <http://www.wzb.eu/sites/default/files/veranstaltungen/miguelmadurothreeclaimsofconstitutionalpluralismhu-collmay152012.pdf>.
—— "Courts and Pluralism: Essay on a Theory of Judicial Adjudication in the Context of Legal and Constitutional Pluralism," in J. Dunoff and J. Trachtman (eds.), *Ruling The World? Constitutionalism, International Law and Global Governance* (Cambridge: Cambridge University Press, 2009).
—— with L. Azoulai (eds.) *The Past and Future of EU Law* (Oxford, Hart Publishing, 2010).
—— with D. Halberstam (eds.), *The Constitutional Challenge in Europe and America: People, Power, and Politics* (Cambridge: Cambridge University Press, forthcoming).
Mancini, F., "The Making of a Constitution for Europe" (1989) 26 Common Market Law Review 595.
—— "Europe: The Case for Statehood" (1998) 4 European Law Journal 29.
Mayer, F., "The European Constitution and the Courts: Adjudicating Constitutional Law in a Multilevel System" in A. von Bogdandy and J. Weiler (eds.), *European Integration – The New German Scholarship (Symposium),* Jean Monnet Working Paper 9/03 2003.
—— "Competences—reloaded? The vertical division of powers in the EU and the new European constitution" (2005) 3 International Journal of Constitutional Law 493.
—— "The European Constitution and the Courts: Adjudicating Constitutional Law in a Multilevel System" in A. von Bogdandy and J. Bast (eds.): Principles of European Constitutional Law (Oxford: Hart Publishing, 2006).
—— "Supremacy – Lost?" in P. Dann and M. Rynkowski (eds.), *The Unity of the European Constitution* (Berlin: Springer, 2006).
—— with Lenski and Wendel "Der Vorrang des Europarechts in Frankreich (Anmerkung)," (2008) Europarecht 51.
—— "Multilevel Constitutional Jurisdiction," in A. von Bogdandy and J. Bast (eds.), *Principles of European Constitutional Law* (Oxford: Hart Publishing, Revised edn., 2010).
—— "Rashomon in Karlsruhe - A reflection on Democracy and Identity in the European Union" Jean Monnet Working Paper 05/10, 2010.
—— "Van Gend en Loos: The Foundation of a Community of Law" in M. Maduro and L. Azoulai (eds.), *The Past and Future of EU Law: The Classics of EU Law Revisited on the 50th Anniversary of the Rome Treaty* (Oxford: Hart Publishing, 2010).
—— with Wendel M., "Multilevel Constitutionalism and Constitutional Pluralism" (2011) conference paper.
—— "Multilevel Constitutionalism and the Delimitation of Competences – Lessons from the United States for the EU?" in D. Halberstam and M. Maduro (eds.), *The Constitutional Challenge in Europe and America: People, Power, and Politics* (Cambridge: Cambridge University Press, forthcoming).
Menendez, A., "A Pious Europe? Why Europe Should Not Define Itself as Christian?" (2004) Arena Working Paper No 10/04.
—— (ed.) *Law and Democracy in Neil MacCormick's Legal and Political Theory* (2011) 93 Law and Philosophy Library.
Michelman, F., "The Subject of Liberalism" (1994) 46 Stanford Law Review 1807.
—— "Morality, Identity, and 'Constitutional Patriotism'" (1999) 76 Denver University Law Rev 1009.
—— "Dilemmas of Belonging: Moral Truth, Human Rights, and Why We Might Not Want a Representative Judiciary" (2000) 47 UCLA Law Review.
—— "Modus Vivendi Postmodernus? On Just Interpretations and the Thinning of Justice" (2000) 21 Cardozo Law Review 1945.

—— "Morality, Identity and Constitutional Patriotism," (2001) 17 Ratio Juris 253.

—— "Faith and Obligation, Or What Makes Sandy Sweat?" (2003) 38 Tulsa Law Review.

—— "Living With Judicial Supremacy" (2003) 38 Wake Forest Law Review 579.

—— "Ida's Way: Constructing the Respect-Worthy Governmental System" (2003) 72 Fordham Law Review 345.

—— "Proceduralism in Liberal Constitutional Theory: A Fragment," Annual Distinguished Lecture, Boston University School of Law, April 2005, manuscript.

—— "Entrenchment and the Dignity of Legislation," Annual Law and Philosophy Lecture, Columbia University 2006.

—— "A Civilized Man: Morton Horwitz Struggles with 'Fundamental Law'" in D. Hamilton and A. Brophy (eds.) *Transformations in American legal History: Law, Ideology and Methods* (Cambridge: Harvard University Press, 2011).

Morgan, G., *The Idea of a European Superstate: Public Justification and European Integration* (Princeton: Princeton University Press, 2005).

—— "Democratic Equality, Transnational Institutions, and the constraints of Modernity" in B. Morrison (ed.), *Transnational Democracy in Critical and Comparative Perspective: Democracy's Range Reconsidered* (Aldershot: Ashgate Publishing, 2003).

Morris, C., "Justice, Reason and Moral Standing" in J. Coleman and C. Morris (eds.), *Rational Commitment and Social Justice: Essays for Gregory Kavka* (Cambridge: Cambridge University Press, 1998).

Mouffe, C., "Preface: Democratic Politics Today" in C. Mouffe (ed.), *Dimensions of Radical Democracy: Pluralism, Citizenship, Community* (New York: Verso, 1992).

—— With Laclau, E., *Hegemony and Socialist Strategy: Towards a Radical Democratic Politics* (2nd, New York: Verso, 2001).

N

Nagel, T., *The View From Nowhere* (Oxford: Oxford University Press, 1986).

Neyer, J., with Wiener, A. (eds.), *Political Theory of the European Union* (Oxford: Oxford University Press, 2010).

Nicolaïdis, K., (with R. Howse, eds.) *The Federal Vision: Legitimacy and Levels of Governance in United States and the European Union* (Oxford: Oxford University Press, 2001).

—— with S. Weatherill (eds), *Whose Europe? National Models and the Constitution of the European Union* (Oxford: Oxford University Press, 2003).

—— "Our European Demoi-cracy: Is this Constitution a Third Way for Europe?," in K. Nicolaïdis and S. Weatherill (eds.) *Whose Europe? National Models and the Constitution of the European Union* (Oxford: Oxford University Press, 2003).

—— "The New Constitution as European 'Demoi-cracy'?" (2004) 7 Critical Review of International Social and Political Philosophy 76.

—— "We the Peoples of Europe" (2004) 83 Foreign Affairs 97.

—— "Notre Demoï-cratie européenne: la constellation post nationale à l'horizon patriotisme constitutionnel" (2006) 19 Politique Européenne 45.

—— with J. Pelabay "One Union, One Story? In Praise of Europe's Narrative Diversity," in A. Warleigh-Lack (ed.), *Reflections on European Integration* (Basingstoke: Palgrave Macmillan, 2008).

—— "The Idea of European Demoicracy" in J. Dickson and P. Eleftheriadis (eds.), *Philosophical Foundations of EU Law* (Oxford: Oxford University Press, 2012).

—— with R. Kleinfeld "Rethinking Europe's Rule of Law and Enlargement Agenda: the Fundamental Dilemma" OECD-SIGMA Strategy Papers Series, 2012.

—— "European Demoicracy and Its Crisis" (2013) 51 Journal of Common Market Studies 351.

Nussbaum, M., *Frontiers of Justice: Disability, Nationality, Species Membership* (Cambridge: Harvard University Press, 2006).

Nygren, A., *Agape and Eros* (Chicago: University of Chicago Press, 1982).

O

Oliver, P., "Sovereignty in the Twenty-First Century" (2003) 14 King's College Law Journal 137.

Ostrom, V., *The Political Theory of a Compound Republic: Designing the American Experiment* (3rd, Lanham: Lexington Books, 2007).

Outka, G., *Agape: An Ethical Analysis* (New Haven: Yale University Press, 1972).

Ovid, *Metamorphoses* (Book 8), Perseus.

P

Payandeh, M., "Constitutional Review of EU Law after *Honeywell*: Contextualizing the Relationship between the German Constitutional Court and the EU Court of Justice" (2011) 48 Common Market Law Review 9.

Pellet, A., "Les Fondements Juridiques Internationaux du Droit Communautaire," Academy of European Law (ed.), *Collected Courses of the Academy of European Law*, Vol V (1994), Book 2.

Pernice, I., "After the Lisbon Treaty: Multi-Level Constitutionalism in Action," (2009) 15 Columbia Journal of European Law 349.

—— "Multilevel Constitutionalism and the Treaty of Amsterdam: European Constitution-Making Revisited" (1999) 36 Common Market Law Review 703.

—— "Multilevel Constitutionalism in the European Union" 27 (2002) European Law Review 511.

Piris, J.-C., "Does European Union Have a Constitution? Does it Need One?" (1999) European Law Review 557.

Plato, *Euthyphro*, Perseus.

Plato, *Laws*, Perseus.

Plato, *Republic*, Perseus.

R

Rawls, J., "Kantian Constructivism in Moral Theory" (the John Dewy Lecture) (1980) 9 The Journal of Philosophy 515.

—— "The Idea of an Overlapping Consensus" (1987) 7 Oxford Journal of Legal Studies 1.

—— *Political Liberalism* (New York: Columbia University Press, 1993).

—— *A Theory of Justice* (Revised edn., Cambridge: Harvard University Press, 1999).

—— *The Law of Peoples, With the Idea of Public Reason Revisited* (Cambridge: Harvard University Press, 1999).

—— with Philippe Van Parijs, "Three Letters on The Law of Peoples and the European Union" in *Autour de Rawls*, special issue of (2003) 7 Revue de philosophie économique 7.

Raz, J., *The Morality of Freedom* (Oxford: Clarendon Press, 1986).
—— "Disagreement in Politics" (1998) 43 The American Journal of Jurisprudence 25.
Reid, T., *The United States of Europe: The New Superpower and the End of American Supremacy* (New York: Penguin, 2004).
Ress, G., "The Effects of Judgments and Decisions in Domestic Law," in R. Macdonald et al. (eds.), *The European System for the Protection of Human Rights* (Dordrecht: Kluwer Academic Publishers, 1993).
Richmond, C., "Preserving the Identity Crisis: Autonomy, System and Sovereignty in European Law" (1997) 16 Law and Philosophy 377.
Rifkin, J., *The European Dream: How Europe's Vision of the Future is Quietly Eclipsing the American Dream* (New York: Penguin, 2004).
Röben, V., "Constitutionalism of Inverse Hierarchy: the Case of the European Union," Jean Monnet Working Paper 8/03, 2003.
—— "Constitutionalism of the European Union after the Draft Constitutional Treaty: How Much Hierarchy?"(2004) 10 Columbia Journal of European Law 339.

S

Sabel, C., with Gerstenberg, O., "Constitutionalising an Overlapping Consensus: the ECJ and the Emergence of a Coordinate Constitutional Order" (2010) 16 European Law Journal 511.
Sandel, M., *Public Philosophy: Essays on Morality and Politics* (Cambridge: Harvard University Press, 2005).
Saurette, P., "Questioning Political Theory: Charles Taylor's Contrarianism" (2004) 5 Political Theory 723.
Scharpf, F., "Legitimacy in the Multi-Level European Polity," in P. Dobner and M. Laughlin (eds.), *The Twilight of Constitutionalism?* (Oxford: Oxford University Press, 2010).
Schilling, T., "The Autonomy of the Community Legal Order: An Analysis of Possible Foundations" (1996) 17 Harvard International Law Journal 389. "Rejoinder: The Autonomy of the Community Legal Order," in T.Schilling, J. Weiler and U. Haltern, *Who in the Law is the Ultimate Judicial Umpire of European CommunityCompetences? The Schilling—Weiler/Haltern Debate,* Harvard Jean Monet Working Paper Series No. 10/ 1996, 1996.
—— "On the value of a pluralistic concept of legal orders for the understanding of the relation between the legal orders of the European Union and its member states" (1997) 83 Archiv für Rechts-und Sozialphilosophie 568.
—— "The European Court of Justice's Revolution: Its Effects and the Conditions for its Consummation: What Europe can learn from Fiji?" (2002) 4 European Law Review 445.
—— "The Jurisprudence of Constitutional Conflict: Some Supplementations to Mattias Kumm," (2006) 12 European Law Journal 173.
Schmid, C., "From Pont d'Avignon to Ponte Vecchio: The Resolution of Constitutional Conflicts between the European Union and the Member States through Principles of Public International Law" (1998) 18 Yearbook of European Law 415.
—— "The Neglected Conciliation Approach to the 'Final Arbiter' Conflict: A Critical Comment on Kumm, 'Who is the Final Arbiter of Constitutionality in Europe' in this Review" (1999) 36 Common Market Law Review 509.

Schmidt, V., *Democracy in Europe: The EU and National Polities* (Oxford: Oxford University Press, 2006).

Schopenhauer, A., "Die Grundlage der Moral" in his *Die beiden Grundprobleme der Ethik* (Frankfurt am Main: Joch Christ Germanische Buchhandlung, 1841).

Scotus Duns, J., (A. Wolter, tr.), *Duns Scotus on the Will and Morality* (Washington: Catholic University of America Press, 1986).

Schütze, R., *From Dual to Cooperative Federalism: The Changing Structure of European Law* (Oxford: Oxford University Press, 2010).

—— "Federalism as Constitutional Pluralism: A Letter from America" (2010) Social Science Research Network, at <http://papers.ssrn.com/sol3/papers.cfm?abstract_id=1693196>.

Singer, M., Generalization in Ethics (2nd edn, New York, NY: Atheneum, 1971).

Sadurski,W.,"Solange,Chapter3: Constitutional Courtsin Central Europe—Democracy—European Union"(2008)14 European Law Journal 1.

Somek, A., "Kelsen Lives" (2007) 18 European Journal of International Law 409.

—— "Monism: A Tale of the Undead" University of Iowa Legal Studies Research Paper No 10/22, 2010, available also at <http://papers.ssrn.com/sol3/papers.cfm?abstract_id=1606909>.

Spinelli, A., "European Union and the Resistance" in G. Ionescu (ed.) *The New Politics of European Integration* (London: Macmillan, 1972).

Spinner-Halev, J., with E. Teiss-Morse, "National Identity and Self-Esteem" (2003) 1 Perspectives on Politics 515.

Stein, E., "Lawyers, Judges and the Making of a Transnational Constitution" (1981) 75 American Journal of American Law 1.

Stirk, P., *European Unity in Context: The Interwar Period* (London: Pinter, 1989).

Stone Sweet, A., *Governing With Judges: Constitutional Politics in Europe* (Oxford: Oxford University Press, 2000).

—— *The Judicial Construction of Europe* (Oxford: Oxford University Press, 2004).

—— "A cosmopolitan legal order: Constitutional pluralism and rights adjudication in Europe" (2012) Global Constitutionalism 53.

—— "Rights Adjudication and Constitutional Pluralism in Germany and Europe" (2012) 19 Journal of European Public Policy 92.

—— "The European Court of Justice, State Non-Compliance, and the Politics of Override" *American Political Science Review* (2012) 204.

—— "The Structure of constitutional pluralism: Review of Nico Krisch, Beyond Constitutionalism: The Pluralist Structure of Post-National Law" (2013) 11 International Journal of Constitutional Law 491.

T

Taylor, C., *Sources of the Self: The Making of the Modern Identity* (Cambridge: Cambridge University Press, 1992).

—— "Leading a Life" in R. Chang (ed.), *Incomparability, Incompatibility, and Practical Reason* (Cambridge: Harvard University Press, 1997).

Torres Perez, A., *Conflicts of Rights in the European Union: A Theory of Supranational Adjudication* (Oxford: Oxford University Press, 2009).

Tribe, L., "The Puzzling Persistence of Process-Based Constitutional Theories" (1980) The Yale Law Journal 1063.

—— *American Constitutional Law* (2nd, New York: The Foundation Press, 1988).

—— *American Constitutional Law* (2nd, Volume I, New York: The Foundation Press, 2000).

Tully, J., *Strange Multiplicity: Constitutionalism in an Age of Diversity* (Cambridge: Cambridge University Press, 1995).

—— "The Agonic Freedom of Citizens" (1999) 28 Economy and Society 161.

—— "The Unfreedom of the Moderns in Comparison to their Ideals of Constitutional Democracy" (2002) 65 Modern Law Review 204. "Struggles over Recognition and Distribution" (2002) 7 Constellations 469.

Tuori, K., and Sankari, S., (eds.), *The Many Constitutions of Europe* (Farnham: Ashgate, 2010).

V

Van Parijs, P., "Should the EU Become More Democratic?" in A. Follesdal and P. Koslowski (eds.), *Democracy and the European Union* (Berlin: Springer, 1998).

—— with J. Rawls, "Three Letters on the Law of Peoples and the European Union" (2003) 7 Revue de Philosophie Economique 7.

Verhofstadt, G., *De Verenigde Staten van Europa* ("The United States of Europe") (Antwerp: Houtekiet, 2005).

—— "Forging 'United States of Europe' Is Key to the Future," European Voice 2005, at <http://www.europeanvoice.com/article/imported/forging-united-states-of-europe-is-key-to-the-future/53650.aspx2005>.

W

Waldron, J., *Law and Disagreement* (Oxford: Oxford University Press, 1999).

—— *God, Locke and Equality: Christian Foundations in Locke's Political Thought* (Cambridge: Cambridge University Press, 2002).

Walker, N., "Sovereignty and Differentiated Integration of the European Union" (1998) 4 European Law Journal 355.

—— "Flexibility Within a Metaconstitutional Frame: Reflections on the Future of Legal Authority in Europe" in G. de Búrca and J. Scott (eds.), *Constitutional Change in the EU: From Uniformity to Flexibility* (Oxford: Hart Publishing, 2000).

—— "Human Rights and Postnationality: Reconciling Political and Constitutional Pluralism" in T. Campbell, K. Ewing, and A. Tomkins (eds.), *Sceptical Essays on Human Rights* (Oxford: Oxford University Press, 2001).

—— "All Dressed Up" (2001) 21 Oxford Journal of Legal Studies 563.

—— "The Idea of Constitutional Pluralism" (2002) 65 Modern Law Review 317.

—— *Sovereignty in Transition* (Oxford: Hart Publishing, 2003).

—— "Late Sovereignty in the European Union" in N. Walker (ed.), *Sovereignty in Transition* (Oxford: Hart Publishing, 2003).

—— "From Großraum to Condominium: a Comment" in C. Joerges and N. Ghaleigh (eds.), *Darker Legacies of Law in Europe: The Shadow of National Socialism and Fascism over Europe and Its Legal Traditions* (Oxford: Hart Publishing, 2003).

—— "Europe's Constitutional Momentum and the Search for Polity Legitimacy" (2005) 4 International Journal of Constitutional Law 211.

—— "Constitutionalism and New Governance in the European Union: Rethinking the Boundaries" EUI Working Papers LAW No. 2005/15, 2005.

—— "Legal Theory and the European Union: A 25th Anniversary Essay" (2005) Oxford Journal of Legal Studies 581.

—— "Europe's Constitutional Engagement" (2005) 18 Ratio Juris 387.

—— "The Migration of Constitutional Ideas and the Migration of the Constitutional Idea: The Case of the EU" EUI Working Paper LAW 2005/04, 2005.

—— "A Constitutional Reckoning" (2006) 13 Constellations 140.

—— "EU Constitutionalism in the State Constitutional Tradition" (2006) 59 Current Legal Problems 51.

—— "Post-Constituent Constitutionalism" in N. Walker and M. Loughlin (eds.), *The Paradox of Constitutionalism* (Oxford: Oxford University Press, 2007).

—— "Beyond Boundary Disputes and Basic Grids: Mapping the Global Disorder of Normative Orders" (2008) 6 *International Journal of Constitutional Law* 373.

—— "Taking Constitutionalism Beyond the State" (2008) 56 *Political Studies* 519.

—— "Denizenship and the Deterritorialization in the EU" *EUDO Citizenship Observatory Robert Schuman Centre for Advanced Studies*, EUI LAW 2008/08 (European University Institute, 2008).

—— "Europe at 50. A Midlife Crisis: Democratic Deficit and Sovereignty surplus" (2008) 15 Irish Journal of European Law 23.

—— "The Variety of Sovereignty," in R. Adler-Nissen and T. Gammeltoft- Hansen (eds.), *Sovereignty Games: Instrumentalizing State Sovereignty in Europe and Beyond* (London: Palgrave, 2009).

—— "Beyond the Holistic Constitution?," Edinburgh School of Law Working Paper 2009/16, 2009.

—— "Reframing EU Constitutionalism," in J. Dunoff J and J. Trachtman (eds.) *Ruling The World? Constitutionalism, International Law and Global Governance* (Cambridge: Cambridge University Press, 2009).

—— "Out of Place and Out of Time: Law's Fading Co-Ordinates" Edinburgh School of Law Working Paper No. 2009/01, 2009, at <http://ssrn.com/abstract=1367591>.

—— "Multilevel Constitutionalism: Looking Beyond the German Debate" in K. Tuori and S. Sankari (eds.), *The many Constitutions of Europe* (Farnham, Ashgate, 2010).

—— "Surface and Depth: the EU's Resilient Sovereignty Question," in J. Neyer J. and A. Wiener (eds.), *Political Theory of the European Union* (Oxford: Oxford University Press, 2010).

—— "Constitutionalism and the Incompleteness of Democracy: An Iterative Relationship" (2010) 39 Rechtsfilosofie & Rechtstheorie 206.

—— "Constitutionalism and the Incompleteness of Democracy: A Reply to Four Critics" (2010) 39 Rechtsfilosofie & Rechtstheorie 276.

—— "The Anti-Political Polity" (2010) 73 Modern Law Review 141.

—— "Constitutionalism and Pluralism in Global Context" NYU Colloquium on Global and Comparative public Law, December 2011, at <http://www.law.nyu.edu/ecm_dlv2/groups/public/@nyu_law_website__academics__colloquia__global_and_comparative_public_law/documents/documents/ecm_pro_070600.pdf>.

—— "Reconciling MacCormick: Constitutional Pluralism and the Unity of Practical Reason" (2011) 24 Ratio Juris 369.

—— "The Cosmopolitan Local" in A. Menendez and J. Fossum (eds.), *Law and Democracy in Neil MacCormick's Legal and Political Theory* (Berlin: Springer, 2011).

—— "The Place of European Law" in G. de Búrca and J. Weiler (eds.) *The Worlds of European Constitutionalism* (Cambridge: Cambridge University Press, 2011).

—— "Postnational Constitutionalism and Postnational Public Law: A Tale of Two Neologisms" (2012) 3 Transnational Legal Theory 61.

—— (ed.), *MacCormick's Scotland* (Edinburgh University Press, 2012).

Weatherill, S., "Competence" in B de Witte (ed.) *Ten Reflections on the Constitutional Treaty for Europe* (Florence: EUI 2003).

—— with K. Nicolaïdis (eds.), *Whose Europe? National Models and the Constitution of the European Union* (Oxford: Oxford University Press, 2003).

Weber, M., "Politics as a Vocation" in H. Gerth and C. Wright Mills (eds.), *From Max Weber: Essays in Sociology* (Abingdon: Routledge, 1991).

Weiler, J., "The Transformation of Europe" (1991) 100 Yale Law Journal 2403.

—— "Does Europe Need a Constitution? Demos, Telos and the German Maastricht Decision" (1995) 1 European Law Journal 219.

—— "The State 'Uber Alles': Demos, Telos, and the German Maastricht Decision" in O. Due et al. (eds.), *Festschrift für Ulrich Everling* (Baden- Baden, Nomos Verlag 1995).

—— with Haltern, U., "Response: The Autonomy of the Community Legal Order–Through the Looking Glass" (1996) 37 Harvard International Law Journal 411.

—— "European Neo-constitutionalism: in Search of Foundations for the European Constitutional Order" *Political Studies* 44 (1996) 517.

—— "The European Union Belongs to Its Citizens: Three Immodest Proposals" (1997) 22 European Law Review 150.

—— "The Reformation of European Constitutionalism" (1997) 35 Journal of Common Market Studies 97.

—— "Europe: The Case Against the Case of Statehood" (1998) 4 European Law Journal 43.

—— with Haltern, U., "Constitutional or international? The Foundations of the Community Legal Order and the Question of Judicial Kompetenz- Kompetenz," in A.-M. Slaughter et. al. (eds.), *The European Court and National Courts: Doctrine and Jurispudence (Oxford: Hart Publishing*, 1998).

—— "Europe: The Case Against the Case of Statehood" (1998) 4 European Law Journal 43.

—— *The Constitution of Europe: Do the New Clothes Have an Emperor and Other Essays on European Integration* (Cambridge: Cambridge University Press, 1999).

—— "Why Should Europe Be a Democracy: The Corruption of Political Culture and the Principle of Constitutional Tolerance" in F. Snyder (ed.), *The Europeanisation of Law: The Legal Effects of European Integration* (Hart Publishing, Oxford 2000).

—— "Federalism and Constitutionalism: Europe's Sonderweg" in K. Nicolaïdis and R. Howse (eds.), *The Federal Vision: Legitimacy and Levels of Governance in the US and EU* (Oxford: Oxford University Press, 2002).

—— "In Defense of Status Quo: Europe's Constitutional Sonderweg" in J. Weiler and M. Wind (eds.), *European Constitutionalism Beyond the State* (Cambridge: Cambridge University Press, 2003).

—— "Faith in the Agnostic State" interview in Nextbook (26. March 2004) at <http://www.nextbook.org/cultural/feature.html?id=1>.

—— (M Ožbolt, tr.) *Krščanska Evropa: Raziskovalna Razprava* (Christian Europe: An Exploratory Essay) (Ljubljana: Claritas, 2005).

—— "Prologue: Global and Pluralist Constitutionalism – Some Doubts" in G. de Búrca and J. Weiler (eds.), *The Worlds of European Constitutionalism* (Cambridge: Cambridge University Press, 2011).

—— with D. Halberstam, "Dialogic Epilogue" in G. de Búrca and J. Weiler (eds.), *The Worlds of European Constitutionalism* (Cambridge: Cambridge University Press, 2011).

—— "Deciphering the Political and Legal DNA of European Integration: An Exploratory Essay," in J. Dickson and P. Eleftheriadis (eds.), *Philosophical Foundations of EU Law* (Oxford: Oxford University Press, 2012).

Wiener, A., with Neyer J. (eds.), *Political Theory of the European Union* (Oxford: Oxford University Press, 2010).

De Witte, B., "Sovereignty and European Integration: The Weight of Legal Tradition," in A.-M. Slaughter et. al. (eds.), *The European Court and National Courts: Doctrine and Jurisprudence* (Oxford: Hart publishing, 1999).

—— "Do Not Mention the Word: Sovereignty in Two Europhile Countries," in N. Walker (ed), *Sovereignty in Transition* (Oxford: Hart, 2003).

—— "The European Union as an International Legal Experiment" in G. de Búrca and J. Weiler (eds.) *The Worlds of European Constitutionalism* (Cambridge: Cambridge University Press, 2011).

Wood, G., "Democracy and the American Revolution," in J. Dunn (ed.), *Democracy: The Unfinished Journey* (Oxford: Oxford University Press, 2000).

Z

Zakaria, F., *From Wealth to Power: The Unusual Origins of America's World Role* (Princeton: Princeton University Press, 1998).

Ziller, J., "Multilevel Governance and Executive Federalism: Comparing Germany and the European Union," in P. Birkinshaw and M. Varney (eds.), *The European Union Legal Order After Lisbon* (Kluwer Law International 2010).

Zurcher, A., *The Struggle to Unite Europe 1940–58* (New York: New York University Press, 1989).

Index

The manufacturer's authorised representative in the EU for product safety is Oxford University Press España S.A. of el Parque Empresarial San Fernando de Henares, Avenida de Castilla, 2 – 28830 Madrid (www.oup.es/en or product.safety@oup.com). OUP España S.A. also acts as importer into Spain of products made by the manufacturer.

www.ingramcontent.com/pod-product-compliance
Lightning Source LLC
LaVergne TN
LVHW011908200926
848484LV00002B/563